TRAVELLERS *through* EMPIRE

McGill-Queen's Native and Northern Series
(In memory of Bruce G. Trigger)

Sarah Carter and Arthur J. Ray, Editors

TRAVELLERS

through

EMPIRE

Indigenous Voyages from Early Canada

Cecilia Morgan

McGill-Queen's University Press

Montreal & Kingston • London • Chicago

© McGill-Queen's University Press 2017

ISBN 978-0-7735-5134-3 (cloth)
ISBN 978-0-7735-5210-4 (ePDF)
ISBN 978-0-7735-5211-1 (ePUB)

Legal deposit fourth quarter 2017
Bibliothèque nationale du Québec

Printed in Canada on acid-free paper that is 100% ancient forest free (100% post-consumer recycled), processed chlorine free

This book has been published with the help of a grant from the Canadian Federation for the Humanities and Social Sciences, through the Awards to Scholarly Publications Program, using funds provided by the Social Sciences and Humanities Research Council of Canada.

McGill-Queen's University Press acknowledges the support of the Canada Council for the Arts for our publishing program. We also acknowledge the financial support of the Government of Canada through the Canada Book Fund for our publishing activities.

Library and Archives Canada Cataloguing in Publication

Morgan, Cecilia, 1958–, author
Travellers through empire : indigenous voyages from early Canada / Cecilia Morgan.
(McGill-Queen's Native and northern series ; 91)
Includes bibliographical references and index.

Issued in print and electronic formats.
ISBN 978-0-7735-5134-3 (cloth).–ISBN 978-0-7735-5210-4 (ePDF).–
ISBN 978-0-7735-5211-1 (ePUB)

1. Indians of North America–Travel–Great Britain–History–18th century. 2. Indians of North America–Travel–Great Britain–History–19th century. 3. Indians of North America–Canada–History–18th century. 4. Indians of North America–Canada–History–19th century. 5. Voyages and travels–History–18th century. 6. Voyages and travels–History–19th century. I. Title. II. Series: McGill-Queen's Native and northern series ; 91

E78.C2M646 2017   971.004'97   C2017-904208-4
                                    C2017-904209-2

To the Memory of the Travellers
And to Paul

Contents

Illustrations

Acknowledgements

My great thanks to the Social Sciences and Humanities Research Council of Canada for providing me with the assistance I needed to write this book. Although the digitization of newspapers and genealogical sources means that much research now can be done online, nevertheless following the archival traces of these travellers across the Atlantic, south through the United States, and across the Pacific to Australia was an essential, if expensive, part of my work. My thanks, too, to archivists and librarians in the following institutions: the Archives of Ontario; Victoria University Library, Toronto; the Woodland Cultural Centre, Brantford, Ontario; Grey Roots Archival Collection, Owen Sound, Ontario; Library and Archives Canada; the Hudson's Bay Company Archives and the Public Archives of Manitoba, Winnipeg; the Newberry Library, Chicago; New York State Public Library, Albany; Victoria State Archives, Melbourne; and in Scotland the Dunfermline Historical Society; Inverness Public Library; Highland Archive Centre, Inverness.

I'm very grateful to Mark Abley, my editor at McGill-Queen's University Press, for his support, good advice, and great efficiency in the publication process. It's been a true pleasure working with Mark and with the other staff at the Press: Joanne Pisano, Ryan Van Huijstee, and Filomena Falocco. Thanks, too, to David Drummond and Elena Goranescu for such a beautiful and inspired cover. Patricia Kennedy's copy-editing improved this book a great deal; I hope our paths cross again. I owe Sarah Carter, co-editor of McGill-Queen's Native and Northern Series, a great debt of thanks for her enthusiasm for this book and her wise counsel. It's always a pleasure, Sarah.

Thanks as well to Mary Chaktsiris, Martha Donkor, Kristina Llewellyn, Alison Norman, Melissa Otis, Joan Simalchik, and Nicole Woodman-Harvey for their research assistance over the years. A special thank you to Alison and Melissa for sharing their insights and thoughts on Indigenous-settler relations. Marion Press – now, sadly for me, retired from OISE/U of Toronto's Education Commons – gave generously of her extensive knowledge of genealogical sources, particularly for the children of the fur trade. Thanks to Marion, any doubts I might have had about the value of genealogy to historical research are long gone.

Portions of this book have appeared in the following:

"Celebrity Within the Transatlantic World: the Ojibwa of Upper Canada, 1830–1860," in *Celebrity Colonialism: Fame, Power and Representation in (Post) Colonial Cultures*, edited by Robert Clarke (Newcastle, UK: Cambridge Scholars' Press, 2009), 15–36.

"Kahgegagahbowh's (George Copway) Transatlantic Performance: *Running Sketches, 1850,*" *Cultural and Social History Journal* 9, no. 4 (Fall 2012): 527–48.

"Creating Interracial Intimacies: British North America, Canada, and the Transatlantic World, 1830–1914," *Online Journal of the Canadian Historical Association* (New Series) 19, no. 2 (2008): 75–104.

"'A Wigwam to Westminster': Performing Mohawk Identity in Imperial Britain, 1890s–1900s," *Gender and History* 25, no. 2 (Aug. 2003): 319–41.

(I would like to thank the publishers for permission to use these works, which form part of Chapters 2, 3, and 6, respectively.)

The support of SSHRC also allowed me the privilege of testing this work out on a number of audiences: the Australian and New Zealand Studies Association of North America, Berkshire Conference of Women's Historians, British World Conference, Canadian Historical Association, Ethnohistory, Irish and Scottish Encounters with Indigenous Peoples (Universities of Guelph and Toronto), Maastricht Centre for Transatlantic Studies, North American Conference on British Studies, Northeast American Society for Eighteenth-Century Studies, and the Rupert's Land Colloquium. Audiences at Griffith University, Guelph University, McMaster University, Monash University (Prato Campus), Montreal History Group, University of Bristol, University of Melbourne, University of Saskatchewan, and Western University also provided thoughtful feedback. I'm particularly grateful to Tolly Bradford, Jane Carey, Chelsea Horton, Zoë Laidlaw, Alan Lester, Jane Lydon, Kristine Moruzi, Fiona Paisley, Kirsty Reid, and Michelle Smith for their invitations to participate in a number of workshops that dealt with the themes of colonialism and transnational mobility. I would also like to thank the anonymous reviewers for their insightful comments and suggestions. Overall, this is a much better book for all of those discussions and contributions.

Over the (many) years it's taken me to research and write *Travellers through Empire*, I've had the great pleasure of talking about the British Empire and settler colonialism with a group of very smart and very generous historians: Jane Carey, Paul Deslandes, Elizabeth Elbourne, Victoria Haskins, Fiona Paisley, and Angela Woollacott. These conversations have occurred in places ranging from staid conference and seminar rooms to restaurants, pubs, patios, a boat in Sydney harbour (thanks, Fiona), and lovely walks around Brisbane, Saskatoon, and Sydney. I also am very grateful to Jill McConkey for suggesting that an Ontario historian should explore the travels of fur-trade children.

Nancy Forestell and Su Morton have always been there for matters both personal and professional. They have given wonderful advice and support and have a sense of humour, even about (especially about) things that at first glance didn't seem all that funny. I couldn't have got through the years without them.

This book is about people crossing borders and breaching boundaries, those that all too often were set up to effect their dispossession. As I finish it, borders around the world again are being reinforced in the face of human movement underpinned by suffering and dispossession. I can't speak for the people I've written about: I don't know what they would have made of these events. But I do hope that their histories make us pause when Western societies seek to deny mobility to others or value it only when it benefits nation-states and the interests of capital. So I dedicate this book first to those travellers. I'm grateful to them for leaving me their archival traces and count myself very privileged to write about them.

And, lastly, this is for Paul Jenkins, for his love and support and, too, for making me laugh.

TRAVELLERS *through* EMPIRE

Introduction:
Travelling through Empire

In the pages that follow you will be introduced to a range of individuals. Many of them were born into Indigenous communities in the British colony of Upper Canada; others came from the northwestern fur-trade country, their very existence a product of the racially charged encounters engendered by that trade; and the subject of Chapter 1, John Norton, was born in Scotland to a Cherokee father and a Scottish mother. The central thread that ties these men, women, and children together is that of travel and mobility, movements that took them across the Atlantic Ocean to Britain, parts of Europe, and, for some, to British colonies such as Australia and India. A number of them also journeyed back and forth across the (very young) border between Canada and the United States. Some returned to their home communities, while others created new spaces for themselves in Britain or elsewhere.

The histories of these people span the nineteenth century, a period in which the geographic, political, social, and cultural reach of the British Empire grew extensively, settler colonies such as Upper Canada were created (and would be followed by settler nations), and Indigenous people in a number of colonial sites found their worlds changing in multiple ways.[1] In part, this book argues that these travellers used mobility and movement across numerous boundaries and borders as a kind of resistance and reaction to these changes, a form of agency that became increasingly important as their worlds became, at least geographically, smaller, more confined, more restricted. However, not all of these Atlantic crossings should be seen in this way: the overseas voyages of fur-trade children, for example, were rarely undertaken through their own volition. Nevertheless, for many in this book, the decision to board an ocean-going ship was one deliberately and often carefully taken. Whatever the trip's purpose, it was often provoked by imperial expansion and the depredations of settler colonialism: the actions of settler governments, for example, who encroached on the traditional territories of Indigenous people, or who wished to restrict their mobility and confine them in a multitude of ways, geographic, political, cultural, and social.

These voyages, though, were sparked by both disruptions *and* as part of a continuum of motion and movement. While there is no disputing the changes to their lives brought by settler expansion in British North America during this time, we also should not lose sight of the fact that the mobility of Indigenous people was not something only sparked or set in motion by imperialism. Indigenous movement, whether for trade or warfare, and encounters with strangers in other Indigenous nations had been a long-standing feature of the histories of those communities. Moreover, crossing the Atlantic was not a practice initiated by the increased arrival of Europeans in the nineteenth century: this is not a story that depends on the upending of pristine and unspoiled cultural innocence for its telling. Historians of early modern European meetings with the Indigenous inhabitants of North America have pointed to a number of occasions on which members of their communities – from those Innu who arrived in sixteenth-century England to Joseph Brant's appearances in the late-eighteenth-century English court – met and mingled with various strata of British and French society.[2] As Nicholas Thomas argues in his study of Pacific Islanders, to see Indigenous people as being "in situ," local and bounded by place, is to ignore and dismiss their histories of travel and mobility.[3]

Nevertheless, the nineteenth century brought significant changes for Indigenous people in British North America (as it did elsewhere): changes to national borders, changes to political structures – not least the creation of the settler state of Upper Canada – and changes to social and cultural meanings and practices.[4] While I do not claim that my coverage is completely comprehensive – other Indigenous leaders from British North America and Canada made trips to Britain and Europe in the nineteenth and early twentieth centuries[5] – in conjunction with the growing body of scholarship on Indigenous mobility this book suggests that the experiences of these men, women, and children were far from being unique.[6] Nor were these individuals so singular that their travels can be dismissed as being exceptional, an historical curiosity without wider meaning and significance. They may have been distinctive in some respects, not least because of their fluency, both oral and written, in English (a subject which I take up later in this chapter). However, the reasons for their travels were the challenges, and sometimes the possibilities, that faced many Indigenous communities throughout British North America and other settler colonies in the British Empire.[7]

Those whose voyages are at the heart of this book both experienced and were emblematic of these changes. Far from being idiosyncratic or atypical, in many ways their oceanic voyages register the reordering of their communities. The aftershocks of transatlantic democratic and religious revolutions of the late-eighteenth century were felt, for example, by John Norton, whose intimate and public life was bound up with, and indeed created by, the imperial and transcontinental warfare of the eighteenth and early nineteenth centuries; it would also be shaped by the philanthropic and religious sensibilities of London's abolitionist movement. The voyages undertaken by the Anishinaabe people of Upper Canada, discussed in Chapter 2, were the direct result of religious and humanitarian interest in their communities, settler expansion that threatened them, and a colonial government's policy aimed at their removal from traditional territories and restrictions on their movement. The way they reached across domestic boundaries and created new forms of intimate relationships, familial structures, and friendships, the subject of Chapters 3 and 4, was, as a host of scholarship has demonstrated, a phenomenon engendered by imperial expansion. These travels became so frequent that they should be seen as fundamental to empire's spread, as was the circulation of ideas, institutions, and material culture.[8] Chapters 5 and 6 explore Indigenous celebrity; they examine the appearances of a number of Indigenous performers, Anishinaabe and Haudenosaunee, in Britain (most notably London). While the display of Indigenous people in metropolitan centres was not unique to the nineteenth and early-twentieth centuries, over the course of the nineteenth century imperial expansion meant that such displays became more numerous. They took forms that ranged from the presentations by individual promoters of Indigenous bodies to more widespread circuits of performance, such as Wild West shows and state-sanctioned spectacles of Indigeneity in colonial and imperial exhibitions.[9] These performances built on earlier popular displays of the curious and unusual – commonly known as freak shows – while at the same time they intersected with the rise of anthropology as a mode of both popular and academic inquiry.[10]

As these chapters demonstrate, Indigenous people from, first, British North America and then the Dominion of Canada participated in these circuits of performance and the discourses that helped shape them, albeit with their own motivations and purposes. After concluding reflections on the meaning of these travels, the Epilogue suggests the ways in which Indigenous mobility from Canada has both been remembered and has continued in the twentieth century.

Those who appear in *Travellers through Empire* will be familiar to some historians. Although perhaps not quite as well-known as some, John Norton's multiple movements, not to mention his excursion into Cherokee country, captured the imagination of literary scholars Carl F. Klinck and James J. Talman. Their discovery and publication of Norton's journals in 1966 provided an important, albeit relatively (at least until recently) under-explored, dimension to our understanding of transatlantic exchanges and the complexity of Indigenous identities in late-eighteenth-century British America. As well, scholars of Indigenous history in Canada have explored the lives of Peter Jones, John Sunday, George Copway, and Nahneebahweequa (Catherine Sutton), those Anishinaabe people from the Mississauga band whose communities were drastically affected by the spread of settler society after the end of the War of 1812.[11] Maungwudaus, their contemporary, has been looked at within the context of "performing Indians," as too have been those Ojibwe performers brought to England and Europe by Arthur Rankin.[12] Moreover, while the life of John Brant-Sero has attracted somewhat less attention than that of his fellow Mohawk performer, E. Pauline Johnson's poetry and performances have been the subject of a number of recent studies that have been informed by postcolonial and feminist theory and Indigenous knowledge.[13] Finally, work by Jennifer S.H. Brown, Jacqueline Peterson, and Sylvia Van Kirk drew the attention of historians to the experience of the northwestern fur trade's mixed-race children, both those who remained in Rupert's Land and Red River and those who were sent across the Atlantic. Their scholarship set out a framework for our understanding of racial intermarriage and mingling, one that has proven highly influential both within Canada and beyond.[14]

Travellers through Empire also joins wide-ranging studies of the journeys of Indigenous peoples across both the Atlantic and Pacific oceans. For example, Kate Fullagar's study of New World visitors to eighteenth-century Britain, *The Savage Visit*, argues that so-called "savage visitors" became popular in Britain because they were, in her words, "good to think," as their presence in the metropole could "enable or enhance" debates over British civilization, and, in particular, the question of British imperial expansion.[15] Visitors from both North America and the Pacific could be seen, Fullagar argues, "as *memento more* of the innocence lost in the move away from classical political economy, or they could be demonized as spectres of the dependent brutishness entailed in embracing an exchange culture."[16] But as debates over Britain as an imperial power were resolved in favour of expansion, Fullagar argues that "symbols of fundamental difference were no longer as potent in the more reform-minded debates that followed": not only was the notion of "savagery" a "less *useful*" idea after the 1780s, it also became an increasingly inflexible and much narrower one.[17] The lukewarm reception of an Australian Indigenous man, Bennelong, and his fellow countryman in 1794 was an example, she suggests, of such a shift.[18]

In contrast, literary scholar Kate Flint's *The Transatlantic Indian, 1776–1930* picks up the narrative of Indigenous travellers to Britain where Fullagar's work ends and focuses exclusively on the visits of North Americans. Like Fullagar, though, Flint too explores Europeans' perceptions of Indigenous travellers who, as she points out, were ubiquitous in Britain throughout the nineteenth and into the early twentieth century, both at the level of representation and as actual embodied presences. Although published prior to Fullagar's work, Flint's book takes up the question of the wider significance of these "transatlantic Indians" to both British and American nationalism, their visits to Britain, and the use of their images in material culture, fiction, poetry, and other texts. As Flint argues, "the capacity of Indians to inhabit British public, intellectual, and social spaces attests to their participation not just on the troubled terrain of the United States and Canada, but within a yet broader transatlantic context of developing modernities."[19] The "intermingled geographies" of Britain, the United States, and Canada, as Flint describes them, "were sites for disrupting categories like the 'modern,' the 'savage,' and the 'civilized.'"[20] As Flint points out, no small part of that disruption took place because of the agency and activism of Indigenous people themselves: one of the great strengths of Flint's work is the attention she pays to the voices of travellers such as Peter Jones, George Copway, and E. Pauline Johnson, men and women who spoke up and back to imperial audiences, providing consistent commentaries on metropolitan practices and insisting that their voices be heard.[21]

More recent works have joined Flint in arguing for bold reconceptualization of categories or frameworks through the inclusion of Indigenous travel. Jace Weaver's *The Red Atlantic: American Indigenes and the Making of the Modern World, 1000–1927* covers a wide swath of time, from the arrival of the Vikings in North America to Charles Lindbergh's solo flight across the Atlantic. Weaver argues for the centrality and importance of Indigenous movement and Indigenous peoples' presence in the Atlantic world, pointing out that reinserting narratives of Indigenous captives, slaves, prisoners, soldiers and sailors, diplomats, and celebrities into it calls our attention to very long-standing patterns of Indigenous agency and, too, Indigenous cosmopolitanism.[22] In contrast, Coll Thrush's *Indigenous London: Native Travellers at the Heart of Empire* examines the journeys of Indigenous people from North America, Australia, Aotearoa New Zealand, and Hawai'i to London, arguing that from the sixteenth century until well into the twentieth century their presence "indigenized" the city, making it a cosmopolitan site of encounter and, at times, exchange. Thrush points out that these travellers were not, at the time, hidden or obscure: in fact, they were highly visible. It is only, he contends, through acts of forgetting that their movement around the metropole has been concealed. Like Flint and Weaver, Thrush points to the consistent and recurring theme of Indigenous peoples' agency as they came into contact with, and at times confronted, imperial perceptions of them and their cultures. And, like Fullagar, Thrush is also concerned with the encounters of Londoners with individuals such as Pocohontas, Joseph Brant, Samson Occom, Maungwudaus, and Queen Emma of Hawai'i, the shifting meanings of these meetings over time, and their consequences for Londoners' understanding of empire, race, and their city.[23]

What, then, does this book contribute to our knowledge of these people and their voyages through the British imperial world? How does it differ from the studies discussed above? While it certainly shares much with these works – not least the foregrounding of the experiences and agency of Indigenous peoples – this book departs from them in a number of ways. For one, the Canadian-based scholarship generally focuses on particular Indigenous communities and tends to discuss transatlantic movement in the context of very specific causes, such as the redress of settler governments' infringements on treaty rights, missionary fundraising, or careers in performance. In contrast, similar to the international work cited above, *Travellers through Empire* brings together a range of individuals from various communities – Haudenosaunee, Anishinaabe, and the fur trade – looks at a spectrum of mobility and travel, and argues that mobility also needs to be mentioned in our understanding of the experiences of nineteenth-century Indigenous peoples, not least their encounters with settler colonialism. Furthermore, like Fullagar and Thrush's studies of Indigenous mobility, my arguments and frame of reference are situated more closely in British imperial history than is the case for Flint and Weaver or, too, the majority of work by Canadian scholars.[24]

Yet *Travellers through Empire* also differs from the international historiography in a number of ways. While many of these will be elaborated on in the following paragraphs, some central distinctions are worth discussing. For one, in varying degrees Flint, Fullagar, Thrush, and Weaver all pay attention to imperial and metropolitan perspectives on and conceptions of Indigenous people.[25] I agree with these scholars that the reactions of Europeans to Indigenous travellers was a critical dimension of these encounters, not least because it demonstrates the ways in which cross-cultural conversations were shaped by glimmers of understanding, but also by ambiguity, confusion, and at times downright hostility. Wherever my sources permit, I have attempted to discuss audience reception, both its content and timbre, as well as the receptivity of metropolitan audiences to the messages brought by these voyagers. I also pay attention to the shifting imperial context in which these men, women, and children found themselves. Nevertheless, I have chosen to keep my focus on the travellers themselves, to look at their narratives, their experiences, and their voices, all of which had much to tell both European audiences (and present-day historians) about the complex and creative ways in which they approached the steadily increasing power of the British Empire.

Moreover, while Weaver's rethinking of "the Atlantic" through the lens of Indigenous experiences adds much to our understanding of both histories, those whose lives I explore were part of not just Atlantic worlds but also those of the Great Lakes, the fur trade, nineteenth-century settler society, and the British Empire more broadly.[26] While the Atlantic Ocean connected these worlds, to make that the sole means of conceptualizing their experiences overlooks the importance of the multiple linked sites and places that played important roles in their lives and identities. Also, while I admire both Weaver's and Thrush's choices to cover much longer periods of time and a wider-ranging cast of characters than does *Travellers through Empire*, I have focused on a much narrower slice of time and individuals who shared territorial and political ties. Such "contextual specificity" has as many rewards, as does a broader, more extensive, chronological and geographic framework: not least because it allows us to understand the details and, thus, the nuances of relationships between the imperial and the local frameworks that shaped the movement of these people.[27] Moreover, although Thrush provides a compelling and beautifully crafted portrait of London as an Indigenous space, one which overlaps in some ways with the arguments presented in this book, my work adds other spatial dimensions to these travellers' experiences: they could be found in both London and in many other parts of Britain and Europe, not to mention in Australia and in the territories of other Indigenous nations in North America. London's importance to their voyages cannot be denied, but neither can their widespread presence throughout Britain – and beyond.

Furthermore, unlike many of the other studies cited above, *Travellers through Empire* juxtaposes the highly visible mobility of adults alongside the less-celebrated movements of fur-trade children as a specific group. It thus contributes to our knowledge of childhood within the nineteenth-century British Empire and suggests the ways in which children's mobility was both similar and different from that of their adult counterparts, not least around the issue of racial visibility and identification.[28] As well, while other studies have discussed the interracial marriages of individuals such as Peter Jones, Catherine Sutton, George Copway, and John Brant-Sero, *Travellers through Empire* places these forms of intimacy within a framework of imperial, and in some cases transnational, movement. While this book points to new forms of domesticity as an effect of such movement, it also argues that intimacy needs to be understood as a form of mobility, one that carried as much weight and import as other kinds of movement (political activism, for example, or missionary organizing).

It also seeks to explore the range of ways in which these men, women, and children were linked, both to the metropole and, at times, to each other, through multiple, sometimes overlapping, networks and circuits. Scholarship in imperial history and historical geography has pointed to the centrality of networks, circuits, and webs to empire's expansion, those networks that linked a range of individuals and that conveyed news, ideas, goods, and people to various metropolitan and colonial sites.[29] At times their travels overseas were clearly grounded in their ties to assemblages of individuals and organizations: this was most obviously the case for those Anishinaabe male missionaries who were part of the British Wesleyan missionary movement, for example, or Nahneebahweequa (Catherine Sutton), whose journey to Britain was sparked by the actions of the colonial government, but who made the trip with the aid and assistance of transatlantic humanitarians. Such contacts and connections, in both colonial and metropolitan contexts, were critically important to their ability to move back and forth between these varied places. In the case of John Norton, historic ties between the Haudenosaunee and the British military were the filaments that took him back and forth across the Atlantic. Simultaneously, networks of British abolitionists provided him with exposure to groups outside the military and, too, the means to convey particular forms of technology and knowledge to the Grand River territory. Out of these humanitarian networks emerged ones of intimacy, whether of friendship or of kinship, that further linked Upper Canada and Britain.

Although the world of the fur trade is not often placed alongside that of the settler colony of Upper Canada, it too consisted of those commercial ties that linked London, Scotland, and the Northwest. These ties also helped create new networks of kinship and friendship, intimate connections that, as Chapter 4 explores, overlapped in various ways and that at times also connected Rupert's Land, Red River, and Britain to other colonial settings. While promoters of Indigenous performers, such as Arthur Rankin and George Catlin, may not have operated as deliberately as part of a large-scale transatlantic network as did, for example, the missionaries, their entrepreneurial ambitions were shared with similar impresarios who brought spectacles of "exotic" people from their homelands to the metropole.[30] Furthermore, those who appeared before late-Victorian and Edwardian audiences made use of connections and patrons. They could be those of imperial governance, such as Pauline Johnson's ties to the British aristocracy and Lord and Lady Strathcona, or of circuits of knowledge, such as John Brant-Sero's links to anthropologists and archaeologists in Ontario, the United States, and Britain.

Moreover, the networks that Indigenous people themselves created also underwrote a number of these circuits. While at times less obvious to the eyes of the press, for example, or public officials, such ties often drew these travellers together long before they left on their journeys. Norton's adoption into the Six Nations not only underpinned his political and military career: it also provided him with family and kin who, as we shall see, influenced his trajectory in multiple ways. As Chapter 2 demonstrates, the Anishinaabeg who travelled overseas were already linked through clan and kin relationships or had forged their own ties as members of a Christian Ojibwe community (or both). Chapter 3 suggests the ways in which marriage might also help forge new bonds or reinforce existing ones. To be sure, Indigenous networks per se come less to the fore in discussions of the fur-trade children, yet individuals such as Matilda Davis and Alexander Isbister connected Britain and Red River in ways both intimate and public. Maungwudaus and other Ojibwe performers were very explicitly tied to a range of Anishinaabe communities in Upper Canada, not least through their performance troupes, the latter consisting of family and kin. In the case of Pauline Johnson, her more attenuated connections to the Six Nations, particularly in the aftermath of her father's death, provided an impetus for her travels. Overall, their ability to mobilize existing connections and the need to forge new ones, both formal and informal, was an important way in which Indigenous travellers maintained visibility and voice in a settler society that would prefer they remained unseen (for the most part) and unheard.

There are other questions that surround these networks. As Zöe Laidlaw has argued vis-à-vis networks of governance in the early nineteenth-century Empire, they connected people first and places second, an argument with which I concur.[31] Throughout the following chapters we will see how these transatlantic ties linked, for example, John Norton to Robert Allan or Nahneebahweequa to New York and British Quakers, connections that enabled them to press for their particular goals. Yet although ties between people were fundamental, place mattered too, and in a number of ways. For one, those who were public figures attempted to convey to their audiences a sense of their homes, whether Christian mission villages or traditional territories, the landscapes and histories that had shaped them. These travellers, then, offered their audiences the opportunity to be conveyed across the ocean and to appreciate places and communities they probably would never see in person. Although not unlike "armchair tourism" tinged with – at least from the listeners' perspective – more than a little voyeurism (especially when the topic was the missionary appeal for the "poor Indian, suffering in the woods"), in other ways they presented different messages. As Thrush has argued for individuals as diverse as Mohegan missionary Samson Occom, the Inuit shaman Atajuq and his family, and the Haudenosaunee leader Joseph Brant, these travellers "reasoned themselves and the city into a broader transatlantic world."[32] In so doing, the struggle of Indigenous travellers to impress upon a wide swathe of metropolitan audiences that they emanated from a particular place was evident in their critiques – sometimes gentle, sometimes more stinging – of British society. Strung throughout their assessments and evaluations of the metropole were metaphors and comparisons based on the fish, fowl, and animals that helped constitute specific Indigenous topographies and landscapes. English women, for example, resembled particular birds and fish from Anishinaabe territories. The travellers also discussed Indigenous social and cultural practices that seemed more reasonable and logical to them than those they witnessed in Britain.

Yet places feature in other ways throughout these histories, as assemblages of geographies, communities, and institutions. Because of its centrality to many of these travellers' journeys, London assumes a particularly important role in this book, as it went from an early-nineteenth-century burgeoning imperial city to the Edwardian "heart of the empire" traversed by Pauline Johnson and John Brant-Sero. Yet, as pointed out earlier, it was not the only place that was touched by the presence of these men, women, and children. Throughout these narratives, wherever possible I have attempted to highlight and underscore particular characteristics of the places through which they moved, whether as sojourners or, in some cases, as "settlers." At times their own words do that, as when John Davis and Albert Hodgson wrote to their aunt, Matilda Davis, to tell her of their schools in Walthamstow and Jedburgh. When such descriptions were lacking or scanty, I have attempted to create pictures of Dunfermline in the late-eighteenth century, the Grand River territory across the nineteenth century, Inverness in the 1830s, Port Phillip in the 1840s, and mid-nineteenth-century Nairn, using mixtures of primary and secondary sources. In this way I have attempted to determine the kinds of sights and, where possible, sounds and smells that confronted these travellers, to pay attention to the different physical environments they encountered, the lived and material consequences of the networks that took them far from their homes.

However, connections between people and communities were also consolidated through a world of print.[33] Exchanges of paper, often brought these people into their initial contact with organizations and individuals. After those meetings ended, the written word and, for some, visual and material culture maintained these ties, at times over thousands of miles. The majority of these travellers were, after all, fluent in English, cultivated primarily because of their missionary education, familial relationships with British settlers, and negotiations with the colonial authorities. (Indeed, my choice of these particular individuals was shaped by the availability of the trails of written sources, whether published or manuscript, that they left). At times they used public forms of communication, such as addresses, interviews, open letters, and articles published in newspapers on both sides of the Atlantic. A few – Maungwudaus, George Copway – also wrote travelogues that described their overseas journeys.[34] In addition to these better-known genres, these travellers also left an equally valuable epistolatory trail across the Empire, the "cold communications," as Norton and others called them, sent to both family and friends. Their letters not only conveyed news of events, intimate and public, back and forth across the ocean: as I have argued elsewhere, they also provided a kind of stage on which their senders' subjectivities could be explored, rehearsed, and performed.[35]

While historians have made us aware of the very real and very deleterious effects that colonialism exerted on Indigenous forms of communication, particularly oral transmissions of history, culture, and spirituality, these collections of correspondence left by Indigenous and mixed-race travellers demonstrate the varied ways in which their authors appropriated and used the written word to help create and sustain their own imperial networks, in which the worlds of formal and domestic politics intermeshed.[36] Moreover, they also deployed the medium of writing to narrate the histories of their lives and their communities, blending autobiography within larger contexts. In so doing, they staked claims to personal and political visibility within transatlantic worlds that primarily preferred they exist only as relics of a dying culture, living outside modernity's temporality.

Although networks and connections were critically important, each chapter focuses on individuals within this context of mobility and movement. Such an approach is based on my belief that we need to ensure the biographies of these men and women, their negotiations and struggles with colonial and imperial rule, are given equal weight with those of the Europeans with whom they met, mingled, and (in some cases) married.[37] As much recent work has demonstrated, narratives of individuals and their experiences of colonial rule have taken on a new importance as historians grapple with the contours of the histories of colonialism and imperialism. A number of historians of empire have shown that adopting a biographical approach can help us to understand the interplay between individuals, with their own specific circumstances and trajectories, and the large macro-level of historical processes and institutions and of imperial networks and colonial formations. Historians must be mindful of the power relations that shape our ability to write such narratives: some lives have been deemed more worthy of documentation than others, the life stories of some individuals can be told only through the lenses of others. Nevertheless, work on a range of imperial projects has demonstrated the very rich possibilities that arise when individual and collective biographies take centre stage in our research and writing.[38] The ways in which we contend with questions of negotiation, cooperation, collaboration, and resistance can become more nuanced when we try to determine the meanings of colonial and imperial rule for those individual men and women –colonizer and colonized – involved. As historians David Lambert and Alan Lester write, "each colonial life provides insight not only into the heterogeneity of the empire and the multiple subject positions that arose from the 'variegated terrain.'"[39]

Yet, as we explore this terrain for this particular group of actors, it becomes clear that, just as place mattered, so too did gender. Gender relations, whether as lived experience or as constructs that permeated and shaped discourses about and by Indigenous people, were also a critical part of these histories. For one, my research suggests that fewer women than men travelled from Upper Canadian Indigenous communities. Of those whose lives are explored here, only two, Nahneebahweequa and Pauline Johnson, were able to speak, read, and write English, and thus establish a speaking presence for metropolitan audiences. Such an imbalance may have been the result of a number of practices: the Methodist missionaries' preference for formal male leadership; the insistence of the colonial and imperial governments on conducting negotiations with male Indigenous leaders, and the latter's seizing of that opportunity to establish their own forms of patriarchy under colonial rule;[40] Indigenous women's responsibilities for child-rearing, which, perhaps, made mobility more difficult for them; and the gender-specific dangers that surrounded their public visibility, problems which, I believe, both Nahneebahweequa and Johnson experienced.

However, this does not mean that gender relations were of less consequence or played an unimportant role in these travels. Here, too, this study differs from that of others in its insistence on the significance of gender. Weaver's work has little to say – at least explicitly – about gender; other books, such as Flint's *Transatlantic Indian* or Thrush's *Indigenous London*, discuss gender relations as being important at particular moments in the history of Indigenous travel. However, *Travellers through Empire* sees gender as a central category of historical analysis throughout.[41] For one, Indigenous and mixed-race men were also confronted with either new forms of masculinity in their travels or experienced gendered discourses and practices that might have been only tentatively sensed in the colonial context. How these men refashioned themselves as, for example, men of humanitarian sensibility, integrating British norms of manhood with Indigenous practices, forms an ongoing thread in these stories; so too does their confrontation with imperial notions of militaristic masculinity and tensions over Indigenous men's sexuality. Moreover, just as nineteenth-century missionaries and anthropologists seized on gender relations as indicative of a society's place in the hierarchy of civilization (often insisting on the deficiencies of Indigenous societies in that domain), Indigenous travellers reversed this discourse, pointing to the shortcomings of gender roles in British society and holding up their own communities' practices as superior and desirable.

Finally, for the children of the fur trade, education and mobility was imbued with lessons about British gender norms and standards, although, as we shall see, not all transformed these lessons into the kinds of attitudes and practices desired by their tutors.

Gendered attitudes and practices also evoke the question of another set of boundaries, categories, and meanings: those of the multiple emotional communities and frontiers that these travellers encountered and, too, those that accompanied them on their travels.[42] To be sure, the role of emotions has not been entirely absent from other studies of Indigenous mobility, most notably that of Kate Flint. Flint has pointed to the central place that "Native Americans" played in the work of British women writers, who were especially attracted to the former as a "suitable object on which to expend the fashionable literary currency of sentimental compassions" and, too, as an analogy for their own place in British society.[43] *Travellers through Empire*, though, takes up the question of emotions in multiple ways and engages in varying degrees with the historiography on emotions. For a number of years, scholars have been historicizing emotions, seeing them to be as valid and important a subject of inquiry as those other categories – gender, race, sexuality, nation, and empire – that have increasingly shaped the writing of social and cultural history. Emotions, a diverse group of historians have argued, do not exist outside of culture and society, but rather are embedded within these entities and, as such, perform a number of roles and functions.[44] It is not my intention to engage in a lengthy discussion of the varied approaches to the history of emotions that have been advocated by these scholars, not least because to date little has been written in the Canadian context that explores emotions and sensibilities explicitly.[45] However, a number of concepts appear to me to be particularly pertinent to these travellers. They range from Barbara Rosenwein's framework of "emotional communities," in which certain emotions are defined as being valuable or harmful to their members, to Monique Scheer's arguments for the importance of "emotional practices," with their "habits, rituals, and everyday pastimes" that serve to achieve particular emotional states, and Nicole Eustace's analysis of colonial and early nineteenth-century America, in which expressions of particular emotions were bound up with power, both its demonstration and its contestation.[46] These perspectives are particularly useful in understanding these travellers' discussions and reflections on the way in which they conducted themselves, in both public and intimate settings, and the reactions of their audiences to their presence in the metropole. While their performances of self and community were always

shaped by racially charged meanings and frameworks, they were also emotionally charged ones, in which feeling and affect came to the fore, and in
a range of ways. Hurt, anger, anxiety, sympathy, affection, desire, longing
(for various entities), happiness, and contentment: these travellers' writings
register a range of emotional states that formed a significant aspect of their
imperial encounters. The geographic and political borders that they crossed
were also those of affective culture, shot through by a number of emotional
codes. John Norton, for example, found new networks of masculine companionship and affection in London and Cambridge, while Indigenous
performers encountered reactions from their audiences that were highly
emotionally charged, and which ran the gamut from delight to disgust.

Moreover, new insights into the relationship of emotions and the history of childhood provide important lenses through which the experiences
of fur-trade children can be viewed. As the editors of a recent collection on
childhood and the emotions point out, children and youth have always had
to learn to navigate divergent emotional spaces and collectivities, whether
that of the school, the orphanage, or the workplace.[47] To this list I would
add the new kinds of families and schooling encountered by children sent
from Rupert's Land to England and Scotland. These were places where they
acquired skills in masking certain emotional states, such as great homesickness for the North American woods, and displaying others, such as
gratitude and affection for newly met grandparents, uncles, and aunts. As
Jan Plamper has argued, "the traffic of emotions between cultures, spaces,
regions, languages, groups, individuals, etc., is often *multi*directional ... historians of emotion benefit from remaining aware of this multidirectionality.
This multidirectional traffic comes in many forms, including the deliberate
closing-off of certain routes."[48]

While I hope, then, that this research demonstrates the richness of
the experiences of these men, women, and children, I do not intend this
account of their travels to be a celebratory one. It is, perhaps, logical that
early twentieth-first-century historians might see Indigenous mobility and
movement as a positive sign. They might provide a way for people to come
together for activist reasons, for example. They also might be a means of
circumventing and negotiating around the kinds of restrictions – preventing
people from holding membership in their Indigenous nations or trying to
keep them out of certain cultural and economic spaces – that settler societies
and their governments imposed on them. Yet we also need to acknowledge
that the networks Indigenous people created and the transatlantic and
imperial networks in which they participated might have been forged out

of crucibles of desperation, dispossession, and the traumas of colonial struggles, a response to the loss of territories, languages, practices, and people. For indigenous peoples, imperial connections could be far more than just interesting social and cultural ties: "connections" or "networks" could be maintained through the linkages of a shared history of defeat, loss, and grief.[49] While some travellers – John Brant-Sero, for example, or George Copway – often treated their metropolitan audiences with a degree of insouciance that suggested a certain disregard for imperial power, they also displayed very real flashes of anger when the latter refused them certain rights or treated them as living stereotypes.

These characteristics – and much more – can be seen in the travels of John Norton, Teyoninhokarawen, whose narrative is the subject of the following chapter.

. 1 .

"Of Pleasing Countenance and Pleasant Manners": John Norton's Transatlantic Voyages

Introduction

He was baptized John Norton on 17 December 1770, in the parish of Crail, Scotland. The parish register lists his father as "John Norton, soldier" and his mother as Christine Anderson; two witnesses were present at the baptism. His mother, it seems, was probably from Dunfermline or nearby, while his father was originally from the Cherokee nation, "having been taken, a boy, from Kuwoki [Keowee], when that village was burnt by the English" as part of the British army's campaigns against Cherokee towns from 1759 to 1761.[1] While the details of Norton's father's experiences are hazy – all we know is that he was brought from Keowee in present-day South Carolina to the Dunfermline area by a British soldier – an account of Keowee's destruction by James Grant, second-in-command of the British troops, suggests what Norton's father might have seen. Sixty to eighty Cherokee lay dead; forty men, women, and children were taken prisoner; and many more had fled over the mountains "in a miserable situation," not having had time to take provisions of any kind. "The surprise in every town" taken by the British, Grant concluded, "was almost equal, as the whole affair was the work of a very few hours."[2] From its inception, then, Norton's was a narrative of racial entanglement, one created in the context of transatlantic imperial warfare and settler colonial violence. Such a story might have been familiar to his fellow Scots who had either served in North America or had read tales of captivity generated by frontier conflicts, albeit ones in which the captives were European.[3]

We don't know much about his life in Crail parish; nor, it seems, are there travellers' accounts that describe the area in 1770. However, if the late-eighteenth-century *Statistical Account of Crail* in any way represents the area during Norton's childhood, it is perhaps not surprising that the family chose Dunfermline. According to the *Statistical Account*, the six-mile-long parish of Crail occupied the easternmost end of the County of Fife, reaching inland towards the city of Dunfermline and bordered by the North Sea and the Firth of Forth. "The general appearance of the country is flat and naked," wrote the Reverend Andrew Ball, of St Andrew's Presbytery, "the few trees and hedges here are reared with difficulty, and have an unhealthy appearance."[4] Despite its unprepossessing appearance, though, the countryside produced "plentiful" crops of wheat, oats, and barley; as well, coal pits and mines had left their marks on eastern and western Crail. Overall, though, Ball's description of the area suggests a place that an energetic young man was more likely to leave than choose to put down permanent roots. "The whole town bears evident marks of having seen better days," Ball remarked.[5] The fisheries had been declining for over fifty years, the result of the North Sea storms breaking up the shoals, of Dutch, Swedish, and Norwegian overfishing, and of a poor harbour. Such a dwindling of the industry was no small problem, since the majority of men in the parish had made their living from the sea. To make matters worse, trade had dropped off. As Ball reported, "the reader must not expect to hear of the flourishing state of trade and manufacturers in this parish. They are indeed in a very languishing situation."[6] Commerce had migrated to larger centres, and goods were now exported from Edinburgh, Dundee, or Leith. Education was not in a good state, as "the school of Crail has experienced a proportional decay with the town, as the people in general are not able to afford their children a liberal education."[7] Crail had "no peculiar advantages" over its neighbours, then. As well as a deteriorating economy, it suffered from a "lack of shelter, which exposes it to the blast from every quarter … its irregular situation … circumscribes its intercourse to a small district of country, and a scarcity of running water."[8]

Despite Ball's picture of economic stagnation, a poorly educated population, and unwelcoming topography, he admitted that at least Crail's residences were built on high ground and the air was "pure and healthy."[9]

Moreover, "the credulity of former times with respect to witches [was] almost extinguished" and superstitions were "losing ground" (although Ball noted that inoculations against smallpox had been "held back" through a combination of religious scruples and expense). Crail's residents were starting to pay more attention to "the cleanness and commodiousness of their habitations" and "when dressed they are decently neat, rather than fine. If they are not remarkable for sobriety and industry, neither do they deserve to be stigmatized as dissipated and idle." Ball concluded that perhaps things were not quite so dire, since the good folk of Crail were "becoming more liberal, decorous and mannered" and could be described as "peaceful and loyal subjects."[10] Just as Indigenous people around the globe were increasingly being observed and categorized by Europeans, so too might Scotland's residents come under similar gazes.[11]

Norton's family took him to Dunfermline, where his biographer suggests he attended a good school and may have worked in a print shop.[12] Dunfermline might have appeared to the Nortons as a more promising place than Crail. The same volume of the *Statistical Account* describes it as "most pleasantly situated, and the prospect it commands remarkably various, beautiful, and extensive," as it was possible to see Edinburgh Castle and Arthur's Seat across the Firth of Forth from a number of streets. A climb of the church steeple would afford a view of Berwick, Lanark, Perth, Stirling, and Midlothian.[13] With a population of over two thousand, the town boasted eight public fairs, ten alehouses, and "one very commodious inn," although the Reverends Allan Maclean and John Fernie regretted that the local ale had "sadly degenerated," becoming "weak and insipid," with the result that the alarming and evil practice of drinking whiskey had taken ale's place.[14] Fortunately for the residents, though, the local slaughterhouse had been moved outside the town's limits, and the town had appointed an officer to inspect weights and measures, enforce street cleaning, and move on vagrants begging in Dunfermline's streets.[15] Agricultural improvements had been taking place, the reverend gentlemen noted with approval; it was a welcome trend, since mining, a significant part of the local economy, had affected the quantity and quality of the local water supply.[16] The population spoke a mixture of "Scotch-English" and "in general, the people are strong, and abundantly quick in learning mechanical employments"; they were also "remarkably ingenious, industrious, and frugal." Nevertheless, there was room for concern, since there also were "many idle, factious, discontented persons, who are greatly divided in their political, moral, and religious sentiments. In gratifying their capricious humours, and supporting their respective parties, they sometimes involve themselves in unnecessary expense, and defraud their just creditors" (these expenses were incurred on items such as "dress" and "furniture"). "Increasing trade, manufacturers, and the rapid circulation of money, has had an unhappy influence on their morals," was the gloomy conclusion of the good reverends. Matters were not helped by the lack of attention to education: in general, it was neglected, and many could not read. "Proprietors are not sufficiently attentive to the instruction of youth," who, lacking proper guidance, become "grossly ignorant and profane."[17]

Ingenious, industrious, but also living beyond his means: all of these qualities might be said to characterize Norton later in his life. As we shall see, though, education certainly played a more central role in his career than in the lives of those "grossly ignorant and profane" youth of Dunfermline. As the *Statistical Accounts* were being created, Norton had already left Scotland; in 1784 he enlisted in the British Army in Ireland and arrived in Canada the following year. Norton's early military career was not a distinguished one: he deserted the army at Fort Niagara in 1787 and went on to teach at John Desorontyon's Mohawk settlement on the Bay of Quinte. Apparently, he found teaching school tedious and its confinement unbearable, preferring instead to spend time "with the young Indians in all their diversions."[18] Upon his resignation from his teaching position, Norton travelled again, this time to the fur trade of the upper Great Lakes; here he worked for John Askin's Detroit-based company. The Battle of Fallen Timbers in 1794, which resulted in the defeat of the important Indigenous confederacy of western New York, Great Lakes, and upper Ohio River Valley tribes, saw Norton on the move again, both geographically and in his work. He returned to Upper Canada and became an interpreter for the Indian Department at Niagara.[19]

At the Grand River, he met Haudenosaunee Pine Tree Chief Captain Joseph Brant, who took him into his service as an interpreter and emissary; Brant also adopted Norton as his "nephew," deputy, and successor.[20] Norton subsequently left the Indian Department's employ and moved to the Grand River community of the Six Nations. In 1799 Brant appointed him a diplomat and war chief. While, unlike the titles of other Confederacy chiefs, that of a war chief was not hereditary, it recognized his abilities and courage and gave him authority to act with and for the Confederacy in specific situations.[21] Norton also was given the name Teyoninhokarawen, or "it keeps the door open," an honorific that both reflected his position and abilities and proved to be, in many ways, prophetic. From that point he took on a recognizable, albeit at times contested, role whereby he mediated between the hereditary chiefs and the Indian Department. It was in his capacity as Teyoninhokarawen that Norton embarked on the portion of his career that has attracted the attention of historians: that of a negotiator who represented Brant's interests concerning the sale of Haudenosaunee land at the Grand River. As such, he travelled both within North America and overseas, voyages that attracted varying degrees of attention from a number of his contemporaries. Not surprisingly, then, it is at that point that the colonial archives also begin to provide us with more information about Norton and the transatlantic networks that shaped the rest of his life.

1804: From the Grand River to London

By the time Norton arrived at the Grand River, the members of the Confederacy had established themselves in areas that, as historian Charles M. Johnston has pointed out, "duplicated the separate and distinctive communities they had left behind in their New York homeland."[22] Close to two thousand members of the Confederacy made their homes at the Grand River in 1785; the Mohawk formed the largest group. Settling around the area near present-day Brantford, they created the Mohawk village of Oshweken, or "Brant's Town."[23] Through his relationship with Brant, Norton would have been most familiar with the Mohawk village: it too also asserted continuity for its residents, as it "recreated the layout, architecture, and geographic prominence of the Upper Mohawk Canojoharie settlement left behind in New York."[24] The settlement was organized around a frame-and-steepled church, and the Brant family home was also prominent; moreover, it sat on an important transportation route between Lake Ontario and Detroit. The subject of a great deal of attention from travellers, Moravian missionaries, and prominent colonial figures (including Elizabeth Simcoe, wife of the lieutenant-governor, John Graves Simcoe), the Mohawk village left, as archaeologist Neal Ferris has argued, a "greater descriptive legacy than any other on the Grand."[25] In particular, Brant's home offered a high level of hospitality, one marked by both the adaptation of European material culture – tea, china, spirits and wine, a hand organ, beds with sheets and blankets, and uniformed slaves – and a clearly expressed Mohawk identity. As Ferris points out, for Brant and a number of other Mohawk families, "being able to demonstrate an understanding of and the ability to live within both Iroquois and colonial cultures was an important expression of continuing cultural relevance, visibility, and autonomy."[26] It is not surprising that Norton, with his ability to move across ethnocultural boundaries, felt an affinity with Brant and his supporters.

Yet Norton's entry into the Grand River community also occurred at a period of controversy and conflict, discord shaped by the trauma suffered by the Haudenosaunee in the American Revolution. Indeed, the settlement at Grand River had been created by the events of the 1770s: the challenges Norton experienced, both from Indian Department officials and from Haudenosaunee chiefs, might best be described as the aftershocks of the 1770s and 1780s, rippling through the villages of the Confederacy into their council meetings and clan relations.[27] In particular, such aftershocks could be seen at work around the question of land and Indigenous sovereignty. Upon arriving at the Grand River, Brant and a number of fellow Confederacy members realized that hunting and farming would not be enough to support the community. As a way of ensuring Haudenosaunee independence, they argued that selling a portion of the community's lands to those white Loyalists with close ties to the Confederacy would generate much-needed revenue. These funds could then be used to promote economic development, prevent the community from becoming overly reliant on the Crown, and reinforce the Six Nations' claims to sovereign political status and not, as the imperial and colonial governments would have it, a dependent racial group. Moreover, establishing a block of white supporters in the community, Brant thought, also would reinforce ties of friendship and alliance. In a new settler colony, such networks might prove strategically useful to the Haudenosaunee. In early 1787, Brant and other Six Nations leaders sold several thousand acres to ten Loyalist families.[28]

While this transaction pleased Brant and his supporters, it was met with great hostility by the colonial and imperial governments, who had no interest in recognizing the sovereignty of the Six Nations and argued that the terms of the Haldimand Grant (the deed that had transferred land at the Grand River to the Six Nations from its Mississauga residents) gave the Haudenosaunee only usufruct rights and not full title: they could sell or lease land only to the colonial government, not to any other parties.[29] Brant, in particular, objected strenuously to the government's position. Not only did he oppose any attempt to encroach on the Six Nations' ability to act as the Confederacy saw fit, he saw in the government's desire to limit land sales echoes of American practices: the new United States government profited by being able to purchase lands from Indigenous communities cheaply and then reselling them to settlers for considerable profits.[30] Over the course of the 1790s, Brant and his supporters negotiated with the new colonial government for a resolution to the question of the Six Nations' control of land and sovereignty. (Although the colony's administrator, Peter Russell, had confirmed Brant's land sales, he did so without the support of the colonial executive council or the permission of the Duke of Portland, the British home secretary). By the end of the decade, though, London-based officials, Indian Department agents, and Upper Canadian government administrators had obstructed Brant's efforts, and he decided to explore new strategies. The latter included working on internal improvements at the Grand River and completing any outstanding land sales, a task which would involve a direct appeal to the Privy Council in London.[31]

Norton, it seemed to Brant and his supporters, was an ideal emissary. Not only was he familiar with the situation at the Grand River and shared Brant's hopes for the community's political independence and improvement, Norton was well-acquainted with the Indian Department. The latter, Norton felt, had become an impediment to the Haudenosaunee's prosperity: its treatment of the Six Nations was becoming increasingly autocratic, while simultaneously the department wished to reduce its financial obligations for the community. (It also helped that Norton spoke three European languages in addition to English, and twelve Indigenous languages and dialects).[32] Thus it was Norton who went as the Six Nations' representative to England to try and resolve the question of land, its ownership, control, and the relationship of these question to matters of political sovereignty.

In early February of 1804 Norton left the Grand River for Niagara, travelling first with a group of friends and then with an elderly man and a woman. A snowstorm led his male companion to leave the group for the shelter of a nearby village; Norton and his female companion continued on foot, running into a friend with a sleigh and good horses. Norton, it seems, preferred to walk, while another member of the group drove the sleigh. Whether he did so out of gallantry or pragmatism is unclear; he claimed to have passed the sleigh once it met a three-mile ascent, so perhaps it was a mix of both. From Niagara, Norton's route took him to New York City, where he lodged in a boarding house for three days before embarking for Liverpool. Norton's stay in the city included befriending an (unnamed) Quaker, who provided him with letters of introduction to individuals in England, a gesture that points to both the strength of humanitarian ties and, too, Norton's ability to create relationships of affection and sympathy.[33]

We don't know if he was seasick on the voyage, if he was excited or apprehensive about seeing Britain again, or if the dual purposes of his mission – to see that Brant's wishes were respected and to enlist again in the British army to fight against France – preoccupied his thoughts and emotions. We do know that, as well as the letters of introduction provided by his New York Quaker acquaintance, he also brought with him similar documents from Brant that introduced him to Hugh Percy, the second Duke of Northumberland, Sir Evan Nepean, and the Earl of Moira, Secretary for War and the Colonies.[34] Although he first stayed at a hotel, by the end of June Norton was lodging with Quaker chemist and humanitarian William Allen at 2 Plough Court, Lombard Street. Norton's networks had brought him to an area that was itself "the heart" of international and imperial trade, a street that, with its many banks, would become the capital's financial centre.[35]

A good portion of Norton's time was taken up with writing to Edward Cooke, the undersecretary to Earl Camden (Moira's successor), and trying to find a copy of the Haldimand Grant in order to strengthen Brant's case. Although he came close to success, having persuaded Lord Dorchester (Sir Guy Carleton), the governor-in-chief of British North America, to testify on his and Brant's behalf, Norton's hopes were crushed. In early July, correspondence from Upper Canada arrived in the metropole that stated two Grand River councils had denounced Norton's mission.[36] Yet Norton's disappointment over the failure of both his endeavours (he was unable to enlist in the army), was mitigated by the reception he received from William Allen and his contemporaries.[37] Allen, along with his friend Robert Barclay, represented multiple and linked currents in early nineteenth-century Britain. As well as being part of the Society of Friends, Allen was an abolitionist and promoted science, education, and philanthropy.[38] Originally from a prominent Quaker family in Philadelphia, Barclay had lived in England for over forty years and had become a well-known brewer; he also had a keen interest in literature. As well as introducing Norton to like-minded humanitarians and proponents of education and reform, William Owen and William Wilberforce, Allen and Barclay also helped house and support Norton in both London and at Barclay's homes in Bath and Sussex.[39]

Owen, a fellow of Cambridge's Corpus Christi College, took him to the university in March 1805. There Norton transported his listeners across the Atlantic, giving talks designed to educate his English audience about Upper Canada; Iroquois history, culture, and spirituality; and the more recent history of his voyage to Britain, all of this recorded by "Headley" (in all likelihood Charles Allanson Winn, Lord Headley, a fellow of Cambridge's Trinity College). In Headley's account, Norton features as an ethnographic lecturer, as he told his listeners of hunting practices, Mohawk women (better-respected than their English counterparts, he noted), education, marriage practices, the Iroquois creation story of Sky Woman, trade, medicine, dreams and predictions, government, warfare, and language.[40] During his discussion of warfare, Norton decided to provide his audience with a war dance, using another man as a partner. He also sang two war songs, one for his dance and one addressed to women, accompanied by a flute "similar to a clarinet." During his dance, though, Norton, who had impressed Headley with his "mild and humane" countenance, "instantly changed" his appearance and became a ferocious warrior. He took on a "most savage and terrific look; he sprang forward to seize the enemy with amazing ferocity; the action was both manly and graceful."[41] Overall, Norton struck Headley as possessing traits both similar to and distinct from British culture. "Tall, about six feet high and well made, very active, rather dark complexion, but by no means sallow nor so dark as many Englishmen, who have lived in hot climates, his countenance is remarkable mild and pleasing; his manners are perfectly surprising. He has a native politeness, which makes him act with the greatest propriety in all companies. I do not know anyone who relieves or gives anything at table with so pretty and pleasing a grace."[42]

Headley was impressed by Norton's dress but, based on his own gender, felt obliged to profess his lack of experience in such matters, admitting "it will not be so easy for me to give an intelligible description of his dress as I am not skilled in the delicate terms which ladies are upon these occasions." His powers of sartorial observation may have been more acute than he realized, as he went on to list the items of clothing Norton sported. Working his way from head to toe, Headley noted Norton's headdress of red silk and ostrich feather, a "tail [that] consist[ed] of the hair which grows at the top of the head," moving to a blue calico shirt with small white stripes, a silk belt studded with silver brooches, high leggings, and shoes made of "leather obtained from the beasts killed in hunting," tied with leather strings. "The shoes are just like our shoes, only the soles are of the same substance with the rest w[h]ere the opening is for the foot to go in. There is a part which folds over outwards ... I suppose it is the part which the Ladies embroider." Headley felt that Mohawk dress had an "elegance in it which gave a manly appearance to the whole person."[43] He also was struck, albeit not favourably, by Norton's "large silver" earrings: "this was the only part of the dress that I would wish omitted; as it was the only article that reminded you of a barbarous, that is an uncivilized nation."[44]

Earrings aside, though, Headley also rejoiced "to find that the Bible Society has offered to print in the Mohawk language and part of the scripture if Mr. Norton would translate it." Norton's professed devotion to this task was unequivocal, as he vowed to rise each morning "before sunrise and not leave off till midnight if they would but print it." This work might serve as both compensation and consolation for the dashing of Norton's other hopes: "if Mr. Norton does not succeed in the causes for which he first undertook mission he ought to comply to be satisfied with the comforts which his tribe will receive from this translation of the Gospel."[45] While earrings (and possibly war dances) might strain the bonds of empathy and interest that Headley felt for Norton and his people, Norton's keenness to disseminate Christian teachings brought him back into the circle of amity and warm attachment.

Headley clearly admired Norton for his intelligence, strength, and manliness; equally importantly, his admiration translated into a belief in his friend's authenticity. "I am not writing in a cold manner," he admitted, and so far as the "identity of Mr. Norton which I understand has been questioned I will mention once for all that he has credentials which I have read from the same council which informs our government of the election of their chiefs and also from Capt. Brant – he is acknowledged by our government."[46] Moreover, Norton "was personally known to the Duke of Northumberland, when in America, and has been noticed by his grace in the most handsome manner since his residence in England." Noting that both Northumberland and his son, Lord Percy, had been incorporated into the Mohawks through adoption, Headley also referred to the attention Percy paid to Norton while at Cambridge, calling on him and leaving a "visiting ticket for him with his Mohawk name upon it ... Mr. Norton was very much delighted." "I have observed a very high degree of honour and regard for his word it is natural to suppose that he is much mortified that his business is not yet finished." After all, when pressed for the written text of the "original grant," one that he could not produce, Norton offered to recite it, a presentation which was not permitted. "He seems more hurt by their doubting his word," Headley observed, "than by the delay in completing the object of his mission."[47] Norton may have been affronted by both the slight to his honesty and, too, by his British audience's questioning of the legitimacy of oral testimony.

Norton's ability to respond to myriad questions about his people – a number of which were quite simply "foolish" – and to do so with grace and intelligence, also impressed Headley.[48] His answers were "shrewd," and his command of English "elegant." Norton had a "very nice selection of words, and uses them with great propriety," having learned his English from his Scots mother. When asked by one of Headley's friends if the Mohawk used metaphors drawn from the animal world to describe their warriors, fighting like tigers or bears, for example, Norton's response was clear but firm. His people having "contemptible opinion of the abilities of those animals," they instead "say that a warrior who distinguishes himself in battle, had conducted himself as a man ought; that he has proved himself to be a true son of the Five Nations." Headley believed that Norton's presence and charisma held his audience and that he had witnessed a truly masterful performance, in which imperial perceptions and concepts of the Mohawk had been challenged, perhaps even undermined. "The attention paid to Mr. Norton at Trinity College was very great; he was listened to, with the utmost silence; no other voice but his could be heard in a room containing about forty people the surprise of different persons was very astonishing almost all came with the Idea of seeing an uncivilized Savage; but after they had been for a short time in his company, the story was materially changed, & this is the man we call a savage said one; these are the people we think absolute Cannibals. Each according to his ruling passion expressed his astonishment – one wondered where he could get his Information; another his money, another his politeness."[49]

Like those of other Indigenous travellers, then, Norton's was an appearance framed within the theatrical and performative milieu of eighteenth- and early nineteenth-century imperial expansion, a milieu that, as Headley's comments suggest, was fascinated with Indigenous people's dress, body ornaments, and enactments of their culture. Yet as art historian Ruth Phillips has pointed out in the context of settler colonies (most specifically that of Upper Canada), such fascination was often no guarantee that the historically and culturally contextualized meanings represented in dress and ornament were conveyed by European observers.[50] Despite Headley's admiration for many of Norton's qualities and character and his detailed description of Norton's appearance, it is likely that the cultural messages represented in Norton's clothing and bodily ornaments were lost. Norton's insistence that his audience understood the rules, protocols, and rituals that governed both Haudenosaunee warfare and society in general was not an aberration or personal quirk: as Thrush points out, other Indigenous visitors to London brought "their own systems of ritual and protocol [ones] as complete as those of the Regency and the early Victorian city."[51] However, the onlookers' comments concerning Norton's acquisition of knowledge, financial support, and manners suggest how deep-rooted their incredulity at a "civilized Indian" might be.

Moreover, in the particular imperial moment in which Norton appeared in Britain, both south Asia and, in particular, British exploration in the

Pacific were very much on the minds of his audience members.[52] Drawing connections between different Indigenous cultures, then, might help reaffirm the status of one's own as important and worthy of attention, part of a global phenomenon. In discussing Mohawk war songs, Norton suggested Trinity's collection of Tahitian drums, brought back by Captain Cook, were similar to those of his countrymen.[53] Simultaneously, however, it was important to differentiate oneself from other Indigenous peoples, to insist on a specific history and particular characteristics, and, equally importantly, to assert knowledge superior to that of British "experts" and collectors.[54] Headley recounted the tale of Mr Betson, a "fat man who shows many wonderful things" at Trinity's library, who pointed out a "pouch ... for provisions, worn by the East Indians; 'no' said Mr. Norton, 'it is a tobacco pouch. I wear such a thing as that myself.' Next on display were items from the South Pacific. After Norton dismissed the librarian's claim that 'Queen Obordas' apron' was made of tree bark and stated that it instead consisted of hemp, grown 'not far from our village' a statement that perfectly astounded Betson who began to distrust almost every word he uttered."[55] Asserting signs and symbols of indigeneity was a fraught and contested enterprise, one that, as we will see, affected other travellers.

As Headley mentioned, Norton's other activities while in Britain included translating the Gospels into Mohawk. This was more than just a passing fancy on his part. Accompanying Norton on his 1805 trip back to Upper Canada was a printing press that, he told Wilberforce, Captain Pelly (the captain of the ship on which Norton sailed) had taken on board after the watermen had told Norton it was too large for their wherry.[56] Two years later, Norton also was grateful to receive five hundred Bibles from the British and Foreign Bible Society, telling Owen that he wished the society would send more, as he hoped that literacy would become more widespread among the Six Nations. He also planned to send them to the Roman Catholic Mohawks "who inhabit lower down among the St. Lawrence."[57]

As much as Norton's transatlantic voyage brought representations of Six Nations' society to Europe, then, it also assisted in the circulation of European technology to British North America. Furthermore, along with religious and intellectual knowledge, Norton also was keen to become up-to-date with scientific advances in agriculture and bring them to the Grand River. The Bath and West of England Society for the Encouragement of Agriculture, Arts, Manufacturers, and Commerce made him an honorary member in 1804, at which time Norton thanked the "Great Spirit" for influencing the society to think about the "arts of peace" during the "bustle of war." He hoped "some rays of knowledge and the fruit of your persevering researches, may illuminate our Western woods, and there also increase the comforts and happiness of life." In his address to the society, Norton sketched a vision of the spread of knowledge from east to west across the Atlantic, arguing "formerly no other cultivation was known among us but that of maize and beans. No occupation was thought so worthy the attention of a man by which to supply all his wants, as that of the chase. The part from which I came, it is hardly thirty years since cattle was first seen; therefore whatever we perform in Agriculture, being but an imperfect imitation of what originates from this quarter, no communication from us could be in any wise instructive to you." Nevertheless, "if there should be anything in the manner in which we blend our ancient mode with European culture, that might be gratifying to the curious in research, it would be with pleasure communicated to you."[58] Norton's statement that current practices were only "imperfect imitations" suggests metropolitan notions of Indigenous people as capable only of a flawed mimicry.[59] Perhaps, though, his promise that the blending of "ancient modes" with European ones can be read as a subtle hint that such hybridity could be instructive to metropolitan audiences, possibly even presage future agricultural practices.

As well as these personal appearances, Norton also sat for a number of different portraits, an act that both affirmed his celebrated status within certain circles and suggested that such status might be perpetuated even after he set sail for Upper Canada.[60] The American-born, British-based artist Mather Brown depicted Norton in ways that suggested both his Indigenous and Scottish backgrounds. Sporting the earrings that had so distressed Headley, Norton stands in front of a background reminiscent of romantic depictions of Scotland.[61]

In addition to Brown's portrait, Robert Barclay presented the Bath and West of England Society with an oil portrait of Norton, although unfortunately that painting appears to have been lost.[62] He was also painted by Thomas Phillips, a portrait commissioned by the Duke of Northumberland. The latter painting depicted Norton in a Romantic pose, reminiscent of Phillips's portrait of Lord Byron in Albanian clothing.[63] Norton's networks, then, were instrumental in the creation of these artifacts.

As art historian Kristina Huneault has suggested, it is likely that Norton was introduced to one of his portraitists, the London-based, twenty-eight-year-old miniaturist Mary Ann Knight, by John Owen; we know that Mary Ansted gave the miniature to Owen. The latter received Ansted's gift with much delight: on receiving the news that his request for the painting had

Fig. 1.1
Portrait of Major John Norton as Mohawk Chief Teyoninhokarawen,
by Mather Brown, c. 1805.

Fig. 1.2

Major John Norton, by Thomas Phillips, RA

Fig. 1.3

Major John Norton, Teyoninhokarawen, the Mohawk Chief, by Mary Ann Knight,
1805. The many silver brooches Norton wears represented wealth and status in
Haudenosaunee society. (Many thanks to the anonymous reviewer
who reminded me of the brooches' significance.)

been granted, Owen wrote to her from Cambridge "the intelligence afforded me very considerable pleasure; and I should be more unworthy of such an act of kindness than I really think myself I were to be either slow or cold in acknowledging the obligation." Judging "by my own feelings," Owen acknowledged that "an accommodation to my wishes in this instance" must have been painful for Ansted. While

> She knew (it is true) less of the extraordinary man whom it so faithfully represents than I did; and therefore may be supposed to have valued him less. I am however well convinced that she saw and knew enough of him to make the preservation of his memory, and consequently the possession of his image, an object of peculiar interest. I do then most sincerely assure the Lady to whom I am so much indebted, that I am deeply affected with her kindness in sacrificing to my ardent wishes so important a treasure; that I shall always connect the generosity by which I acquired the portrait with the memory of the great original.[64]

John Norton's Transatlantic Communities of Affection and Sociability

Delight, pleasure, and overall warm feelings: not only did Norton stir up these emotions in Owen, he also evoked such sentiments in his other acquaintances. On 14 August 1805, William Allen bade farewell to his newly met friend, an event he remembered with regret shaded with fondness. "I walked with John Norton to Harley Street, Cavendish Square, where we took an affectionate leave. I felt much at parting with him: he is certainly a very extraordinary man: with great mental powers, he combines sweetness of temper and a dignified calm. He is to sail from Portsmouth to Quebec, in the Mercury frigate, (with) Captain Pelly."[65] William Wilberforce confided in his diary that his circle of friends was "extremely struck with Norton, the Mohawk chief (Teyoninhokarawen); his blended modesty and self-possession; his good sense and apparent simple propriety of demeanour." He was, though, relieved that "he again danced his war dance more moderately."[66]

In turn, Norton shared in these sentiments of good-fellowship and happiness. On board the *Mercury*, Norton's thoughts turned to his new English circle, writing to Owen "my heart shall ever glow with gratitude for the many favors I have received from my much to be esteemed English friends."[67] His correspondence depicts a man who embraced the opportunity to participate in networks of friendship, politeness, and sociability. To be sure, these were not exclusively masculine, since he did not fail to send his good wishes and pay his respects to the wives of his new acquaintances. In turn, he hoped that they would remember him: male sociability, after all, was mediated by wives, mothers, daughters, and sisters.[68] He also asked Barclay to tell Miss Agatha Goreghwens to excuse his delay in writing to her. In a letter to his English friend Samuel Thornton, director of the Bank of England and a well-known humanitarian, about his arrival home at the Grand River in March 1806, Norton told him that he had hoped to tell Mrs Thornton "and the young ladies" of the event.[69] Nevertheless, the bulk of his correspondence was sent to his male friends and discussed their company as well as the "exquisite pleasure" brought him by the sight of "an English letter."[70] "I really think of all my friends and regret that the wide water between us prevents me grasping them by the hand," he told Barclay.[71]

Once at home, he eagerly awaited letters from these men. In 1807, he was happy to hear that the Owen family was well, but regretted that "many circumstances have concurred to constrain me to give up the idea of recrossing the Atlantic at present and of again enjoying the pleasure of seeing you all. The only compensation I can now hope for is this mode of conversation, and although it be a cold medium of communication, I must content myself with it, until it may please God to grant me one more congenial to my feelings of gratitude and affection."[72] Transatlantic correspondence was a poor substitute for dinners at Cambridge and walks around London, practices which helped cement networks and communities that merged the political and emotional.

Yet as well as the sentiments of politeness and emotional connection, Norton's military ambitions and identity were not far from his mind. Being in Britain in 1804 and 1805 likely reinforced his determination to re-enlist and strengthened his sense of himself as a solider: the capital increasingly represented imperial military might, while simultaneously memorializing "complex notions of military masculinity," in which both valour and decorum coexisted.[73] As historian Gillian Russell has pointed out, from 1793 to 1815 British society was marked both by its militarization, as local voluntary groups formed to protect the country from a French invasion, and by the theatricality of this patriotic mobilization. Military pageantry, parades, and commemorative ceremonies took place in the streets and other public spaces, while at the Covent Garden or Drury Lane playhouses, dramas, pantomimes, songs, and other theatrical displays were infused with military themes and images.[74] In all likelihood Norton was not immune from such displays and spectacles, including the desire to see the royal figure who presided over much of them. As he told Owen while he waited to sail from Falmouth, "although I have not had the pleasure of seeing the good old King tête-à-tête yet I have had many meetings on the road, and here even in the wide road of the British Channel it seems I could not miss him, we met him in his pleasure yacht off Weymouth, and our ship along with the rest saluted him and regaled us with the smell of gunpowder while at our dinner." Norton may have been slightly disappointed, though, by the encounter, as he concluded "however I only saw the vessel that contained him after all."[75] His wish to meet the King was undoubtedly heartfelt and also, it is likely, influenced by the knowledge that such meetings had been important features of the travels of Brant and other eighteenth-century Indigenous people.

Even while professing his support for Crown and empire, though, Norton suggested that he did so as a Mohawk ally, not a British subject. Writing to Wilberforce at the same time, he was pleased to see "how God with your Navy protects your shores; no enemy dares approach while their coasts are encompassed with your ships. It calls to my recollection our situation with the Americans before the peace of 1795; that while we hunted on their frontiers, they could not with safety leave their fortifications." Furthermore, Norton was extremely grateful to Lord Barham

for the kind favor he has granted me of a passage in this frigate, in which I certainly see a very pleasing specimen of the British Navy. Discipline regular and strict at the same time preserved with the greatest mildness and moderation. It resembles more what is practiced among our Tribe, than from description I had reason to imagine. Commands are given with that energy concordant with circumstances that generally ensures a ready obedience. (I must however observe that our Warriors in common are generally treated with that deference shown to Midshipmen), but the regular system of discipline is a sufficient remedy for any inconvenience that might arise in your service from the variety of characters of the lower ranks that are necessarily admitted therein. The blustering language and imprecations which I have heard in Merchant ships have never assailed my ears. All this prophane [sic] and useless appendage to commands seem here wisely to be laid aside.[76]

He made similar observations to Owen, remarking "the regular system of their discipline seems to render it almost unnecessary for good officers who know how to command to call severity to their assistance except in rare circumstances, and from what I have already seen I have reason to hope that our voyage will not furnish any such."[77] Despite suggestions from some contemporaries and nineteenth-century historians that the "warrior" image rested on foundations of individual male heroism and, so far as Indigenous men were concerned, lacked restraint and self-discipline, Norton's notions of such ideals thus merged manly courage with continence and polite behaviour.[78] As we have seen, Norton also wanted his English audiences to understand the kind of Indigenous manhood that went into battle. He stressed that bravery and fine character, not the ability to purchase office, were the qualities that constituted a Confederacy war chief.[79]

As well as being both a warrior and a sociable man, Norton also saw himself as a loving father and family member. Norton sent the Thorntons a more detailed account of his return to the Grand, something that he had promised Mrs Thornton and the "young ladies." Despite his hopes of a surprise arrival, news of his coming had preceded him. Since the roof of his own home had blown off, he went to "the older brother's house," thinking that he would find the

> little ones and their mother there. A young lad his son was sitting by the fire, on entering and saluting him in English he was not deceived by the change of language, he knew my voice for I was not sufficiently an adept in disguise. He ran to the old family house to the rest. In the instant the door opened, it was again darkened by the sortie of the children and their joyful shouts … in a few moments I had some in my arms and others by my side.

An elderly warrior who knew Norton was there and was at first "deceived by my change of language but soon became undeceived by the noisy acclamations of the children and joined in the general salutation. The congratulations were sincere but shaded with a gloom – not long before the mother of the family the grandmother of the children had left them for a better abode." Here too Norton was philosophical: "God gives and takes. He has the lives of all in his hand."[80]

One year later he was happy to tell Barclay "I have got a little boy in addition to my family of a year and a half … his name is Tehonàkaraa (or young buck in the second year) but we have lost his poor grandmother a little before I arrived. It is the fate of mortals thus to drop off one after the other," Norton mused, "but the time shall come when we shall meet again."[81] Divine intervention notwithstanding, Norton continued to be delighted in his family.

"My little family are very well in health," he told Owen in the summer of 1806, "a fine little boy that is now about two years old and two months old takes up most of my time – We are too fond of each other, and he too much inclined to join me in whatever I am doing, for to leave me much time to write unless he is absent."[82] Happy domestic scenes thus appealed to Norton's sensibility, whether those of his own mixed-race household or those of his English friends. "Although I cannot take a view of you with the eyes of the body," he wrote to Owen in the same letter, "yet the eyes of the mind have you all perpetually in sight when I read your letter I almost imagine myself in the room where you are Mrs. Owen on right hand and the dear lively little ones running about with their delightful prattle – remember me most affectionately to all and my dear little Henry and Stephen I may see in England before they come to shoot squirrels."[83] He also wrote his English friends of his hopes to improve his acres and his plans for the weaning of his calves, even though he often found that the politics of the Six Nations' land claim took time away from his farming.[84] In turn, the Earl of Northumberland passed on information to him of his family estate, particularly the fate of his cabbage crop.[85]

1807–1810: From the Grand River to Cherokee Country

When Norton returned to the Grand River, he may well have found the correspondence from his English friends provided a welcome relief from conditions there. Despite his domestic happiness, the situation was not a promising one. Joseph Brant was becoming weaker as he aged, and his son John was still too young to take on his father's role at the Grand River (although he would do so later in the decade).[86] Norton attempted to carry on his work, but found himself frustrated by the Indian Department, by Lieutenant-Governor Francis Gore, and by some of the civil chiefs in the Confederacy's council.[87] He expressed his frustrations to Owen, writing to him of the "the private ambition or selfish views of the [Indian] agent," ambitions and views which threatened to lead "to the corruption, and perhaps ruin of a people, who were ever faithful to Great Britain, and were once united among ourselves." Norton also felt that the Indian Department "encouraged idleness; instead of virtue vice has been cherished, and instead of endeavouring to unite us in the brotherly bonds of amity and unity – discord distrust and all their gloomy attendants have been introduced and fomented amongst us."[88] After Brant's death in 1807, Norton felt increasingly besieged by those who attacked him for being greedy for land and excessively loyal to Britain at the expense of the Haudenosaunee.

Curiosity about his Cherokee ancestry, a desire to educate audiences on both sides of the ocean about Indigenous people, and dissatisfaction with matters at the Grand River led Norton to leave for a year-long and two-thousand-mile trip through Ohio, Kentucky, and Tennessee to visit Cherokee territory. Norton kept an extensive journal of his trip, one that combined the perspectives of both insider and outsider. As well as being a travelogue, the journal combined ethnography and history, along with an analysis of the political challenges that faced the Cherokee. Pressured by both the United States government and the prospect of future white settlement, the Cherokee debated whether they should move further west or remain on traditional lands.

While Norton's writing can be read for its content, as a portrait of the southeastern landscape and its people, it also suggests the ways in which the journal reflected his particular preoccupations, perspectives, and personal history. The reverberations of the Revolutionary War were felt everywhere, it seemed, as both the Indigenous and American people he met told him of their experiences and expressed a fervent desire that peace would prevail.[89] An elderly justice of the peace in Ohio spoke of white avarice and the need for "peace with Aboriginal Tribes," recounting to Norton the injuries inflicted on them by whites; the American government, he felt, should end land speculation and the greed it unleashed.[90] As he travelled through the southeast, Norton himself recounted Indigenous histories replete with conflicts with Americans, both settlers and the government: burnt villages, maimed and dead men, women, and children, and displaced communities were part of this landscape's past.[91] Warfare, though, was not confined to struggles between Indigenous people and imperial and national powers, as Indigenous people had also fought among themselves for control of territory. Norton's reflections on the southeast's history included discussions of conflicts between the Cherokee and other Indigenous nations, such as the Pawnee, the Osage, and the Natchez.[92] To be sure, Norton's fascination with the histories of the Cherokee and other Indigenous nations in the region was not limited to war. He discussed their different languages, spiritual beliefs and practices (including different creation narratives), and social customs.[93]

War, though, occupied a particular place in Norton's journal, not least because he saw inter-Indigenous warfare as a phenomenon that was undeniably part of the history of Indigenous peoples, but should not shape their present or future. Despite his own military background, Norton saw the unity of Indigenous people as a critical part of their resistance to the United States government and white speculators' attempts to take their lands. Although Norton attempted to remain impartial when asked for his opinion about the Cherokees' options – whether to hold onto their territory or move west of the Mississippi – his invocation of the Haudenosaunee's fate, caused by British duplicity and, in his opinion, divisions within the Confederacy, was telling. Presenting a gift of wampum from the Five Nations to a gathering of Cherokee chiefs, Norton included a warning to "seek and encourage unanimity of sentiment throughout the Nation, as the surest preservative of its respectability and permanent welfare ... and to be resolute in holding fast their territory, to take warning from the fate of the Nottowegui or Five Nations," who had given up much of their ancestral territory, had "confided in European friendship [and] had suffered their Villages to be enclosed in the bosom of their Settlements," and had subsequently been offered "every indignity," even by those "whom they had thought their best friends."[94] Norton, it seems, had learned an important lesson: not all "friends" were true and loyal, particularly when the negotiation of political boundaries was at stake.

War, though, could also provide the conditions for leadership to emerge. Norton reported "it is a general complaint in the Nation, that, since the decease of Kenniteagh" and other elderly respected chiefs, that the Cherokee "have suffered for want of men of abilities to govern them and direct their affairs." These problems, though, seemed to him to stem from "want of opportunity" to call such leaders forth, rather than "a scarcity of talents." Norton mused:

> In a time of war and trouble, those who lead the warriors with success against the enemy, and who shew more than a common address and intrepidity in extricating them from difficulties, acquire a degree of renown and respectability above the reach of the assaults of the vain and malicious, who have shrunk into their natural nothingness in the time of danger and difficulty. Thus supported by the love and gratitude of their countrymen and recommended by the voice of Fame with a moderate share of good sense and eloquence, they are enabled to calm the passions of contending parties, and to unite and lead them to promote the National Welfare.[95]

Here, too, his own situation, in which he felt assaulted by the "vain and malicious" at the Grand River and within the Indian Department, most likely shaped his thoughts. Whatever the case, though, for Norton history provided clear warnings. Narratives of the recent past could help anchor political strategies for the Cherokees' future, one in which unity and independence must prevail.

Yet that same more recent past also gave hope for that future. Norton was struck by the changes brought by contact with Americans, particularly Quakers and other religious groups. Hunting remained important to the Cherokee; indeed, Norton and his party hunted throughout their journey. Norton was impressed, though, by the prosperity of many individuals and communities he met during his travels, a prosperity that arose from a range of enterprises.[96] He admitted that this was not because the Cherokee had proved to be model agriculturalists, citing Chief Kennetea (Little Turkey), who told Norton that, although Cherokee men had done little with their crops, they were raising large herds of cattle, which they sold for great profit.[97] The villages Norton visited appeared to be pleasant places, with cultivated landscapes, neat houses, and "well-arranged plantations," places where Norton and his companions were "entertained with a profusion of good things."[98] A number of individual men embodied such adaptations and cultural mixing. For example, on meeting the Cherokee translator John Thompson, Norton initially thought Thompson was an Anglo-American, until he heard him speak fluent Cherokee. Thompson, Norton discovered, was a man of considerable property and was also one of the nation's great hunters; at his home Norton saw many cattle, several slaves, and some Anglo-American servants.[99]

Norton believed the women of the nation had also made a great contribution to its well-being and had demonstrated their ability to adapt. Cherokee women's skills in spinning and weaving impressed Norton: his journal charts such work, it seems, wherever he found it. "Everything about these houses denotes more than ordinary industry and neatness," he mused, not least because "many of the women were busily employed in spinning cotton on the large wheel."[100] Norton also recorded his conversations with various chiefs or prominent men who told him, with apparent pride, of women's progress in such industrious pursuits.[101] Whether Norton had been influenced by European notions of women's work and status as being the cornerstone of a civilized society, or whether he felt that Cherokee women wielded great influence and thus needed to form the vanguard in adapting European technology, is not clear (like the Haudenosaunee, Cherokee descent and membership was matrilineal). Nevertheless, while Norton – like many other male travellers in the nineteenth century – negotiated and spoke primarily to other men, his account foregrounds Cherokee women and their work as harbingers of future prosperity.

While taking up spinning and weaving could be seen as straightforward indicators of assimilation to European norms, matters were not so simple for Norton. His journal does not suggest that the Cherokee should simply integrate into American society, losing their lands and identity. Instead, Cherokee prosperity and industry would provide the wherewithal for the Cherokee nation to protect their territory and stand united against the American government and land speculators. Although Norton did not approve of some Cherokee practices – believing, for example, that Christianity must replace traditional "superstition" – he was confident that Indigenous people were fully capable of change and adaptation. Norton did not agree with those who believed in "natural" tendencies, whether for better or worse. If "Aboriginal Americans" lacked "such a persevering industry," such deficiency stemmed from "the diversity of their occupations [more] than from any inferiority, in the natural powers of mind or body, to other nations." Conversely, "I have also endeavoured to shew that it is ... their way of life, and the nature of their ordinary employments, [to which] is to be attributed their excelling in attainments which display no small degree of sagacity, rather than to the possession of any peculiar natural faculties, uncommon to those which it has pleased the Benevolent Author of our Being to bestow, generally, in various proportions, on the whole human race."[102] Indigenous people, then, were not a "race apart," but instead shared fully in the humanity of others: culture, not nature, shaped their abilities and tendencies. Norton made a similar argument about the Shawnee, who appear in his account to be a good-humoured, affable, energetic, vivacious, frank, and hospitable tribe. Although they had made "less rapid progress" in the "arts of Civilization" than the Cherokee, Norton thought this was the result of a "less advantageous situation" rather than any aversion to labour or "inferiority in genius." He noted that Shawnee men were not prevented "by a vain pride" from working in the cornfields, a point he may have intended as a not-so-subtle poke at his Cherokee relatives, who preferred herding cattle to ploughing.[103]

Yet, if hunting and herding were more prevalent than raising crops, Norton was impressed by other Cherokee practices. For one, Norton was invited to political gatherings of the Nation and to social events, where he witnessed dancing, ball playing, and other forms of leisure.[104] Cherokee hospitality within individual households also features throughout his account, as when a "well informed Cherokee" "entertained us with the easy and kind hospitality of his Nation, which seems to make the guest forget that he is from home."[105] Hospitality was not limited, though, to the ready and generous provision of food, drink, and shelter. As in the case of Norton's London acquaintances, it also meant a willingness to converse, to share information openly and freely, particularly one's thoughts on matters within the Nation: Norton's meetings in Cherokee domestic spaces encompassed both intimacy and political developments. Furthermore, in Norton's account, many of these households reflected Cherokee willingness to welcome strangers in other ways. The journal contains multiple references to mixed-race households, the homes of Cherokee women and Anglo-American or British men, such as that of a Scots farmer and trader, whose Cherokee wife was "very respectable" and spoke good English.[106] Norton also met Tekighwelliska (Mr McDonald), the former Deputy Agent of the Crown to the Cherokee in the Revolution, who had married a Cherokee woman and "at the Peace of 1783 his affection for his wife and children had induced him to remain, and share the fate of the Cherokee." Tekighwelliska had spent forty years in the Nation and spoke their language "elegantly, having acquired it much more correctly than has ever been known to be done by a foreigner" and "entertained me with the hospitality of an ancient Caledonian or a modern Cherokee."[107] Here, it seemed, was a society in which racial crossings and the formation of mixed-race households, created through the reach of imperial trade and imperial warfare, was not only prevalent but desirable.[108]

Given Norton's own background and his desire to find his Cherokee family, it would have been odd if he had been troubled or disconcerted by such racial entanglements. His friend Selukuki Wohhellengh told Norton that the chiefs believed Norton's father was the brother of Chief Kennitea's widow, and that Norton must seek her out and speak to her.[109] At their meeting, Norton's aunt "expressed great satisfaction in seeing the son of her brother, and derived much pleasure when she perceived that I could understand her language." She told him of seeing "the scene in which her brother was taken from her: she said, that she saw the officer rescue him after he had been scorched, on which account he was taken away in a wagon – and they were separated." His aunt also hoped that Norton might return "to fix my residence" amongst his Cherokee family, to which he replied that he "could not ascertain the time of my return to them." Norton felt that he was welcomed with great kindness: other family members brought in wild turkeys and tobacco; his cousin, "a young man of about thirty years … of an athletic proportion," took him to meet other relatives, including Innoligh, "the leading Chief at present," and the latter group held a dance for him.[110] From Norton's perspective, the family reunion had gone well.

As well as mixed-race families, the journal also points to other complexities that Norton found within Cherokee society. At John Thompson's household, he noted the presence of Anglo-American servants and, too, African-American slaves, while his census of the Cherokee villages included both 314 American tenants and servants, but also 583 "Negro slaves."[111] Norton's silence on the implications of Cherokee slave-holding is intriguing, given that Cherokee independence was so important to him, as well as his connections to the abolitionists in England. To be sure, he saw "poor, half-naked creatures" working on a Kentucky plantation,[112] and heard of two fugitive slaves who had been discovered living alone by Cherokee hunters on the banks of an Alabama creek, before the Cherokee villages had spread south. They had made "an improvement and planted there," on the banks of the creek, a state of affairs that touched Norton. "How insupportable must slavery be! When these two fellows, to escape from it, were content to purchase liberty at the expense of being sequestered from all mankind; happy in breathing the air of freedom in this solitary asylum, where the chaunting [sic] of birds must compensate for the social converse of a friend to cheer the hours of repose."[113] (For Norton, who particularly relished sociability and companionship, such solitude must have seemed unfathomable). Yet his sympathy for these two individuals did not translate into a straightforward condemnation of slavery. Norton told of a "good farmer's supper" he enjoyed at the home of a man who declared "slavery itself is *contrary to justice*" and yet who also "had some slaves himself, yet they looked plump and had every appearance of being well used and seemingly connected."[114] A friend's brother-in-law, Norton reported, had a number of "negroes" newly arrived from Africa. While they spoke neither English nor Cherokee, and were of a smaller stature than American-born blacks, the new arrivals were "simple and honest, for which reason, the Cherokee esteem them more than those who are brought up in the United States."[115] Such a passage suggests that Norton's sympathy for those who, like his father, had been torn from their homes and forcibly removed across the ocean only went so far.

The War of 1812 and Another Transatlantic Voyage

The situation he found upon returning to the Grand River in June 1810 kept Norton from publishing his findings. Matters had not improved vis-à-vis his position, so much so that Norton considered another trip, this time to the West. The outbreak of the War of 1812, though, kept him in Upper Canada, and Norton went on to distinguish himself, commanding warriors from both the Six Nations and other Indigenous nations on the Niagara frontier. When the war ended in 1814, Norton retired from fighting and received a pension of £200 per year. He also ended the war as a husband; in 1813 he married Karighwaycah, also known as Catherine, in Niagara in an Anglican service conducted by the Reverend Robert Addison. A member of the Delaware nation, Catherine was around sixteen years old and Norton was forty-three.

The end of the War of 1812 saw Norton on the move yet again. In 1815 he travelled back across the Atlantic with Catherine and his son John, with the intent of putting both of them in school and seeking promotion for himself to an officer's position in the British army. The Nortons went first to Scotland, where Catherine and young John were placed in the school run by John and Christian Isobel Johnstone in Dunfermline. By this point the town (including its suburbs) had grown to over eleven thousand residents; although lacking a public coach connection, it boasted four banks and fifteen Friendly Societies.[116] During the Nortons' stay, Dunfermline also saw the foundation of the Dunfermline Philanthropic Society. By the time they were home at the Grand River in 1816, the town's educational establishments included a Lancastrian School, a High School, and a commercial school (the Nortons were probably grateful to escape the torrential rainfall that occurred in June 1816, though).[117]

A married couple for about three years at the time of the Nortons' arrival, the Johnstones were involved in a number of enterprises. Not only had Christian Johnstone been previously married and divorced, she had just embarked on her career as an author, with the publication of *Clan Albyn, a National Tale*.[118] Possibly, as Carl Klinck suggests, Norton's relatives in the area had ties to the Johnstones.[119] Whatever the links and connections were that led the Nortons to the Johnstones' schoolhouse door, Norton's decision to send his wife, Catherine, and his son John to school in Dunfermline suggests a conception of himself as a head of household more closely related to British norms and values. As Chapter 4 will discuss, some of the mixed-race children of the fur trade were sent by their British fathers to school in England and Scotland to equip them for better positions within these commercial enterprises.[120] Although there are fewer sources for the Norton family's progress than fur-trading families have left us, those that have survived suggest that his concerns and those of the school did not differ dramatically from the hopes and fears of other British fathers for their dependents. J.O. Johnstone, the school's headmaster, wrote Norton in December 1815 that both Mrs Norton and John were "in very good health and spirits and were very much rejoiced to hear from you particularly the former who is happy in the thought of your journey here so soon. She still continues a very keen student so much so that I sometimes think this over-anxiety defeats its own purpose. Too close application is certainly not a fault of John's but he comes on very well nevertheless and I have no doubt he will make a very good scholar." Johnstone emphasized Catherine's diligence again in his letter, telling Norton that the school had not had a dancing master since his wife's arrival. Nevertheless, "though we have abundant opportunities for cultivating music Mrs. Norton can hardly be persuaded on to quit her spelling book and writing for anything else." John, though, was in danger of becoming "quite effeminate – he hardly ever goes out of doors." Young John's perceived lack of ambition, particularly in contrast with the drive of his stepmother and father, may have exasperated his teacher: "Mrs. Norton Mrs. Johnstone and myself had a pleasant walk of nearly two mile [sic] today but John complained of cold and would not accompany us."[121]

Despite his son's apparent idleness – and possibly hypochondria – at the time of the Nortons' departure from Greenock, Norton must have been pleased with his trip. His friendship with the Duke of Northumberland, maintained between 1805 and 1815 through the medium of "cold conversation," resulted in a portrait of Catherine being commissioned by the Duchess. On 4 June 1816, Dunfermline town council granted him the freedom of the burgh, a mark of recognition that would have been gratifying.[122] Furthermore, Norton's quest for a more desirable rank was successful. He became a major in the British army, a promotion that Northumberland found very satisfying, since it was "completely a Royal, and not Provincial Commission."[123] Just as Norton had arrived home with his printing press in 1805, this time European technology also followed him across the Atlantic, although on this trip the technology was military. Northumberland sent him rifles and a "Wall Piece ... most properly and carefully proved at Woolwich" (the wall piece was a firearm designed to be mounted on the walls of fortifications or on light carriages). He hoped that Norton would approve and "find it most useful, and formidable, weapon against an enemy."[124] Norton replied with both gratitude and humour, telling the Duke "since I have opened at the Grand River the last mark of your friendship, the wall-piece we have not ceased to admire it, and with some of my companions, we flatter ourselves that even should we be too old for active exertion when another war takes place we may yet be able to injure the enemy at long shots."[125]

To be sure, another war that involved the Six Nations did not take place within Norton's lifetime; moreover, future conflicts saw the Six Nations fight not as allies but, from the Crown's perspective, as its wards. As well, warning signs of the Haudenosaunees' fate in the years after the end of the War of 1812 began to emerge more clearly. More British immigrants to Upper Canada arrived, looking for land on which to settle, and the Indian Department shifted to a civilian arm of the colonial government, charged with assimilating those who had been Britain's allies.[126] On their return to Upper Canada, though, John and Catherine Norton were preoccupied with other matters. Norton now possessed a large parcel of land (possibly just over nine hundred acres), next to the Grand River and south of Caledonia. Here he started building a new home, Hillhouse. At the request of Reverend Robert Addison, he continued his work as a translator, completing the translation of the Gospel of St Matthew into Mohawk (his more ambitious project, to translate all the Gospels, was not completed).

Norton also continued his work on behalf of Brant and his supporters at the Grand, making use of his transatlantic ties to English officials. When John Brant travelled overseas to London in 1821, accompanied by Robert Kerr (the widower of Brant's cousin Elizabeth Johnson Kerr), to pursue the question of land title at the Grand, Norton wrote a letter of introduction to the third Duke of Northumberland, just as he, Klinck points out, had been introduced by Brant to the second Duke. "The kind attention with which your Grace has honored me and our concerns," he told the Duke, "induce me to take the liberty to introduce to your notice Mr. John Brant alias Ayaewacs (a son of the late Col. Jos. Brant) and his cousin Mr. Robert Kerr alias Thayendangea. Their intention is to seek redress at Downing Street for an encroachment made by the Council of York, on the Upper part of the Grand River lands." Brant was a "gentleman [who] served with me in the Indian Department in the late war, and the proofs which he gave of his fidelity and courage, indulges me with the pleasing hopes, that he will support with credit to his family, the character which his father left behind him."[127] Brant and Kerr were ultimately unsuccessful, telling the Duke after they returned that the colonial government had started a settlement "merely to deter our people from receiving the Deed" (the Haldimand Grant). However, they received a "warm welcome" from Northumberland, and their trip made it clear that Norton was part of a "line of spokesmen" for their community, not an "intruder whom future generations of Brants should ignore."[128] On his return, Brant also sent Northumberland news of their mutual acquaintance, telling him that the last time he saw "Colonel Norton he was quite well and the whole of his time occupied in clearing new land, and improving his old fields, he is very much pleased with the Plough, churn, and Flax Machine which your Grace gave in charge to Mr. Kerr and myself."[129] Transfers of technology, then, continued.

Thus, while Norton would not cross the Atlantic again, his links to metropolitan political culture and society continued. He also maintained ties to his friend Robert Barclay, who wrote to him of his domestic affairs and shared news of agricultural developments in Britain.[130] His most immediate connections to Britain, however, brought him his fair share of anxiety. Norton's son stayed with the Johnstones for four years, remaining with them when they moved to Inverness and founded a newspaper. In 1819 John returned home; the next year he was followed by a Miss Macdonald, whom he had met in Scotland and who would become his wife.[131] However, bills for John's education also made their way across the ocean: £184.15s was owed by Norton to the Johnstones, a sum which he could not meet. While Norton's Scottish family members had paid part of his son's expenses, he had already racked up debts in his last trip and did not have the funds to make any new payments. "I was in great despondency," Norton admitted to his relative Adam Wilson, "about that which was due on John's account, for had it not been so I would not have failed making remittance and this failure gave me much uneasiness, lest the extraordinary delay might have put you to some inconvenience"(Wilson's assistance to John Jr included buying him clothes and paying his coach fare from Inverness to Glasgow).[132] The Duke of Northumberland came to his rescue, paying the debt and earning an even greater share of Norton's gratitude. "The generous manner in which my noble friend has relieved me from this anxiety," he wrote to Wilson, "has given me sensations which I cannot describe so readily as I can feel."[133] In his financial straits, Norton was probably like veterans of the Napoleonic Wars, who found return to civilian life an economic challenge.

While he occupied a position of some prestige and prominence at his Grand River home, certifying the war records of other Indigenous people and advising white settlers on various topics, he does not seem to have been suited for a life of settlement himself. For one, he yearned to return to Cherokee country, but lacked the money to undertake such a trip. Perhaps, he thought, the colonial government might help him; after all, like his British grandfather (although without the violence that underpinned Norton's father's trip across the Atlantic), Norton had brought a young Cherokee man back with him in 1811, who now wished to go home, back to Cherokee territory. "A youth, a kinsman followed me to this country," he wrote to Colonel Addison, the military secretary, "the War prevented our return, he served with me throughout. He now sighs to revisit his country and his friends, and I am desirous to see him safe there." However, the young man's home was now west of the Mississippi, his people having moved "more than a thousand miles from our abode on the G[rand] River. The expenditures I have been subject to since the war deprives [sic] me of the means of appearing there in a manner becoming the King I serve. I am therefore necessitated to petition government for the assistance of a hundred pounds for this journey; it might promote the interests thereof, and if I live long enough I will repay it, but as life is uncertain I cannot at present burden my family with it."[134] He did not – at least not then – make that trip.

John Norton's Last Journey

His domestic life shaped the last years of Norton's life in Upper Canada, years that involved Catherine and the breakdown of their marriage. The few earlier glimpses we have of Catherine's relationship with her husband suggest that, at least for a time, the couple were content with each other and their life together. In an undated letter to Christian Johnstone, Catherine wrote of her happiness to hear of her former teacher's good health, sent her "warmest affection," and "how much I learnt that the distance we are apart bereaves me the hopes of ever seeing [you] again and writing is a cold method of conversation between friends." "I have become very industrious," she confided, "and soon expect to enter my little cottage where, if providence should ever give me an opportunity of entertaining my friends from your side of the water I will feel as happy as if it was a palace." Catherine asked Christian to send through John two songs, "Lady Fair," and "Saw Ye Johnny Coming," and closed her letter with a charming pastoral image of a "tame deer at my elbow [that] won't let me write anymore, it is so full of its play."[135]

By 1823, though, the Nortons' happiness had ended. In late summer, while haymaking was underway, Catherine complained to her husband that a young man, Joe Crawford (Big Arrow), had "offered her the grossest insult a woman can receive." To make matters worse, Crawford was no stranger. Norton had "affectionately fostered [him] from his childhood," and he fought alongside Norton in the War of 1812, being wounded at the Battle of Fort George. But Norton also disapproved of Catherine's behaviour and "apprehensive that I once touched on the subject, my feelings might lead me to extremities, I sent notice to him to be gone and the same to her." However, "both had deferred obeying my directions; for when he came to the house she rushed suddenly down stairs, and accusing him to his face, started to upbraid my moderation." In the midst of such turmoil, Norton could not remember exactly what he said at that moment. He did, though, feel both angry and reluctant to hurt Crawford, but in the face of the latter's goading of him, Norton "told him to choose his weapons, for if I did anything he must have an equal chance." Unfortunately for Crawford – and Norton – the duel ended in the former's death, albeit more, it seems, because of Crawford's actions than Norton's. "After firing it appears he sprung upon me: and had seized or in some manner changed the direction of the pistol for the ball passed downward and through his thigh, while his ball grazed the top of my head. When I saw the poor young man stretched on the ground and the recollection of past times crowded into my mind – pity succeeded to every other feeling and to a much higher degree; I was so much distressed for many days on the third my friends prevailed on me to leave home, in hopes that a change of situation might afford the mind relief. You will think me superstitious when I tell you that (notwithstanding the kind attentions and assiduity of my friends to make me easy) the first real consolation I had was in a dream wherein I saw the deceased."[136] It is possible, particularly given his reference to superstition, that Norton was referring to Indigenous beliefs in the efficacy and strength of dreams.

Dreams of Crawford may have consoled Norton; his son, John Norton, Jr, was not quite so sanguine as his father about the reactions of the dead man's family. "Crawford's family say little or nothing to me," he wrote to him, "but from what I can find out by round about way they seam [sic] to be very invited [embittered] against you." Stay away, he warned his father, "until they get a little more calm." Perhaps observing Haudenosaunee custom might help: would Norton "think it proper for me to offer wamping [wampum] and presents to the injured family according to Indian custom which I fancy you know." If covering the grave was a viable option, then Norton would have to authorize his son to do so and tell him "what you would be willing to give and in what way": annual amounts? a lump sum? money? or "goods or grain or cattle"? The support should be offered only to Mrs Crawford and her children, "for certainly the widow and orphans are more entitled than Mrs. Norton that I am sure you are aware of you may do as you please about it."[137] Norton's neighbour, Robert Thomson, echoed his son's concerns. "Anxiety of mind for your safety unfits me completely for either thinking or writing … When I reflect upon your too generous heart, and the ingratitude you have met with I cannot refrain from weeping."[138] One week later, Thomson was still worried for his friend's well-being. He had heard that some Onondagas, members of Crawford's clan, were still

Clearly things had changed greatly for Catherine since she wrote to Christian Johnstone of her tame deer. The letter admits to some misbehaviour on her part, as she pleads to be forgiven for her sins, although she attempted to defend herself against charges of theft from her husband. At the time of her marriage's collapse, Catherine would have been approximately twenty-six, and Norton, fifty-three. The gap between their ages may well have contributed to their alienation; Norton's pride may have been hurt if Catherine was, indeed, involved with a much younger man.

A traveller who crossed both the Atlantic and a number of cultural boundaries, Catherine ended up being a pathetic figure, or so the available archival sources tell us. Norton did not forgive her. She left the Grand River area and was last reported to have gone to Fairfield on the Thames River, close to the ruins of the local Moraviantown mission. Missionaries from that area reported that, in the winter of 1827, they called on an "Indian woman of the Monsey [Munsee] tribe who had formerly been married to a certain Captain Norton," and who, becoming "dangerously ill," died on January 16 of that year. Her father, they noted, had been white: she had been raised by her grandmother (they did not note whether she was white or Indigenous) until the age of sixteen, at which time she married John Norton. Although their obituary noted Catherine's time in Scotland with her husband's family, it also stated "on their return to the Grand River they led a wild and dissolute life. Her husband having killed an Indian in a duel on her account, he left her and took up in the south among the Cherokee nation." While it's possible that Catherine remembered at least some aspects of her life at the Grand as "wild and dissolute," the missionaries also might have been influenced by gossip and rumour, since the Norton case became the stuff of local legend in southern-Ontario histories.[143]

After attempting to protect his father by, amongst other things, expunging his stepmother from their lives, John Norton, Jr, went on to live in the area with his Scottish wife. It is not clear if he moved into his father's home, although as it was left in Thomson's care, it seems unlikely. Thirteen years after John Norton's departure, his son received a patent for 388 acres in North Cayuga Township; the Nortons sold it in 1840, and may have moved further south and west to the Upper Canadian town of Thamesville.[144]

And what of John Norton? After leaving the Grand River in 1823, he was next reported to be in his young Cherokee ward's community in the Dwight mission in Arkansas. Norton then may have set off on a journey westward, as his 1821 and 1822 letters to the Duke of Northumberland and to his friend Henry Goulburn told of his desire to make his way to the Pacific along the

Santa Fe trail.[145] Here Norton's story ends: he may have died in October 1831, although the place of his death remains unknown.

John Norton and Self-Fashioning within the Imperial World

In many ways this tale of Norton's life resembles a late-eighteenth or early nineteenth-century novel: making something of oneself from humble beginnings; the restless movement and voyaging from place to place; heroic deeds and a rise to prominence, partly through the patronage of important persons (whether Joseph Brant or the Duke of Northumberland); a journey to find one's complicated family roots and a keen desire to leave a record of those experiences; successful and then thwarted romance; and a sad, pathetic end. His narrative may well have served as an inspiration for a work of fiction: his contemporary, the Upper Canadian novelist (and fellow major) John Richardson, is said to have created his protagonist Wacousta in his novel of the same name with Norton in mind.[146]

Fictional creations aside, though, perhaps what is intriguing about Norton's life are the choices available to him and those he made. It would have been possible, for example, for him to identify as a Scottish soldier, fur trader, and teacher, to fashion himself as primarily "British" at a time when British imperial power was expanding and opportunities to fight in the country's defence were on the increase. That he decided to ally himself with the Six Nations, despite the tensions and conflicts that such a choice entailed, suggests that such an alliance held out possibilities for Norton that the British army or a life back in Dunfermline did not: the opportunities for different kinds of movement; for new alliances, both political and intimate; for new forms of knowledge and experience, whether journeying to the Cherokee or joining the Bath Agricultural Society. Norton's own personal drive for adventure, his intellectual curiosity, his courage, and his ability to adapt to new situations, new social circles, and new forms of emotional communities played an important role in his life.

He was not, though, unique. As the lives of diverse individuals, such as anti-slavery campaigner Gustavus Vassa and the English traveller Elizabeth Marsh demonstrate, eighteenth-century transatlantic, imperial, and global routes and circuits had afforded others opportunities to circumvent social, cultural, and political norms and structures, to experience both danger and pleasure, upheaval, and new places to call home.[147] Closer to Norton in time and place, the travels of Abu Taleb bin Muhammed Isfahani, the Shi'ite Persian scholar from north India's Muslim elite, provide a useful point of comparison to Norton's movement (not to mention those who would follow him). Invited in 1799 by the Scots military officer Captain David Thomas Richardson (who also was a Persian translator for the East India Company) to join him on the latter's return to Europe, from his arrival until he departed in 1802 Taleb became a celebrated figure in London, painted by James Northcote, RA, and lionized by the press and the London crowds. "An accomplished gallant and flirt," Taleb gained social status and an entree to circles of elite masculine power through his relationships with London's upper-class white women. He also enjoyed the city's public and private entertainments, its coffee houses, clubs, societies, and House of Commons debates, which he likened to "flocks of Indian parakeets, sitting upon opposite mango trees."[148] Upon his return to Calcutta, Taleb recorded a narrative in Persian of his travels; it was sent to Charles Stewart, a professor of Persian at Oxford's Haileybury College, who translated portions of it and published it as *The Travels of Miza Abu Tableh Khan*.[149] Norton and Taleb thus shared similar traits and experiences, which included portraits, patronage, and personal charm. We can, though, surmise that class distinctions and different valences in their crossings of racial boundaries distinguished their travels from each other. Although Norton's work as a translator and journal-keeper demonstrated a keen intellectual interest in bridging two cultures, one that foreshadowed the nineteenth century's anthropological fascination with North American Indigenous culture, at the time of Norton's British sojourns there were no Oxford professorial posts in Mohawk, Ojibwe, or other northeastern Indigenous languages.[150]

Nevertheless, like other transatlantic and global travellers, Norton was an individual shaped by different worlds and the nature of the borders that he traversed. His movements were made possible and, at times, orchestrated by his particular transatlantic contexts and networks. In his case, they were ones of both imperial warfare and humanitarianism, which provided opportunities for him, while, simultaneously, acting as a crucible of colonialism for communities such as the Six Nations. Such contexts and networks would shift in the years after the War of 1812, as Indigenous people in British North America saw their military role decline precipitously, even as the British Empire's military strength grew. In some ways, then, Norton's travels represent the end of one era, the closing of a "military moment," in which alliances between nations of the Great Lakes and imperial power came to an end. But he also represented degrees of continuity that became even

. 2 .

Missionary Moments and Transatlantic Celebrity, 1830–1860: The Anishinaabeg of Upper Canada

Introduction

While John Norton was making his way south into North America's interior, another group of Indigenous people were contending with events that would lead to their own transatlantic voyages. From 1831 to 1860, members of the southern Upper Canadian Anishinaabe (Ojibwe) band of Mississauga – Kahkewaquonaby (Peter Jones), Shahwundais (John Sunday), Pahtahsega (Peter Jacobs), Kahgegagahbowh (George Copway), and Nahneebahweequa (Catherine Sutton) – travelled across the Atlantic.

Like Norton's 1804–05 trip, some of this travel was undertaken to resolve disputes over land, to protect the Mississauga's claims to territory in a colony increasingly populated by white settlers. Moreover, as with Norton's reception in Britain, these travellers experienced degrees of popular exposure, becoming part of a growing culture of colonial celebrity in the metropole. Yet there were also important differences from Norton's travels, differences produced by historical circumstances and contingencies. Although humanitarian circles and networks shaped and mediated Norton's time in Britain, they did so after his voyage had begun: these Anishinaabe voyages were even more directly implicated in religious movements. They were sparked by the global missionary movement of the early nineteenth century, which played a direct role in Upper Canada through (amongst other things) the conversion of many Mississauga people and, in the case of Jones, Sunday, and Copway, the recruitment of Mississauga men as missionaries. Furthermore, the type of celebrity culture in which the Anishinaabeg participated differed from the attention given to Norton, who was admired and had his mission promoted by influential, yet small, numbers of the British aristocracy and middle-class Londoners. Although a number of the Mississauga met with royalty, they gained public attention through the medium of the British press, both missionary and secular. Their appearances also were staged in front of those ever-growing crowds who came out to support the missionary cause and, it is likely, to gaze with wonder on the "Red Indian" who spoke for it.

As well, the travels of Jones, Sunday, Jacobs, Copway, and Sutton were distinguished from Norton's transatlantic crossings by the absence of the military and the aftermath of the War of 1812. Despite the important role played by the Ojibwe as British allies in the War of 1812, by the 1830s their military services were no longer needed. Instead, in the decades after the war, the status of Indigenous people shifted to that of wards and dependents of the Crown, their future – so far as colonial authorities were concerned – one of assimilation into Christianity and Euro-Canadian notions of "civiliz-ation." Such a policy, historians suggest, was motivated partly by the need to secure land for the steady influx of British immigrants who arrived in Upper Canada after the end of the Napoleonic Wars, a group that included those dislocated by the social and economic changes of a Britain engaged in post-war reconstruction. As well, the Mississauga found themselves the target of intensified missionary endeavours by British-based Wesleyan Methodists. Missionary proselytizing, on hiatus during the War of 1812, resumed after 1815 with (as we will see) mixed results for Aboriginal people. In addition to demographic shifts and the spread of evangelical religion, the colony's political changes – challenges to its conservative elite, calls for reform, the Rebellion of 1837, and the movement towards responsible government in the latter's aftermath – had mixed, sometimes contradictory, implications for its Indigenous population. Mindful that the colonial reform movement repre-sented a shift towards liberal definitions of citizenship that excluded them, and wary of any connections between the reformers and the United States in light of the treatment of Indigenous Americans during the Revolutionary War and after, Indigenous people turned out in support of the Crown during the rebellion. However, they found their loyalty rewarded in 1857 with the Gradual Civilization Act, aimed at their assimilation.[1]

Yet the story is more complicated than it might appear. The impetus that brought missionaries to the colony also brought humanitarian perspectives towards Indigenous people to the fore, attitudes that saw them as particularly vulnerable to settler violence and the depredations of colonial governments.[2] Furthermore, Indigenous people were not helpless victims of colonial history, since they engaged in negotiations and, at times, direct opposition to policies and practices of the colonial government. Three months before the rebellion, for example, Peter Jones could be found in London, appearing before Queen Victoria and voicing his people's opposition to the colonial government's plan to remove his people to Manitoulin Island. The Prince of Wales, on tour in British North America in 1860, was met by Aboriginal delegates who presented their people's histories of support for the Crown, but also reminded him of the inequities of their treatment by colonial governors and assemblies.[3]

Anishinaabe Biographies

Of the Mississauga Methodist missionaries whose fundraising efforts for their church took them overseas, the best-known was Peter Jones. Born in 1802 to an Anishinaabe mother, Tuhbenahneequay (Sarah Henry), daughter of the Mississauga chief Wahbanosay, and a Welsh father, the surveyor Augustus Jones, until 1816 Jones and his brother, John, grew up under his mother's tutelage, learning Mississauga customs and religion. At that point his father sent him to school near his Stoney Creek farm, where he was taught to speak, read, and write English; the following year Jones's father moved him again, this time to his Grand River lands (Augustus Jones was legally married to Sarah Tekarihogen, daughter of a prominent Mohawk chief), where the teenaged Jones learned to farm and care for livestock. For the next seven years, Jones lived with his father and Mohawk family at the Grand River; he eventually decided to return to school (working in a Brantford brickyard to pay his fees), as he hoped to take up a clerk's position in the fur trade. Although he was baptized in the Church of England in 1820, in 1823 he attended a Methodist camp meeting with his half-sister Polly Jones, and experienced a profound religious conversion. It would lead him to teach Sunday school, help build a chapel, and convert half of the Mississauga band to Christianity.

In 1826, Jones moved to the Credit Mission, a village of twenty dwellings built on the Credit River. The mission had been built by Lieutenant Governor Sir Peregrine Maitland for the converts. Received on trial for the

Methodist itinerant ministry in 1827, Jones extended his missionary work, both within the Mississauga band and across the colony. Working alongside his brother, John, the village schoolmaster at the Credit River, Jones oversaw the creation of a successful agricultural community; the two also translated the Bible into Ojibwe. While Jones believed that the Mississauga's future would be best secured by making a transition to farming, and that accepting Christianity was integral to this shift, he was also a staunch advocate for his people's interests, protesting, for example, about the encroachment of whites on the Mississauga's salmon-fishing grounds at the Credit River, or the Indian Department's failure to pay the full annuity owed to the band. In 1829, the Mississauga of the Credit elected Jones one of their three chiefs: such a position gave him considerable influence within his own community and as its official representative to settler society.

Jones's overseas trips, which began in 1831, were undertaken as a result of his own success in Upper Canada. While he travelled extensively throughout Upper Canada, preaching to white audiences of his people's need for Christianity, he also appeared in a number of Ojibwe communities across the province. Jones's preaching helped lead to the establishment of a number of new missions, all of which needed more financial support than the Upper Canadian church could muster. He first toured the northeastern United States in 1829, along with the American-born Methodist leader William Case and several Indigenous converts. In 1831 Jones travelled to Britain, where he made 150 appearances and raised over £1,000; he also petitioned the Colonial Office concerning Indigenous land claims in Upper Canada and had a private audience with King William IV. It was on this tour that Jones met his future wife, Eliza Field, the daughter of a prosperous industrial and evangelical London family. By the time he left for home in 1832, the two were engaged, an event discussed in more detail in Chapter 3. The following year Eliza herself sailed for New York, where they were married. Jones and Eliza returned to Britain in 1837, his trip prompted by Lieutenant-Governor Francis Bond Head's decision to move the Mississauga of the Credit to Manitoulin Island. As well as conducting another speaking tour, he met with Queen Victoria, an audience that resulted in the Mississauga being granted title to their lands on the Credit. In 1845 Jones, accompanied by Eliza and their sons, crossed the Atlantic again for yet another fundraising trip. During his year abroad, he not only toured England and Scotland and made a stop in Ireland, but, with a French-speaking friend, visited France for medical consultation. Although Jones continued to travel in British North America and the United States, and Eliza took their son Peter

Edmund to England to visit her family in 1854, his poor health prevented him from making another transatlantic trip. Suffering from Bright's disease, Peter Jones died in his Brantford home, Echo Villa, in 1856.[4]

As well as Jones, the Mississauga Methodists John Sunday and Peter Jacobs appeared in Britain in the 1830s and 1840s.[5] Sunday converted to Methodism around 1824 and then helped to found the model mission village of Grape Island on the Bay of Quinte, then moved on to take up a position as an itinerant minister under the direction of the Methodist Episcopal church's superintendent of Indian missions, William Case, and Jones. By the time he travelled to England in 1836, a trip that followed his ordination in the church, Sunday had already covered considerable ground, visiting Ojibwe communities around Lake Superior. While in England, Sunday spoke as at fundraisers for Indigenous missions in Upper Canada and, like his fellow Mississauga Jones, was presented to the Queen. Sunday then served at a number of mission stations, including that of Alderville (near Rice Lake), where he retired from active church work in 1867 and died in 1875.[6]

His contemporary, Peter Jacobs, was one of the first Mississauga converts of the 1820s. He then went to school in Belleville, at the Grand River community, and at the Credit River mission. He began preaching to the Ojibwe at St Mary's River in 1836, and then travelled to the upper reaches of Lake Superior; by 1840 he was working as a missionary at fur-trade posts. Jacobs's ordination took him across the ocean to London, where he lived with Robert Alder, Wesleyan missionary secretary for British North America. Jacobs's return to British North America saw him posted to Fort Frances until 1850. After a short stay in Canada and England, in 1852 he voyaged from Rice Lake to York Factory and published an account of both the trip and conditions at the various mission stations that he visited along the way. Jacobs spent the next few years back in Canada West, first at the Saugeen Reserve and then at the Rama Reserve. However, he became disillusioned with the church, and became less effective as a missionary. He did not receive a mission post in 1857, and after travelling to the United States for an unauthorized fundraising trip, in 1858 was expelled from the Methodist Church as a minister. Upon his return to Rama, Jacobs took up school teaching, interpreting, and selling goods; like a number of his contemporaries, he also worked as a hunting and fishing guide. Jacobs died in 1890, outliving Jones and Sunday, although, according to his biographer, he suffered from alcoholism and lived his last days in acute poverty.[7]

Like Jacobs, the experiences of Anishinaabe missionary and speaker George Copway (Kahgegagahbowh) with both Methodism and forms of border-crossing were mixed. Partly because of Copway's complicated history, his life has attracted considerably more attention than those of some of his fellow-Mississauga. He was born in 1818 and his father, John, was a medicine man and chief. Copway grew up in the Rice Lake area, his childhood years shaped by his parents' practices of hunting, trapping, and fishing. Along with Jones, Sunday, and Jacobs, he and his family also experienced the conversion "wave" of the 1820s. After attending the local Methodist mission school in the 1830s, Copway was invited to work for the church as an interpreter and teacher in its missions along the southern shores of Lake Superior and in Wisconsin; it also sent him to study at the Ebenezer Manual Labor School in Illinois. Upon returning to Upper Canada in 1840, he married English immigrant Elizabeth Howell. Their initial meeting was at the Jones's Credit Mission home, where Peter had acted as a spiritual guide and father to Copway; Elizabeth also was a friend of Eliza Field Jones. After their wedding, the couple travelled to Minnesota, where he had been sent to establish a mission post amongst the upper Mississippi Ojibwe, a posting that involved many moves, because of the ongoing war between the Dakota Mdewakonton Sioux and the Ojibwe. Copway's work for the Methodist church took them back to Upper Canada in 1842, where he served as a Methodist minister for Ojibwe communities at Saugeen and Rice Lake. However, in 1846 he was imprisoned for embezzlement and expelled from the Canadian Congress of the Wesleyan Methodist Church.[8]

Copway quickly refashioned himself as an American-based advocate for Aboriginal rights: he published his autobiography in New York in 1846 and wrote the history of the Ojibwe, gave well-attended lectures along the Atlantic seaboard from South Carolina to Massachusetts, and made friends of American writers and politicians such as James Fennimore Cooper, William Wadsworth Longfellow, and William Cullen Bryant. He also promoted his vision of Kahgega, a territory of over eighteen-thousand square miles that he wished to see established in South Dakota as an alternative to the United States government's removal program. Populated by over one hundred thousand Ojibwe and other Great Lakes Algonquin peoples and run by both non-Indigenous and Indigenous governors, the territory's occupants would hold permanent title to the land and would be encouraged to adopt Christianity and western forms of education.[9] There is no evidence to suggest that Copway had been inspired by John Norton, who also envisioned a "confederated Native state" on western lands, removed from the influence of white settlers and consisting of the Six Nations, but also Ojibwe, Ottawa, and

Pottawatomi peoples, but the similarities between both men's concept of a pan-Indian, "modern," and "agricultural" homeland are striking.[10] Although his efforts in establishing this area were unsuccessful, Copway continued to speak for, in his words, the "Christian Indians of North America." In 1850 he travelled to Britain and Europe to speak at the Frankfurt International Peace Congress in this capacity. Upon his return, Copway founded a New York–based but short-lived newspaper, *Copway's American Indian*. However, by that time his financial difficulties were beginning to prove intractable and became more pressing over the decade.[11]

Perhaps related to these problems, his movements in the late 1850s and early 1860s are difficult to trace. In a one-line article published 1 April 1857, the North Carolina newspaper the *Raleigh Weekly Register*, stated "George Copway, the Chippewa Chief, has gone to Nicaragua, to join Walker's army."[12] To date it is impossible to know if this was a rumour or if he had indeed joined John Walker, the American adventurer who made himself president of Nicaragua in 1856 and who would be defeated by a coalition of Central American states on 1 May 1857. Whatever the case, it seems that the former peace advocate had abandoned the cause of pacifism; in 1864, he and his brother David worked as recruiters for the Union Army in New York and Upper Canada. After the war ended, he advertised himself as a healer in Detroit. Copway died in July 1869 in Ypsilanti, Michigan, having spent his last years estranged from his wife, Elizabeth, and their daughter, Frances Minnehaha Copway.[13]

While the Methodists' adherence to patriarchal structures of mission work meant that Anishinaabe women could not work as ministers to convert their fellow Mississauga, in the case of Catherine Sonego Sutton (Nahneebahweequa), the gendered inequities of colonial rule, combined with her own position within her community, took her overseas. Born in 1824 at the Credit River to Mississauga parents, Catherine was Jones's niece; a family visit to her uncle at the Grand River just after his conversion to Methodism may have persuaded the Sonego family to follow his example. They moved to the Credit River Methodist settlement, where Catherine attended school; in 1837, she accompanied Peter and Eliza Jones to London. Two years later, at the age of fifteen, Catherine married the English carpenter and lay preacher William Sutton, who had immigrated to Upper Canada in 1830. As well as starting a family at the Credit, Catherine also worked as a Methodist class leader.

In 1846 the Suttons first embarked on a number of moves, when they relocated to Owen Sound along with two other families from the Credit.

There the Newash band allocated the family two hundred acres, based on Catherine's Indigenous status, and the family cleared and cultivated at least forty acres of their land and built a house, barn, and stable.[14] In 1852 the Suttons moved again, this time to the Garden River Reserve close to Sault Ste Marie, where they supervised the reserve's mission farm. Two years later, they crossed the border to Michigan, where, until 1857, William worked in one of the state's Methodist missions. Although it is likely they envisioned a peaceful return to their farm once William's work was finished, the colonial government's actions made this impossible. During their absence, the Indian Department had gained control of their land and other band lands, put them up for sale, and then refused to let the Suttons bid on these lands. After the failure of petitions filed by her and other members of her band, Catherine was chosen to represent them in London. While en route, in New York City, she received support from the city's Quaker community, a group that also helped her in England. Like Jones and Sunday, Catherine received a royal audience and was able to regain her land. Sadly, she died five years after her return. William continued to preach until his own death a few years later.[15]

Mobility, Continuity, and Change

As their biographies suggest, these travellers were already part of networks and communities: they were tied to Anishinaabe families, kinship systems, clans, and villages, and, equally importantly, to circuits of Christian Anishinaabeg and to the missionary movement. Historians depict these communities as struggling to negotiate with the changes discussed above: encroachments on land by settlers, the decline of the fur trade, contagious diseases, and a colonial government that increasingly saw Indigenous people as wards, not allies, of the government.[16] As well, those who had converted to Methodism and moved to sites such as Rice Lake or the Credit Mission village were faced with the challenges of adopting new cultural, social, spiritual, and emotional regimens, which – at times – taught them that their traditional ways of life and relationships, both to each other and to the natural world, were "heathenish" and must be left behind.

Yet to see the changes in Mississauga life in the 1820s and 1830s as only those of great disruption is not the entire story. For one, as Katherine Murton Stoehr has noted, the Christianity of figures such as Jones might be far more syncretic than historians originally thought.[17] As well, while Anishinaabe people's adoption of various kinds of self-regulation and discipline, such as temperance or the incorporation of European dress, might differ in form from traditional habits and practices, like other Indigenous peoples their use of particular social and cultural strictures to govern behaviour continued, whether it involved hunting protocols, the gathering of medicines, or attitudes towards elders and clan relationships. Indeed, to see such changes as a rupture or as something completely new that entered their worlds is to risk replicating the discourses of missionaries and colonial officials, who might be oblivious to the structures and forms that shaped the lives and practices of Indigenous communities. For example, temperance, with its connotations of self-control and abstention from harmful practices, was also a feature of traditionalist revival movements, such as the Haudenosaunee Code of Handsome Lake. To be sure, I do not want to suggest that certain practices adopted from Methodism – the corporal punishment of children or increased forms of patriarchal control in Anishinaabe households, for example – did not represent a significant shift in Mississauga communities. Nevertheless, to see these men and women only as victims of historical change does a disservice to the persistence of Indigenous practices and to their practitioners' resourcefulness and determination.[18]

Moreover, although as we shall see these travellers made a habit of commenting on new sights and sounds, peoples and places, they happened upon overseas, their biographies also demonstrate that they had experienced their fair share of mobility and movement before embarking on transatlantic voyages. Whether such movements were those of the itinerant minister who spoke before communities of other Indigenous people in Upper Canada, the Northwest, and across the border or, in Catherine Sutton's case, those tied to her family's relocation and the work she and William did for the missionary cause, these were men and women accustomed to travel and meeting strangers. In addition to the histories of migration for hunting and war undertaken by their own peoples, they had been part of networks, both Indigenous and European, which then facilitated their travels in North America and also helped take them across the ocean to London, Edinburgh, Manchester, Dublin, Paris, and Frankfurt. Rather than seeing their overseas travel, then, as a new and distinct phenomenon, it should be viewed as part of a continuum of mobility. While going to Britain might have been caused by the incursions of settler society, it also represented carefully made choices and decisions.

Missionary Moments in the Metropole

Like John Norton's travels on the Atlantic, we know little about their experiences on the voyage out, whether they all suffered dreadfully from seasickness on the rough waters of the North Atlantic, what they thought of their cabin and fellow passengers, if the days became unbearably tedious (many of these voyages were undertaken before steamship travel shortened the time at sea), and if they were relieved, excited, or apprehensive on sighting the coast of Ireland or England (perhaps all three). For some, the former might present an opportunity to educate transatlantic audiences in the histories of colonialism. In his travelogue *Running Sketches*, George Copway mused on seeing the Irish coast that he was reminded of that country's "history of misfortunes," which he compared to those suffered by Indians. These "the Irishman" nobly struggled against and "though physically defeated, he is in mind unconquered, and has still a name in the world." The Irish in Canada, he told his readers, who "frequently lament their departed country," were a people characterized by wit, feeling, eloquence, warmth, passion, nobility, and hospitality. Copway also thought of visits to an Irishman's cabin in Upper Canada, where he and his father heard about the greatness of Daniel O'Connell, the Irish political leader and reformer.[19]

However, their more intimate experiences of sea travel can only be the subject of speculation. A number of these travellers, though, left no doubt about their first impressions of England once they left the ship. While eighteenth-century voyagers landing in Plymouth might have been impressed by the British naval dockyards and professed awe at the power of the British navy, their nineteenth-century counterparts landed in Liverpool, where they were struck by the spread of industrial and urban growth.[20] At times their observations were enthusiastic. For Copway, Liverpool's docks were a "piece of master workmanship – a noble monument of untiring industry" and the homes of its city's merchants were "tasteful," with their parks, fishponds, gardens and hedges."[21] As we shall see, though, Copway – and others –also had other things to say about British streetscapes and their inhabitants.

Tasteful homes and lovely gardens aside, these were interesting, often quite critically important, decades in which to be an Indigenous visitor to Britain. For one, Jones and Sunday came to the metropole at the moment when the treatment of Indigenous people by British settlers in the Cape Colony, New South Wales, Tasmania, and Upper Canada was the subject of religious and humanitarian movements across colonial and metropolitan centres, a concern that would crystallize in the creation of the Aborigines'

Protection Society.[22] The abolition of slavery within the British Empire took place two years after Jones's first trip to Britain, bringing to fruition the work of John Norton's circle of friends, although its replacement by apprenticeship schemes remained the subject of critique and debate.[23] Moreover, as scholars such as Catherine Hall and Leonore Davidoff, Susan Thorne, and Alison Twells have pointed out, over the course of the 1830s and 1840s, the global missionary movement became increasingly important to middle-class definitions of self and subjectivity.[24]

Along with the climate of heightened religious interest in the protection, salvation, and civilization of Indigenous peoples and African slaves, the travels of the Indigenous visitors were affected by technological and demographic shifts. For one, the growth of Britain's rail network and its urban centres made it possible for these travellers to make more appearances and to do so more quickly, while simultaneously increasing the mobility of their audiences. Not only did those who turned up in person to hear them preach or lecture about Upper Canada's Indigenous people form part of an ever-increasing group, hungry to see "converted savages" onstage, but the spread of cheaper, more widely disseminated publications also helped create larger reading audiences who might be struck by an article about the "Red Indian" who was giving a talk at the local Mechanics' Institute or Lyceum. Furthermore, the urban British public's appetite for exotic spectacles of race had been honed by the shows of the eighteenth century and whetted by the well-publicized appearances of the South African Khoi woman Sarah Baartman in London. Jones, in particular, would discover to his dismay that this fascination was far from exhausted.[25]

Given that their task was to raise funds for the mission villages, it is not surprising that Jones and Sunday worked diligently to transport their audiences through both space and time so that they could appreciate these settings. Although this was a strategy Norton also employed in much of his transatlantic correspondence and in his public pronouncements, nevertheless immersing their listeners and readers in the worlds of the Credit River or Rice Lake villages was crucial for these travellers. It also was critical that British sympathizers, as well as those who might be curious but not yet won over to the missionary cause, appreciate the different chronologies of development that Jones and his contemporaries had moved through. Of course, it is not surprising that those caught up in the evangelical revival of this period should stress temporal dimensions in their discussions, since the contrast between old and new spiritual states was a common means of delineating the process of salvation. The autobiographical focus of evangelical confessions, the intricate tracing of one's individual progression to salvation, also emphasized change over time (even if that change might be a dramatic rupture and break with the past, as opposed to incremental shifts). Yet important though their own autobiographical accounts of conversion and salvation might be, these men needed to speak for more than themselves. It was their community, whether in a more abstract sense or in the specific locale of the mission village, that embodied the changes brought by religion. Furthermore, to their audiences, growing accustomed to hearing about the struggles and successes of British missionaries around the globe, these places might have appeared familiar in their intent and purpose, even if the details were new.

And humanitarian efforts were working. "The people," Jones wrote in a letter, "every where have received me with open arms and in the name of the Lord ... (they) are all alive for the Missionary cause." At times hundreds had been turned away from the meetings he addressed, but those who did hear his "'statement of facts' have been gratified by his addresses." Jones had no doubt that his words would "have a tendency to stimulate them to a greater zeal for the conversion of our perishing countrymen in the woods. The collections that have been made for the Wesleyan Methodist Missionary Society at those Meetings where I have been present have amounted to more than those made the last year. So you may judge that the hands of our English brethren do not yet hand down in the good work of faith and love."[26]

Jones's letter (and others like it) can be analyzed in a number of ways. Most obviously, it points to the support he had received from English audiences, their donations being evidence of the missionary and colonial link between the residents of Manchester and those "perishing in the woods" in Upper Canada. As well, though, Jones's letter also suggests the multiple ways in which he was a link between the British people, Upper Canadian settlers, and the Ojibwe, his writings and persona the vehicle by which a certain type of transatlantic community might have been forged, one better than either the settler colony or the metropole. Furthermore, his work, conveyed to an English audience, might also help to create interrelated communities in a number of ways. The English enthusiasm for the missionary cause might help prod and stimulate those who were much closer geographically to his people to feel empathy and to develop connections to them. The metropole, then, might serve as the moral arbiter and compass for the settler colony, doing so by a display of its emotional and affective ties to the Mississauga, a transatlantic community created out of such bonds.[27]

Villages such as the Credit Mission, then, with narratives of past declension (especially with the arrival of white fur traders and, to some degree, godless settlers) that were then replaced with tales of progress, not only held out utopian hopes for a better future for the Mississauga; they also had their counterparts in contemporary missionary discourse, particularly the free black communities of Jamaica.[28] While focusing on the specifics of time and place, Jones's and Sunday's narratives were intertwined with the languages of humanitarianism found in both the abolition movement and in attacks on settler violence.

The interlinked relations of gender and race also helped mould these communities. He also commented on the work of the English "ladies," a group who appear in his correspondence as crucial in forging these connections. "The Ladies in some of the towns," Jones noted, "have been very busy in collecting and making articles of clothing for the benefit of our Indian missions in Canada; and also provided several school rewards. Please to tell our Ladies at the River Credit [of] this pleasing intelligence of the industry of the English Ladies, several of whom have signified a wish to go to America and teach the Indians to be good and how to make nice work."[29] Thus Jones's set of transatlantic communities was created not just through financial donations or prayers: it also consisted of the work of middle-class women and the bonds of sisterly, Christian affection between two groups of "ladies." The material objects these women created, such as clothing or the "school rewards" (possibly missionary publications aimed at children), were both emblematic of these worlds and helped form them. Moreover, English women's work in London, Manchester, and York was having tangible benefits. In a letter to the London Wesleyan *Methodist Magazine*, Jones described the situation of the Mississaugas at their village on the Credit River, "where they are now learning to become good Christians and good farmers, like the good white people." Living in log homes and enjoying the benefits of a chapel, schoolhouse, carpentry workshop, and hospital, the Mississauga community had made great progress as farmers and livestock keepers. Boys and girls had their own schools, where they were taught in English and were learning to read the Gospels and write. Furthermore, as well as these skills, "the Indian girls are taught to sew and knit and to keep a house clean and nice, like the clean white women."[30] These transformations in domestic life were given material form, since during his talks Jones produced "specimens of needle-work" created by Indigenous women, such as samplers and reticules; these items, along with dresses and pants provided by the Dorcas societies, groups organized to provide clothing for the poor, served to represent the transatlantic networks of mutual support and dependency.[31] Material culture thus was clear evidence of the links between missionary enterprises and colonial projects.

Jones also told his audiences of the changes wrought in Indigenous men's behaviour through their embrace of Christianity and "civilized" social mores. Perhaps the most frequently cited evidence of such a shift was men's renunciation of alcohol (even though support for temperance was not a strictly British or European stance); they also, though, were depicted as having given up other forms of noxious and unchristian behaviour, such as swearing. Altering Indigenous masculinity, however, was not undertaken just for the sake of Indigenous men's souls. In an 1838 speech to a London Methodist meeting, Jones remarked that he saw a "great many ladies" in the audience and thus wished to tell them "that the Gospel of God has done much for the Indian women. Before the Gospel was preached to us, the Indian women had to do all the hard work, and the Indian men considered the women as inferior beings." Not only that, a lack of sociability between the sexes marred Indigenous society: when Indigenous men visited other "wigwams" in their village, "the men would go a great way ahead, the women a great way behind. They never walk arm in arm. I don't think the ladies here would agree to that." Fortunately, Jones pronounced, "since the Gospel has been introduced among us, the poor Indian women has been better treated."

As well as changing their treatment of Indigenous women, men now expressed their emotions freely by weeping, something forbidden in Indigenous conceptions of manliness that relied on physical self-control and stoic acceptance of pain and suffering.[32] Building on these sentiments in the metropole, Jones and his fellow ministers also invited their audiences to look into their hearts and the heart of the speaker, so that they might judge their compassion and sympathy, once again creating bonds of love and intimacy. Yet although these invitations might suppose the Mississauga's acceptance of British tutelage in all matters domestic and personal, not everything could be attributed to the latter's examples. Jones made a point of "shaking hands in his heart" with his audiences when they were too large for him to do so physically; he also did so with those who might have been absent (such as Queen Victoria), but with whom he wished to connect. As Jones told his listeners, this gesture of peace and amity was one practised around Ojibwe councils by the chief, who shook hands with all individuals there.[33] In Britain, the metaphorical handshake became a personal, intimate, and embodied means of linking the world of the council with the missionary meeting and chapel, a gesture with which his British audience was familiar but which Jones claimed was a practice innate to Indigenous culture.

Handshakes aside, such constructions of Christianized Indigenous societies were not unique to Jones or Sunday. White missionaries were eager to offer changes in gender roles and relations in both Indigenous and non-Indigenous communities in the colony as proof of Christianity's benefits and as testimony that it had firmly taken hold.[34] When Jones, Sunday, Jacobs, or Copway, though, presented this narrative, notions of their "authenticity," both as "Indians" and missionaries, were at play, notions that were mediated by the texts and conditions of their performance of such identities. Both these men and their presenters stressed that here was a "true" representative of both categories; their (auto)biographical narratives and the history of their people were emphasized as proof of their representative status and their ability to perform as a speaking subject for the Ojibwe (notwithstanding that Jones, for example, was mixed-race and had married a white Englishwoman).[35] In their public writings, Indigenous identity became a textual device that needed to be stated and restated for their readers, with the repetition of images and motifs such as the wigwam, the hunt, and the forest setting of the revival that brought them to Christianity.[36] In these men's appearances there were clearly discernible traces of the imperial need for those "mimic men," as post-colonial scholar Homi Bhabha has described them, so close to being English but embodying an always-discernible difference that could be authenticated and verified.[37] These Ojibwe men were presented and, to some extent, presented themselves as proof of transformed Indigenous manhood, not someone who would work women to death or refuse to appear alongside them in public. They thus might be seen as a synecdoche for the larger transformation that Indigenous societies would undergo as they experienced both Christianity and civilization. Such performances of authenticity have historically been, as a number of scholars have argued, part of colonialism's cultural apparatus, usually mediated by the need to find evidence of the "vanishing race" that would soon be lost to Europeans. This loss, then, might be mourned by the latter without making substantial changes to the behaviour that had led to the (supposed) disappearance of Indigenous peoples: not all expressions of sentiment led to political change.[38]

However, stating one's authenticity was never a straightforward act. For one, colonial and imperial authorities might question an Indigenous representative's authenticity, motivated by a wish to undermine Indigenous lobbying and claims for land and resources. Just as John Norton had to contend with the government's opposition to his legitimacy, at times Jones was faced with colonial officials who raised questions about his status as a "true" representative of his people, while British politician Richard Cobden suspected Copway of being "a humbug" in his desire to represent North American Indians at the 1850 Frankfurt International Peace Congress.[39] As well, the demand for a "true" representative of the "North American Indian" was shaped by the desire of evangelical and humanitarian audiences for transparency, honesty, and sincerity.

Yet this was not quite the entire story; other narratives, other perspectives, intruded. Although their travels, appearances, and public statements were mediated by Europeans' desires and aspirations for Indigenous communities, it would be condescending to assume that these travellers simply acquiesced in the metropole's wishes or in its conceptions of Indigenous societies. It also would be simplistic to assume that they did not share at least some of the latter's hopes. For one, in his writings Peter Jones refers to Ojibwe women not as "pious Indian women," the term commonly employed by non-Indigenous missionaries, but as "Ladies." Such usage symbolized his desire that his people be granted the dignity and respect afforded to their non-Indigenous counterparts. For his part, Copway opened his 1850 travelogue, *Running Sketches*, by vowing to "uphold my race ... endeavour never to say nor do anything which will prejudice the mind of the British public against my people – In this land of refinement I will be an Indian – I will treat everybody in a manner that becomes a gentleman – I will patiently answer all questions that may be asked me – I will study to please the people, and lay my own feelings to one side."[40] Although it's doubtful that Copway was ever able to completely put aside his own feelings, his travelogue is marked by his self-identification as a "Red Indian," a term that, for all its stereotyping of Indigenous peoples, also appears in his work in numerous modes and with different, albeit related, valences. Copway used it to claim both individual and collective dignity, as it connoted to him gentlemanly and proper conduct and manners, courtesy, patience, and self-abnegation.

Although their support for the temperance movement – one particularly pronounced in Copway's case – might signify assimilation into the missionaries' civilizing program, this too was a more complicated matter for Indigenous people of the Great Lakes area (and elsewhere). For one, Indigenous prophetic movements, such as that of the Shawnee Tenskwatawa, the Prophet, or that of the Seneca Handsome Lake, insisted that renouncing alcohol would aid in the revitalization of Indigenous societies and help lessen their dependency on whites.[41] It is also worth considering that even those who were more clearly committed to certain aspects of assimilation – such as Jones – did so not simply out of a desire to mimic Europeans but, rather, to banish from their societies forms of contamination that originated with whites and that left them vulnerable to colonial exploitation, particularly of their land and resources. As Maureen Konkle has argued for Copway's other writings, if the Ojibwe were to cease drinking they would not abandon each other but, instead, would unite as a nation and fight for their territory.[42]

Copway's work for temperance, then, was a complex negotiation between both Ojibwe needs and the expectations of his British audiences. As with Jones, Sunday, and Jacobs in their work for the missions, being a temperance lecturer allowed him to claim public stages in which he might perform the persona of an Ojibwe man who, contrary to white expectations, was able to exercise discipline and self-restraint – not just to please missionaries and reformers but for his own advancement, and that of his people. Copway's father had sworn off liquor and had thus regained his role as a father in Ojibwa society. Temperance might – at least from Copway's perspective – help bolster his claims to masculine leadership in the eyes of multiple audiences.[43]

Renouncing warfare was also a complicated act, particularly when performed in front of British or European audiences who most likely believed the warrior signified "Red Indian" more than any other set of representations. Like the Six Nations, the Ojibwe had proved themselves valuable allies of the British in the War of 1812. However, for Copway, either renouncing warfare altogether or embracing the peace movement was a critical – while not permanent – aspect of the way in which he constructed his public self. In addition to appearing as a representative of the "North American Indians" before the 1850 International Peace Congress, throughout *Running Sketches* his persona of a modern and activist "Indian man" was one who shunned war. As he commented, Prussian soldiers who were being reviewed by Prince Frederick made a "brilliant and formidable appearance, but such things are altogether repugnant to my feelings since my warrior's creed has been changed to a harmless one."[44] While his may have been a more general and abstract objection to war partly shaped by his conversion to a particular form of Christianity, events of the early to mid-nineteenth century would have left him with more immediate and personal reasons to object to the use of force. The memory of the forced removal of the Cherokee in the United States, for example, was not a distant one. Furthermore, he and his wife, Elizabeth, had lived through war between Indigenous people and had seen its deleterious effects.

As well, embracing other means of resolving conflict did not necessarily mean assimilation to Western values. Rather, it could stem from a belief that mid-nineteenth-century warfare involved battles in which his people would suffer disproportionately. It might also invoke the role of peacemaker and treaty negotiator, one with a long history in Ojibwe and other Indigenous societies.[45] Thus, as part of his self-transformation and his work for the Ojibwe, Copway might be said to have waged "war" on a different type of front, translating the meaning of "the warrior" into a different kind of idiom and performing it in a different kind of theatre, as he took up the struggles of political and social reform. As Kevin Hutchings has pointed out, in his autobiography Copway spoke of transforming the hunter's tools of the bow and arrow into those of the writer: the goose quill became his bow and its point his arrow, as he hunted not wild game but an audience of readers. Just as a clever Ojibwe hunter might change his tactics and strategy to lure his prey, Copway would do the same to lure in audiences of white readers to advance his people's cause.[46]

Indigenous Ethnographies of the Empire's Heart

Not only did these travellers lay claim to a more fluid, multi-layered performance of Indigeneity than that of the assimilated convert, they also assessed, commented on, and judged British society, highlighting both its assets and its foibles. While Jones shaped the world of the Ojibwe for a variety of audiences, he also told his Upper Canadian audiences about England, reversing the customary pattern of the period's travel literature and nascent ethnographies in which the colony was brought to the metropole. "I thought you would be glad to hear my remarks, as an Indian traveller, on the customs and manner of the English people," he wrote to the *Christian Guardian*. He found the English generally a "noble, generous minded people – free to act, and free to think – they very much pride themselves in their civil and religious privileges, in their learning, generosity, manufacture, and commerce, and they think that no other nation is equal with them in respect to these things." Jones found them very "open and friendly … ready to relieve the needs of the poor and needy when properly brought before them."

He did, though, characterize the English as very fond of "novelties" – no nation, in fact, was as taken with new things. Here, Jones displayed an acute awareness that his appearances in Britain were performances staged and enacted before an audience, part of the theatre of both the missionary and the British colonial worlds.[47] "They will gaze and look upon a foreigner as if he had just dropped down from the moon: and I have often been amused in seeing what a large number of people, a monkey riding upon a dog, will collect in the streets of London where such things may be seen almost everyday." Jones went on to hint at the tensions he faced. "When my Indian name (Kahkewaquonaby) is announced to attend any public meeting, so great is their curiosity that the place is always sure to be filled; and it would be the same if notice was given that a man with his toes in his mouth would address a congregation in such a place, and on such a day, the place without fail would be filled with English hearers."[48] Jones's causes might benefit from the attention paid him as an "Indian," but he was acutely aware that his audience might see him as both a celebrity and an exotic spectacle in a theatre of colonial attractions, one whose novelty might wear off as other, even more exciting, representatives of "otherness" appeared.

While appreciative of the English support for overseas missions and English philanthropy, Jones noted the hold that commercial capitalism had on his hosts. "Their close attention to business, I think, rather carries them too much to a worldly mindedness, and hence many forget to think about their souls and their God … 'Money, money, get money – get rich and be a gentleman.' With this sentiment they all fly about in every direction like a swarm of bees in search of that treasure which lies so near their hearts." Here, too, gender relations played their part: "This remark refers more particularly to the men of the world, and of such there are not a few." (Although he was, perhaps, too polite – or politically savvy – to mention it, it's hard not to imagine that Jones knew there was a clear link between the metropolitan desire for "money, money" and settlers' desire for his peoples' traditional lands.) Jones went on to describe British eating habits. "They are very fond of good living," a desire which manifested itself in a diet that, for many, revolved around roast beef, plum-pudding, and turtle soup. The English, he stated, "get very fat and round as a toad," mostly, it seems, from eating four times a day. Jones gently mocked such food and its frequent consumption; he may also have been making an implicit comparison to Indigenous eating habits, which, while healthy, tended not to leave his countrymen "fat as toads."

He also attempted to describe Englishwomen's dress for his audience, although he felt that it was so changeable that he could not do it justice. "I will only say that the ladies of fashion wear very curious bonnets, which looks something like a farmer's scoop shovel and when they walk in the tiptoe style, they put me in mind of the little snipes that run along the shores of the lakes and rivers in Canada. They also wear sleeves as big as bushel bags, which make them appear as if they had three bodies with one head." Yet, just in case his audiences had forgotten his recognition of English "Ladies'" charitable work, he adds "with all their big bonnets and sleeves, the English ladies I think are the best of women." Jones closed his letter with a desire to be "in the midst of my friends and brethren" in Upper Canada and asked any who saw his "Indian brethren" to tell them he prayed for them daily.[49]

Like many other Indigenous travellers, Copway also shifted between admiring Britain's "progress" and exposing the nation's flaws. At times he became almost lyrical in his encomiums to the country's greatness. Approaching Birmingham, he mused on the

> heart of that commerce whose broad wings are spread over every country in the world. It was here the Anglo-Saxon Race was cradled; here they were educated and from this place they have gone forth; distinguished wherever they have gone, for enterprise, perseverance and intelligence. These are the qualities which characterize England, and will perpetuate its existence. Its power is concentrated in the intelligence and education of the people, and whatever adds to these will strengthen the bonds that bind it, and consolidate the foundation of its government.[50]

Liverpool's docks were a "piece of master workmanship – a noble monument of untiring industry," and the residences of its city's merchants were "tasteful," with their parks, fishponds, gardens and hedges."[51] London, in particular, gave him much to enjoy and wonder at, not least of which were the Houses of Parliament, the place from which

> will emanate laws that will tell upon the destinies of British subjects throughout the world, and upon the destinies of the race. Before this Hall shall have crumbled into dust, it will have resounded with the eloquence of generations of the greatest and best of the noblest races on the face of this earth. A thousand years hence, the true-hearted Britons will hold on to its tottering walls, and cling to every stone, because those who now occupy it, and the many generations that shall follow, will have made it venerable.[52]

Yet his praise also was undercut by social and political critique. Liverpool's streets were full of impudent beggars who appeared to multiply when one of their numbers was successful.[53] Steel made in Birmingham would go forth to do immense good, but, once turned into armaments, it also would commit evil deeds by destroying life and despoiling the earth.[54] Moreover, on returning to London from Europe, he found "the noise and confusion which reign over this great city, would make stronger heads than mine to turn and ache."[55] The Cheapside stores seemed very narrow to Copway, and those on Regent Street, while "in point of richness surpass anything I have ever seen," still could not match the size, elegance, and convenience of New York's Bowen and McNamee silk store. London's older areas felt cramped and potentially dangerous, their narrow, long, and crooked streets were "high and dark, dismal, smutty-looking." The churches and chapels in which he preached were "old-fashioned," their pulpits so cramped that he was forced to stand in one position. "There is no animation," he lamented.[56]

It is more than likely that Copway was fully aware of similar pronouncements made by those who had gone before him. Such travelogues and commentaries also grew over the nineteenth century, as other Indigenous travellers to Britain produced, in historian Antoinette Burton's words, "new cultural geographies of the imperial metropolis."[57] Both commentators on and participants in "imperial modernity" – urban centres, commercial and industrial capitalism, the formation of European nation-states, to name but a few subjects covered by these Ojibwe travellers – Jones and Copway helped produce and make known the metropole for their readers, crafting images that stressed both its delights and its deficiencies.

Political Humanitarianism: Nahneebahweequa

Their travels also, though, provided them with the opportunity to do more than offer a critical ethnography of metropolitan society. Imperial travel might also provide wider audiences for subtle – and not-so-subtle – attacks on the wrongdoing of settler colonialism. Such attacks were common in the writings of Indigenous travelers. For Catherine Sutton (Nahneebahweequa), her entire trip was aimed at righting the wrongs settler officials had committed against her people, a strategy that involved deploying a range of stances and tropes. On the one hand, she frequently depicted herself as possessing a transparent persona, fixed, centred, and not contingent upon its context, telling her "American Friends" that they would be welcomed "at my humble forest home" and promising them they "will find Nahneebahweequa at New York and London to be Nahneebahweequa at Owen Sound."[58] However, Sutton's creation of a public identity within the transatlantic world may have been a somewhat more complex process. In many of her public letters and addresses to the Quakers and to periodicals such as the *Colonial Intelligencer; or Aborigines' Friend*, she alternated between the use of what may have been, according to some ethnohistorians, the Ojibwe "language of pity" (her constant use of the phrase "poor Indian"), appeals to Christian sentiment, and clear denunciations of colonial injustices.[59] In a fairly typical letter to the "Friends of New York," published in the *Friends' Intelligencer* in 1861, "Nahneebahweequa" blesses them for taking in "an unprotected Indian woman, a lonely, solitary wanderer, a foreign pilgrim in a strange land … all of you did something in this great effort that was made by my poor, despised, downtrodden people." Comparing her people to Lazarus, waiting at the rich man's gate for a few crumbs, she hopes that they will someday find rest in heaven, where "the white man that now holds his sway over the poor Indian will have to give an account, as well as the poor Indian, to his maker. Now he feels strong: in a word, they have the unlimited control of all the Indian's funds, and disburse or withhold them as they please; but God has said vengeance is mine." For Nahneebahweequa, both white and Indigenous people were equal in God's eyes and would be equally accountable for their actions on earth. Her letter also suggests that she had been exposed to colonial discourses that characterized Indigenous women as deficient in their performance of gender roles. "Though I am an Indian woman, I know what it is feel the affection of a mother's heart," to be driven out of a hard-built home and lose all claims to it.[60]

While it may have been politically strategic, as well as integral to her Christian beliefs, for Sutton to perform as a supplicant who appealed to her audiences' sympathies and sensibilities, hers was not a message delivered only in that idiom. Rather than accept a subservient place in a colonial hierarchy skewed by distortions of gender and race, she pointed to the ways that Indigenous women in particular suffered from such deformations of the law. "All in a land where the poor slave can come and be a man and a citizen; while the poor Indian woman that is married to a white man can be driven from her home and taken for a white woman; but, when she offers to buy her own land, she is an Indian." Nevertheless, despite the Indian Department's imposed categories, "I am an Indian; the blood of my forefathers runs in my veins, and I am not ashamed to own it; for my people were a noble race before the pale faces came to possess their lands and homes." Yet despite having been well received by the Duke of Newcastle and the Queen, the Duke had betrayed her. He had pretended that the Indian Department was innocent of any charges of wrongdoing. Instead, ignoring Sutton's male fellow-petitioners, Newcastle claimed that her marriage had turned her into an Englishwoman and that she had no claim to her lands. Nahneebahweequa disputed these charges, pointing out that she had been married since 1839 and only now been told of her changed status; she also argued that the numerous other Indigenous women who were married to non-Indigenous men had not suffered such discrimination.[61]

Her English sponsor, Christine Alsop, believed "a poetical character ... has been given to her visit, which cannot fail to exercise a beneficial influence." While "public sympathy has not been allowed to concentrate itself exclusively upon this noble-minded lady" (possibly because of the Civil War in the United States), nevertheless "she has been the means of exciting interest in the fortunes of her race generally" and making their wrongs known. Covering her address to the Liverpool branch of the Aborigines' Protection Society, the *Liverpool Courier* reported that "with great composure [she] delivered a peculiarly effective address, in a clear, natural, and rather melodious voice." "Nahneebahweequa," the reporter claimed, was "'glad to see so many'" friends to her "'poor destitute people that can't help themselves.'"[62] Yet this position was not quite that of a supplicant, as her appearance in the pages of the transatlantic religious press provided a counterpoint to such a stance. Far from being helpless, Sutton herself had been wronged and was determined to right that fact.[63] Overseas travel, then, might mean the chance to defend rights to land and call attention to the betrayals of colonial administrations, as well as giving Christian Indigenous people a platform from which they could demand humanitarian support and sympathy from their audiences. Emotional bonds might lead, not to mourning, but to political activism.

Indigenous Celebrity

As well as linking Upper Canada and the metropole in a variety of ways, Jones and his contemporaries were part of the humanitarian movement's culture of celebrity. As historian Anna Johnston argues, the nineteenth-century British missionary movement was not above creating prominent figures, such as David Livingstone, as celebrities.[64] Moreover, although missionary promoters may not have been completely cognizant of their debt to eighteenth-century theatrical celebrity, they often appear to have drawn upon the latter. For one, its forms of representation and practices inflected evangelical religion's creation of "larger-than-life" figures who were meant to inspire sentiment and sympathy in their audiences. The crafting and manipulation of images and reputations through prints, pamphlets, paintings, and material artifacts; the development of an obsession with bodies; the circulation of details of domestic or private matters which collapsed the distinction between private and public; and, finally, the cultivation of the notion of an achieved, rather than ascribed, celebrity: all of these can be found, in varying degrees, in these travellers' representations in Britain.[65]

Perhaps not surprisingly, as he made the most trips overseas, circulated amongst more cities and towns, and was seen by his Methodist Upper Canadian contemporaries as a religious leader, Peter Jones can be said to have achieved the status of a religious *and* Indigenous celebrity. Jones's arrivals, departures, and lectures throughout Britain, particularly in England and Scotland, received considerable coverage in both the secular and religious press. Such reports also helped create interest in and excitement about Jones's appearances. While at times he appeared before gatherings held within religious institutions, such as the Church of Scotland's Synod of Glasgow and Ayr, his other appearances were widely publicized. The press noted the large crowds that gathered, and sometimes ran advance articles that announced a forthcoming talk.[66] As we have seen, these appearances were well-attended, something that the press was happy to report. As well as in newspapers, Jones and his fellow-ministers' narratives and images were circulated through other media: handbills that advertised their appearances, portraits, and, for Jones, early forms of photography.

Copway's *Running Sketches* depicts his temperance lectures as also contributing to his celebrity, as he shows great pleasure in discussing the large crowds that, he claimed, turned out for them. While his emotions were no doubt heartfelt, such numbers also drew attention to his own status and reputation as a lecturer. His speech in London on the subject drew a large crowd, with many turned away for lack of room, and "the papers are full of notices of it. Some applaud and some condemn the speeches."[67] Crowds of three to four thousand turned out in Edinburgh, Glasgow, and Paisley, which roused the many children who attended to give "three cheers for the young teetotallers in Europe," whose numbers were joined by like-minded children in America.[68] His numbers are, it must be admitted, difficult – and in some cases impossible – to verify. Many newspaper reports of his temperance lectures mention "the large crowds" that attended, while a few lament that only a small number turned out (although that is generally attributed to poor advance coverage or the meeting having been organized hastily).[69] Attendance aside, though, newspaper coverage of his temperance lectures ran the gamut of responses. Some reporters saw his message as being primarily that Indigenous peoples needed to assimilate, to become "Christian and civilized."[70] Others repeated his statements about his peoples'

PROGRAMME OF SOIREE

IN BEHALF OF THE

NORTH AMERICAN INDIANS,

IN THE TRADES' HALL,

On Thursday Evening, 30th Oct. 1845.

REV. DR. SMYTH IN THE CHAIR.

TEA.

CHAIRMAN'S ADDRESS.

JOHN DUNLOP, ESQ.
TO INTRODUCE THE INDIAN CHIEF.

KAHKEWAQUONABY, THE INDIAN CHIEF,
On the Customs, Manners, Religion, and Superstitions of the RED INDIANS.

REV. DR. KING,
On the Claims of the NORTH AMERICAN INDIANS on our Sympathy and Support.

SERVICE OF FRUIT.

REV. DR. BUCHANAN,
On Native Agency.

REV. DR. JOHN M'FARLANE,
On the utility of Mechanical Arts, as a handmaid to Christianity, in the Advancement of Civilization.

REV. ANDREW KING,
On the Present Condition of Canada.

REV. DR. EADIE,
On Education, and its special importance with reference to the youth of Heathen Lands.

D. MACDONALD, PRINTER.

Fig. 2.1
Address on behalf of North American Indians

innate intelligence and focused, instead, on his indictment of the behaviour of whites towards Indigenous people. Such reports highlighted the former's dishonesty and hypocrisy and pointed to those portions of his lectures that placed blame for Indigenous social problems squarely on the shoulders of white missionaries and governments.[71] But whatever his reading audiences took away from the content of Copway's talks, they also were told that this "Indian Chief" was an articulate and fluent English speaker (despite his own protestations to the contrary); physically striking; dignified but also capable of wit and humour; and a man with great public presence.[72] Furthermore, while politician and reformer Richard Cobden may have worried about the authenticity of the "Ojibway chief," newspaper reports of his temperance tour accepted it, seemingly without question.

The international networks that brought these travellers to Britain also brought them into the orbit of prominent and well-known figures within British society, figures whose patronage helped shape their movements within metropolitan centres. A range of politicians, religious leaders, and prominent philanthropists – Daniel O'Connell, the politician John Bright, and the Queen's cousin and leader in the Aborigines' Protection Association, Sir Augustus d'Este – met with them. These meetings were publicized and promoted as proof of their visibility and the potential of increased assistance that they might receive from such contacts.[73] In particular, an audience with Queen Victoria was a significant moment in their metropolitan tours. Eliza Jones noted that, on 18 July 1837, she began to help her husband prepare for his interview, which took place almost two months later, on 14 September.[74] To be sure, her description of the audience does not suggest a great deal of pomp or spectacle, except for Jones's Indigenous dress, worn on the advice of his patrons. "When the folding doors were thrown open, we saw the Queen standing about the middle of the room, each advanced bowing several times till at last they met, when Peter went down on his knee holding up his right arm, on which the Queen placed her hand, he then rose and presenting the Petition said, he was much pleased to be introduced to Her Majesty, explained the nature of the petition and the wampum chain." Victoria smiled and "appeared pleased to hear that the prayer of the petition had been granted." Jones then told her that he thought she might like to keep the petition "as a curiosity," which she accepted and, having asked about his visits to England, "she bowed to indicate the visit was over, he did the same, they then receded backwards, at length the little Queen turned her back, and the interview was over."[75]

A royal audience added a degree of lustre and prestige to the status of a colonial subject. Moreover, their position as a celebrated representative of their people also could be underscored by links to historical Indigenous individuals who had been attributed a semi-monarchical or regal status. Jones stated that he was part of a long line of Indigenous people, such as Pocahontas and King Philip, both of whom had enjoyed an elevated position within their own nations and had also been highly visible actors within metropolitan and colonial society.[76] Copway's connections with particular members of English society, many of them committed to liberalism and reform causes (abolition and penal and educational reform, to name a few), are interwoven throughout his book, offered as proof that he was recognized as an important figure. While in Liverpool, he was entertained by Richard Rathbone and his brother, the former mayor of that city, along with the "chief magistrate" E. Rushton, who had previously accompanied Copway to watch Police Court proceedings.[77] In London he actively sought out a number of English politicians. Copway dined at Fintan's Hotel with Mr Brotherton, "the vegetarian MP"; breakfasted with Richard Cobden, whose "solid English look I very much admire" and who asked him a number of questions about his country and people; and went to dinner at Lord Brougham's, where he met lords and a marquis, "a nobler set of Englishmen I never beheld." The company also included Mr Gambardilli, the "celebrated portrait painter."[78] After leaving his lodgings from Randall's Hotel in Cheapside in favour of Hanover Square's much quieter (and likely more elite) George Street, Copway found "an abundance of cards on my table. O fie, fie: these English will spoil me." Gambardilli, Dr Wiseman (quite likely the Roman Catholic cardinal), E. Saunders the "celebrated dentist," and Lady Franklin and her brother, Sir Simpkinson: all extended dinner invitations, which he was happy to accept (although he was left exhausted by them).[79] Upon his return to London, Copway feared he would disappoint his many callers. He was running out of time in London and, as well as receiving numerous letters and cards, also had invitations from two committees who wanted him as a speaker.[80]

While it is difficult to determine whether all these meetings took place, the political and social concerns of many of these individuals makes it quite plausible that they would be sympathetic to and curious about the "Ojibway chief" who was so concerned about the well-being and advancement of his people. Copway's own network of contacts with well-known American literary figures such as Longfellow likely added to his cultural and social cachet in Britain. He also used his appearance at Jenny Lind's Liverpool concert to underscore his own popularity, in an account notable for its multiple layers of meaning. In that city to give a public lecture at the Mechanics' Institute on "Indians' religious beliefs, superstitions, legends, origins, and history," he found its residents very excited about the arrival of the "Swedish nightingale." Not even standing room was left in the concert hall, and even "ladies and gentlemen" from Ireland, it was reported, had booked tickets to hear her. Copway, who had appeared "in Indian costume" to give his lecture, was surprised on arriving at his own venue to find "a crowded house," which received him very kindly. However, he was eager to hear Jenny Lind "for the first time," and was therefore "glad to escape from the sound of my own voice." Copway then included his letter to "B.T." of the *New York Tribune*, in which he described Lind's performance and his own appearance. "I have just heard the identical and far-famed Jenny Lind!" One hour before, her voice had filled the Philharmonic, the largest hall he'd seen, which held six thousand people. From its shop windows and splendid halls to its cellars, Liverpool was filled with Jenny Lind souvenirs and memorabilia. Copway wished to capture the "Lind-mania" that was galvanizing the city. "All things are baptized with the all-potent name of the Swedish young squaw!" He had cut short his own lecture to arrive at the concert hall without a ticket, and found mass confusion and a "besieged" entrance; however, two of his "best friends" in Liverpool happened to be at the door and escorted him to an aisle seat. At intermission, he was given a tour of the hall "and my dress excited as much attention as any one there, for Jenny Lind had not come out then." When Lind appeared, presenting the "sight which my very black eyes were aching to see," it was to deafening cheers, applause, and the waving of handkerchiefs. Still he was not moved, as she was wearing a plain, albeit graceful, dress, with no elaborate floral arrangement or hairstyle. When she began to sing, though, he was thrilled and left breathless. "O, what unearthly and heavenly music," he wrote, adding that he was transported to Eden. He closed his letter by asking his friend to tell his readers that Lind had been poor and obscure; they could imitate her example "and be something while they live."[81] Of course, the same lesson might also apply to Copway's own life.[82]

Copway's account, then, pointed to his multiple locations: a public figure who also appeared before audiences and whose presence in Lind's audience stirred up excitement and interest; a knowledgeable commentator who could contribute to the creation of Lind's own transatlantic celebrity by writing about her concert to a major newspaper in a city in which Lind would soon appear; and an audience member who, by witnessing and appreciating

Lind's appeal, was part of urban popular culture. The use of such vantage points are not unique to his account of Lind; rather, they mark a number of Copway's narratives of his public appearances. At times he speaks in the first person, attempting to convey to his readers his impressions and feelings of new places and people, as well as reporting on his own performances in ways that are at times quite critical. At other times, though, as well as the newspaper accounts threaded into the text, Copway speaks as a European or English spectator who observes and remarks upon the presence of a "North American Indian" (to be sure, these descriptions are invariably couched in an overawed or flattering tone), authorial stances that underscore the fluidity with which he crafted his public persona in text.

Such references, combined with their meetings with the British monarch, were attempts by the travellers to confer an aura of legitimacy on their persons and their missions. Equally importantly, they also were statements that symbolized the speaker's authenticity as a representative of their community or nation. While, as previously discussed, imperial observers who discussed Indigenous authenticity often projected their own desires and fantasies onto Indigenous subjects, an individual's claim to authenticity and representative status within this context had both cultural and political implications. As art historian Stephanie Pratt has argued, one of the most popular images of eastern North American Indigenous people that circulated in Britain during the early to mid-nineteenth century was found in travel narratives of Canada and the United States. In these publications, Indigenous people are said to be a dying race and are "reduced to an exotic ensemble; but no tribal affiliation, names of individuals, or explanations of culture or of history are offered."[83] While celebrity status did not mean that Jones and his contemporaries could escape such suggestions, it offered audiences the possibility of seeing them not as anonymous stereotypes but as individuals with names and histories, products of particular times and places. Politically ineffective mourning, previously mentioned as a European response to such developments, could be replaced by a more sincerely felt sympathy and, possibly, an anger that would lead to politically effective action.

Intimacy and Colonial Celebrity

The creation of private lives for public consumption was another, ongoing, feature of the travellers' British appearances, and it also played an important role in the colonial context. Perhaps the most common demonstration of the private was the conversion narrative, both to Christianity and to "civilization." Of course, this display of the intimate was demanded by the religious and humanitarian contexts in which their travels took place. Upper Canada conversion narratives, both for Euro-Canadians and Indigenous people, were important forms of testimony to the success of evangelical initiatives and a significant form of memorializing and commemorating church members.[84] Through public lectures and writings, these travellers gave accounts of the transformations of their souls, subjectivities, and bodies for audiences on very public platforms, whether in lectures delivered directly to a group of listeners or to readers of a newspaper. As we have seen, these conversion narratives follow a trajectory from a state of unenlightened, ignorant (albeit often happy) paganism to that of growing dissatisfaction with one's spiritual and material state, an acceptance of one's state of sinfulness, dedication to Jesus, and transformation into a state of spiritual grace and enlightenment, which was needed for entrance into the evangelical community.

They also, though, dealt with the theme of achievement in their narratives. It took hard work to achieve this state of affairs, to continue renouncing certain practices and beliefs, to constantly scrutinize self and behaviour to avoid backsliding into heathen ways. As Peter Jacobs told the 1843 Wesleyan Missionary Conference, not only had he thrown away tomahawks, his former "heathen idols," and his belief in the worship of the sun and moon, he had also embarked on lengthy and arduous missionary tours of northwestern Canada, building mission houses and schools on the shores of Hudson Bay to persuade his fellow-Indigenous to renounce Satan and embrace Christianity.[85] This state of affairs – which, after all, was what made these individuals valued representatives of the "Christian Indians of North America" – was not an ascribed, but rather an achieved, status.

Private lives also became public in other ways. While most of the press coverage was quite flattering in its descriptions of their appearances, speech, and comportment, when Peter Jones married Eliza Field in New York, the intimate space of their life became the subject of far-less-complimentary discussion. One of the city's newspapers linked the couple to Othello and Desdemona and the practice of sati; a number of Upper Canadian newspapers subsequently picked up and reprinted the article.[86] As well as seeing his and his wife's name linked in the press in ways that evoked global practices of brutal Indigenous masculinity's destruction of white womanhood, Jones also experienced first-hand the reception of their marriage. Writing to Eliza in 1837, he told her of a discussion with an anonymous "Yankee," whom he had recently met in Oswego, New York State. During their conversation,

Fig 2.2
Reverend John Sunday,
Wesleyan Methodist Magazine, 1839

Fig. 2.3
Peter Jones, c. 1837–38

Fig. 2.4

George Copway, photograph, c. early 1860s

the general question of "Indians in Canada" came up and, specifically, the subject of Peter Jones. Upon assuring the stranger that he was "well acquainted" with Jones, he was asked about the "English lady" that Jones had married: "How does she stand it 'out there in the woods. Does she seem happy amongst your people?'" He assured the "Yankee" that she seemed contented, and on being asked "what do the Indians think of her do they like her?" replied "very much, they think the world of her." His interrogator "seemed disappointed when I gave him such a good account of Peter Jones and his English wife. I had a good laugh."[87]

The state of these travellers' health was also a subject of public discussion and at times concern, to no small extent because of the memory of other celebrated Indigenous and Inuit travellers, past and present, who had been taken seriously ill and, in some cases, had died while on overseas tours.[88] When Jones spoke in Bristol in 1831, the audience that heard him "was much delighted, but expressed great concern to his debilitated and sickly appearance. He ended up in bed for three weeks with such a bad cold that his doctors feared he might not recover."[89] Their improved health was cause for pleasure, possibly celebration. On John Sunday's 1837 departure from England, the Wesleyan Mission House noted his accomplishments in Britain and was particularly happy to announce that "his health, which had been impaired by journeys, exposure, and severe labour in the wilds of Canada, has been restored and established."[90]

These travellers also had to deal with reactions to their personal appearance. As we have seen with John Norton, clothing, jewellery, hair, and gesture were integral to a celebrity's self-fashioning: the fetishization of such markers within the context of imperialism meant that they were even more important for colonial celebrities. At times Jones and his contemporaries chose black suits, a form of male dress that had come to signify sober, industrious, respectable middle-class masculinity.[91]

On other occasions, though, Jones and Peter Jacobs presented themselves in "authentic" Indian dress. In the words of the *Aberdeen Journal* in 1845, Jones was "arrayed in full Indian chief costume," an outfit which "excited much interest" with its tunic, leggings, and moccasins, "all of dressed deerskin, and beautifully embroidered. On his head was a cap to match, crowned with waving plumes." Jones also wore silver medals presented to the Ojibwe: one from William IV, the other from George III.[92] In addition, he appeared with Indigenous spiritual artifacts or, as they were described by his promoters, "heathen idols" that were used to demonstrate his people's spiritual progress in renouncing such things for Christian artifacts, most notably the Bible.[93] However, Jones became extremely uncomfortable with wearing Ojibwe clothing. Writing from Glasgow to Eliza, he ended by noting that he had "been requested to appear in my odious Indian costume so I must begin at once to dress."[94] It is possible, of course, that "odious" was meant either sarcastically or playfully: Jones possessed a sense of humour that is sometimes overlooked by his biographers. (It is also possible that his Ojibwe clothing was uncomfortable in hot and crowded British halls and meeting rooms.) However, eventually he refused to wear anything other than his black suit, for, when "clad in the garb of an Englishman," he attracted "little or no notice" when not making public appearances.[95]

For her part, Catherine Sutton shared the ambivalence of her uncle, Peter Jones, about wearing Indigenous clothing for public appearances. In Queen Victoria's account of Sutton's audience with her, the monarch described her as being "of the yellow colour of the American Indians, with black hair, and was dressed in a strange European dress with a coloured shawl and straw hat and feathers." However, Sutton's wearing of a "strange European dress" was no accident, nor was it simply the result of decisions made by her patrons.

Figs. 2.5
Peter Jones in Ojibwe clothing

Figs. 2.6
Peter Jones in Ojibwe clothing

She refused to wear "Indian dress," telling the *Aborigines' Friend* that, while her band council had decided she should "dress in an Indian style," she had refused. As she told them, if they

> had chosen me to go, I was not to go back to paganism after the Missionary had tried to civilize the Indian, and make us like white people: and was I to go back and dress like pagan Indians, and come over here to shew myself? I told them I was not going to do that; and some said, "it is best to let her go in her simple Christian dress, and the Queen will know that we are civilized." And I have been asked by different people why didn't I fetch my Indian dress. I tell them I had none, this was my dress; this is the way we dress. I tell them we are not pagan, that we try to be like white people – to be clean and decent, and do what we can to be like the civilized people.[96]

Thus, Sutton wanted to demonstrate the extent to which she – and perhaps by extension the Ojibwe – were fully capable of engaging with European cultural and social mores. Rather than seeing the issue as simply or only one of assimilation, though, in all likelihood she knew of her uncle's frustration in being treated like a "curiosity" when he appeared in Ojibwe clothing. And if an Indigenous man such as Jones, well-spoken in English, versed in European ways and mores, and from a mixed-race background, experienced a level of visibility so high as to cause him embarrassment or frustration, the stakes of being a public spectacle may have been even higher for an Indigenous woman. As Carol Mattingly has written of black women activists' use of the attire of middle-class ladies in the nineteenth-century United States, such women needed modest and respectable dress to draw attention away from their physical being. In a context in which black women's bodies had been sexualized or made grotesque, choices concerning dress were rhetorical strategies with important political and social implications.[97] Sutton might well have been aware of such constraints on her own person.

Furthermore, the difference that gender made in this respect becomes even more evident when we compare Sutton's reticence about public appearances with Copway's delight when audiences paid attention to his person. According to the newspaper reports that he included in *Running Sketches*, Kahgegagahbowh was a "fine, noble-looking man, very intelligent, and speaks the English language with great fluency, correctness, and thoroughness."[98] The *Liverpool Standard* "found him a very intelligent man. His complexion is of course rather dark and his hair long and black, and

Fig. 2.7:
Nahneebahweequa/Catherine Sutton, c. 1860

he is a tall, well-proportioned, and handsome man, with the manners and graceful dignity of a perfect gentleman. We hail his presence amongst us as a token of spreading intelligence among the North American Indians."[99] Although he probably found the *Standard*'s appraisal flattering, Copway may well have squirmed inwardly at the article's last line, with its suggestion that "intelligence" was growing among his people. Later, in *Running Sketches*, he stated "Indians" had always possessed intellectual capacities, ones that predated the arrival of Europeans.[100] At the peace conference in Frankfurt, a reporter was equally impressed with Copway's speech and deportment. He possessed "an aristocratic bearing – and is not the orator a Prince? – an earnest, calm, countenance, well-toned voice," as well as "few, but natural gestures, and an epic manner, as if he stood in the middle of his tribe, relating clearly, and without passion, some important occurrence."[101]

As much as *Running Sketches* constructs its author as a public-spirited reformer, then, it is not above subtly tweaking British and European sensibilities around interracial sexuality, something that, as the next chapter will explore, Copway's own choice of wife had done quite openly. For one, he was pleased by the attendance of "the ladies" at both public and more intimate events, such as certain meetings at the Frankfurt International Peace Conference or gatherings in private homes (the companionship of his wife, who accompanied him on both legs of his British tour but not to Europe, is rarely mentioned in *Running Sketches*). The gaze of white women did not seem to discomfit Copway. At the peace congress, attended by approximately 154 women, "the ladies" also found him a compelling and attractive figure, although he appears to have been careful to not disrupt – at least not overtly – racially charged notions of appropriate sexual behaviour. He does not acknowledge his potential sexual appeal directly and in his own voice; rather, he quotes the account of his appearance by another as evidence of his audiences' appreciative gazes. The report of his speech at the congress notes "the ladies direct their looks no longer to the finely bearded men on the left; the beardless Indian chief, with the noble Roman profile, and the long, shining, black hair, takes their attention."[102] Although carefully couched, such an account suggests that here is proof not only of his own masculinity but, particularly when placed alongside his critiques of Britain and Europe, that "'English' civilization was not antecedent to colonial masculinity, but in effect created in dialectic tension with it."[103] Overall, Copway had the freedom to enjoy being a gendered, sexualized, and racial spectacle, a freedom that was not available to his countrywoman, Catherine Sutton.

Conclusion: Complicating Colonial Celebrity

The celebrity fashioning of these Ojibwe people, however, was complicated by the religious and imperial context in which it took place. They did not travel across the Atlantic solely to become celebrities: they came for religious and political reasons. Moreover, despite the fact that the appearances made by these travellers resembled in some ways features of commercial theatre and organized spectacle, British evangelicals were well-known for their attacks on the theatre. While the Methodists were eager to display their converts as proof of the church's effectiveness, such tactics also had the potential to contradict spiritual teachings, both Christian and Indigenous, concerning public modesty and the subordination of self. For the evangelicals, individuals

Fig. 2.8
George Copway, c. 1860

were meant ultimately to subvert their own sense of self and will to that of God, and were meant to be representative – not to be unique or to stand out in front of crowds as singular personalities.

The process of shaping their images, too, was not one in which these travellers participated wholeheartedly or without reservations, particularly as this process took place within an ever-expanding metropolitan market-place for people and goods from across the empire and a well-established history of "freak shows" within British popular culture.[104] As a number of these travellers realized, they risked objectification as merely one more spectacle of empire, their social and political messages unheard or ignored and their individual histories dismissed, as more colonial subjects appeared in exhibitions and popular theatrical productions. (Some of these performers, as Chapter 5 will discuss, were their relatives.)[105] Furthermore, whether their audiences outside the networks of friends and sympathizers also remembered other Indigenous people who had appeared in Britain is a question that is difficult to answer. Although Jones pointed out that his lineage reached back to Pocahontas, we do not know if any who saw him, shook his hand, or read about his lectures remembered – or were aware of – John Norton's efforts to bring Bibles and new agricultural techniques to the Six Nations (let alone his military achievements). Nor we do know if the general public linked Nahneebahweequa to her uncle, if they saw her as unique, or, perhaps, as merely one of the many oddities brought to Britain's shores by the dynamics of imperial expansion.

In conjunction with the question of the reception of British audiences of this "missionary moment," there is, too, the impact of these travels on the home communities of the travellers, an impact that is equally complicated. To be sure, many of these travellers met their immediate goals: raising funds, the return of land, or the prevention (at least for a time) of relocation. Their travels also brought a greater degree of familiarity with the metropole, politically, socially, and culturally. However, determining precisely the effect of that familiarity on their fellow Mississauga is no easy task: the expansion of settler society in the years after 1815, particularly the growth of the missions, meant a greater knowledge of British social and cultural norms, not to mention the English language. Such an expansion propelled and assisted these travels, so to claim, for example, that Peter Jones's time overseas was responsible for introducing European notions of gender relations or of child-rearing practices would be to place too much responsibility on such movements across the ocean.

Their travels, though, serve as testimony, in all their multi-layered ways, to these actors' understanding of the need to engage with the metropole directly, whether that meant challenging imperial power head-on or forging sympathetic alliances (or both). In doing so, they presented themselves before imperial audiences as knowledgeable subjects, fully cognizant of the changes and challenges that confronted their communities and, thus, armed with an intelligence, comprehension, and understanding that their audiences did not possess.[106] In their speeches and writings addressed to both British and colonial audiences, Indigenous travellers emphasized such abilities. And, as work on other settler colonies has shown, affective bonds of humanitarian sympathy might also be undergirded with paternalistic notions of Indigenous peoples' need for European leadership and guidance.[107] These Anishinaabe travellers attempted to make use of such bonds in order to further their own ends, whether better support for mission villages or the prevention of further loss of land.

They also, though, made connections with the metropole in other ways, through intermarriage and the creation of new families. As the next chapter will discuss, humanitarian and commercial networks both created and were underpinned by other ties, those of domesticity and intimacy. Such ties were important in the movement of Indigenous and mixed-race peoples to Britain – and, in some cases, to other parts of the British Empire.

. 3 .

Intimate Entanglements within Empire

Introduction

As historians Antoinette Burton and Tony Ballantyne have argued, the spaces of empire were "animated … by the collusions and collisions of imperial bodies with colonial power and colonial bodies with imperial regimes," encounters which "sponsored historically specific, and often politically unsettling, forms of intimacy across a variety of interconnected worlds."[1] For the travellers we have just met, and those who will be introduced in the next chapter – men, women, and children from the Northwest fur trade – movement and circulation meant crossing a number of boundaries: oceans, national borders, class divides, educational systems, frameworks of knowledge, and communities of emotion and affect, all shaped and inflected by racially charged constructs and practices. They also, though, circulated through the thresholds of households and family relations. In so doing, they both met with and created significant spaces of intimacy and new networks of family and kin between British North America and the metropole and, in a few cases, between these sites and other colonial locations.

Some of these relationships were long-lasting, and brought comfort and sustenance to both partners. Such was the case for Peter Jones and his English wife, Eliza Field, as well as for his niece Nahneebahweequa and her husband, William Sutton, an English shoemaker, farmer, and Methodist lay preacher (1811–1894). Other relationships, though, were marked by considerable tensions and stress, where individual personalities meshed with the exigencies of colonial relationships and history. The marriage of George Copway (1818–1869) and English-born Elizabeth Howell (1816–1904) demonstrated how fraught such intimate ties might be. As we shall see in Chapter 4, for those boys and girls who travelled across the ocean to meet British families and to be educated in their fathers' home countries, such experiences might evoke the excitement of finding new familial networks, and with them new opportunities, personal and professional; they also might, though, bring emotional turmoil and, for some, crushing disappointments.

The trajectories of these relationships did not fall into any one pattern or category: their varied paths suggest the complexities of such intimate relations, forged both within and against colonial power. As historian Damon Ieremia Salesa has argued, "the relevance, focus, and meanings of race crossings differed from one locale to another."[2] At times the creation of these "intimate zones" within the colonial context might require that an individual move across national and colonial boundaries. Nahneebahweequa, for example, her land taken from her partly because of her marriage to Sutton, travelled to Britain in 1860 to gain an audience with the Crown. Others, such as Jones, developed such relationships because of their transatlantic travels. The children of the fur trade, themselves already examples of intimate boundary-crossing within a transatlantic economy with a long history of movement and cultural exchange, were caught up in myriad networks of family that encompassed Rupert's Land, Red River, Britain, and, at times, other points in the British Empire and beyond.

Moreover, for these men, women, and children, the boundary-lines of empire – particularly those fundamental markers of belonging aligned with notions of "home" and "away" – were far from precise, fixed, or unambiguous. For one, they were created and re-created within the context of transatlantic movements, in which being Indigenous might have great meaning and weight or – at least publicly – became so muted as to almost disappear from the historical record. As well, while these ideas of home and away might resonate across gendered and racialized boundaries, they also could hold very different implications for precisely those very reasons. Finally, the span of time in which these relationships unfolded, the 1830s to the late-nineteenth century, saw critically important shifts in the policies of both the colonial government and the Dominion of Canada towards Indigenous and mixed-race people, as well as related changes, at the global and imperial levels, of the meanings of indigeneity, race, and "civilization." Yet, despite such large-scale transformations in national and imperial policies and practices, racial intermingling and intimacy persisted.

Beloved Friends in Upper Canada: Eliza Field and Peter Jones, Catherine Sunego, and William Sutton

As a number of scholars of empire have pointed out, colonial encounters at times quite literally "got under the skin," sometimes to the dismay of colonial authorities, whose attention to classifying, managing, and segregating bodies from both sides of the colonial divide intensified over the course of the nineteenth century.[3] The tenor of these relationships has been studied by scholars of imperialism and slavery in the United States and in the fur trade; their work has told us much about the (at times brutal) racially charged dynamics at work in relationships between Indigenous women and white men.[4] As we also know, however, such attempts were never entirely successful and do not constitute the entire story of lives affected by the growth of imperial power. Other historians, such as Martha Hodes, Katherine Ellinghaus, Victoria Haskins, and John Maynard, have pointed to the related-but-different dynamics at work when cross-racial intimacy involved white women and Indigenous men.[5] Furthermore, there were moments when racial intermingling was seen as a worthy, at the very least tolerable, practice, one to be encouraged in discrete places and times by fur traders, missionaries, and educators.[6] As Salesa points out, racial crossings might challenge colonial power, but were not "intrinsically troublesome" to it; rather, they could be seen as a solution or as "benefit strategies of colonialism."[7]

Relationships that took place in Upper Canada between these Anishinaabe men and English women also encompassed a range of varied combinations.[8] Perhaps the best-known and most-studied couple is Eliza Field and Peter Jones, who, as Chapter 2 has discussed, met in London during his tour of Britain in 1831–32, married in New York City in 1833, and travelled back to Britain for his 1837–38 and 1845 tours. Although Eliza was the daughter of a wealthy manufacturer and had grown up in a comfortable Lambeth household, she and Jones shared much, including mutual religious convictions and evangelical fervour for missionary work amongst the "poor Indians" of the colony, not to mention an intense personal attachment. Their marriage was not only long-lived, it also left behind a wealth of documentation in which they recorded their feelings for each other. While we are

Fig 3.1
Portrait of Eliza Field by Matilda Jones, 1833

not fortunate enough to have a record of Eliza's first impressions of Jones, her diary records the growth of her very strong attraction to Jones and her desire to spend the rest of her life with her "beloved friend."[9] Despite these feelings, Eliza's diary entries for 1832 and 1833 map a trajectory of emotional upheaval that alternated between great joy and deep depression, as she anticipated both the pleasures and challenges that her hoped-for future "in the wilds of Upper Canada" might bring. At times his presence in her life in London was a source of delight. On 19 March 1832, "my dearest friend came about one o'clock and stayed the rest of the day. How sweet the society of a Christian friend, we do indeed love one another and we feel that it would be our mutual comfort and delight to promote each other's happiness, oh that the Lord would in his own good time give us the desires of our hearts and unite us in the dearest ties of affection and love."[10]

Yet even the happiness of that day was underpinned by her fear of "how hard the separation will be, and the time drawing nigh soon … the ocean will roll between us but there is one sacred spot where we can always meet. May that be our solace and happy place of meetings."[11] This was not the only time when thoughts of the "rolling ocean" that awaited her "dear K" (Kahkewaquonaby) and other obstacles tormented Eliza during Jones's stay in Britain. Once she had admitted her attraction to Jones, Eliza was initially wracked with apprehension as she considered breaking the news to her intimate circle. "My spirits were much depressed in the evening," she wrote on 17 February, "the delicacy of my situation not allowing me to make any feelings known to any of my friends, a word touching the subject so near my heart was enough. I found relief in a flood of tears, and sweet consolation in being able to pray to my God in this time of need."[12]

Her family, though, regarded her care for her "dear friend" and her desire to join him in Upper Canada with varying degrees of ambivalence. Talks with both her mother and father that reassured Eliza of their blessing, or letters from "her dear K" "in which I have the happiness to hear that his mind is much relieved by his last interview with my dear Parents,"[13] were followed by other, more wrenching, scenes. In late June, a family encounter occurred in which "the conversation I so dreaded was introduced, it was a very great trial to me as my brother J.D. looks on the affair with horror, I am sure prejudice and ignorance are causes of many of his objections." Eliza was gravely disappointed in herself for not "better bearing his remarks and because I was so much dispirited the rest of the day."[14] Four months later she recorded a tear-filled exchange with her father, who begged her not to go to Canada, telling her that she would break his heart if she left, because they would never see each other again.[15]

Fears for the health of her "beloved K" while they were separated by the Atlantic (not to mention fears for his safety during the crossing itself); concerns that, despite her deep desire to take up God's work and join him in the Upper Canadian mission, she would not be up to the hardships of being a frontier missionary's wife; and anxiety that her family and friends would oppose her marriage to "an Indian chief" in a faraway land: even one of these problems might have been difficult to bear, but, combined, they could appear insurmountable. Eliza repeatedly attempted to calm herself with the thoughts that "God's will" would be done. Divine providence, not humans, would be the arbiter of whether she married "my dear K." However, at times her entreaties to the divine will had the ring of abject desperation.[16] And while the fears of her family and friends seem to have been partially motivated by the distances involved and the imagined rigours of her future life, Jones's race influenced their notions of the match's suitability, despite their approval of his work, his character, and his own mixed-race status. Although it was not a secret that Jones was the son of Augustus Jones, a Welsh surveyor, and Tuhbenahneequay, a Mississauga woman, as we have seen in Chapter 2, he was customarily presented – and presented himself – in Britain as an "Indian Chief" or a "Red Indian."

Transatlantic networks maintained the couple's relationship once Jones returned, in April 1832, to his work in Upper Canada. "Oh what a privilege it is that we can convey our words, feelings, and desires to each other by the means of *writing* and the *post*!!" he told her in January 1833. Jones could not, however, help but be keenly aware of the problems they faced, as he negotiated with Eliza's parents, particularly her father, for their blessing. While news of his work at the mission took up part of this letter, her parents' attitude towards him was the most important concern. "And now, my beloved Eliza, a few words with respect to our very important affairs. The anxiety your dear Papa feels on the subject is no more than what I expected, surely he is perfectly right in gaining all the information he can as to my character, connections, and reputation, and I highly approve of the plan of his writing to Mr _ on the subject." Mr _, it seems, had a good knowledge of Upper Canada "and is as good a judge to give an opinion as to the trials and difficulties that are to be met with as any one I know." While Jones waited "anxiously" to hear "the result of his remarks," like Eliza he stressed that "it is far from me … to desire to do anything contrary to the will of the Divine Mind. Should the desire of our hearts ever be realized, I shall endeavour to do all in my power to make you happy and comfortable as far as human efforts may contribute." While Jones knew "real happiness does not consist in the things of this world but in the service and worship of God," he considered Eliza's "greatest sacrifice … would be the want of such society, as you have been accustomed to enjoy, there are however a few pious, sensible friends with whom you could take such counsel." Moreover, he had started to make plans "to build a suitable house for your accommodation, and am now making preparations to accomplish this." In the meantime, he assured her that he was "very comfortably situated, I sleep, write, read, and pray in my study, and board at my brothers."[17]

Yet even as Jones continued in his work of creating a welcoming domestic space for his future wife, he too confronted the fact that their relationship was far from "private" or a matter that should be determined by themselves and Eliza's family circle. As we have seen, her parents' concerns were not couched only in terms of race; the Fields were also worried about the distance, the harshness of conditions in Upper Canada, and the loss of friends and religious community that Eliza would endure. Yet Jones was well aware that, for some of his contemporaries, race was the central – and only – ground on which the marriage could be discussed. Four months after he began to imagine their home, Jones wrote Eliza with regrets that

> some of my white friends in this country, who have heard of my attachment to an English lady, have expressed their fear as to the results of such a union. My heart has been much grieved at some of their insinuations in supposing that I had not been candid in telling you my actual state … But the fact is my beloved Eliza, it is that feeling of prejudice which is so prevalent among the old American settlers (not Indians) in this country. They think it is not right for the whites to intermarry with Indians. Now if this doctrine be true, what must we poor fellows do who in the order of God's providence are brought to be united in heart to those of a white hue? However, I am happy to state there are those who take a right view of the origin of nations, and their relationship to one another. In my opinion *character* alone ought to be the distinguishing mark, in all countries, and among all people.[18]

Jones attempted to soften the brutality of his contemporaries' racism by reminding Eliza that God "was no respecter of persons" and "If God be for us who can be against us?"[19]

Nevertheless, Jones was never able to entirely escape public interest in his domestic affairs. As well as enduring the controversy stirred up by the press when he married Eliza in New York City, one that evoked the spectre of white womanhood meeting a sorry fate at the hands of brutal savagery, Jones directly encountered the prurient curiosity of strangers.[20] In a discussion with an anonymous "Yankee" whom he had met in Oswego in 1837, mentioned briefly in Chapter 2, he told Eliza that the question of "Indians in Canada" came up, particularly the question of Peter Jones. Upon assuring the stranger that he was "well acquainted" with Jones, he was asked about the "English lady" that Jones had married: "how does she stand it out there in the woods. Does she seem happy amongst your people?" Upon assuring the "Yankee" that she did indeed seem contented and, on being asked "what do the Indians think of her do they like her," Jones replied "very much, they think the world of her." His interrogator "seemed disappointed when I gave him such a good account of Peter Jones and his English wife. I had a good laugh."[21] Tricking the curious and ill-informed was a mild form of reprisal for the taunts and attempted humiliations that Jones, in particular, endured.

Yet if his relationship with Eliza brought a degree of public opprobrium, or at least voyeurism, it is equally clear that their relationship also was a profound source of emotional and spiritual strength to him. When they were both in Britain but separated by his tours, Eliza remaining in her family's Lambeth home while Peter visited cities and towns across England, Scotland, and Wales, he wrote constantly and at great length to her, telling her of his reception by British audiences (including that all-important information: the amount of money raised), the state of his health, the details of his travels, and, most frequently and consistently, how much he missed her and hoped to receive more of her letters. Posted from cites such as Aberdeen, Edinburgh, Manchester, and smaller towns in England and Wales, the letters are also marked by his frequent use of Ojibwe: Eliza often was "my dearest Newish" (Jones's Ojibwe name for his wife); Jones sometimes wrote passages to her in Ojibwa (telling her that his niece Catherine, who was with her in England, would have to translate), and he often signed himself "your dear hubby Kahkewaquonaby" (or Kahke).[22] As historian Donald Smith has argued, Jones's adoption of some aspects of British social and cultural norms and practices – his great fluency in English, Christianity, European dress, and an acceptance of many aspects of British gender roles – did not prevent him from maintaining strong ties of emotional devotion and political commitment to the Ojibwe.[23] His letters to Eliza also suggest his ability to embody and incorporate seemingly disparate worlds and to do so with confidence, humour, and affection.

Yet although Jones frequently reminded Eliza that she was, in his words, married to a "Red Indian," it would be a distortion of their histories to reduce their mutual attraction and shared lives to a discussion of racial differences alone. As Katherine Ellinghaus has observed of interracial marriages in the late-nineteenth-century United States, the issues surrounding such unions "can disguise the real similarities a couple may share."[24] As we have seen, despite their different backgrounds, Eliza and Peter also resembled each other in many ways: their shared religious convictions, their beliefs in the power of humanitarian sympathy, and their desire to serve in the Upper Canadian missions. Moreover, their sons, born in 1839, 1841, and 1843, were a powerful link. His letters to Eliza from Glasgow in 1845, for example, are full of longing to see "my darling boys" and entreaties to her to kiss them and embrace them.[25] While both settler and metropolitan society would not let them forget the racial dynamics of their union, such dynamics may have been muted as Jones sat in his Glasgow lodging-house, writing to his dear Eliza of his blistered feet, worn out through tramping the streets of that city.[26]

Far fewer sources have survived that would allow us to understand more fully the texture and timbre of Nahneebahweequa's relationship with her husband, the English-born Methodist lay preacher and missionary William Sutton, whom she married in 1839. Unlike the case with her Aunt Eliza and Uncle Peter, Nahneebahweequa's meeting with Sutton took place not in a London drawing room or missionary meeting, but at the Credit Mission village. Furthermore, Eliza married as a young woman; Nahneebahweequa was only fifteen at the time of her marriage to twenty-eight-year-old Sutton. We can only guess at Nahneebahweequa's motives for marrying Sutton; there is no wealth of correspondence or diary entries to suggest if he, too, was her "dearest friend." Probably her own family ties to one of the most prominent mixed-race families within the Christian Mississauga community and her own position in this group as a respected Methodist class leader made marriage to Sutton both logical and desirable. Her uncle's marriage may well have suggested to "Nahne" that a union with a non-Ojibwe who shared her religious values and, unlike other British immigrants, desired her community's well-being might bring her both domestic and spiritual happiness.

As Chapter 2 has shown, the Suttons' marriage was also marked by geographic mobility within the colony, across the Canada-US border, and, for Catherine, across the ocean. In many ways, her travels across the ocean

Fig 3.2
William Sutton, n.d.

and through multiple social settings were the antithesis of those models of domesticity urged upon Ojibwe women by the Methodists, models that emphasized the primacy of the home and immediate community setting for Christian Indigenous women. However, the need to act as her people's representative and counter the colonial government's assimilationist program was more significant for Nahneebahweequa and, it seems, for her husband, who appears to have supported and encouraged his wife's journey to the metropole.[27] Furthermore, unlike that of others, the Suttons' marriage did not result in desertion or breakdown. It lasted for twenty-six years, produced eight children, and ended with her death in 1865, at which time Sutton provided a public testimonial to his wife. His tribute spoke warmly of her many qualities and abilities, describing a life dedicated to the service of her people and to God. She loved Jesus and was "capable of describing her feelings and enjoyments with a fluency and clearness that but few were capable of doing." A "warm friend and a good mother," she had often wrestled for her children's souls.

While lauding her deep piety and domestic devotion, Sutton also celebrated Nahneebahweequa's ability to move between multiple locations, pointing out that his wife was very much of the world and able to circulate easily in a variety of social settings. Catherine, as he called her, had travelled to England to lay before Queen Victoria "the wrongs of her deeply injured race," but she was also

> A general favorite among both Indian and White people there was something in her natural appearance and behaviour which at once introduced her to the notice and attention of all with whom she came in contact without any effort of her own. I have known her to go on board of a Large Steamboat where the Large Salon was full of Ladies and Gentlemen and all entire strangers and in an almost incredible short time [she was] Personally introduced to the whole and become the Belle of the Salon, she was equally at home among all classes of the People whether in the Mansions of the Rich, the Poor Man's cottage, the back woods shanty, or the Bark of rush wigwam of the Indian, and she was capable of enjoying any and travel under almost all circumstances whether by the noble steamer, the swift canoe, or the slow coasting of small row boats, or bivouacking for the night on the wild uncultivated shore of our Northern Lake, her disposition uncommonly buoyant and no difficulty in finding a subject for conversation she was kind to all and a special friend to the Poor and suffering.[28]

Thus, for both the Joneses and the Suttons, shared Christian beliefs and their desire to help "the poor and suffering" were mutual sympathies that both attracted them to each other and helped provide a foundation for their relationships.

To be sure, class relations, as they intertwined with those of gender and race, had different meanings for these couples. William was a lay preacher, not an ordained minister. While sought after by the Methodist Church as an instructor, he lacked Jones's prominence and social capital in both the colony and abroad. Furthermore, his background was not as prosperous or as privileged as Eliza's. His obituary states that he left his parents' Lincolnshire home at the age of eleven to learn a trade as a shoemaker and then left England for British North America eight years later in order "to get away from parental restraint."[29] Although the Suttons' home at the Credit River was, as Smith argues, "the second most valuable" on the reserve, nevertheless in 1847 the Jones's home was worth £124, four times more than that of Nahneebahweequa and William.[30] By the early 1850s, the Suttons were deemed to have made a success of their Owen Sound farm, a not inconsiderable feat considering the area's poor soil; they had cultivated around fifty acres and built a house, barn, and stables.[31] In contrast, by 1851 the Joneses had built a large brick home, Echo Villa, near Brantford, which sat on a thirty-acre lot and featured a neoclassical design and eight fireplaces, and was surrounded by carefully tended lawns and gardens.[32] As Smith argues, it is likely that Eliza's father helped finance the construction, thus providing a very comfortable home for the couple, one beyond the means of the Suttons.[33] Photographs of Echo Villa and the remains of the Sutton homestead underscore the different material conditions that shaped the lives of these couples.

Moreover, by mid-century the different racial locations of Eliza and Nahneebahweequa resulted in different articulations of gender and class for each woman. While her husband's race meant that at times she experienced degrees of social opprobrium, Eliza Jones gained a home in Upper Canada at the Credit while simultaneously maintaining her links to her English family (to be sure, a home life that was complicated by her inability to speak Ojibwe and by her husband's sometimes controversial stance on the reformation of Ojibwe society).[34] In contrast, the colonial state's realignment of racial and gendered categories resulted in grave threats to Nahneebahweequa's home and livelihood. In 1847, the Suttons received their Owen Sound property because of Nahneebahweequa's Ojibwe heritage; the couple's economic position thus was shaped to no small extent by her

Fig. 3.3
Echo Villa, 2016

Fig. 3.4
The Remains of Catherine and William Sutton's Homestead, 1928

racial identity and not solely by William's abilities as a breadwinner. Ten years later, the government attempted to supersede that history by denying her membership in the Nawash Band because of her marriage, thus placing her in a position of economic dependency on her husband. Although her subsequent activism demonstrates that the government failed in its efforts to strip of her identity as an Ojibwe woman, such actions foreshadowed more widespread changes that would occur nine years later, with the passage of the Dominion government's Enfranchisement Act, legislation that revoked the status of Indigenous women who married non-Indigenous men.[35] To be sure, her family did not forget their mother's struggle. In 1899, Catherine Sutton, daughter of Nahneebahweequa and William, petitioned for her reinstatement to the Nawash Band list, arguing that her mother and her children had been unfairly removed from it.[36]

A "Less Than Perfect" Union: George Copway and Elizabeth Howell

The Field-Jones and Sunego-Sutton marriages have left records that suggest relationships that, despite being negotiated within the parameter of colonial power structures, nevertheless were marked by mutual affection, stability, and respect. Moreover, they also were forged within and shaped by the evangelical movement of the late-eighteenth and early nineteenth century, one that posited reformed and reshaped gender relations and the heightened importance of domesticity as the central foundation of society. These ideals and practices were disseminated and refined through those missionary and humanitarian networks in which these couples were embedded. While as Chapter 2 has argued, historians should not overlook the colonizing implications of missionary discourses on domesticity, particularly as they advocated the submission of Indigenous women as Christian wives and mothers, in these cases the companionate aspects of marriage advocated by evangelicals (and others) may have mediated the tensions and stresses of these intimate colonial encounters. As we have seen, Jones's public persona was that of an example of reformed masculinity that respected women, Indigenous and white, both as wives and mothers and as participants in transatlantic benevolence and charity. The religious community, then, also had the potential to create new emotional communities, those that might foster closer and more affectionate ties between spouses.[37]

But the evangelical movement's efforts to reshape categories of masculinity and femininity could not guarantee that a relationship would withstand the strains brought on by movement within transatlantic and transnational borders, or the shifting forms of identifications that such circulation might create. In 1840, George Copway married Elizabeth Howell, a friend of Eliza Jones and an English immigrant to Upper Canada. The couple had known each other for five months, having met at the Jones's Credit Mission home shortly after Copway returned from mission work in the United States; he also attended the Ebenezer Manual Labor School in Illinois. Jones, who acted as a spiritual father to the younger man, performed the ceremony and, with Eliza, advised the Copways about the settler society's likely opposition to their marriage. Elizabeth Copway may well have already come up against such attitudes. For example, her family did not act as witnesses at her wedding, possibly because they lived in Scarborough (eight miles east of Toronto) or because they did not approve of Copway's Indigenous background.[38] After their marriage, the couple travelled to Minnesota, back to Upper Canada in 1842, and then, after his imprisonment and expulsion from the Canadian Conference of the Wesleyan Methodist Church in 1846, to the United States.

As with the Suttons, little private correspondence has survived that attests to the couple's feelings for one another; there are no letters or diary entries that parallel the rich archive left by Peter and Eliza Jones. However, it is not difficult to understand Copway's attraction to Elizabeth. She shared his religious perspective, assisted him with his religious and political work, and helped compose some of his correspondence – and, possibly, a number of his publications.[39] Copway's 1850 *Reflections on a Forest Life* was one of the rare occasions in which he discussed his marriage and paid public tribute to Elizabeth. His wife, he told his readers, had arrived with her family in Toronto from England; six months after she met Copway, they were married.

> My wife has been a helpmeet indeed; she has shared my woes, my trials, my privations, and has faithfully laboured to instruct and assist the poor Indians, whenever an opportunity occurred. I often feel astonished, when I reflect upon what she has endured, considering that she does not possess much physical strength. I can truly say that she has willingly partaken of the same cup that I have, although that cup has often contained gall. I trust that I have not transgressed the bounds of delicacy,

in speaking of one who has sacrificed so much in becoming the partner of an Indian missionary.[40]

In his autobiography, *The Life, History, and Travels of Ka-ge-ga-gah-bowh*, Copway did publicly what Jones had done privately, as he castigated white Americans for their rude, inquisitive, and racist prying into his marriage.[41] Yet, while Elizabeth and their child accompanied him on his 1850 trip to Britain and Europe, Copway had little to say about her in his account of that journey. He pointed out to his readers, though, that their trip to England included a visit to Knaresborough, his wife's birthplace, where he found many "curiosities" in that "romantic wilderness" (although the Town Hall, where he lectured to a group of "warm hearts," was a "wretched" building).[42]

If he said little about his wife publicly, Copway may well have provided an apt assessment of her character in *Reflections on a Forest Life*. Elizabeth's forbearance, tolerance, and patience were all qualities, it would seem, much needed over the course of their years together. Leaving the Methodist Church, struggling to support his family, and constantly negotiating his public voice and presence appear to have led Copway to abjure the evangelical model of gender relations, at least so far as his personal life was concerned. It appears that maintaining a commitment to domesticity was a considerable effort for him. His biographer suggests that Copway crafted a public persona that was more aggressive and self-promoting than that of Jones.[43] Over time, he may also have become unable – or unwilling – to emulate Jones's domestic and familial devotion. To be sure, the Copways' marriage survived the death of three children in a short period, between August 1849 and January 1850; six years later, though, Copway abandoned Elizabeth. Their reconciliation in 1858 resulted in the birth of their daughter, Frances Minnehaha, in 1860 or 1861.[44]

In a reversal of the customary scenario faced by historians of imperial and Indigenous relations – although one all too familiar to women's and gender historians – we know more about Copway than we do of Elizabeth.[45] Like her friend Eliza, Elizabeth may well have been attracted to Copway because he represented opportunities for meaningful work and experiences outside of the more confined realm of domesticity offered by her life in Upper Canada. Moreover, Copway's personality and charm may well have had a strong romantic appeal to the young Englishwoman. As Copway himself admitted, Elizabeth also stood by her husband during their most difficult times, such as composing his 1851 appeal to James Fenimore Cooper

Fig. 3.5
Elizabeth Howell Copway, c. 1860s or 1870s

when Copway was searching for financial support for his paper.[46] Their 1858 reconciliation came at Elizabeth's instigation, after she made a heartfelt plea to her husband: "Oh George reflect for one moment for heaven's sake have mercy upon me let your heart relent and breathe the word forgiveness, have you never needed it."[47] Yet she was not oblivious to his shortcomings as a husband. In July 1856, she had contemplated a final separation, telling her sister Sarah "it is very desirable to be loved but to be a slave to an unworthy object is revolting to our pride."[48]

When Copway remained in the United States, he did so without his legal wife and their daughter. In the mid-1860s he had contracted a short-lived bigamous marriage with Sarah Van Gleson in Geneva, New York; by 1867 he was living in Detroit. Copway died in Ypisilanti, Michigan, in July 1869. By that time, Elizabeth had returned to Canada and was living with Frances near her family, in the village of Port Dover, on the Canadian shore of Lake Erie.[49] Although we do not know much about the details of Elizabeth Copway's reunion with her family, it appears to have lasted until her death in 1904, as a number of censuses list her and Frances as living together in the area.[50] Mother and daughter continued to be described as Methodists; by 1891, Frances had become a music teacher.

When Elizabeth Howell Copway died and was buried in the Woodhouse Methodist Church's cemetery (now the Woodhouse United Church Cemetery) in Norfolk County, the gravestone that marks her final resting place is inscribed "Elizabeth Howell, Wife of G. Copway." While it is not clear why Elizabeth Copway's inscription reads as it does – the marriage's break-down? a feeling that, as a white woman, she deserved to be remembered separately from her Indigenous husband? the perception that, as a wife who had been treated shabbily by a poor husband, she deserved to be remembered separately from him? – nevertheless in death she earned a degree of distinction, unlike many other nineteenth-century women whose gravestones generally registered only their first names and their husband's surnames, not their birth names.[51] On 16 December, one year after her mother's death, by then in her mid-forties, Frances married Samuel Francis Passmore. Four or five years her senior, Passmore was a Classics teacher at Brantford Collegiate Institute and a member of the city's Masonic Lodge. Frances died in 1921; her husband outlived her by three years.[52]

Somewhat ironically, given the Canadian government's desire to disenfranchise children of Indigenous mothers and white fathers from their mothers' communities, Frances seems to have been cut off from her Mississauga heritage, in all likelihood a rupture caused by her father's peregrinations,

Fig. 3.6
Frances Minnehaha Copway, c. 1870s

Fig. 3.7
Frances Minnehaha Copway, c. 1870s

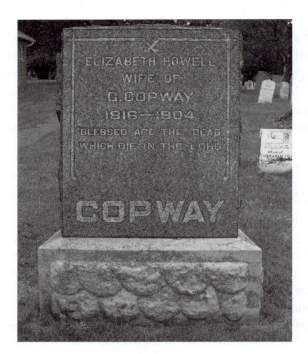

Fig. 3.8
Elizabeth Howell Copway's gravestone,
Woodhouse United Church Cemetery, Norfolk County, Ontario

Fig. 3.9
Frances Minnehaha Copway Passmore's gravestone,
Greenwood Cemetery, Brantford. Note that Frances's birth name is given on
the inscription, although not her full second name of Minnehaha.

complicated relationships with his people, and the broken marriage. In contrast, Catherine Sutton junior, the daughter of an Indigenous woman and white man, appears to have been identified with her mother's community, an identification shaped by Nahneebahweequa's activism and the family's proximity to an Indigenous community. It doesn't appear that Frances Copway had any links to Mississauga members on the nearby New Credit Reserve.

Intimacy in the Imperial World: The Marriages (?) of John Ojijatekha Brant-Sero

The Copways' marriage was not the only such union that began with romantic promise and shared communities, only to end in disappointment and collapse. Near the close of the nineteenth century, the twenty-four-year-old Mohawk performer, lecturer, and would-be imperial soldier John Ojijatekha Brant-Sero met Mary Ann McGrath in Blackburn, Lancashire.[53] Originally from the Six Nations community at the Grand River, his mother a descendant of Joseph Brant, in 1891 Brant-Sero was appearing in a touring production of the play *On the Frontier*, a Wild West show in which he played a white man (and which is discussed in more detail in Chapter 6). According to the *Derby Mercury*, McGrath, a "good-looking" twenty-year-old "tailor ... fell in love with the chief." Over the next two years they courted, and then, according to McGrath's testimony in a Blackburn courtroom, "went through a form of marriage" in Liverpool, after which they lived together "in a house furnished" by Brant-Sero in Blackburn, where McGrath gave birth to a son, John Edward, in 1894.[54] It appears that, at the time of the birth, McGrath considered herself Brant-Sero's wife, as she described him as her husband on John Edward's birth certificate.[55] However, in 1896 Brant-Sero apparently told McGrath that "a lady had taken a great fancy to him and would educate him for the ministry if she would release him for two years." Not disposed to lose her partner, McGrath refused, whereupon Brant-Sero vanished "and the next thing she heard of him was that he had been married at Preston to Mrs. Kirby, widow of a Church of England clergyman, and reputed very wealthy." Brant-Sero did not appear too disconcerted by the court proceedings, as he admitted to being John Edward's father and declared his pride in his son. His admission did not save him, though, from being ordered to pay the full amount of child support requested by McGrath and from being served with a writ of breach of promise.[56]

Fig. 3.10
John Ojijatekha Brant-Sero. From David Boyle, *Ontario Archaeological Report*, 1898.

One month after the case, Brant-Sero brought his new bride, forty-eight-year-old Frances, to Canada, where they settled at Pinder Lodge, a house on a large estate outside of Hamilton. Not unlike Joseph Brant and John Norton, who established themselves in similar domiciles, here the Brant-Seros conducted a busy social life and hosted large parties, including a lavish, well-reported celebration of the 1897 Golden Jubilee that included the visit of a large group from the Six Nations. The *Saturday Globe* quoted Chief David Thomas, the Mohawk deputy-speaker of the Six Nations Council, who spoke, on behalf of his fellow-councillors, as being

surprised at Mrs Brant-Sero; she is open-hearted and kind. She is a superior white woman in the matter of education and true womanly sympathy for the welfare of her Indian friends. It will not soon be forgotten by the Six Nations. Our thanks to her is mingled with regret that because she has not yet learned our language, consequently it must be through an interpreter. My chiefs hope she will realize our good wishes. Especially do we admire her for having had the good sense to fall in love with our fellow young Indian.[57]

In 1901 the couple were back in England, "living on [their] own means" in the parish of Liscard in Cheshire in a house that they shared with five others, including a fine-art dealer.[58] Brant-Sero had not seen the last of his courtroom appearances, though; in 1902 he was charged in Liverpool for failure to pay child support (presumably for John Edward).[59] After this point, it is difficult – in all likelihood impossible – to know whether Brant-Sero maintained a relationship with his son. Although his mother listed him in the 1901 English census as John Edward McGrath, later in his life John Edward went by the surname "Brant," and kept genealogical records attesting to his descent from Joseph Brant. At the very least, then, he was aware and proud of his Mohawk ancestry: what he thought of his absent father is another question.[60]

Although not quite as clearly expressed as those of her fellow country-woman, Eliza Field, Frances Kirby's motivations can be pieced together from a range of sources and contexts. Perhaps Kirby linked both the publicly expressed and sanctioned late-Victorian metropolitan fascination with Indigenous "others" and their artifacts with more private sexual fantasies and desires. Motivated, it seems, by William Cody's Wild West Show, in 1890 Kirby travelled to Alberta, where she amassed a collection of artifacts from the Kainai (Bloods), a division of the Blackfoot.[61] Prompted by her existing interest in Indigenous people and culture, back home in England she may well have made a point of seeing Brant-Sero perform in the Wild West Show (I would like to think that she was in the Leeds audience that, in February 1896, gathered to hear him lecture on "Marriage: Ancient and Modern").[62] She may have come to regret her decision to "fall in love with the young Indian," as her later letters to a mutual acquaintance suggest that she found her husband unpredictable, possibly untrustworthy.[63] Moreover, during his 1900 travels abroad, Brant-Sero appears to have left her in Canada without any means of support.[64] Initially, though, Kirby seems to have been fascinated by this articulate, attractive man who presented himself as both Mohawk and British and did so seemingly without contradiction and with great confidence. The prospects of a life in Canada, albeit in a region with a longer history of settler presence and prosperity than Alberta, yet still close to her husband's Haudenosaunee community, also may have appeared far more exciting than life as a clergyman's widow in Preston. At this point I do not know how long Frances remained with him after their return to England; his estate records suggest that, by his death in 1914, they had been estranged for a number of years.[65]

In contrast, what of Mary McGrath's role in his life and her desires? There are only fragments out of which the outline of McGrath's life may be constructed. The little we know of her comes not from coverage of her social life or the extensive correspondence of an Eliza Field but, rather, from the census and the newspaper account of her court case against her child's father. McGrath came from a very different echelon of British society than Kirby or Field: born in India to an Irish mother; young, single, and working as a "machinist" or "tailoress."[66] Was she won over by Brant-Sero's charm as a "Mohawk prince," an enactment of masculinity that combined elements of those captivity tales and Wild West narratives that circulated within British popular culture at the turn of the century with that of the worldly traveller who played a white man in *On the Frontier* in her hometown of Blackburn? Just as Eliza Field may have seen Peter Jones as the personification of the early nineteenth-century missionary movement's achievements and, simultaneously, her "beloved K" – an "Indian chief" who was also her "dear hubby Kahke" – so too might McGrath have seen Brant-Sero as the embodiment of late-nineteenth-century wider, racially inflected desires and fantasies. Such a figure might then have been overwritten by that of an unreliable partner who deserted her and their child in order to better himself economically and socially.[67]

While the sources tell us little directly about Brant-Sero's motives and feelings towards his partners, the ethnic and, in particular, class differences between McGrath and Kirby surely shaped the type of relationship he forged with these women. His union with McGrath appears – at least on the surface – to have been shaped by romantic and sexual feelings. Certainly McGrath could not offer him the chance to move into the English middle class and finesse the imperial connections that Brant-Sero prized in his professional life.[68] Frances Kirby's respectability as a clergyman's widow, her interest in Indigenous cultures, and the financial stability that she apparently offered may well have been attractive to him; all would have advanced his career as a lecturer and authority on the Mohawk. When Kirby and Brant-Sero married, his inability to produce a baptism certificate from the Methodist church led him to be rechristened in the Anglican church (at which point he officially added "Brant" to his name). In all likelihood, this christening was part of the bargain struck between the two as part of their marriage.[69] Brant-Sero was not a notably religious man, at least not so far as Christianity was concerned, and changing denominations may have seemed to him a matter of convenience and expediency. Furthermore, officially adding "Brant" to his name may well have been a way of proclaiming his authenticity in both metropolitan and settler contexts and of reminding both of his people's ongoing presence. As we will see in Chapter 6, asserting that his people were not a dying race was important to Brant-Sero.

When put alongside his public performances in both Canada and Britain, his unions with these two British women also suggest that the intimate might be used to reinforce publicly performed personas. As Chapter 6 demonstrates, like John Norton and George Copway, Brant-Sero performed a highly physical, often very flamboyant, type of masculinity that merged Haudenosaunee and Western dress and sensibility. Far from being content to be confined to categories of either "Indian" or "British," he enjoyed displaying his abilities to move across racial and imperial boundaries, claiming multiple spaces and identities in the process.[70] Unlike Jones or, in the early stages of his marriage, Copway, for whom domestic life was fundamental and underpinned public work and achievement, Brant-Sero seems to have reversed these relationships. Creating intimate relationships and, in the case of McGrath, new kin networks with white women may well have been yet another marker of his desire to counter imperial discourses which frowned upon such liaisons and also saw his people as a dying race, incapable of contending with the stresses and strains of modernity. Although the trajectory of his intimate relationships was not, as we have seen, completely under Brant-Sero's control – he was not able to escape the magistrate's court order for child support, for example – nevertheless his conception of gender relations and domesticity merged both personal longings and political desires.

"Home" and "Away" in the Nineteenth-Century British Empire

These stories encompass a range of outcomes and suggest that, within these networks of empire and transatlantic movements, encountering an intimate "other" might end in any manner of ways, none of them predictable. Colonial circuits of religious benevolence of the early nineteenth century brought Eliza Field and Peter Jones together; they also underpinned the union of George Copway and Elizabeth Howell. For Brant-Sero, Mary McGrath, and Frances Kirby, metropolitan fascination with "wild Indians" provided a stage – figuratively but also literally – on which new forms of intimacy might be created. While the structures of nineteenth-century empire and movements across and outside formal imperial boundaries shaped the subjectivities and experiences of these peoples, where possible we also need to consider the specific trajectories of their lives, their own personal predilections and traits. These were ideas, practices, and identities that, as historians David Lambert and Alan Lester point out, "developed trans-imperially as they moved from one imperial site to another."[71] To these practices and identities, which in Lambert and Lester's study are primarily those of the public realm, I would add those of husband, wife, father, and mother. It may be that the domestic happiness Peter Jones experienced, for example, strengthened his resolve that the Christian Ojibwe of Rice Lake and the Credit River mission villages would benefit from the same model of domesticity and piety that shaped the Jones household.

Moreover, while imperial networks were both "constructed and maintained by colonial interests," we also should not "overlook the fact that colonized subjects themselves could and did forge new networks which similarly spanned imperial space, some of which were assimilationist and others more deeply anti-colonial in their effects."[72] The "new networks" of family ties engendered by these travellers' movements fall in between these polarities, occupying a complicated, shifting, and sometimes ambivalent relationship to them. Peter Jones preached of the Mississauagas' need to take up models of European Christian family life, while at the same time fighting for his peoples' right to their land, addressing his English wife as "Newish," teaching her Ojibwe, and signing himself "your dear hubby, Kahke." His niece

Nahneebahweequa wrote to her Aunt Eliza for spiritual guidance; twelve years later, self-styled as a "Christian Indian," she vociferously rejected the colonial government's seizure of her land, making use of those humanitarian networks that brought her husband into her life to mount a political protest.[73] Copway pointed to the voyeurism that surrounded his marriage to critique American society and to claim, as literary scholar Cathy Rex points out, a stance that merged both Ojibwe and British subjectivities.[74]

These familial networks and intimate spaces might help bind metropole and colony together even more tightly. In the case of a couple such as Eliza and Peter Jones, they could provide justification for and proof of the superiority of the missionary movement's efforts. However, while some viewed the creation of the family relations and households that emerged from these meetings approvingly, as evidence of much-desired assimilation, others viewed them with an ambivalence that at times erupted into the hostility encountered by Eliza Field, Peter Jones, Elizabeth Howell, and George Copway. Not all racial crossings were equally sanctioned by imperial authorities and settler societies. Taking this hostility seriously entails, too, that we appreciate, as Victoria Haskins and John Maynard have argued in their article "Sex, Race, and Power," the great sacrifices and courage these relationships required of these individuals.[75]

Moreover, including these networks within the ambit of others which are better-known might make us reflect on the meanings of commonly used concepts of space, place, and, in particular, home in the nineteenth-century British Empire. As Catherine Hall and Sonya Rose argue, the categories of imperial and domestic are often used to delineate "away" and "home" and are usually linked in oppositional forms. Furthermore, "the metaphorical connections between domestic, home, and nation on the one hand, and their opposition to the Empire on the other, were especially evocative during the nineteenth and early-twentieth centuries as the Empire expanded and the ideology of domesticity in middle-class England held sway."[76] There is no disputing the power of these connections, yet I would point out that, for these men and women, they occupied a very complicated position in their lives. Those whose intimate connections took them back and forth across the ocean, whether as a result of the missionary movement or because of heightened interest in Indigenous cultures in the late-nineteenth century, experienced the imperial and domestic mingled at a number of levels: emotional, social, cultural, and material.

To be sure, these experiences would not have merged seamlessly. Eliza Jones, for example, became accustomed to hearing her husband preach in

Ojibwe, longed to speak to the Ojibwe women at the Credit River village in their own language, and was exceedingly proud of her husband's work as a representative of his people.[77] Simultaneously, she also wished fervently that she could teach Ojibwe children – particularly the girls – to wash their faces and hands, and was very gratified when they did so; she also hoped to eradicate Indigenous men's habit of spitting and improve the level of cleanliness in Ojibwe homes.[78] One month earlier, though, she had been woken from a dream of her English family and friends by her "dear husband's voice."[79] For their part, Elizabeth Howell Copway and Frances Kirby Brant-Sero found that, no matter how intense or genuine their interest in their Indigenous husbands' cultures and no matter how supportive and proud they were of their spouses' work as public Indigenous figures, such a commitment could not offset the upheaval and tribulations of their lives, as well as their husbands' characters.

For Peter Jones, Nahneebahweequa, Copway, and Brant-Sero, "home" as a space within imperial networks and circuits held somewhat different, albeit no less complicated, implications and values than it might for their English partners. First and most importantly, there was the "home" represented by ancestral lands and by networks of kin and community, both traditional and those reworked by the political, social, and religious upheavals of the mid-eighteenth to early nineteenth centuries, whether at the Credit or Grand rivers. There were, too, the physical spaces of "homes," whether created at the Credit River (Jones, Nahneebahweequa), at mission posts in Michigan or in the Upper Mississippi Valley (Nahneebahweequa, Copway), or in a boarding house in Blackburn or Liscard (Brant-Sero). Furthermore, for Jones, Nahneebahweequa, and Copway, places that evoked "home" might well encompass the spiritual family of the church, physically manifested in chapels, revival meetings, and parlours in which prayer meetings were held, and which might be found on both sides of the Atlantic. However, as we know from other colonial contexts, for Indigenous and non-Indigenous people home and domesticity, the intimate and familial, were concepts and places that, over the course of the nineteenth century, became increasingly subject to the intrusion and regulation of colonial governments and nation-states.[80] To be sure, couples such as Jones and Field or Copway and Howell experienced the opprobrium of the popular press, the racist curiosity of individuals, and the disapproval of networks of family and friends. However, the state did not intervene to prevent these marriages, nor did it seize their children.[81] It may well have been that their movement across national boundaries put them into a somewhat different relationship to the state than those who lived within the confines of reservations or mission villages. Others, though, occupied a different relationship to state power.

The movements of these individuals also occurred within temporal contexts that shifted in tone and timbre over the course of these decades. Unlike those of their seventeenth- and eighteenth-century predecessors, as we have seen, these travellers' journeys were not taken to underscore or strengthen military and political alliances but, rather, to contend or engage with the ongoing spread of settler colonial power across British North America. Peter Jones, Eliza Field, Nahneebahweequa, William Sutton, George Copway, and Elizabeth Howell met and married during and in the aftermath of a large influx of British settlers to Upper Canada, an influx that itself brought both Sutton and Howell to the colony. But their unions also took place in a framework of widespread transnational and imperial concern about the "plight" of Indigenous and enslaved peoples, particularly within new settler societies in the British Empire. Their encounters with one another were framed by humanitarian concerns for those whose lot, it seems, could be inestimably and infinitely improved by social and cultural changes. Nahneebahweequa and Sutton saw those sentiments start to wane (although they did not die out completely, as her relationship with the Society of Friends shows), to be replaced by an international hardening of attitudes that reoriented discourses about race and civilization from cultural adaptation towards questions of fixed biological traits.[82]

Moreover, and not coincidentally, the lives of the Suttons were also shaped by more determined attempts by the imperial and the settler state to place Indigenous people *and* white settlers into categories marked by notions of gender and race, categories that assumed the dependency of Indigenous and white women on husbands and fathers, whether Indigenous or not. Nahneebahweequa thus lived to see the beginning of an increase in the colonial and then Dominion state's legal, political, and economic power over Indigenous people, forms of control that became broader and deeper as the nineteenth century wore on.[83] It is telling that it was an Indigenous woman, Nahneebahweequa, whose movement across both racial and national boundaries brought her into a confrontation with the state that revolved around matters of intimacy. Even a respectable, Christian woman was not free from state regulation that sought to confine her and curtail her location, a point that she understood all too well.

As well as these questions of imperial and settler politics, their relationship to these "moving bodies," and their domestic matters, these mixed-race unions also produced children: Eliza and Peter Jones's sons,

. 4 .

Intimate Networks and Maps of Domesticity: The Northwest Fur Trade

Introduction

Peter Jones and Eliza Field, George Copway and Elizabeth Howell, Catherine Sunego and William Sutton, and John Brant-Sero, Mary McGrath, and Frances Kirby were not the only couples who forged intimate relationships in the context of transatlantic and imperial movement and networks. From the early 1800s until the 1870s, changes in the transatlantic fur trade and the spread of settler colonialism, represented most clearly by developments at the Red River colony, sent a number of children of Cree-British backgrounds to Britain to attend school and, equally importantly, to become part of English and Scottish family networks. In some cases, they returned to British North America. Others, though, because of familial decisions and/or their own marriages, remained in Britain or moved beyond its shores to other parts of the Empire, sometimes beyond the Empire's borders.[1]

The travels of these boys and girls, young men and women, both resembled and differed from those of others discussed in this book. For one, as we have seen, a number of their adult counterparts were either mixed-race (Jones, Norton) or had created new networks of family and kin (Copway, Sunego, Brant-Sero) with people from the British Isles. Placing the travels of these children, then, within the framework of imperial voyagers reminds us that, although the settler colony of Upper Canada is rarely looked at alongside the northwestern fur trade, political and economic differences between the two should not obscure their shared histories of intimate racial crossings. Furthermore, while located far from the Atlantic Ocean, both Upper Canada and Rupert's Land were tied into a transatlantic world, one in which Indigenous movement and mobility figured. Although children arguably played far less of a role in choosing whether they would cross the ocean, they shared with their adult counterparts a mobility brought about through British imperial expansion. Also, just as Jones or Sutton experienced the heightened scrutiny of metropolitan observers over matters such as dress and comportment, so did these children undergo degrees of scrutiny of their clothing and conduct.

There were, however, important differences between these two groups. In the case of the children, such scrutiny appears to have taken place and have been felt most intensely not on the public platform or church pulpit but, rather, within the new homes and schools that these children entered. Furthermore, it was exercised by those charged with their care, both material and emotional. While Peter Jones might escape such examinations of his conduct and appearance in the bedroom of his boarding house, such a refuge was not always possible for children. In addition, while, as we have seen, adult travellers might participate in those emotional networks and communities – humanitarians' sympathy and sociability for example – they found overseas, such exchanges often were extensions of those they had experienced at home and did not differ drastically in timbre or tone, and they also entered into these networks on far more egalitarian terms than children. Although fur-trade children would have experienced emotional connections with their parents, kin, and friends in Rupert's Land and Red River, once in Britain they had little choice but to form attachments to new guardians and caretakers, men and women who might demand they conform to new habits and disciplines, both physical and emotional. Furthermore, while the places through which adult travellers moved were important to them, Edinburgh, Liverpool, or London were temporary stops in voyages meant to end back in these travellers' homes: children had no such reassurance that they would return to Rupert's Land or Red River. Finally, while displays of Indigenous identity might be troubling to some adult travellers, for many of their supporters and audiences it was expected that they would be identified as "Indian." In contrast, the children of the transatlantic fur trade were in Britain not to demonstrate their Indigenous ancestry but, rather, so that they could become transformed, taking on the customs, traditions, and practices of their British fathers. In these processes, they might suppress, perhaps even shed, the customs, traditions, and practices of their Cree mothers' forebears.

A Dutiful Daughter and Caring Aunt: The Family Networks of Matilda Davis

While a handful of children moved back and forth from Rupert's Land to Britain in the late-eighteenth century, the travels of Matilda and Elizabeth Davis in the 1820s signalled an intensification of such mobility; they also suggest the various ways in which family networks across the ocean were created throughout the generations. The sisters were the daughters of Ann (also referred to as Nancy) Hodgson (1789–1849), a Cree-Scottish woman, and John Davis, originally from London's Clerkenwell, who entered the service of the Hudson's Bay Company (HBC) in 1801. By 1821 Davis had become a chief factor; the following year he returned to England, taking the very young Matilda and Elizabeth with him. In 1824, en route from Moose Factory to his new posting as chief factor at Mistassini, John Davis drowned, leaving Ann a widow with at least seven children, six of whom were daughters.[2] His will left money to be shared between Ann and their children, funds that were to be executed by his siblings, William and Ann, in London. However, to ensure that Ann and the children who remained in North America were dealt with fairly, thus relieving John "of a load of anxiety," he also included a codicil that appointed fellow HBC officer Thomas Vincent a joint executor, "as my highly esteemed friend is one to whom I can look up to with confidence."[3] It may have been that Vincent, himself the father of Cree-English children, appeared to Davis as one experienced in dealing with the tensions that surrounded mixed-race families, a parent who would appreciate the need for precautions in providing for the children's future.[4]

Matilda spent at least seventeen years in Britain, as pupil, governess, and – judging by letters she later received in Red River – as a niece and cousin. She returned to North America and opened a school at Red River in the 1850s.[5] The school held approximately forty female students, many of them daughters of fur-trading families; judging from Davis's correspondence, for a time she also admitted a few young boys.[6] Like many female-run academies in British North America (and elsewhere), the school was a family enterprise. Nancy Davis, Matilda's sister, taught alongside her (Elizabeth had died in 1854 in England) and helped run the school; their niece Alice Davis also appears to have been involved in some capacity.[7]

Fig. 4.1
Matilda Davis, c. 1860s

Fig. 4.2
Matilda Davis's School for Young Ladies, photograph taken c. 1970s

Told in this manner, then, Matilda's history appears to be one that, while marked by upheaval and separation, was ultimately a "success" story, as she achieved the status and respectability her English education was designed to provide. Yet, although such a narrative would not be inaccurate, it also hides the tensions and, at times, the sorrow that the complications of her family history brought to Davis. Such complications can be traced through the rich correspondence that Davis left, an epistolatory trail that wends back and forth across the ocean.

A theme that emerges most clearly from Davis's writings is her hope that her family would be a site of mutual affection and support. Given that her father was dead and that her mother, Ann, might not have been able to read and write English, letter-writing to her siblings played an important role in Matilda's world, especially in the times when they were separated by half a continent and the Atlantic.[8] Writing in 1843 from London to her brother, George, in Red River, for example, Matilda declared herself "quite proud of my brother he will I know be worthy of such a father as he had." "I think of him often dear boy," she mused and, although John Davis died before George was old enough to know him (Matilda and Elizabeth were too young to really know him as well), "our dear mother can tell you all about him I can assure you that my greatest happiness has been to know that I had so good a father." In his daughter's eyes, John Davis's goodness was linked to his religiosity. "He I know studied the Bible and endeavoured to imitate an example there given by our saviour Christ. Can we as Christians have a better example, certainly not." Matilda closed her letter by asking her brother about his faith and religious practices.[9]

Matilda and her sister Elizabeth may well have had good reason to hope that, in choosing a particular model of masculine behaviour, her brother would follow his father's example of moral conduct, not that of their Uncle William. Writing to George and another sister in the early 1840s, Matilda told her siblings of their uncle's betrayal of his nieces and nephew. When their father died, she and Elizabeth "had the highest opinion of our uncle's integrity and honesty and you may imagine how surprised we all were when we found out how shamefully he had acted towards us." The Davis children did not receive any money from their father's estate until 1841, seventeen years after his death; moreover, they did not even know about their inheritance until 1838. John, it seems, had owned a number of houses in Finsbury; the rent – or at least a portion of it – from these properties was to be passed on to his wife and children. Matilda had asked for her mother's and siblings' shares to be sent to them, but had heard from George

Simpson that the money had not arrived. However, the correspondence about the houses does not tell us only about William's apparent breaking of his promise to his brother's family and of his niece's disappointment in him. Matilda's letter also suggests that she and Elizabeth sent at least part of their salaries as governesses back to their mother and siblings. That year, though, despite having been promised a salary of eighty to one hundred pounds a year, she had been paid only sixty; Elizabeth had been paid only twenty pounds. However, she reassured her brother and sister that she had left her situation for one in the north of England, which "promises to be very comfortable ... I think I may remain some time in it."[10]

Davis's letters raise multiple questions about both her family's inheritance and her uncle's motivations. Was there some misunderstanding about the inheritance and the money owed to Matilda and her siblings? Did William get into financial trouble and decide to dip into the rents from the houses? Had William Davis decided that his brother's mixed-race family were not truly "family," and thus did not deserve an uncle's protection and loyalty? By this point, Indigenous and mixed-race wives and children were becoming less acceptable within fur-trade circles in Rupert's Land and Red River; William might have been influenced, via transatlantic correspondence, by such attitudes.[11] Davis's letters, regrettably, do not tell us.[12] However, this would not be the only example of such children's inheritance apparently vanishing into a British relative's bank account.

Whatever the case, later in life Matilda may well have remembered the hurt William had caused her and have determined that, as an aunt, she would support her siblings' children and try to provide education and professional opportunities for her nephews. After returning to Red River, she began with Albert Hodgson, her sister's son, arranging for him to stay with Janet (or Jane) Braby, a dressmaker who, judging from her letters to Matilda, may have been a friend from either Red River or from Matilda's years in London.[13] In 1861 the ten-year-old Albert boarded with Jane in Walworth, a district of the south London borough of Southwark in Surrey; the following year she moved to Brighton, taking Albert with her. The two arrived during a spate of building in the seaside resort town, which by that point was connected to London by the London and Brighton Railway, and was undergoing rapid growth. Albert may well have witnessed the construction of its luxurious Grand Hotel, completed in 1864, although, if he did, he did not leave a record of his impressions.

Despite Brighton's growth and many attractions, the arrangement does not seem to have been a happy one. In May 1862, Braby wrote to Matilda, telling her how sorry she was to hear of her anxiety about her nephew. "My dear friend you do not know me, or you would have known that whatever I undertake to do, that be done, or in no way neglected." (Janet Braby's declaration of her devotion might not have been completely reassuring, since she then told her friend that she had been away for a few weeks, leaving Albert in the charge of her friends, the Masons.) Albert's future schooling, it seems, was the subject of the tension between the two women: Matilda was considering sending him to a boarding school, a move Braby thought unwise. She doubted that Albert would be better fed, clothed, and lodged than if he stayed with her, or that he would receive "better instructions even at a boarding school, which requests two suits of clothes in the year and boys like him wear out many boots, they cannot dress here as in Red River." Moreover, except for short stays with some of Braby's female friends, Albert had not been away, "and you know if the children are away already at the holidays it does make a difference." However, Braby vowed to do her duty by him so long as Albert remained with her "and we are rather attracted to him but he is not petted or spoiled quite the contrary, we shall be very glad to see him placed anywhere you think to place him." Moreover, if Matilda wanted him to "have sea air," Albert was welcome to stay with Braby during his holidays. Generally, Albert was well and happy; he suffered from toothache, but it had abated somewhat.[14]

Albert's education was a troubling question for his aunt and for those who looked after or taught him in England. Former Red River resident Alexander Isbister, a prominent educator and humanitarian, who had become a well-known advocate for the colony, had recommended the Forest School for Albert, as Isbister was well acquainted with its headmaster.[15] Braby, though, believed "strict school discipline" would not suit him. At Albert's present school his sums "at first used to give him bowel complaint but has got over that now." Although he was supposed to learn French and Latin, his teachers had decided to concentrate on his English until he was "well versed" in that subject.[16] By April 1863, Albert had been moved to Walthamstow in northeast London, where he was enrolled in the Forest School on the edge of Epping Forest.[17]

Concerned about his progress and the fact that he had not written much to her, Matilda wrote to D. Grey, the school's headmaster. Although he reminded her that "backwardness in letter writing is not an unusual failing on the part of boys so young," he promised to remind the twelve-year-old Albert of his duty. "It is only fair that you, to whom he owes so much, should hear frequently." Matilda would not be surprised, he told her, "to hear that your nephew is backward. I don't think it of serious importance as he has the ability and I attribute a good deal of his poor progress since arriving in England to the shy and timid seriousness which I hope he is learning to throw off." When spoken to, Albert appeared frightened and replied with his teeth shut, which made it difficult to converse with him. Nevertheless, his writing had improved, he appeared to enjoy games, and his conduct pleased Grey.[18] However, the headmaster ended his letter with reflections that might not have encouraged an aunt with hopes for her nephew's future and who, moreover, was paying about £100 per year for Albert's board, tuition, allowance, clothing, pocket money, and travel expenses.[19] "It is quite a matter of uncertainty yet as to what his strong point may be and in which direction his tastes may be. All we can do is to ground him well in the regular routine of schoolwork."[20]

For his part, Albert's letters to Matilda spoke of the daily routine of the school: the Forest School's success at football, the muddy conditions of the playing fields, the older boys' trip to the Crystal Palace, the presence of mice in the cellars, the lack of snow in England, his marks (Fourth in Latin, Second in Dictation, Fifth in Arithmetic), and the arrival of an "Indian box" with maple sugar.[21] He was quite happy at Forest School, he told her: "the boys are very kind to me here. I do not get bullied and [am not] played any tricks with."[22] Yet Albert was lonely, it seems, missing both his family and the landscape of the Canadian northwest. Although he had enjoyed himself on his holidays at Miss Braby's, "the worst was I had no companion to accompany me in my walks so I had to go by myself sometimes I used to take my dinner with me." He wondered when his cousin John would join him and, just as significantly, wondered "when I should come over to America. I should like to know very much. I like this place because there is forest only not so thick as the American forest. It is not so thickly wooded. I can hardly remember anything about America I have been away so long but all I know I hope I am coming over soon."[23] While Albert may have tried to mask his emotions in order to save his aunt concern, he had yet to submerge them under a veneer of dutiful cheerfulness. Furthermore, although he might have forgotten much about his home, its landscape still tugged at his memory.

Despite not being bullied and feeling that he had a place in the social life of the school, Albert did not, it seems, thrive academically or impress his teachers. In June 1865 Grey wrote again to Matilda, apologizing for not having been in touch for some time but telling her that there was "little to say" about her nephew. He then proceeded, though, to say quite a lot, stating that

I cannot hold out grounds for any sanguine assessment of his intellectual progress. He somehow does not seem to receive all the impressions that the school ought to convey. There seems to be in his nature traces of a strong early bias which do not easily [bend?] to our conventional ideas. We think, as I told you the last time that he does exhibit mental prowess beyond those of mere apprehension, and therefore there is no reason why he should not persevere. But it is an expensive and, it may be, an unsuccessful course. One great difficulty with me, as well as with my coadjutors, is that we cannot get the boy to speak up, even in the most ordinary conversation, either in the holidays or during school time. His great delight is, to get away rambling in the forest, and I suppose fancy himself free from all our English restraints.[24]

Was Albert's refusal to "speak up" to his elders and his persistence in "rambling" a stubborn assertion of his Indigenous background? Of course, he simply may not have wished to engage with adults who might not have hidden their low opinion of his intellect. However, Grey's reference to "our English restraints" on Albert's mobility suggests that he did not take kindly to this type of discipline. Nevertheless, Albert's education was not a complete waste of the school's time and Matilda's money. His Latin and Greek teacher had reported an improvement, his French exercises were written "fairly," and his French dictation was respectable; however, they too reported that getting Albert to speak up in class was proving impossible. "He can make a tolerable map and has some idea of Drawing. His Arithmetic is the best part of his work."[25]

Perhaps Matilda's decision to support the education of another nephew, in this case John Davis, provided the impetus to move Albert to The Nest Academy, a boys' school in Jedburgh (close to the border with England), before John's arrival in Scotland. The school was founded in 1824 by the Reverend Alexander Burnett, and by the time Albert arrived it was run by headmaster George Fyfe. The son of an Edinburgh glazier, Fyfe may have had an entrepreneurial streak, since under his mastership the school expanded its curriculum and drew in an increasingly international group of pupils and teachers. Indeed, the school advertised itself as having adapted itself for boys of "delicate constitution" or those who had "recently returned from India, or other warm countries."[26] Marion Millar, sister of the recently deceased Reverend John Millar, Fyfe's predecessor, who taught at The Nest and acted as a matron or nurse to the boys, told Matilda of Albert's arrival in January 1866.[27] He had travelled from London to Jedburgh by himself, but had reached the school safely. "We are much pleased with what we have seen of him and I think he continues to improve on further acquaintance with him he is a very nice looking boyo and very quiet and modest." She also reassured Matilda that Albert "will find always a good example in his companions Master[s] Alick and James Christie and he seems to have quite taken to them both."[28]

John arrived later that year, and he too received a good report: "we think Master John a very sweet pleasant little boy ... he took to his companions and went direct to the gymnastic ropes in the playground. Master Albert takes quite a fatherly charge of him, and the Christies seem to have so much to talk about with him." Albert too was "much improved." All at the school were very fond of him, as he was noted for his kindness and good behaviour. Millar was also pleased that he had "got so stout since he came to Scotland" and had not suffered any illnesses since starting at The Nest.[29] The following December, Millar sent Albert to stay for a few days with her sister in Edinburgh, as she had taken a "great fancy to him" after a summer trip to Whitby sponsored by the school. Albert departed for the city "in great sprits," accompanied by the Christie boys, who were taking him to see their grandfather, retired Hudson's Bay Company chief factor Alexander Christie, and show him "all the wonders of Edinburgh." His holiday was well-deserved, Millar thought, as the schoolmaster Mr Fyfe was very pleased with his progress in the last session. John too was doing much better that term "and is getting more steady and attentive."[30] "Master Johnnie," Marion Millar told his aunt, "is improving very much, he looks much better than on his arrival. I daresay he suffered a good deal during the Passage, tho' they all said it was not at all a rough one, but at any rate it was a long holiday to him." Millar went on to reassure Davis that Albert also was doing well. "He is most attentive to his studies and although he seems to keep up the character of the American Boys, for good conduct in every way, Master Albert continues well and always a good Boy, and keeping up well in all his classes. He is a favourite both with his Masters and companions." Moreover, "he is growing up a tall gentlemanly looking young man and I have no doubt will turn out a good and amiable member of Society."[31]

Matilda did not have to rely exclusively on Marion Millar's appraisal of her nephews, since both boys continued to send letters home. Like those sent by Albert from Forest School, their letters home are both mundane and remarkable: mundane because many of the details they relate were so common to schoolboys' experiences for this period; remarkable because their commonplace nature gives us rare glimpses into the daily rhythms and immediate concerns of these two Cree-British children, living far from their homes and immediate family circles. The boys played cricket and football; received boxes from America (including those containing mittens made by "Aunt Nancy" and maple sugar sent by "Aunt Matilda"); learnt their lessons in History, Geography, Latin, French, English, and Arithmetic; celebrated Hallowe'en with apple dunking, eating nuts, and magic lanterns; went for nice walks by the river Jed, which flowed past the schoolmaster's garden; and enjoyed their seaside vacations at Whitby.[32] However, John's health was a source of anxiety for his parents and his aunt. He sought to put her mind at ease in 1867, telling her "I never had a headache whether at lessons or at play. I do not know what makes you think I am ill, I am as healthy as anyone here."[33] Three years later his sister Alice told him that she was glad to receive his "most kind and welcome letter" and was very glad to hear from their father that he was very well and that his cough was better.[34]

All of this correspondence might well have suggested to Matilda that her confidence in The Nest was well placed. The cousins' relationship at the school seemed to have been a happy and close one. John told her of Albert's kindness to him, confiding in her in 1868 that "I will miss him very much when he leaves." Moreover, the masters also were kind. "There is no flogging here but when a boy does anything wrong he is corrected, and there is no caning here. Mr. Fyfe punishes any boy who beats another."[35] As well as the absence of corporal punishment and the discouragement of bullying and physical aggression, The Nest also may have been better suited to the needs and backgrounds of the "American boys" than the Forest School. As Albert's letter home indicated, other fur-trade families – the Christies, the Cowans – sent their Cree-Scottish children there.[36] Writing to his sisters in 1869, John told them "a boy has come from Vancouver Island, name of Graham, he was at Norway House when I was there."[37] The 1871 Scottish census shows that, as well boys from Edinburghshire, Aberdeen, Roxburghshire, and Renfrewshire, the school also took in pupils from British North America (Jason, John, Robert, and William Christie; Henry, James, and John Stewart), Vancouver Island (James Helmcken), and India, South America, Syria, Singapore, and Italy.[38] While it is clear that George Fyfe and his colleagues strove to give their pupils a British education designed to provide them with opportunities for professional careers, either in Britain or in the Empire, the school's experience with boys "from abroad" may well have suited John and Albert better than an English boarding school with a more homogenous student body.[39]

It is not entirely clear when John left The Nest; it seems, though, that his family's fears for his health were well founded. He died in 1873, the same year as Matilda.[40] Unhappily for himself and his family, Albert and his situation also continued worrisome. He left The Nest in 1868 before his education was completed and went to London, where he stayed with Matilda Hunt, his aunt's cousin, who was most concerned about his future. It was a great pity, she told Matilda Davis, that Albert had left school. "Young gentlemen" were finding it difficult to be "placed in society" in England at the present, and she lacked connections with "influential gentlemen" who might help him. "I am without a male friend," she confessed to her cousin, "and Albert certainly wants a man to see after him. *I can do nothing.* We had all agreed that he had much better return to America." She was more than willing to help Albert, she assured her cousin: "You must not think dear Matilda that I wish to get rid of him *far from it.*" However, Albert was wasting time and money. Again, Alexander Isbister, "the one good and kind friend" that she knew, was invoked as a potential source of help. Albert might, she hoped, study with the mathematics professor until something turned up.

He wants to be *drilled* in a knowledge of arithmetic he is so very backwards in figures. Mr. I might bring [him] forward for he cannot go into a merchant's office without a knowledge of figures and A says he has no wish to be a Missionary as to his attending classes at King's College, it seems quite absurd, he requires *personal* attention and I am sure he could do nothing, and having to go backwards and forwards would be very dangerous at his age and it would cost a great deal in addition to your present expenses for him. I could not get Albert a place in a respectable family under 10/ [shillings?] per week. I dare say that you know everything is changed since you left England – provisions are enormous and *money very scarce.*

Others who might understand Albert better and might be more adept at "drawing him out" were unable to help. The fault, it seemed, was not with Albert's willingness but with his abilities. "I know poor boy, he is most anxious to get some thing … he does not recommend himself unfortunately – he said the other day he should like to be with Henry in his office *but that never can be,* he [Henry] *has no openings. Unhappily.*"[41]

Isbister may have helped tutor Albert; at any rate, by the following March his prospects were brighter. A "Mr. Hadon" had taken Albert into his office, and Hunt was happy to report "he has become much more business like and conversational." Moreover, he was making preparations to return to the Northwest. "He has been with Mr. Dickeson lately laying in a stock of things he was wanting." Hunt also had been to see Mr Dickeson to arrange Albert's berth.[42] Although other letters continued to pass back and forth across the Atlantic, no more was said about Albert: presumably he returned home without much incident.[43]

It was not just news of her nephews' education in Britain, though, that filled these letters. Matilda Davis also heard about engagements, weddings, births, and deaths of relatives and friends; of holidays spent in the Western Highlands; and of family members who had gone to Sydney in search of new opportunities.[44] Sometimes the correspondence went even further to reinforce intimate imperial ties. Even though Matilda Hunt was happy to send her cousin good news of Albert, she wished that she could leave for Red River to provide the assistance Matilda now needed. Davis's school, she was glad to hear, "was being so flourishing as to require extra help." "I am miserable and desolate enough and gladly would I go out to you if I were in better health." Apparently in a previous letter, Davis had reminded Hunt that she had "plenty of friends, and so I have," nevertheless "I have no one to fill the place, *the vacant chair*." Hunt's mother had recently died and, to make things worse, the friends that Davis had mentioned were going through bad times: poor health, alcoholism, and potential financial ruin. But above all it was her mother's death that weighed so heavily on Hunt. She was left facing a number of bills, since her mother had been ill for some time; worse for her, though, was the sudden nature of her death. "The particulars of my dear Mother's death you ask for but the bare remembrance is so painful *it was so sudden as this*." They had gone to dinner and, upon returning home, her mother had gone to bed and had died quickly of bronchial pneumonia and "softening of the brain."[45] Perhaps in asking for the "particulars" of her aunt's death, Matilda in some ways relived that of her own mother and was reminded of Ann, by then dead for twenty years.

Transatlantic ties to her own relatives are not the only ones that emerge in Matilda Davis's papers. The letters she received from parents who wished to send their children to her school suggest that, through education and the care of children (both Cree-British and white), Davis resided at the centre of networks of families and friends brought together by the fur trade – networks that, moreover, extended across both the Northwest and the Atlantic. It was probably no coincidence that Matilda sent her nephews to school with the grandsons of Alexander Christie, the chief factor and administrator for the Hudson's Bay Company, who had married Ann Thomas, the Cree-Welsh daughter of the company's surgeon, Thomas Thomas, and Sarah, a Cree woman.[46] For one thing, she also was godmother to Agnes Christie, Alexander's daughter, a responsibility that Alexander felt she more than amply undertook.[47] Those Christie family members stationed at posts such as Fort Chipewyan and Norway House sent their daughters to Matilda Davis's school in Red River, hoping that the girls would impress, be dutiful, and give satisfaction to their teacher.[48] Though Davis's English education and experience may have been an attraction, these families may also have felt that the alternatives had been far from satisfactory. In 1843 Letitia Hargrave, the Scottish wife of trader James Hargrave, described "Mr. MacCallum's" school at Red River (the Red River Academy) as "going to wreck." Children who had been fed on duck, geese, and venison three times a day were given only milk and water breakfasts with dry bread, and were punished with "severe floggings," confinements, and the withholding of food. What was more, she told her mother, MacCallum refused to allow his female pupils to wear their "Indian stockings" when they went for mandatory walks in the snow, with the result that their feet and lower legs became very cold and wet. Even worse, those mothers who were not legally married to their children's fathers were forbidden from seeing their offspring.[49]

However, Lydia Christie, whose sons were at The Nest, thought her daughters should join her in Scotland (she appears to have been helping to look after their grandfather). Writing to Matilda to discuss their future, she mused about a number of possibilities. Their father was not sure what to do with them and was considering a school in Toronto, while Miss Millar at The Nest had advised her that it would be

> more advantageous for the girls to go either to England or Scotland for two of three years. It's true it's pretty expensive but I think it would be well to give them every advantage we can. I hope you will give Mr. Christie a hint to that effect when you see him. I have long wish [sic] them to have been sent to Scotland when they might have been at school. I was so much pleased to hear such good account of my 2 dear boys at the Nest. Also the other "American" Miss Millar mentions both your nephews being well. In the event of the girls remaining again at R.R. which I hope they won't if I have to pass another winter here again will you please send me a list of what they may require. Annie did mention some articles but I fancy she might have overlooked something.[50]

If Matilda Davis was insulted or hurt by the suggestion, however veiled, that her school was not good enough for Anne and Lydia Christie, she gave no hint of such a reaction. However, once in Scotland, young Lydia Christie wrote to her from Edinburgh to tell her that she did not like it as much as she had Canada. Perhaps she should not say so, Lydia confessed, as she hadn't been long in Scotland; however, she found the Scots not as kind as the Canadians.[51] One wonders if she passed those sentiments on to her mother or if Matilda, reading them, might have experienced a twinge of satisfaction that in some ways Canada was better.[52]

Two years after Matilda's death in 1873, the Anglican clergyman and missionary Abraham Cowley reflected on the changes in education at Red River. Writing to Matilda's brother, George, Cowley expressed his belief that two schools would emerge from Matilda's and mused "it made me think of your late excellent sister, her great labours, and her wonderful success. Oh that dear Miss Alice could walk in her good aunt's footsteps!"[53] Davis's stay in England and her work as a teacher provided her with both practical experiences and a type of cultural capital that stamped her identity as a teacher and thus her school with authority and legitimacy. Such experiences played an important role in her ability not just to earn a living but also to gain respect from her contemporaries. Unlike some of her male counterparts in Red River or elsewhere, she was able to craft a space for herself – cultural and physical – within settler society. Although John Davis's financial legacy to his children might have been compromised by his brother's lack of family feelings, the cultural and social dowry that her English education and socialization had bequeathed were, at least, some compensation. As Janet C. Myers has argued for mid-nineteenth-century English governesses who emigrated to Australia, literacy and education could be a middle-class woman's "inner dowry."[54]

In many ways, Matilda Davis's narrative resembles those nineteenth-century novels that told of the struggles of British middle-class women emigrants in colonial settings, as well as the histories of their real-life counterparts, whose participation in emigration schemes became increasingly important for colonial promoters and settler governments. In their work as mothers, wives, governesses, and teachers, it was hoped that such women would domesticate and civilize colonial frontiers.[55] Yet simultaneously, Davis's story also needs to be told in a different register, one that also incorporates her particular history, a path that led her from colony to metropole and then back to her colonial birthplace. Moreover, although the circulation of children through the households of other family members was a familiar practice in middle-class Victorian society, Matilda's was not entirely a "typical" trajectory.[56] The potentially painful process of a child's acculturation to a world that did not include her mother or her Cree ancestry is one that at this point can only be imagined. Such a process, though, can be glimpsed in discussions about her nephew, Albert, and in Albert's own words. Along with his lessons in arithmetic and Latin, like many other children Albert was "subject to a variety of attempts at emotional enculturation" at the hands of well-meaning adults. Janet Braby, D. Grey, Marion Millar, and Matilda Hunt all hoped he would develop both his intellect and "certain sensibilities and habits of feeling," such as the expression of gratitude towards his aunt and being able to project confidence when speaking to adults.[57] As we have seen, some of these sensibilities and habits may have conflicted with those he had learned from his Cree kin.

Wives and Daughters of the Fur Trade in the Metropole

Matilda Davis's travels and movement, although distinct in the detailed archival traces they have left, was not unique. Like those of the Davis family, networks of family and friends, many of them created within the fur trade and operating on both sides of the ocean, underpinned the travels of other girls and young women from the Northwest and Red River to Britain and, for some, back across the Atlantic. Although generally a more privileged and elite group than those who remained "in country" with their mothers' families or who were educated at Red River or in the Canadas, other Cree-Scottish girls and young women appeared in the classrooms and drawing rooms of London, Liverpool, Edinburgh, and Aberdeen, their movements glimpsed in the correspondence of their British fathers. In some cases, their racial identities were either unremarked or not spoken of by their parents, as their education was discussed on the same terms as that of their British fur-trade counterparts. In an 1851 letter to fellow trader Donald Ross, Alexander Christie informed him that "Mr. Ballenden," a member of the trade with a Cree-Scottish family, had visited Edinburgh to place his children in school.[58] Christie was happy to hear that Ross's daughter Annabella had "been placed under the charge of our ... worthy friend, Mr. and Mrs. Allan, where she will enjoy every *possible kindness*, and comfort, as well as being in the *immediate vicinity* of the Miss Allport's School for attaining the best instruction." The Christie family, it seems, "would have been most happy to have afforded her all the assistance in our power ... we have the pleasure of seeing our friend Nicol Finlayson's daughter who is residing at the Miss MacKay's in this city, which is a very respectable establishment, the terms are however about the same as the Miss Allport's school."[59] (Although unnamed in Christie's letter, the daughter residing at the "respectable establishment" was Mary Finlayson, whose mother, Betsy Kennedy, had been born to Chief Factor Alexander Kennedy and his Cree wife, Aggathas; moreover, Betsy's siblings included Mary Kennedy, mother of Alexander Isbister, Matilda Hunt's "one good and kind friend" and Albert Hodgson's possible tutor).[60] One year later, Christie had happy news of visits between the Misses Christie and Ross in London. He had also heard that Ross had directed Annabella to return home "by the next ship to York Factory," a "favourable opportunity," Christie felt, as Mr and Mrs James would be on the ship it and could accompany her.[61]

In those letters, we can catch sight of the roles played by family, fur-trade, and settler networks. Relationships of intimacy were enmeshed with those ties initially generated by commerce and migration; over time they might become ones of friendship and mutuality. For these young women, no matter what their racial background, their time at school and with their British family was made possible by such links. For one, by the mid-nineteenth century middle-class norms concerning the need for children and young women to be accompanied in public spaces meant that, lacking available and suitable family members, friends or respectable, reliable acquaintances were pressed into service for the ocean voyages, rail journeys inland, and steamer trips up the British coast. The helpful "Mrs James," for example, the wife of the Anglican missionary at York Factory, turns up in the correspondence of Letitia Hargrave. "Poor Mrs. James had to take to her bed with seasickness on board the *Prince of Wales*," Letitia informed her husband, while accompanying "a half-breed Miss she has undertaken to chaperone."[62] Here, though, class-based conventions were inflected by the racial dynamics of the fur trade. While British children and young women such as Annabella Ross might have travelled under their mother's chaperonage, mixed-race daughters, it seems, could not be entrusted to their mothers' protection. In most cases, Indigenous and Cree-Scottish mothers remained in Rupert's Land or Red River, with little or no expectation by their fur-trading husbands (or the company) that they should enjoy a passage to Britain. In those rare instances when wives and mothers travelled overseas, they did so with their husbands, the latter either on furlough in Britain or returning home for retirement.[63]

It may well have been, too, that some women were not sufficiently fluent in English to cope with overseas travel by themselves, let alone with the responsibility of small children. Those few women who made the journey did not leave travel diaries or letters home to the Northwest. However, the writings of the indefatigable Letitia Hargrave suggest the ways in which the Cree-Scottish women of the Christie family, along with Mrs Nanette Keith, the wife of trader George Keith, and her daughter, Mrs Betsey Swanston, created new homes in the Aberdeen area.[64] During her 1852 stay in England, Letitia stayed with the Christies, as they lived just outside of Aberdeen, their home "a very nice and convenient place. They live very quietly and well and their circle seems to be one that has raised itself as they have done." To be sure, a visit to the neighbours left her feeling "a little uncomfortable," as she was in a "very beautiful house ... where the inmates were gaily dressed and spoke queer grammar &c. but I soon composed myself – They all appear very kind to Mrs. Christie who is much as she was in the country, to me she was more kind and Mr. C. toiled morn noon and night to make me comfortable." It was not just the Christies who linked Letitia to the fur-trade network, though. She had seen Nicol Finlayson's daughter at her school in Aberdeen: she was very like her father, she told her husband, "but fair."[65]

A week later Letitia wrote again to James, as she was still staying with the Christies and had more news of their fur-trade acquaintances. After telling her husband of the Australian gold rush, Letitia confided that the Christies continued to be most hospitable. "Mr. Christie's kindness to me knows no bounds the old lady and her daughter are more than agreeable. They are very comfortable here, and their little circle is most respectable. We would not like it, but I will tell you more about it when I see you." As for Mrs Keith and Mrs Swanston, they had called on Letitia shortly after she had arrived. "The Duchess (Mrs. Keith) is splendid in her own way and they both precipitated themselves upon me and declared themselves my friends. We are to dine there this evening."

Letitia, it seems, was fascinated by the household. In her estimation, Mrs Swanston spoke high English and "well can she speak it," and "told me that she called upon me that my brother might see that she did not neglect his sister after his kindness to her. She has 5 children home with her and the Duchess complains bitterly of the expense of feeding so many. The old lady trades a little, keeps fowls and sells their eggs and also disposes of her garden produce. She is hideously black and ugly but is wonderfully lively, even hilarious in her manner. Old Squirly gives utterance to the most fearful Indian yell and her daughter and she are too much for a small room when they express astonishment."[66] There is no denying that Letitia viewed these women and their families condescendingly, assessing them through a lens shaped by her own class and racial perspectives, in which both culturally inflected emotional practices – "the most fearful Indian yell" – and physical appearances – Mrs Keith's "black and ugly" countenance – served to classify and categorize them. Yet it is also possible to snatch glimpses of these households as more than sites for white traders' amusement. Just as South Asian women of the late-eighteenth and early nineteenth century, their lives intertwined with those of East India Company traders, created domestic spaces in which both British and Indian practices and material culture mingled, so too did the Christie and Keith families configure their households. Country and Indigenous practices, such as hospitality, "Indian yells," and a trade in poultry and garden produce were combined with the accoutrements of a respectable middle-class Scottish home, very like the "Indian boxes" that contained maple sugar and moccasins and reminded Matilda Davis's nephews of home.[67] Moreover, as Nanette Keith's "bitter complaints" about the cost of "feeding so many"indicate, the chickens and vegetables were needed to support her daughter and her grandchildren.

The fur-trade networks which drew together Letitia Hargrave and the Christie, Keith, and Swanston households also placed fur-trade daughters of both British and Cree-Scottish background. Scattered throughout the fur traders' correspondence are references to institutions such as those run by Miss Allport or Miss McKay that Christie regarded so favourably. Furthermore, these men did not rely strictly on word-of-mouth: the Ross family papers include prospectuses from Scottish boarding schools. Miss Lucy Evershed's school, located first on Cumming Street and then at 26 Grey Friars Street in Elgin,[68] offered instruction in music (singing and playing the harp), drawing, Italian, and French (which the English-born Miss Evershed was happy to announce "is spoken in the house"), as well as composition, history, geography, the "use of the globe," writing, arithmetic, and English reading and grammar. "Each young lady to bring one suit of bed linen and six towels," the school warned potential students, and also a "silver fork and spoon which will be returned." Three months' notice was required "for removal," and the entire year's tuition would come to £7 30s.[69] Miss Carnaby's Boarding School in Inverness offered a very similar curriculum and asked its pupils to bring one pair of sheets, one bolster case, and six towels. It did not require them to supply their own cutlery. Whether its higher fees (£10 39s 6d) were meant to compensate or whether Miss Carnaby believed she offered superior instruction or accommodations (or both) is impossible to know.[70]

The records of other schools do not seem to have survived (and may not have existed); while regrettable, such an absence is not uncommon in the history of small boarding and day schools. However, judging from the available records, like Matilda and Elizabeth Davis, these girls and young women, regardless of their backgrounds, travelled across the Atlantic to receive a certain amount of instruction in academic subjects – English grammar, history, geography, and arithmetic – and, perhaps not surprisingly, to receive an education in manners, comportment, accomplishments (singing, playing musical instruments, speaking French), and other kinds of embodied gentility. As Letitia Hargrave told her mother in 1844, at the age of twenty-one, Jessy Ross (Annabella's sister) had "gone home to a London boarding school, just to see the world, her mother says, for she has got plenty of 'book learning.'"[71] As in the case of the Davis sisters and their nephews, these girls and young women were also sent to be introduced to their British relatives, to forge "family ties" with grandparents, uncles and aunts, and cousins. It was hoped that such ties might reinforce the sense these young women had of themselves as ladies, bind them closer to metropolitan and settler society, and teach them various forms of emotional self-control and behaviour. Ultimately, then, they would acquire the social, cultural, and racial capital to make a respectable marriage in the fur trade, in Red River or, in a few cases, in Britain.

Unfortunately, the girls themselves have left little direct evidence of their thoughts and feelings about their voyages. How did they experience leaving fur-trade posts and Red River homes and, in particular, their mothers, siblings, and friends, for places and people with whom they might have only degrees of familiarity? Were they coerced or manipulated; did they step on board the company's ships with feelings of trepidation about their futures or were they excited, full of eagerness to discover the "old world"? To some extent, of course, their attitudes would have been shaped by their age, their family backgrounds, and the circumstances that surrounded their departure. At twenty-one, Jessy Ross, eager to see the sights of London, appears to have made a deliberate and conscious choice to leave her immediate family circle. This was not the case for the children of Captain Matthey, who, in November of 1824, were forcibly taken from their mother by their father at the York Factory beach and put on a ship bound for England. Although certainly many traders ended their relationships with country wives and took at least some of their children to Britain, the sudden manner in which Matthey ended his country marriage, making his intentions clear to his wife only at the very moment of his departure, shocked at least one fellow trader.

G. Barnston described the scene to James Hargrave in some detail: "the Brute then appeared … desiring at the same time some of the men standing by to drag the children from her to whom she clung in this her last extremity. No one being willing to perform this most unpleasant duty – he was constrained to try it himself, but her resolute behaviour utterly precluded his succeeding in this attempt." Although Matthey may well have had his reasons for his decision, Barnston believed,

> no one can defend him for the manner in which he set about it, it evinced him to be destitute of feeling as well as every generous and honourable principle. To conceal his intentions till the very moment they were burst upon her, while in distraction at a sudden separation from her children, and to dispose of his property, inducing her to do the same with hers, that he might decamp with the cash, leaving her the poor woman in wretchedness and poverty, would stamp his character a cruel one under any circumstances in any age or in any country.[72]

Other departures, while not quite so clearly marked by such a violent exercise of colonial patriarchy, emphasize how little choice children and their mothers might have had in these matters. Letitia Hargrave's uncle, John George McTavish, decided on his departure from York Factory to take his young daughter Anne, on whom, it seems, he doted, leaving behind her mother, Nancy McKenzie.[73] As Letitia told her mother, as McTavish's baggage was being loaded onto the ship, Anne "was playing on the river side so he told Hargrave to get her into the boat with him. Her mother was standing at a little distance half distressed and half sulky for she knew she would not see him again. Hargrave lifted Miss Anne into the boat and off they rowed." Once in London, McTavish was said to have "spoiled" Anne, taking her to large dinner parties that Frances Simpson, Governor George Simpson's English wife, appears to have thought unsuitable for a young girl. Perhaps not surprisingly, given the circumstances of her departure from Rupert's Land, in turn Anne "would not let him out of her sight."[74] All this, it is worth noting, Letitia Hargrave recounted to her mother without reference to the fact that Anne McTavish was her cousin.

Anne McTavish might have exercised what little power and agency she had by demanding her father's attention, or perhaps she clung to him simply out of a sense of dislocation and emotional need (or perhaps both motivations shaped her behaviour). In the case of Jane Ross, the dutiful Annabella's older sister, a trip overseas seems to have been an opportunity to exercise her own emotional and sensory desires and to delight in the material goods offered by the metropole.[75] It also, though, suggests the extent to which being identified with the fur trade might combine to undermine such a young woman's claims to respectable middle-class Britishness, even when she was not of Cree ancestry. Described by Letitia Hargrave, who sailed with Jane Ross from Gravesend to Stromness in the late spring of 1840, as "rather fierce altho' good-looking – she has a very dégagé appearance," the seventeen-year-old was, it seems, very fond of fashion.[76] During their trip up the coast, Jane Ross, "rather a large Miss," appeared in "a muslin gown bare neck curls down back slippers and cotton stock. On deck she wears a very expensively trimmed bonnet, primrose gloves and a striped satin bag with lots of black lace and everything new." Letitia found the young woman "very forward and at the same obliging." She, in turn, accused the first mate of "great haughtiness and arrogance," although to the older woman he seemed nothing more than a "good natured reckless looking boy." It may have been that the first mate – himself related to the fur-trade official Governor Pelly, Hargrave believed – had treated Jane Ross with less respect than she believed was due to a chief trader's daughter. Had he slighted her because of her association with the fur trade, seeing her as a colonial, not metropolitan, subject? While we cannot know, it certainly appeared to Letitia that Jane Ross lost no opportunity to display, perhaps even flaunt, her new wardrobe. "Miss Ross had made her appearance in a scarlet and green Saxony cloak, bare neck in the cabin except a pink crepe scarf and boots elegantly glazed – She has bought rosewood dressing case and work box, pale grey satinet gown short sleeves &c. and paid 18/ for a scarf – Altogether her outfit is perfect – Mrs. Finlayson says she means the lilac satin for marriage dress – Mr. Ross has not saved sixpence there, so he will not easily meet the consequences of her extravagance on the dividend of this year."[77] While "perfect" might be an example of her acerbic tongue, despite her British background, clearly Letitia was as fascinated by Miss Ross as she was by the Cree-Scottish household of the Keith family.

Jane Ross's love of fine clothes and furnishings continued to be the subject of fur-trade gossip. Back at York Factory, Letitia told her father, Dugald McTavish, of Donald Ross's recent promotion and suggested that it had come none too soon, as he was "much alarmed and dispirited by the heavy accounts Miss Ross brought upon him." Ross had confided in both Nicol Finlayson and James Hargrave "that it would embarrass him before they were settled. One of them amounted to £85 for dresses, another for a shawl satinet gown lace mitts embroidered with gold of £20 – and many others – He says that her residence of two years and a half in London has cost him

£500 – Her board at school was £30 – and she only studied the ordinary branches, not the piano, which was the principal thing he had in view when he sent her."[78] Jane Ross apparently sensed her father's displeasure about her lack of musical training. She "took the alarm three months before she left school paid ten guineas for a guitar and a music stand for it which would have looked showy in the first drawing room and began to practice singing." However, it seems Jane was not gifted with any musical abilities. "I did not hear her sing," Letitia wrote her father, "but Hargrave said it was shocking."

Perhaps Mary Ross, Jane's mother, was to blame, as Letitia found her "extravagant … if I may judge from the absurd quantities of absurd things she sent for." Jane, for example, "had boots and glazed shoes innumerable but not a pair could be supplied at the store." They were impractical: "even at Stromness the streets were so dirty that she had to borrow a pair of mine." To make matters worse, the young woman still lacked manners, having treated Miss Allan, the English teacher who had travelled to Rupert's Land with them, "very badly," being "impertinent" and deliberately insulting her. Although Miss Ross "was anxious to spend the winter" at York Factory, Letitia told Mrs Finlayson, "who informed her that it was likely her mother would wish her company more than I could do." Jane then expressed a desire to travel with Miss Finlayson so that she might be with her mother; Mrs Finlayson, however, "told her husband on no account to permit her."[79]

Sorting through the thicket of different perspectives on Jane Ross and her spending habits is a task complicated by the lack of her own writings. As we have seen, Letitia Hargrave was a woman of strong and, at times, quite stinging opinions on fur-trade society; she was far from being a disinterested observer. Her letters to her parents depict a community both divided and stratified by class and racial hierarchies, yet it was one that was also confronted with evidence, most visibly embodied by the presence of mixed-race children, that those hierarchies were constantly being challenged and were far from stable and secure. Moreover, in her correspondence we can see a sensible wife and mother shaking her head at the irresponsibility and extravagance of a young, single woman who was frittering away her father's salary on scarves, shawls, gowns, and dressing cases, not to mention completely impractical footwear. Married to a Bay official with her own children's futures to consider, Letitia may well have inwardly shuddered at the prospect of her own daughter falling prey to the allure of fashion. As well, she was intrigued by the dress of Indigenous and Cree-Scottish women, finding them both compelling but also unsettling: Letitia Hargrave thus participated in a wider imperial discourse, in which Indigenous and mixed-race women in "European" clothing were often mocked for their (supposed) attempts to mimic white female gentility.[80] No matter that Jane Ross was not mixed-race: her love of fine clothing, as well as her forward behaviour and seeming independence, may have suggested to Letitia (and other British residents of York Factory) that all fur-trade children, even when they were of solely British ancestry, might end up appearing no better than their Cree-British counterparts. Like those "poor whites" in colonies such as India and the Dutch East Indies, whose inability to retain their racial status concerned late-nineteenth-century colonial officials, young men and women such as Jane Ross might evoke unease about the prospect of class, gender, and racial degeneration, an unease that not even sojourns in Britain (let alone at Matilda Davis's boarding school) could completely assuage.[81]

Finally, how might we assess Jane's own desires and motivations? Despite Hargrave's concerns, her love of fine clothing and expensive furnishings was one shared with a number of other young women in Britain during this period.[82] It should not be dismissed merely as an example of a young woman taking advantage of her father's desire that she become a "lady" to indulge her own acquisitiveness and vanity (although that may well have been the case). Jane Ross had grown up surrounded by the commercial transactions of the fur trade that paid for her gowns and music lessons, so it should hardly be surprising that the material delights of London's stores caught her eye: consumption may not have had the same negative connotations for her as it did for Letitia Hargrave. Furthermore, while her guitar-playing and not-very-melodious singing appear in the correspondence as an amusing, even rather satirical, anecdote, they also might be the attempt of a daughter to please and placate her worried father by giving evidence that his £500 had not been completely wasted. Perhaps Jane Ross was not entirely an inconsiderate and selfish daughter.

Whatever the case, though, it seems that Jane's father, Donald Ross, worked to ensure that her sister Annabella did not succumb to bad influences while in the metropole. Letitia felt compelled to tell James about the latest controversy in the fur traders' metropolitan circles, one that involved a father's patriarchal control exerted across the ocean and made it clear that the company's hierarchies were not confined to Rupert's Land or the Red River colony. Upon hearing that Maggie Mowat, daughter of retired company employee Edward Mowat, was in London, both Donald and Sir George Ross wrote to the Allens, with whom Maggie boarded, that Mr Allen "was not to allow Annabella to visit at Mrs. Arnold's if there was any likeliness of her meeting with Miss Mowat there – Poor Annabella was sorely grieved at this interdict," not least because she would then miss out on Mrs Arnold's "routs, which Miss Ross had to eschew as Maggy [Maggie] was in possession and danced the Polka which must have appeared a war dance to the Cockneys. Annabella informed the Allens Sir George and 'Pap' did not wish her to meet Miss Mowat since they feared that it would get back to Red River that she, a Chief Factor's daughter, had associated in London (where good company could be had) with 'old Mowat's' daughter." Their attempt to quarantine Annabella from such social stigma was, Letitia felt, extremely hypocritical. "Donald is a miserable sinner – and Miss Mowat's criticism upon him is correct. She said to me once he's a seedy old fellow is Mr. Ross."[83] Seedy or not, though, Donald Ross clearly believed that Maggie Mowat's background was a source of class-based and racial infection that would jeopardize the standing of his daughter within both the metropole and the settler colony of Red River.

What Maggie thought of the matter has not, it seemed, survived, although her stay in London may not have been a happy one. A year earlier, Letitia had told her husband that "Maggy Mowat," who had been in the party that had sailed with Letitia, was living with the Reverend James ("a Missionary for Red River and a very dry preacher"), his wife, and their three children in London; they too had returned to London on the same ship.[84] Mr Smith, "who seems moved with compassion towards Maggy Mowat … called at Mr. James's lodging and found her nursing the children and otherwise unpleasantly occupied. I know Maggy would give her £2000 to have me for her duenna instead of the parson's lady."[85]

Imperial Marriages and Metropolitan Respectability

Other girls and young women do not seem to have succumbed to the metropole's temptations, whether the delights of fashionable consumption or the lure of déclassé companions, though, to be sure, they may have found the experience gratifying, a place to have new experiences and meet new people. Isabella Hardisty, daughter of the English fur trader Richard Hardisty and a Cree-Scottish mother, Margaret Sutherland, told her brother Richard how much she had enjoyed her time in England and that she had "many kind friends there, who were all very sorry to part with me. I certainly think London a most wonderful place."[86] Later in life, Isabella Hardisty would marry Donald Smith, Lord Strathcona, and spend a great deal more time in the "wonderful place," although, as we shall see later, her experiences with London society might not have made the metropole seem so wonderful.

Education and marriage in Britain formed yet another route to middle-class respectability. In 1858 Mary Finlayson, in all likelihood the Finlayson daughter boarding at the very respectable Miss McKay's Edinburgh school in 1851 and the "fair" daughter visited by Letitia Hargrave in Aberdeen, married James Dunbar Lamb. Lamb was a solicitor and agent of the National Bank of Scotland in Nairn, a town she had come to "as a very young girl." Marriage to a man with a steady and respectable middle-class occupation was no doubt an attraction, and Nairn might have appeared a very pleasant place to Mary Finlayson. By the time of her marriage, Nairn, a port town surrounded by an agricultural hinterland, was well on its way to becoming the "self-styled 'Brighton of the North.'" Being on the railroad line and having salt-water baths and pleasant sea bathing allowed Nairn to develop a genteel, yet brisk, tourist trade. By the 1880s, a number of tourists from London and southern England came to bathe, play golf, stay at one of the town's prestigious hotels, and enjoy its bandstand. The town supported three banks and a number of schools, including the Nairn Academy and Rose's Academical Institution.[87] Along with the influx of summer tourists, Nairn also could boast other connections to the outside world. Male members of the Cumming family from nearby Moray, for example, served in India and, in R.G. Cummings's case, travelled in South Africa and gave lectures about his experiences. His sister, Constance, travelled through India, Sri Lanka, the Pacific, Japan, California, and Egypt, leaving travel accounts and watercolours of her expeditions.[88]

Whatever she made of Nairn, Mary Finlayson Lamb had obviously paid attention to the lessons she learned in Scotland. When she died in 1923, she was remembered in the *Nairnshire Telegraph* as having "dispensed the hospitality of the Bank House in a charming manner." After her husband's death, Mary "spent the evenings of her days" in Redgeugh, the next home she "acquired" (presumably having had to make way for the next agent of the Bank), where she continued "to interest herself in all good work and contributing in the most general manner to the support of local institutions of a benevolent character. Her private charities were widely extended and were at all times associated with that personal sympathy and grace which so much enhance a gift. Spending her long and beautiful life in our midst, she will be much missed in the community, and her memory will long be cherished and revered by all who knew her."[89]

Fig. 4.3
National Bank Building, 20 High Street, Nairn

Fig. 4.4
The Lamb Family, c. 1860s/1870s. Mary Finlayson Lamb is most likely the centre,
seated figure, holding a child who may have been her youngest, John William Lamb.

It was not just for her charitable work, though, that Mary Finlayson Lamb might be remembered. She and James were the parents of nine children, a number of whom led lives embedded in the filaments of imperial and transnational networks. Four of the Lamb children remained in Nairn. Anne married Donald Michael, a solicitor and notary public, while James married, worked as a solicitor and bank agent in the town, and was active in the Nairnshire Farming Society ("held in high regard by all who knew him"), the Town Council (where he was remembered as "burly and uncompromising"), and the Nairn Parish Church.[90] Others, though, moved beyond Scotland. Elizabeth Lamb married John Shearer Middleton, a tea planter and landowner in Mysore (and sent at least one of their sons to Rugby, the elite English public school); her brother Alexander James, who managed a tea plantation of over a thousand acres, died in Assam, two years before his mother's death. In 1916 the Lamb's seventh child, Roderick, took passage on the *Tuscania*, sailing from Liverpool on a voyage that would take him to New York, then Honolulu (where he worked as a plantation manager), and, finally, Fanning Island (Tabuaeran).[91] While we can't know whether her children's movements around the empire and globe caused her concern or, on the other hand, appeared quite natural to someone with her history of mobility, the fate of the youngest child of her marriage might well have caused Mary Finlayson Lamb great heartache. In 1901 John William Lamb, a law clerk, was certified as a patient in the James Murray Royal Asylum for Lunatics in Perth; sixteen years later he was killed in the First World War, fighting with a Canadian regiment.[92]

Returning to the metropole might also be an attempt to escape the gossip and scandal of the colony, although, in the case of the Ballenden family, gossip and whispers may have dogged them across the Atlantic. Sarah Ballenden, the Cree-Scottish daughter of Chief Trader Alexander McLeod, became the subject of rumours at Red River during the absence of her husband, John, on company business, rumours that suggested she had committed adultery. While her detractors were tried and found guilty of slander, the trial did little to restore Sarah Ballenden's reputation; she left the settlement, taking their seven children with her to Edinburgh. John Ballenden's poor health forced him to go on furlough, and in 1853 he reunited with his wife and family. Sarah, however, did not live long in her new home, and died in December. John returned to his duties at Red River, but illness, perhaps exacerbated by Sarah's death, forced him back to Scotland in 1855. After formally retiring from the company's service on 1 June 1856, John Ballenden did not long outlive his wife, dying in Edinburgh

men. Yet their fathers' anxiety persisted (it probably was felt by their mothers as well, although we have fewer records that testify to their concerns about their sons). Sending a child to Britain might not entirely resolve matters, either. Although by 1844 Alexander Christie felt that he had done what he could for one of his sons, he fretted to his colleague Donald Ross that the boy had been under the age of four when he was sent to England. Christie, therefore, could not be blamed for his children "being too old before sending them to school. It was my intention to give the whole of them a good education and then let them find their way through life."[100] Seven years later, Christie was indeed a great deal more anxious about his son, possibly because he was now separated from him by the Atlantic and unable to deal personally with his transgressions. Writing to Ross from his home at Newlands, outside Aberdeen, Christie was "unable to express my gratitude for the very kind manner in which you notice the misconduct of our son, poor unfortunate young man he cannot offer any excuse" for his behaviour. All that Christie could do, it seems, was to "grieve. For what it was not in our power to prevent, that the Almighty of his infinite goodness may be pleased to show him the error of his wicked ways, before being entirely lost, as regards this life, and that which is to come. I trust you will be pleased to excuse my not enlarging upon this very distressing subject, and therefore merely beg to leave this wretched young man's case, for the determination of the Governor and the Council."[101] One year later, Christie was still distressed about his son, telling Ross that he was "under deep obligation for the many kind manners in which you refer to my unfortunate son, for whose misfortunes one can only grieve without being able to prevent."[102] Christie did not specify which of his two sons was causing him such grief, nor did he provide details in his letter to Ross regarding the young man's "wretched case" and "misfortunes": given the way in which news travelled around fur-trade networks and Ross's own involvement in the matter, there was probably no need for him to do so. It is likely that the "wicked ways" were those of Alexander Christie, Jr, whose 1848 affair with the Cree-Scottish Catharine Sinclair Ermatinger (wife to Chief Trader Francis Ermatinger) led to the birth of a child and her husband's discovery of his wife's infidelity.[103] If so, Christie junior's marital prospects may not have suffered too much from the affair; it is not clear what the direct consequences were for Catharine Sinclair Ermatinger, as she was still with her husband upon his retirement to Upper Canada in 1853.[104] In 1849, Christie married Caroline Isbister, the daughter of Mary Kennedy and Thomas Isbister (thus becoming Alexander Isbister's brother-in-law), and continued to work for the company, becoming a chief trader in 1858.[105]

Alexander Christie, Sr, however, lived long enough to see his sons and grandsons educated at The Nest: not all parents of fur-trade children did so. As the case of the McTavish brothers illustrates, Matilda and Elizabeth Davis's experiences of losing a British father's presence and protection was not unique. On 1 May 1849, Donald McTavish sat down to write his mother, Josette McKenzie, confessing his guilt over not having been in touch and conveying news of his and his brother's whereabout in the mid-nineteenth-century Empire. "My dear Mother," he wrote, "I am induced from motives of filial affection to write you these few lines with the full belief that they will be appreciated by you after so long a silence." Sent from, in his words, "Melbourne, Port Phillip, New South Wales," to Josette's home in Sault Ste Marie, Michigan, the letter acknowledged that "this is the first time, more to my shame, that I have presumed to address you since my arrival in this distant part of the Globe; the last time I wrote you was in July 1841 from Scotland but whether that communication ever reached you is to this day to me a mistery [sic]. I doubt not but you will be no little surprised to see from the heading of this letter that I am so far removed from you, but I shall proceed to relate to you the circumstances and causes of my sojourn to so distant a land."[106]

Donald McTavish's "few lines" was, at first glance, a typical emigrant's letter, his tale very much like that of others who had left Scotland in the decades that followed the Napoleonic Wars. In 1841, his brother, Duncan McTavish, left their father's family home in Inverness for Australia, intending to become a landowner and sheep farmer. Donald followed Duncan the following year, arriving in Port Phillip and finding work – "an appointment," as he told Josette – "as a Clerk in a govt office." The superintendent's records for the Port Phillip district tell us that he found such an appointment, since from 1842 until 1850 Donald McTavish worked as the clerk for the jail. Of Duncan, we know less.

By virtue of their Cree-Scottish background, though, Donald and Duncan McTavish were not what historians might call "typical" immigrants to Australia. Their father, Alexander McTavish, born in Dalcragg Parish near the town of Inverness in 1784, had joined the service of the North West Company in 1813; he was then moved into the Hudson's Bay Company when the two companies merged in 1821. McTavish's work in the fur trade took him first to the western Columbia district and then to that of Lake Superior, where he rose from a clerk's position to that of chief trader, first at the Bay's Fort Albany on the west shore of Hudson Bay and then at the Bay's Lake Nipigon post (north of Lake Superior). At some point during these postings

McTavish met and married a mixed-race woman, Josette Monier.[107] Either just before or after McTavish's death in 1832, Josette and Alexander's sons, Duncan and Donald, were sent to Inverness to live with their paternal grandmother, Isabella, and uncle, Duncan McTavish. Two years after her husband's death, Josette remarried. Her second husband, Peter McKenzie, was also a Bay employee; in 1834 he appears in the company's records as a "Clerk in Charge," who moved from posts on Hudson Bay to Lake Huron and then to Lake Superior. Josette went on to have two sons with her second husband. It's not clear from their letters, though, if her McTavish sons knew of their half-brothers' existence.[108]

Described by the writer George Cameron in 1847 as "the capital of the Highlands," Inverness was the "largest and most populous town in northern Scotland." Its population in 1832 was 9,663; by the time Duncan and Donald left in 1841–42 it had grown to over 11,000 people.[109] By the early 1830s, a joint stock company had brought gas lighting to the town's streets and shops, and the streets themselves had been "greatly improved." During their years in Scotland, the McTavish brothers would have seen the launching of the town newspaper, the *Inverness Herald* (1836), the formation of its teetotal society (1838), and the establishment of direct steam service to London (1836).[110] If their arrival coincided with the 1832 cholera epidemic, an outbreak that was experienced both in the Highlands and British North America and which killed 217 people in Inverness, it does not seem to have touched the brothers.[111] Thus, while not quite the metropolitan hub of Edinburgh or London to which other children were sent, nevertheless Inverness was a very different landscape to that of northern Canada's fur-trading posts and forts.

Gaslit streets and a temperance society were not, though, the most apparent differences for Duncan and Donald. "My dear Mother," Duncan McTavish wrote to Josette McKenzie in 1840, "when I arrived in this country I could not understand by seeing the boys with kilts, for when I saw them, I asked, what were these boys with the short pettycots [sic]." Boys in skirts were not the only problem that Duncan encountered: the twelve-year-old became extremely shy at the sight of girls. The second day after his arrival in Scotland, while out for a walk with his cousin to see some friends, Duncan had noticed some girls looking at him and "off I set home but I mistook my way." Fortunately, a shepherd set him on the right path. He also told his mother of his sojourn in the parish school, which he attended while boarding with a Mr Lobban, "but he treated me very ill, for he was always thrashing and abusing his wife and me for he was always drunk." After he informed his guardian of this bad treatment, Duncan was moved to Inverness's "principal boarding school," the Gair Academy.[112] Run by the brothers Walter, John, and Alexander Gair, the Gair Academy boarded a small number of boys. In the words of the academy's own advertisement, the school took pupils at the age of eleven "who have attained a tolerable knowledge of English Grammar," and taught them "to read the Latin Classics with ease *in two and a half years* – making, at the same time, such progress in Writing, Arithmetic, etc., as will qualify them for business."[113]

BOARD AND EDUCATION
A. & W.R. GAIR, A.M., TEACHERS, Bank Street Academy, respectfully intimates, that having taken the commodious House, in Douglas Row, occupied as a Boarding School by the late Miss Wapsho, they will have it in their power to BOARD and EDUCATE Four YOUNG GENTLEMEN, in addition to those who have already made application. As the system which Messrs. G. intend to pursue combines the advantage of Public and Private Instruction, they pledge themselves to Teach Pupils about 11 years of age, who have attained a tolerable knowledge of English Grammar, to read the Latin Classics with ease in two and a half years – making, at the same time, such progress in Writing, Arithmetic, &c. as will qualify them for Business.

Terms for Board and Education, 25 Guineas per annum.

Mr. G. has opened his Private Classes, for Geography and Writing, &c., at his Lodgings, Douglas Row – for Young Ladies, from 12 to 2; Young Gentlemen, from 7 to half-past 8.

For further particulars, apply at Bank Street Academy; or at their Lodgings.

(Not to be repeated)

Inverness, 13th May, 1830

Local histories of Inverness depict the school as an excellent establishment, both for the quality of its instruction and its congenial atmosphere.[114]

Duncan McTavish would have agreed. At the academy, he enjoyed Saturday walks accompanied by the masters, who also hired coaches to take the boys to see "anything extraordinary" in town and who, he told Josette, were also contemplating moving their school to a farm about two miles outside Inverness. Duncan seemed pleased both with his treatment at the school and its cost: "they only charge twenty-five guineas a year." He was happy that his mother had not forgotten him, as witnessed by her sending him shoes through Mr Finlayson (fur trader Nicol Finlayson). Perhaps demonstrating a young boy's somewhat lurid fascination with crime, he informed her that "there are a great number of murders committed in this country, and there is one to be hanged in a few days." However, perhaps conscious that this type of news might not assuage his mother's concerns for him, Duncan reassured her that he would be finished with his trade in five years and would "go to see you. I think I will leave this country in the year 1845 for I will be some time at London to get a little more insight." He closed with reassuring news of his grandmother Isabella's good health, that she sent her love to Josette, and asked his mother to send his love to Mr Mackenzie.[115]

His brother, Donald, also wrote to his mother as both a child and an adult. In May 1838, he told her that his health had improved, that unlike his brother he had been sent to a boarding school almost immediately on his arrival, where he and his fifteen fellow-boarders were "as happy as if we were all lords," and that he was continuously visited by Mr Finlayson, who lived only five miles away and told him that Josette wished to know of Donald's future plans. "I thought, as well as the best thing for me to be a doctor as I was so far advanced in the dead languages. And in that way I may have a chance of seeing you again in about six years. Do not be grieved about me for I am as kindly treated as though I were with yourself." However, Scotland was not Rupert's Land: "what a difference there is between this country and America." In particular, "religion is here kept by everyone," including, it seems, Donald, as he urged his mother to not only "try to save her soul" but "also those of your neighbours for I know that there are many there that don't know that there is a god in it." While now as tall as Duncan, Donald did not share his brother's antipathy to the opposite sex, as he confided to Josette "what a number of bonny girls there are in this town." Although Donald had hopes for his mother's soul, he also harboured his own, more worldly, ones: "I will be soon expecting to get a beautiful gold watch from you in a present." Yet it would be unfair to characterize him as a greedy child, for in his next sentence he implored Josette to "write for any sake write me as soon as possible." A postscript to the letter consists of two very poignant lines: "Write me. Write me."[116]

In July 1841, Donald McTavish wrote again to his mother from Inverness: he began his letter by telling her that he was not able to write until then as he did not have her address, but, having seen "Mr. Alex Simpson late of your company," he'd been able to locate Josette. Donald had news that he felt his mother needed to know.

The only circumstance that will anyways interest you, and which has occasioned some emotion in my feelings is Duncan's departure from this country to a foreign Colony two or three times farther distant from me, than you are from me called South Australia where an immense number of people have emigrated from this Country for the last few years and from which there has been very good accounts both as to the fertility of the soil, and the immense produce of wool which is considered the finest in the world, there he has gone to pursue the business of Sheep and Cattle dealer, not only because he found himself more adapted for that employment – but because it is really the most successful one there, for persons, have been known to accumulate large fortunes in a very few years. And I am sure, at least I hope that Duncan may do the same. He sailed on the 28th of April last from Glasgow, he is by this time halfway on his Voyage. I will let you know how he gets on there, whenever I hear from him. My old Grandmother was nearly breaking her heart when he left, she is keeping wonderfully well considering her old age, and probably may live a good many years yet.[117]

Whether Josette had indeed heard of South Australia is unknown. Donald's letter, though, not only passed on news of his brother's destination, but it also linked Inverness and South Australia for his mother, creating a map of imperial migration.

He was not exaggerating when he told her of the large number of people who had emigrated. Donald would likely have read about them in the *Inverness Courier*; articles about emigration to New South Wales formed a steady stream of news from at least 1837.[118] Quite possibly the brothers knew some of those who had left; they might even have witnessed the ships' departures. Even if the brothers did not attend a public meeting, held 16 May 1838 at Fort William, to promote emigration to Australia, they might well have read the different perspectives on life in New South Wales published in the local paper. In his 1838 letters to the *Courier*, Donald Macleod, who had left Skye for a settlement on the Paterson River, told his fellow Scots of his community's good fortune (including having their own minister).[119] A different picture, though, was painted in 1840 by an anonymous young man, who had also emigrated in 1838. In a private letter home, he told of deplorable conditions in New South Wales and the corruption of the community by the convict system.[120] Yet, whatever the new arrivals' experiences, emigration to the colony was a much-discussed topic during the brothers' time in northern Scotland.

Donald also told her of his own affairs: he had been working for a "respectable Solicitor in this Town" and had been doing so for two years but "not finding myself adapted for that profession, which has fallen off very much." He was trying to find a "situation … in some Mercantile Counting house in London, or some other large Commercial city in this country." Donald had enlisted the help of friends, although "they might do a great deal more for me if they wished," but was confident that he would succeed. "Whenever I have procured a competent sum of money for myself, I am determined I will go out to see you once more."[121]

The "situation" in London or elsewhere did not materialize, though, and in 1842 Donald followed his brother on a ship bound for Australia. By that time, Duncan had become a superintendent on a large "grazing establishment" in South Australia, while Donald settled in the Port Phillip District, which encompassed the city of Melbourne. Here, too, imperial connections came into play. Having emigrated with an acquaintance, Alastair McKenzie, who had been an officer in the West Indies and had been appointed sheriff of Port Phillip, Donald found work in the Port Phillip jail as the clerk. South Australia, Donald told his mother in a letter sent in 1849, held many opportunities: "this is a fine healthy country, no one need be out of employment here, and for persons possessed of small capitals [sic] independences can be realized in a very few years … thousands are emigrating here every year from the United Kingdom." Earlier in his letter he informed Josette that "on my arrival I found many acquaintances from the Mother country; such has been the immense emigration to these parts, that you could scarce know the towns and villages from English ones."

It was not just the healthier climate or the chance for work and independence that propelled the brothers across multiple oceans to another continent. Donald's reference to "small capital" included himself and Duncan for, as he told Josette, the funds that both brothers should have received from their father's estate, and that should have followed them to Australia, had disappeared. Their uncle Duncan McTavish apparently had "turned insolvent, and in some manner or other compromised with his Creditors, however we have not received one single farthing or perhaps never shall, our relatives at home seemed to have completely set their faces against us. I cannot now even receive an answer to a letter, but kept in utter darkness as to their proceedings." Clearly all of this rankled Donald: "If I were possessed of sufficient funds I should certainly go home for no other purpose than to shew them up." Although he promised Josette, "no more at present on this subject," he returned to it three sentences later: "If I had got my money on my arrival I should be now returning home worth thousands I am certain of it." Like the Davis children's English uncle, the McTavishs' Scottish relative may have thought of his nephews as "not quite" family.

By 1849, though, Donald had decided that his future lay in Australia: "I think I shall always remain here. I have made this the 'Land of my adoption.'" He closed his letter to his mother by hoping that Mr McKenzie would write to him and "the long silence that has prevailed will no longer exist, and that we may have frequent opportunities of revealing to one another our destinies ... I shall be anxiously awaiting in about twelvemonths time for an answer to this letter."[122] Unfortunately, we do not know if those "frequent opportunities" of revelation occurred, as the correspondence with Josette ends with this letter.

Donald McTavish's timing was fortuitous, as he arrived in Port Phillip during the expansion of both the settlement and its courts and jail. By 1842, the deputy sheriff of Port Phillip felt that the "the duties of Her Majesty's Gaol Department" had "of late increased to such an extent" that appointing a clerk was "necessary for the good order of this establishment," a necessity of which he didn't hesitate to remind the district's superintendent in their correspondence.[123] In November of that year, Alistair McKenzie informed the superintendent that he had offered the clerk's job (at that moment vacant) to McTavish, "a Young Man of most respectable connection and character who came from England on the same ship as myself. As I have known Mr. McTavish from his early years," he assured his superior, "and can attest to his qualifications I most earnestly but most respectfully trust that Your Honor will be pleased to appoint him to the vacant situation."[124] It seems that Mackenzie's recommendation provided the cultural capital Donald needed to find employment. Described in one local history as a "cut-and-dry Sheriff from Downing Street ... punctual and precise, often rather fidgety, but civil and obliging," McKenzie would remain in office until 1851, when he became treasurer of Melbourne, and spent the rest of his life in Victoria.[125]

If Donald McTavish committed his impressions of Melbourne to paper, they do not seem to have survived. However, according to one local history, he would have witnessed the construction of a new, "massive," jail, complete with a treadmill, that symbol of early-nineteenth-century punishment. As well, he would have seen a number of "firsts" in the colony's courts, as trials for domestic murder, rape, civil and criminal libel, breach of promise, perjury, and conspiracy to defraud creditors came across the docket. He also would have known of white settlers tried for the murder of Aboriginal people and, conversely, those of Aboriginal people accused of murdering white settlers. However, if he thought he had any connection with local Indigenous people by virtue of his own mixed-race background, there is no evidence of such feelings (and I suspect he did not).[126] A hint of how McTavish might have been perceived by his fellow settlers – and may well have presented himself – appears in *The Chronicles of Early Melbourne*, a local history. When a group of "insubordinate" stone-breakers tried to escape from the Port Phillip gaol, they were thwarted by Wintle, the jailer, and by "a strapping young Scotchman named McTavish (the prison clerk)," who "hastened to the scene of action" assisted by the corporal's guard with fixed bayonets. Although the story was not entirely one of great heroism, since Wintle and McTavish were able to get into the yard of the would-be fugitives only because the other prisoners unlocked the door, nevertheless the riot was subdued and the insubordinates were put into solitary confinement, their diet one of bread and water.[127]

The *Port Phillip Herald* tells us that during McTavish's time as the jail clerk a number of institutions were founded in the settlement, such as a Knights of Father Mathew temperance society, a hospital, and a Mechanics' Institute.[128] At least some of these organizations would have been aimed at his cohort of men, predominantly single and between the ages of twenty-one and forty-five. Unlike many of the younger sons who arrived from Britain and squatted on land in Port Phillip, hoping to make money quickly and return home, McTavish came to think of the colony as his home.[129] To be sure, the local press would have kept him informed of events in both Scotland and British North America, as it ran articles about responsible government in the Canadas, New Brunswick, and Nova Scotia. It also told its readers about the 1844 "Indian Marriage" of Sarah Hayes, the daughter of a "respectable carver and gilder" from Hampstead, to Cadotte, the Ojibwe interpreter of George Catlin, the American artist who was taking a troupe of Indigenous performers through Britain.[130]

Thanks to the record-keeping of the colonial government, a narrative can be told of Donald McTavish's work in Port Phillip, even if it is one based on fragments and traces. For one, his salary increased during his time as the jail clerk. He started at a yearly income of £91 5s; by December 1851, McTavish was making £110 per year.[131] For a brief period in 1850 he was appointed acting gaoler, allotted 5s per day for travelling expenses. Unfortunately, there are no other records that tell us where and when McTavish travelled in his new position.[132] At some point in 1844, McTavish was reprimanded by his superiors. A letter from him, dated 22 July 1844, to Superintendent Latrobe expressed his "regret" and said that he felt it "incumbent of me to beg of your Honor to overlook the complaint preferred against me for the detention of the business of the Court on the morning of Wed. last, through I am sorry to say my apparent neglect." Had McTavish overslept, or been incompetent or, perhaps, drunk? He does not tell us, although he continued in this vein, telling Latrobe "it would be needless for me to attempt to vindicate my conduct on this occasion but I must respectfully beg your Honor to forgive this offense [sic] and if so I shall in future be more cautious in doing my duty to the satisfaction of those over me." LaTrobe somewhat grudgingly forgave him, scrawling on the back of the letter "with the concurrence of his honor the resident judge, I consider that the offence may be overlooked this time."[133]

Whatever the circumstances, though, McTavish must have considered them either minor or thought that enough time had passed for him to move on to something else within the colonial civil service. In September 1848, he wrote again to Latrobe, asking him to appoint him "to some other situation." "I take the liberty," he informed the superintendent, "of addressing your honor with the view of, from causes hereafter shown, altering my situation in the service of the Colonial Government." Reminding Latrobe that he had served as clerk in the "Melbourne Gaol" since December 1842, "which duty I trust I have discharged to the satisfaction of my superiors," McTavish felt the circumstances surrounding his job had changed. "The duties of the above office have increased to a considerable extent within the last three years, so much so that my attendance is almost constantly required within the walls of the prison."[134] Clearly such a confinement was not to his liking.

While Latrobe's office told Alistair McKenzie "to inform Mr. McTavish that his application shall be borne in mind," no new appointment was forthcoming.[135] After 1851, Donald McTavish's name does not appear in the new colony of Victoria's government records, nor have I been able to locate him in other parts of the colonial archive. Did he decide that spending his days within the prison walls was no longer tenable and strike out for the nearby Ballarat goldfields? Or did he hear from his brother, Duncan, and join him on a South Australia sheep farm or, perhaps, take a clerk's position in Melbourne, maybe Sydney? Alternatively, did he return to Scotland (if so, it doesn't seem that he went back to Inverness)? Given the desire of the Hudson's Bay Company to track its employees, it is highly unlikely that he found his way back to Canada to take up a position with his father's (and stepfather's) employer: there is no trace of Donald McTavish in the HBC records for the mid-nineteenth century.

Conclusion:
Race, Visibility, and the Meanings of Home

The stories of these children's journeys within and around the nineteenth-century British Empire tell us something about the links that tied British North America's Indigenous people to other parts of the world. They also add yet another layer to our understanding of the flows of people and migration in this period. While these were not the highly visible and influential imperial careers of governors, military officers, missionaries, and social activists, the odysseys of these children suggest the varied dimensions of imperial mobility and the Empire's heterogeneity.[136] They also provide glimpses into the ways that such heterogeneity and mobility might manifest themselves in daily life, in the ordinary, seemingly banal, accounting of details: schoolroom lessons and school outings, the sending of shoes, the purchase of feminine finery, the consequences of music lessons, a young boy's attitude towards the opposite sex, family scandals, pay rates for jail clerks, and a young Cree-Scottish man's desire to move beyond the Port Phillip jail.

Furthermore, as historians and literary scholars have suggested, the importation of middle-class domesticity, manners, and gender relations was a critical dimension of mid-nineteenth-century imperial expansion; these travels, though, suggest that such an importation might run in many directions. Looking at the children of the Northwest fur trade and their passages through empire suggests how large institutions, such as the fur-trade companies, the colonial state, and the intimate, domestic domain of families, themselves forged through and by imperial networks, intersected in multiple ways. Far from being a haven from the British Empire's ever-growing expansion, the homes these fur-trade children encountered in the metropole were, in the words of American historian Margaret Jacobs, "small theatres of colonialism," stages on which these children were meant to enact "colonial scripts" that taught them the meanings of genteel, middle-class British femininity and masculinity.[137] Some, as we have seen, were more adept in learning those roles than others. To be sure, they do not seem to have been treated with the degree of physical and emotional brutality or been confined in as severe and unyielding a way as those children (Indigenous and mixed-race) who were subjected to residential schooling in Canada – a process that was just getting underway on a large scale as these fur-trade children grew into adulthood.[138] Nevertheless, more benign forms of restriction and surveillance should not obscure the racially charged uneven power relations that were at work.

Moreover, although much the same could be said of the other travellers in this book, not all performances were meant to be enjoyed in exactly the same way or in front of the same audience. A significant difference between Matilda Davis, Mary Finlayson, Albert Hodgson, and Duncan and Donald McTavish and John Norton, Peter Jones, and George Copway was the relative anonymity of the former group, at least so far as British society was concerned. Unlike those who travelled overseas as political petitioners, missionaries, and performers, and who often enjoyed high levels of public and political visibility and celebrity, the vast majority of these young men and women experienced Britain within the context of sequestered settings, the classrooms, parlours, and gardens of cities such as Edinburgh, London, Nairn, and Inverness (shops and nearby forests and hillsides also played a role, of course). Unlike the case with figures such as Peter Jones, no newspaper heralded the arrival of Matilda and Elizabeth Davis in London or their departure for Red River. Instead, we catch glimpses of these children and young men and women in epistolary traces, in some cases in their own letters "home" and, for many, in the letters and diaries of their fur-trader fathers, their British families, or other members of fur-trade society.

To be sure, their lower public profile did not mean that these Cree-British children were invisible. As we have seen, within fur-trade circles they might be the subject of considerable informal surveillance. To some observers, they were undoubtedly and irrevocably "half-breeds," boys and girls whose socialization into the norms of white, middle-class gender roles would never be complete. Such was the case when Albert Hodgson preferred to spend time in the woods, free of "English restraints" and would not "speak up" in ways expected of an English boy. Others might run up against such attitudes later in life, as they encountered the hardened racial categories of late-nineteenth-century Britain. Isabella Hardisty (by then Isabella Smith, Lady Strathcona) was mocked by London's elite as a "hoddy-doddy squaw."[139] Still others might – to the best of our knowledge – be able to cross racial boundaries and pass as "British." Mary Finlayson Lamb's obituary, for example, described her only as having been born in Canada, with a father employed in the fur trade. While "Mrs. Lamb ... will be much missed in the community, and her memory will long be cherished and revered by all who knew her," to her social circle her legacy would not be, it seems, that of a Cree-Scottish woman.[140]

The McTavish brothers went even further in their travels. While theirs was certainly not a common experience for fur-trade descendants, the brothers' stories are a compelling example of the possibilities offered by imperial networks combined with particular circumstances. Because of their Cree-Scottish background, their Scottish education, and, quite likely, their uncle's misuse of their inheritance, Donald and Duncan McTavish undertook journeys around and through the British Empire that remade them from fur-trade "half-breeds" to sojourners in Inverness and, in turn, Scottish emigrants, who then became settlers themselves in Australia. In Donald's case, he was a "strapping young Scotchman," who was also a representative of the fledgling colonial state.

If others viewed these children through such lenses, how did they view themselves? As historians have noted, travel and mobility across boundaries can play a crucial role in shaping and reshaping one's identity and sense of place, and the effects of such movement might be particularly significant for children.[141] What of their mixed-race, Cree-British identity? How did individuals such as Matilda Davis, Mary Finlayson Lamb, or Duncan McTavish understand their histories and positions within both Red River and the British Empire, that of children of two intermingled and entangled, yet different, worlds? Perhaps more to the point: did they see themselves in such a manner? We have a few hints that, for some, such might have been the case. Letters from women of another Ross family, for example – their father Scottish fur trader Alexander Ross and their mother, Sally, an Okanagan chief's daughter – address either their mother's racial background or express great unease about circulating in settler society. "I would rather not go to Toronto," Henrietta Ross Black wrote in 1854 to her brother, James, who was living in the city. "How would an uneducated dark half-breed look among the fair and accomplished ladies; how could I act the part which becomes the wife; there are other reasons but this one especially."[142] (It is worth remembering that these sentiments were expressed just six years before Nahneebahweequa appeared as an "Indian woman" before Victoria, acting her "part" with great dignity and confidence). The few letters written by Davis, on the other hand, tell us very little directly about such matters: she appears to have been almost resolutely silent about her Indigenous ancestry. However, such a silence may have many meanings. It is not a simple indication that Davis was untouched by or denied those racial tensions that, as we know, erupted in Red River, while in England public discourses on race became increasingly fixed around notions of biological superiority and inferiority.[143] As well, the letters of parents and other family members to her about their children, wards, or relatives in her care made it quite clear that "education" meant far more than just reading about the kings and queens of England, parsing sentences, learning arithmetic, or memorizing

French verbs.[144] In their correspondence to Matilda, education signified being tutored in the ways of "civilized" society, embodying and performing the manners and decorum of a British middle-class man or woman and displaying the emotional states of being that accompanied such a performance.[145] While attending Miss Davis's school might not eradicate the stigma of being a "dark halfbreed" that so troubled Henrietta Ross Black, it might assuage it.

As well, there is the question of the different meanings of "home" for these children and young adults, one no less important and complicated for them as it would have been for Peter Jones or Catherine Sutton. Where home was located might well depend on the particular moment in their lives. For Elizabeth and Matilda Davis, arriving in London as very small girls, "home" would at first have been their uncle and aunt's house in the city's southern boroughs. Yet as Matilda's letters suggest, it was also represented by her family left behind in Rupert's Land, particularly her mother; then, as an adult, "home" was likely to mean her school, supported by the networks of family and friends in both Red River and in England. Albert Hodgson, though, clearly thought of home as "America," even when his memories of fur-trade country began to fade. These memories may have been shored up by the material goods that arrived from overseas, such as sugar maple and buffalo tongues, a particular favourite of the Christie family.[146] For much of her life, Mary Finlayson Lamb's "home" was the Nairn Bank House. We can only speculate whether Nicol Finlayson told her stories of her birthplace and, if so, whether she incorporated that place into the self that grew up in northeast Scotland. The McTavish brothers' voyages around the British Empire suggest a shifting, if not fragmented, sense of where home might be. If there was any constant or consistent element for them, it was quite likely their mother, Josette Monier. A person, no less than a place (and sometimes more) might embody "home."

Although Alexander Isbister spent his adult life in Britain, his frequent presence in fur-trade networks in the metropole, along with his other activities, clearly suggests he did not forget Red River, in ways both political and intimate. To be sure, after attending King's College at the University of Aberdeen and the University of Edinburgh, Isbister became a very successful educator in England. He was headmaster of London's East Islington Proprietary School, the first headmaster of the Stationers' Company School, dean of the College of Preceptors and editor of its journal, *Educational Times*, and the author of more than twenty school textbooks (he also received a

Master of Arts degree from the University of Edinburgh and an LLB from the University of London). In many ways, then, Isbister would have served as a role model for Matilda Davis and Matilda Hunt, the epitome of the educated, well-connected man they might have hoped Albert Hodgson and John Davis would become. While his biographer points out that race does not appear to have played any role in impeding his career, Isbister became a passionate advocate for his countrymen's rights to free trade, calling an end to the Hudson Bay Company's monopoly in Rupert's Land. In 1847, Isbister headed a delegation which presented a petition of a thousand signatures against the company; he was also an active lobbyist of British MPs, a writer of pamphlets, and a frequent correspondent with the Colonial Office on behalf of the welfare of Indigenous people. Isbister also supported the spread of formal education in Rupert's Land, endowing a prize and scholarship and leaving almost five thousand books to the newly founded University of Manitoba.[147] In addition to his activism on the colony's behalf, he also brought his mother and sister to England, ensuring that they were supported and cared for even after his death.[148]

Yet while these boys and girls, young men and women, were learning to perform (and possibly pass) as British, other kinds of performance, unabashedly Indigenous but no less complex, were being staged in the metropole. They are the subject of the next chapter.

. 5 .

Playing "Indian": Ojibwe Performers, London, 1840s

Introduction

"Arrival Extraordinary," read the headline in *Bell's New Weekly Messenger* on 12 November 1843. Sandwiched in between news of potential press censorship in France and an inquest held in Bayswater, the article informed the paper's readers that "We understand that there are now in Manchester nine veritable North American Indians, real red denizens of the wilds. These remarkable strangers are all of the very numerous tribe of Ojibbeways, whose locality is to the north of Lake Huron, in the vicinity of Georgian Bay, and consequently they are born subjects of her Majesty Queen Victoria. They consist of two chiefs, four warriors, two squaws, and one child, a girl of nine or ten years. They arrived in Liverpool by the packet ship *England*, from New York."[1] Just over a month later the group was presented to Queen Victoria, Prince Albert, the Duchess of Kent, and other members of the court.[2]

While the paper did not mention it, this group of Anishinaabe performers and travellers were not the first members of the Ojibwe to perform in Britain. In 1835, Peter Jones's friend and patron, Sir Augustus d'Este of the Aborigines' Protection Society, had helped the Ojibwe Maconse (Francis Eshtonoquot). Maconse, originally from Michigan, had brought his dance troupe to England, but was left stranded by his English promoter and saw his wife, nephew, and another member of his troupe die of smallpox. D'Este assisted him and his surviving company members to return to Michigan.[3] Both groups were followed by a troupe of Ojibwe performers that arrived in 1845 and were led by Maungwudaus (George Henry), Peter Jones's half-brother. They spent the next three years touring Britain, France, and Belgium, as well as appearing before audiences in New York and Massachusetts before their return to Upper Canada.

As we saw in Chapter 2, by the 1840s residents of London, Liverpool, Edinburgh, and other British cities were not strangers to public displays of Anishinaabe people; nor were they unfamiliar with performances by and exhibitions of other colonial subjects. The appearances of this new group of performers were greeted with the same degrees of curiosity about these "exotic" arrivals that met other Indigenous arrivals in the metropole. The British press enjoyed telling its readers about the bodies, speech, and dress of Maconse and Maungwudaus, for example; it also found the relationships of Ojibwe men with English women a fascinating, if somewhat prurient, topic. At times these men and women and their children attracted the attention of humanitarians, worried about their physical and spiritual well-being. In many ways, then, the discussion of other Ojibwe men and women's celebrity within the ambit of colonialism, which emerged in Chapter 2, are equally pertinent here. But while John Norton, Peter Jones, John Sunday, George Copway, and Catherine Sutton went to Britain for religious and political reasons, Ojibwe performance troupes were there for different reasons. They travelled overseas to display themselves, to be displayed, and, at least for some, to indulge their own curiosity about the countries from which those who had settled on their traditional lands had come, not to raise funds for missions or to impress upon their European audiences their attainment of "civilization." Furthermore, unlike the individuals in Chapter 2, very few of these men and women were literate in English. Instead, they were represented by their promoters, interpreters, and the British press, all of whom were motivated by multiple desires and fantasies to write about and "speak for" these "Red Indians." Yet there is one important exception: Maungwudaus. As he was able to speak, read, and write English, Maungwudaus left a travelogue of his time abroad, one that is compelling for both its similarities to *and* differences from texts left by his missionary contemporaries and by the promoter, Arthur Rankin.

The Ojibwe Tour of 1843

The nine Ojibwe who docked at Portsmouth in 1843 had been brought to England by Montreal-born Arthur Rankin, a surveyor and militia captain who had fought in the Essex militia in the 1837 Rebellion. After leaving the militia in 1843, Rankin had decided to become, like his contemporaries George Catlin and P.T. Barnum, a showman. Although it is not entirely clear how and where he met the group, Rankin is credited with having organized them into a "show" and taking them on tour.[4] His efforts to publicize the group in England were, at least initially, successful. Their presentation to Queen Victoria was duly noted by the press. The *New Bell's Weekly Messenger* noted that the group included a "pretty little girl" in the party, with whom the Queen "was much pleased, and shook hands." The paper also listed their names: Ah-que-we-zaintz, Patronna Quotta-webe, Gish-e-gas-e-ghe, Weenish-ka-weebe, Wasseb-abbe-neuch-qua, Nib-nah-ne-quan, Ne-bet-neuch-qua, and their interpreter, Nottena-akmc (Alexander Cadotte). The latter, the paper was pleased to report, "although not a thorough-bred Indian, is a fine, muscular, and well-formed man, who speaks English with comparative fluency." Speaking through Cadotte, the eldest chief led off the addresses to the royal party; not feeling well, however, he allowed the war chief to complete his speech. Addressing Victoria as "Great Mother," the chiefs spoke of their sorrow about leaving home, the kindness afforded them by the Great Spirit in keeping them safe, their happiness on seeing the "Great Mother's Face," and their impressions of England. The "sagamoshes" seemed to be very happy and have "pleasant looks," although the group had also seen many "strange things" in England, such as larger and brighter wigwams than those of the Ojibwe. They concluded by telling Victoria how glad their hearts were from meeting her and "when we get home our words will be listened to in the councils of our nation." The addresses were followed by the group's performances of "several of their national dances." The paper also commented on the group's appearance, noting that "their faces were elaborately painted" and all the men, except their interpreter, wore silver rings through their noses, "besides a variety of anklets and bracelets." As well, "their costume was the grotesque dress of their country."[5]

"Grotesque" in this period could mean a number of things – fantastic, unnatural, absurd, bizarre, or quaint – and we can only speculate about the writer's intentions in describing the Ojibwe dress in this manner: it may have been synonymous with both fantastic and bizarre.[6] In many ways, the paper's account of the Ojibwe's appearance was redolent of Headley's description of the clothing John Norton wore at Cambridge, although overall it lacked the degree of detail that Headley provided, not to mention his respect for Norton. Whatever the case, though, the London press continued its interest in the group and their activities, reporting that by the end of December they were appearing at Piccadilly's Egyptian Hall. Originally a museum built in 1812 by collector William Bullock to house his artifacts, which included objects brought back from the South Pacific, the Egyptian Hall also served as an art gallery and showcase for other exhibitions, such as a Laplander family and their reindeer, who lived temporarily in the hall.[7]

The group's public visibility also benefited from having George Catlin as their intermediary. An American engraver, painter, and author, Catlin had toured the American northeast and various European cities, including London, with his "Indian Gallery," composed of paintings of western Indigenous peoples and their artifacts, amassed during his travels in Indigenous American territory.[8] Here he introduced "the Indians to their more civilised brethren, and their more civilised brethren to them," a performance that the public "attended in considerable numbers on the occasion." Although seen as "curious," the Ojibwe were yet "loyal subjects of her Majesty," the male members characterized by the reporter as "fine-looking fellows, muscular and sinewy," the women "if not particularly beautiful according to the notions and prejudices of the people of this country, are such as would meet the ideas of a utilitarian, and are reckoned by those to whom they belong good specimens of feminine loveliness."[9] In January, Londoners learned the Duke of Cambridge had presented the group with £10, ten pounds of tobacco, "two very handsome brooches for the squaws, and two splendid silver medals for the two chiefs." This particular writer also noted that they divided the money equally among them, perhaps acknowledging the Ojibwe's egalitarianism. The same article also noted their visit to the Glaciarium in Baker Street, where they were "much delighted. 'Gishee-gosh-e-ghee (the moonlight night)' skated in a beautiful and scientific manner, and drew down several rounds of applause from the spectators."[10]

Yet as interesting as royal audiences, gifts, appearances in Piccadilly Street, and ice-skating displays were, the marriage between their interpreter, Alexander Cadotte (or Not-enn-a-skin) and Sarah Haynes was a central point of fascination for the press. The same union that Donald McTavish might have read about in Melbourne, theirs was an instance of "racial crossing" that was taking place not in a distant colony but, rather, right under the noses of Londoners. On Tuesday, 9 April 1844, in the church of

St Martin-in-the-Fields, *Bell's Weekly Messenger* announced, "a marriage was celebrated between Alexander Cadoe [Cadotte], otherwise Not-enn-a-skin (or The Strong Wind), interpreter to the Ojibbeway Indians, and Miss Sarah Haynes, aged 18, daughter of Mr. Haynes, carver and gilder, Great George St., Hampstead Road."

The marriage was more than a celebration of domesticity and intimacy: in the pages of the press it became a racially charged spectacle. "The windows and balconies of every house in George Street (where the Indians reside)" were filled and "the street itself [was] crowded by hundreds of people, eager to catch a glimpse of this singular bridal party." Riding in a number of "horse-drawn carriages," the bridal party and "the Indians" were met at the church by such a large crowd on the steps and portico that "it was with the greatest difficulty a strong body of police could obtain an opening for the wedding procession. There could not have been fewer than from 2,000 to 3,000 persons assembled. As early as seven o'clock in the morning, a large concourse of persons, the great portion of whom seemed to be of superior rank in society, had assembled to obtain admission to the church." At nine o'clock the clergyman, Rev. Septimus Ramsey, arrived and half an hour later "the tinkling of the Indians' bells and the buzz of the crowd without" announced their arrival. "At this moment curiosity was so intense that the decorum usually observed in a place of worship was simultaneously forgotten, the whole of the spectators rising on the seats." The men of the party were wearing "full Indian dress," augmented with wedding favours of streamers, yet, as the group walked up the aisle, "their dignified demeanour and placid appearance was the theme of general admiration, and though one of their attendants assured the reporter that they had never entered a Christian church before, they exhibited throughout the entire ceremony a devotional observance of all that passed before them."

The bride's party consisted of four bridesmaids, dressed in white, her parents, and "the happy couple." The reporter lingered over their dress and demeanour.

The bride is a delicate looking young person, of pale complexion, with dark hair; she was attired in white, with a veil which reached to the bottom of her dress. The bridegroom was habited in an elegant robe or caftan of blue cloth, handsomely trimmed with shells and Indian needlework round the neck, arms, and edges: he also wore a rich headdress, but somewhat different from those worn by the Indians, and over his surcoat a scarlet shawl of the brightest colour, and his feet were clothed with a pair of moccasins presented to him by the war chief of the most curious needlework, made from the skin of the moss [moose] deer. On taking his place at the rails of the communion, he divested himself of his headdress and shawl.

The couple's taking of their vows impressed the reporter, who thought the groom spoke his "with the greatest solemnity of manner," and that the bride answered "I will" with an emphasis that appeared to show how thoroughly she understood the nature of the obligation she was taking on herself. As soon as Ramsey had shaken hands with the new couple, "the bridegroom instantly, and with much grace, imprinted on the lips of his bride, in the presence of the whole congregation, the hymeneal salute." As they left the church "they received the warmest congratulations," and the crowd outside "set up a loud cheer." The paper also reported that Cadotte, a "half caste, his father being a French-Canadian, who was confidentially employed during the late war, and his mother a full-blooded Indian," planned a return to "his own soil" with his wife once the tour was finished and planned "contrary to the custom of the Indian nation … to devote himself entirely" to her.[11] Rankin also promised on the day of the marriage "Madame Cadotte, the beautiful and interesting bride of Not-een-au-um, Strong Wind the Interpreter, will be presented to the visitors by Ah-Que-Wee-Zaintz the boy chief. Madame Cadotte will pleasingly fill up the intervals between the dances by performing on her pianoforte."[12]

Not all the coverage of the couple's relationship was respectful, though. Six days after the wedding the satiric magazine *Punch* declared that, because of Pocahontas's marriage to John Rolfe, "we owe a large dividend of wives to American savages," so giving the "London Fog" (the paper's name for Sarah Haynes) to the "Strong Wind" was only fair compensation. The writer continued to ponder the possibilities of such unions.

We have a superabundant female population. This fact is on all hands allowed and deplored. We see an easy remedy for this. Let parties of Indians be imported. Let us have samples of the Chippewas, the Dog-Ribbed, the Sioux, the Chactaws [sic] – indeed, a company of every tribe of white men, from Hottentots to Greenlanders – and let them be let loose in our various towns for the sole purpose of captivating the hearts, and so carrying away in lawful wedlock, our superabundant females. By this means we shall honestly liquidate our long-standing debt to the savage, and shall, at the same time, relieve ourselves of over-population.

War-paint, glass beads, tattoo-work, and tomahawks, have a sweet and proper influence on the female mind.

After citing a stanza from dramatist Henry Taylor's play, *Philip Van Artevelde*, which spoke of women's vanity, capriciousness, and susceptibility to the lure of "the new,"[13] *Punch* declared "our too susceptible countrywomen" should understand clearly what their fate would be. A "North American Indian" requires, the writer declared, "of his wife or squaw" ceaseless physical labour, tasks that ranged from tilling, digging, sowing, and reaping to pounding corn, drying buffalo meat, carrying both game and children, hewing wood, drawing water, and building wigwams. "Think of this, young ladies," the writer cautioned, "and ask whether it is not more pleasant to hatch canary birds in white satin and work puppies' heads in Berlin wool!" Clearly *Punch* had been influenced by those commentators who believed that Indigenous women in North America led lives filled with drudgery, existing as little more than slaves to their husbands.

In contrast to *Bell's* description of the ceremony, *Punch* reported that "The Strong Wind," "in the most charming way, took the ring from his nose, and placed it on the finger of 'The London Fog.'" Furthermore, female readers would be "gratified" to learn that the groom had promised to "take no other wife, but to remain constant." If he broke this vow, his wife "would have the readiest redress at any of the Ecclesiastical Courts to be found in the back woods." In the meantime, reports that she was to "have been visible at the Egyptian Hall" proved erroneous, as her friends had intervened to prevent it. "She ought to have been exhibited," the paper believed, as it "would have been in keeping with the pure taste that dictated the marriage," a union "Mr. Rankin, the showman," had managed "with a fine eye to advertising purposes."[14] The publication also illustrated the article with a sketch of the Ojibwe party en route in a horse-drawn carriage, their appearance and behaviour decidedly unruly and in no way resembling the conduct expected for a respectable wedding.

Punch picked up such themes a week later, in a satirical article titled "Important –To the Ladies." Spurred on by their countryman's success in winning a white wife, the paper announced, other Ojibwe men wished to do so the same. Their departure imminent, the men were openly advertising for mates. The oldest chief would consider offers "with any English lady of known property," and "in his admiration of the martial character of England, will have no objection to the widow of a general officer, if under the age of forty." However, "her property must not be secured upon herself"

and "she must know how to cure bear's flesh, to hoe, and rake, and dig, and reap," skin rabbits, and have been vaccinated. The younger war chief was willing to settle "all his scalps" on his wife, but in return "the young lady must have been tenderly and affectionately brought up, as she will have to carry the wigwam poles of the Driving Cloud in all journeys. She must bring a sufficient income to keep her husband in tobacco, rum, and laziness." Weenish-ka-weebe, the "Hereditary Chief," was said to have "inherited his dignity, not won it by any deeds or virtues of his own, advertisers are confidently referred to the *Ojibbeway Peerage*, 4to. The birth of the Flying Gull will not allow him to treat with anybody below a baronet's daughter." As for the other men, while they too had sent in advertisements, *Punch* had discovered that they were married and therefore "with his known devotion to the proprieties has of course refused to insert any such invitations to the connubial state."[15] This article was illustrated with a sketch of an Indigenous man. Although certainly one of the prospective husbands, as it was taken from an illustration in Arthur Rankin's book about the tour, it highlighted certain signifiers, such as the man's tattoo, nose ring worn in a broad nose, and feathered headdress; unlike Rankin's illustration, it also was isolated from the group he portrayed, which included two women and the young girl. Readers of the paper might be forgiven for thinking that this depiction of an Anishinaabe man was a generic representation of "savage" masculinity from anywhere in the world: the South Pacific, Africa, or other parts of North America.

Punch therefore saw the wedding as representing both racial and sexual transgressions of a carnivalesque nature, all of which were an affront to English social and imperial order and, especially, "good taste." To be sure, it might have been forward-looking in its discussions of so-called "surplus" Englishwomen, since the following decade would see efforts to address the problems of single middle-class women, with their emigration to the colonies proposed as one possible solution. However, *Punch* used the spectre of "Red Indians" let loose in England, their intent to carry off English "ladies" to a life of unremitting toil, just as in the following decade the spectre of "savage" women arriving from the colonies to marry English men would be used to satirize the emigration of Englishwomen and manage imperial fears concerning it.[16] By creating such a fantastical situation, in which Indian men advertised for English wives with impunity – a situation that was clearly absurd and would not occur – *Punch* may have assuaged fears that the Cadotte-Haynes wedding represented any great threat. It could easily be dismissed as nothing more than a freakish aberration.[17]

Rankin published his own account of the Ojibwe visit, although, if it was in some measure a response to *Punch* (or other, similar commentators), he did not say so explicitly. Their arrival, he felt,

affords an opportunity, never before presented to the British public, of obtaining a personal acquaintance with the appearances, habits, manners, and customs of these curious and fast-fading tribes. Naturally remarkable and politically important, they have been rendered additionally interesting by the poet and the novelist. Chateaubriand in Europe, and Fenimore Cooper in America, have surrounded the red man with a halo of romance. Their courage, their fortitude, their lofty, yet peculiar, notions of honour and duty, are familiar to all who have mourned over the pages of Attila, or followed Leather-Stocking through the Prairie.[18]

To characterize the Ojibwe as noble-yet-dying savages was to play on a very familiar trope: its use also helped create excitement at the prospect of seeing actual embodiments of such a process. Rankin sketched a picture of the group,

all dressed in the curious and picturesque costumes of their country. Their appearances affords the visitor a correct impression of these people as they are to be met with in their Indigenous prairies. They are all full-bloods, with the exception of the Interpreter, who is a half-caste. The circumstances of so large a number of these interesting people, furnishing specimens of both sexes and all ages, all of them, too, belonging to a numerous and powerful tribe, which has ever been devotedly attached to the British Government, being together in England, is an occurrence which has not previously happened, nor is likely to occur again during the present generation.[19]

As we shall see, these "full-blooded" (and thus "authentic") Ojibwe would not be the "last of their kind" to tour England; the "present generation" would soon have the opportunity to see another group of Anishinaabe performers. Moreover, whether Rankin's audiences made the connection between this group and the Ojibwe missionaries – Jones, Sunday, and Jacobs – whose visits either preceded or coincided with that of the performers, is unclear. Certainly, the British press did not see a link between the two groups.

Rankin was correct, though, in his frequently repeated declaration that they had sided with the Crown in both the American Revolution and the

War of 1812. However, like many others who commented on this history, he cast it as a choice made between the destruction of Indigenous people in the United States and the "much better treatment" they received from the British – treatment that resulted in "these primitive people" developing a "strong feeling of attachment" to "their 'Great Mother.'" While there was a grain of truth in such an analysis, Rankin did not (and possibly could not) imagine that the Ojibwe had their own reasons for allying with the British, such as protecting ancestral territories, motivations that might have had little to do with "British benevolence."[20] In a similar vein, when the question of who should represent the Ojibwe on the tour came up, "such was their confidence and curiosity that nearly the whole tribe were ready to volunteer upon the expedition."[21] Rankin wished to reassure his audience that, unlike other Indigenous travellers to Britain and Europe, the nine who stepped off the ship in Liverpool were certainly not coerced or tricked into leaving their home. However, like their participation in the War of 1812, he did not explore their perspectives and reasons for wanting to travel.

Rankin was not insensible of the fact that the group was composed of individuals, each with their own histories and sensibilities: he introduced each member by name and provided his readers with short biographies and accounts of their relationships with each other. He also, though, ensured that his own biography and relationships with the Ojibwe were included. Having grown up on the "borders of the Ojibbeways' country," he had "spent some of the happiest days of life hunting and fishing with these rude and simple people." His experiences included being fed by them on long expeditions when game became scarce: they denied themselves meals so "the pale face, who was less able to bear short rations, might not faint from hunger" (a gesture that might have been shaped by his hosts' belief in hospitality to visitors but that also might have hidden a degree of contempt for Rankin's weakness). Just like the Ojibwe, Rankin was loyal to the Crown, telling his readers of his voluntary military service in the 1837 Rebellion in the Canadas, service so impressive it was "mentioned by Lord Brougham in the House of Commons." Who better, then, to accompany these men, women, and children across the Atlantic?

Rankin went on to describe their audience with Victoria and their other appearances that he found noteworthy. The group's visit to St George's Archery Club near Regent's Park was one such event. Here, confronted with a different type of bow and mode of shooting, they nevertheless triumphed, winning gold and silver medals and being presented with "a set of Chinese

bells, a tenor drum, a tambourine, and a triangle." They were also invited to a meal, *déjéuner à la fourchette*, "which they partook of with great
gout: their knowledge of the *etiquette* of the table was surprising, and was
a source of infinite amusement to the toxopholites and their guests." The
meal also allowed the Ojibwe to demonstrate their dedication to Britain and
to the Crown, as Ah-que-we-zants addressed his British hosts by speaking
of the Englishmen "as brothers" and toasted the Queen.[22] He did not mention – although he would have been correct to do so – that the Ojibwe men
also had demonstrated their hunting skills and proved themselves superior
to their English counterparts.[23] In their eyes, the Ojibwe's medals may well
have served to affirm notions of Indigenous masculinity

Rankin followed his account of the archery competition with one of their
visit to the Thames Tunnel, which he had taken from the *Pictorial Times*.
Rankin used the newspaper's report to construct the expedition as "'a striking instance of the meeting of extremes': the most primitive encountering
the 'highest grade of civilisation – a group of savages gazing with wonder
upon the latest triumph of engineering skills.'"[24] The party's arrival was
itself a form of public entertainment, as the "'appearance of feathered heads,
painted faces, bear-skin garments, and mocassined [sic] legs, in the classic locality of "Wapping Old Stairs," created a general hubbub. Shops were
deserted, tools and needles were thrown down, and general rush attested
that curiosity was in no wise wanting amongst the amphibious denizens of
this aquatic neighbourhood.'" Rankin announced that the group had "'had
long expressed a strong wish to see this effort of the skill of the "pale faces"
– a desire he was anxious to satisfy.'" By the time they entered the tunnel,
"'their expressions of surprise were surprisingly characteristic-guttural
"ughs! ughs!" attesting their satisfaction. They evidently regarded it as more
wonderful than many of the more showy and glittering spectacles which
their visit to the "old country" has offered for their admiration.'"

The tour became even more of a spectacle when the Ojibwe stopped
at a stall selling medals of "Mr Brunel" (in all likelihood Marc Brunel, the
tunnel's chief engineer), and the stall's owner gave them "specimens of
the showy memorials." Upon reaching the Surrey side of the tunnel – and
still being followed by a crowd of spectators – one of the male members of
the group decided "to acknowledge the boisterous attention of the crowd"
by tossing his medal down to them. "A scramble ensued, which so much
amused the whole party" that the rest followed suit and were given more by
the stall holder.

The humorous scene which then took place defies description. The scrambling among the dense crowd, some fifty or sixty of whom were seen in every variety of attitude, from the tiptoe of expectative position to the various phases of the tumble and somerset [somersault], the shouting and hurrahing, with some attempts at imitation of the cries of delight of the savages, formed an animated tableau, in which it would be difficult to distinguish who were most delighted, the Indians, the crowd, or the more respectable portion of the spectators, including the ladies, several of whom (not the least pretty) pressed forward and shook hands very cordially with the Red-skins.[25]

We can only guess at the Ojibwe's motivations here. Were they bored with being the recipients of what might have become rather predictable and, at times, tiresome attention and wished to create a diversion that they controlled? Were they making a statement that, although they might have been impressed by the tunnel, they were not overawed by the commemoration of the man seen as responsible for it? Did the sight of Londoners behaving in such an unruly manner – one not unlike the kind of "savagery" they were accused of – delight them? Whatever the case, their gesture suggests that they were well aware of the attention and celebrity that they attracted. Moreover, they were not the primitive innocents in the metropole that the press – and their promoter – needed them to be.

Public appearances and demonstrations of their "Indianness" were important, then, to Rankin; like his contemporary George Catlin, though, so too was his role as a self-styled "expert" on Ojibwe society. As previous chapters have shown, the role of women in Indigenous communities preoccupied mid-nineteenth-century observers, whether from a missionary or a secular perspective, a concern Rankin shared. He devoted four pages of his account to "Habits of the Ojibbeways – Condition of the Indian Women," claiming that the Ojibwe women on the tour lived much the same in Britain as they did in their "Indigenous modes," at least as much as "circumstances will admit." All lived in one house, "sitting, eating, and lying upon the floor," as they found tables and chairs "irksome" and, despite having impressed the archery society with their table manners, "only partially" using knives and forks. "Patient and industrious," the Ojibwe women continued their habits of continuous toil, as they spent their days in London making clothes and embroidering them with beadwork (in that respect being not that dissimilar from middle-class British ladies).[26] Rankin saw women as being less-valued by their society than men, telling his readers that the chiefs objected to women accompanying them: "'Why take women? Nobody looks at women.' They imagined, from the conditions of females in their own lands, that Europeans regarded women as creatures of inferior importance to men. Indeed, nothing astonished the Indians more than the consideration shown their squaws in this country." Yet Rankin felt that, despite being "mere drudges" in their own land and having a "desponding, timid look," Ojibwe women were "in reality contented and happy" (one wonders if he had gone to meet Nahneebahweequa in his travels, an Ojibwe woman who was decidedly not timid). Virtuous, modest, and deeply affectionate towards their husbands and children, they also identified, it seems, very strongly with the Queen as a wife and mother: "the tartan plaid given to them by the Queen is a great source of gratification to them, and they are very fond of wearing it before the public."[27] Perhaps for Rankin, the gift of such clothing was a woman's responsibility, and thus may have exemplified a strong emotional bond between the women of the group and Victoria, one exemplified by the "tartan plaid."

To be sure, Rankin subscribed to the image of the lives of Ojibwe women as one long round of unending work: skinning, cutting, and cooking deer, making clothing for all, chopping wood and drawing water. In turn, Ojibwe masculinity was marked by indolence in the domestic sphere and a lack of providence and foresight, the latter leading to periods of deprivation (hence their ability to withstand starvation). "The man does nothing but smoke and enjoy himself till the food is gone," he declared, and a "European can beat them at hard work."[28] Yet he also characterized Ojibwe men as acting "towards their squaws with real, steady, consistent kindness." Furthermore, the lack of hierarchy in their society meant that there was no class-based servitude among them. "The Old Chief has two wives, and they labour equally as hard as the squaws of the young men of the tribe. This arises from the strong and general feeling in every Indian breast *against hiring themselves to work for another. There is no servitude amongst them.* The chief is head of the party, by hereditary descent or by general opinion for his valour in war, but the rest of the tribe are his warriors and his children, *not his servants.* Hence the wives of the chieftains are compelled to wait upon their families in exactly the same manner as the squaw of the youngest warrior."[29] While not marked by an equitable division of labour between men and women, then, gender roles were practised in the same manner by all in the community. While Rankin did not make an explicit comparison to British society, some of his middle-class readers might have done so, noting that Ojibwe men might resemble the idleness of the British male aristocrat, while their womenfolk were similar to hard-working farm wives.

Moreover, Ojibwe women were admirable as mothers. Sparked by the presence in his group of the "Young Child," who "cannot fail to be noticed as an interesting member of the party," Rankin embarked on a discussion of mothers' treatment of their babies. They carried them on their backs, hung them in high tree branches to keep them safe, and taught them not to cry by ignoring their early outbursts. This latter practice Rankin felt might account for their ability to endure suffering later in life, "which has so often displayed itself in acts of decided heroism."[30] Yet Ojibwe children did not seem to be the worse for all of this, as the "young Indian child is as happy as the 'coddled baby' of civilised life." Moreover, unlike the missionary discourses around Indigenous motherhood, which at times portrayed Indigenous mothers as harbouring "unnatural" feelings, Rankin claimed that the mothers' love for their children was "very great," citing the case of a mother who had starved herself to death after her child died. "She made no noisy demonstrations of grief, but formed a resolution to follow it to the land of spirits. No persuasion, no suffering, could change her purpose."[31] Despite not sharing the culture of sentiment and emotional display that was increasingly becoming the hallmark of "true" motherhood in British and North American society by this time, this Ojibwe woman was no less a "real" mother.[32]

In addition to their affection for their children, the Ojibwe of the troupe lived very peacefully among themselves. Even in the close quarters of their London home, they seldom quarrelled, "never has the least ill-feeling prevailed, nor one angry look been seen." Even of temper, happy, and not displaying any kind of disappointment with their trip, they also were very grateful for any kindness shown them. Rankin cited their friendship with their neighbour, a Mr Saunders, who had invited them to his home "and sought means of amusing them and making them happy. They were not unmindful of this, and formed a strong friendship with him" – so much so that they asked Saunders if he would allow them to have a portrait of him to take back to Upper Canada with them, as, having grown to love him, they thought "it would be pleasant to see him still." They also "would then be able to show to their tribe the man who had been a father to them!" Saunders acquiesced and, at their own expense, Rankin told his readers, the Ojibwe "procured a Daguerreotype likeness which will, doubtless, for many years hereafter, be handed down as a heirloom in the forests of the West."[33] Yet while Rankin's account of their happiness and their placidity might imply the Ojibwe were obedient, biddable children, their relationship with Saunders suggests they conducted themselves according to their own norms of loyalty and friendship, honouring one who had shown them kindness and hospitality.

Moreover, they marked their friendship with Saunders with a practice that, as we have seen in previous chapters, was known to both Indigenous people and Europeans, the commissioning of a personal portrait.

Rankin ended his discussion of the Ojibwe with a brief, almost cursory, discussion of their dances: medicine, war, and pipe. The book closed with an account of his own bravery and heroism. Written by Charles Stuart, a retired military officer, the nine-page narrative told of Rankin's rescue of an escaped slave (a young man who had made it to Canada but then been kidnapped from the Windsor area to be taken back to Kentucky), his humanitarianism emphasized by his then taking the "poor fugitive" with him back to Canada.[34] As we have seen, Rankin was far from being averse to promoting his own career and inserting himself into the Ojibwe's story wherever possible. His readers may have noticed, though, that his account of the Ojibwe did not conclude with their parting of ways from Rankin, let alone a safe return to their "forest home." Instead, it ended with Stuart's tales of Rankin's own brave exploits in the service of humanitarianism.

Rankin did not, though, have the last word on the fate of the "Strong Wind" and the "London Fog." Sarah Haynes and Alexander Cadotte returned to British North America, first living at the Walpole Island community of Ojibwa and Pottowatomie on the St Clair River. Approximately two years later, Haynes and Cadotte moved to Sault Ste Marie in Michigan; in 1851 Haynes gave birth to their daughter, Emily Jane Cadotte. She did not live to see her child grow up, as Haynes died 6 May 1852. In 1856, Cadotte would go on to marry again; his new wife, Celenise or Sarah, was seventeen years his junior. Cadotte had two children with her, daughters Mary-Ann (b. 1860) and Sarah-Ellen (1862), and died in 1901 in Sault Ste Marie.[35]

Yet although the marriage was short-lived and the couple did not experience the same degree of heightened publicity afforded their wedding ceremony, their relationship did not completely vanish from local memory. At least two English travellers to the Great Lakes area heard the sad tale of "the young Englishwoman who became the wife of a half-caste Indian, one of the men exhibited as a Red chieftain in Catlin's exhibition in London." At Walpole Island, William Hancock told his readers, "the young English lady ... was taken by her swarthy mate. The fellow treated her as bad or worse than any wife-beating Englishman could have done; but, though many attempts were made to return to England, they all proved unsuccessful, and she died some years since, as she lived, the faithful loving wife of the degraded savage." It may well be that Hancock was more interested in Haynes's story as an example of how "woman's love ... given in all its overflowing richness, depth and purity where least valued and least deserved; to be, by others, sought, and craved and prayed for – in vain," than in any lesson that could be learned about the complexities of interracial intimacy.[36] While sailing on a Great Lakes schooner en route to Sault Ste Marie, William Kingston was told by his purser of the "Poor, poor girl! little did she dream of the sad fate awaiting her, or of the melancholy contrast between the life her romantic imagination had pictured and the reality." Arriving with a piano "and a variety of elegant furniture on board," Haynes was remembered by the purser as a "fine, handsome, intelligent person" who sang and played well, her music being "her only solace when she reached, not as she expected the rustic palace of the great Red chief, but the miserable shanty of the rough half-caste carpenter, her husband, to instruct the young squaws in such music as they were capable of learning." His curiosity sparked by the purser's tale, Kingston made a point of asking about Haynes once the boat docked, finding out that "she had then rested from all her troubles for nearly two years; and should these pages ever meet the eyes of her relatives, it may be a consolation to them to know that, infatuated as she was, she proved herself a virtuous, high-minded, and devoted woman, striving even to the very last, when all feeling akin to love must have fled her bosom, to enlighten the spiritual being of the man who had so deeply wronged her."[37]

From an exotic to a sentimental spectacle, Haynes's life thus served a number of purposes for metropolitan audiences. It may well have been that her marriage was indeed a deeply unhappy one. Other sources speak of Cadotte's drinking and brutal treatment of her; they also depict Haynes as gentle and caring towards her young pupils, the Indigenous children of Sault Ste Marie.[38] What Haynes thought about her life and whether she regretted the decision to marry Cadotte can only be the subject of speculation, since she does not appear to have left any letters or diaries. In many ways, she resembled Elizabeth Howell Copway, although for Sarah Haynes there would be no reunion with her English family, nor did she have, at the very least, the consolation of seeing her daughter grow to adulthood. Like other travellers, though, the story of Haynes's piano suggests how the movement of people also facilitated the movement of European culture and its technologies, although perhaps not in the way she had envisioned. After her death, her rosewood piano first became the property of the Catholic church and was used in the community schoolhouse – against Cadotte's wishes, it seems. According to the local priest, Alexander Cadotte "made a spectacle … because of the piano, which he wants back."[39] Cadotte did not get his late wife's piano back, however, and at some point, it was cut up and made into a "handsome table" for the owner of a summer house in the area.[40]

Maungwudaus in the Metropole

Although at times it is possible to venture – or hazard – a more complicated reading of the 1843–44 Ojibwe tour than the press and Rankin could provide, nevertheless without their own accounting of their experiences abroad we are left with many gaps and absences. Such silences are exacerbated by the cacophony of voices who so often insisted on seeing the tour as an example of "the colonial primitive" brought face to face with the sophistication of metropolitan modernity. Furthermore, while Rankin's account attempted at times to present Maconse, or Francis Eshtonoquot, and his companions in a positive light – as when he told European audiences of the affection of Ojibwe mothers for their children, for example, or of the group's peaceful existence with their London neighbours – his own perspectives, not least his need to be the authoritative voice on the Ojibwe, shade his description of the tour.

The tour of Maungwudaus (George Henry) has left a different archival imprint, given that Maungwudaus himself chose to write an account of his time abroad. Published by "the Author" in 1848 in Boston, his *Account of the Chippewa Indians Who Have Been Travelling Among the Whites in the United States, England, Ireland, Scotland, France and Belgium* promised readers "very interesting incidents in relation to the general characteristics of the English, Irish, Scotch, French, and Americans, with regard to their hospitality, peculiarities, etc." Maungwudaus hoped his work, written by "the self-taught Indian of the Chippewa Nation," would "benefit ... his youngest Son, called Noodinokay, whose Mother died in England." If Rankin hoped to garner his share of fame and create an exciting public persona for himself as the promoter of the "primitives abroad," Maungwudaus appears to have seized the opportunity to tell his people's story in a different, albeit related, timbre. While his document was created within the context of imperial expansion and colonial relations, like those records left by his fellow Anishinaabe travellers, it can be read for its self-conscious and knowing engagement with those relationships.

Although a familiar figure to some historians and literary scholars, it is fair to argue that Maungwudaus has garnered less attention than has his half-brother, Peter Jones.[41] To a certain extent, his being overshadowed by Jones is not surprising, since the latter travelled more frequently, moved in religious and secular circles in both Upper Canada and Britain, and was involved in political lobbying for the Mississauga. Yet Maungwudaus also had his complexities and contradictions. Born to Ojibwe parents, Mesquacosy and Tubenahneequay (Jones's mother) and (unlike Jones) raised primarily in

Mississauga culture, the teenage Maungwudaus converted to Christianity around 1825. Before deciding to lead a troupe of performers, he had been, as historian Donald B. Smith puts it, "one of the Methodists' most promising Indigenous candidates for the ministry," working as a Sunday-school teacher at the Credit Mission and a mission interpreter at Munceytown, and travelling to Sault Ste Marie as part of a missionary party.[42] By the late 1830s, George Henry was the assistant missionary at the St Clair mission station in southwestern Upper Canada. The American Methodist newspaper *Christian Advocate* described him as the peer of Peter Jones, John Sunday, and Peter Jacobs, being "at the head of our chosen pioneers."[43] As Smith points out, he also was respected by the Mississauga at the Credit, who in 1837 invited him to become their third chief.

However, the Methodist Church's disciplinary practices, coupled with attacks on the Mississauga by white Methodists, led to his decision to resign from the Church in 1840 and form a dance troupe, consisting of his own family members and non-Christian Anishinaabeg from the St Clair River community of Walpole Island. Not surprisingly, his decisions saddened and "mortified" his missionary half-brother.[44] In many ways Maungwudaus's story resembles that of George Copway, as he navigated a journey that encompassed Indigenous communities, Christianity, and public performances of "Indianness" in multiple locations.

Yet despite Maungwudaus's unhappiness with the Methodists and his claim to be "self-educated," like Copway his experience with them may well have provided him with enough education and ongoing exposure to the English language to ensure he could leave his own record of his trip. To be sure, his *An Account* cannot be read without some awareness of the complexities of translation, both within the context of the 1840s and that of the twenty-first century. Maungwudaus himself was well aware of the intricacies of speaking across cultural and linguistic divides, as he prefaced his narrative by stating "I will not ask the reader for pardon. The short notice of me on another page will induce him to excuse me for using improperly the English language."[45] Nevertheless, as a number of scholars have noted, his text suggests both important continuities and significant shifts in the cultural frameworks in which Indigenous travellers were placed and, simultaneously, helped create.[46]

Unlike, for example, Norton or Nahneebahweequa, but like Copway, Maungwudaus chose to record in some detail his impressions of the voyage from New York to Portsmouth. Sailing across the Atlantic in March, he found the journey eventful: the middle mast was blown away, "the waves

Fig. 5.3
Daguerrotype of Maungwudaus

were like mountains," and at times the passengers "got a good ducking with salt water by the waves, pouring into our cabin." Although no one was seasick, they were a "little hurt" when thrown out of their berths by the ship's tossing. Moreover, the supplies of flour and corn were spilled, so "the rats had good feasting. Every night after they had their bellies full [they] were very mischievous; they helped the waves by tormenting us, by biting us on our toes and noses." Yet despite these discomforts, "the sea in the night was a blaze of fire."[47] Leaving behind bothersome rodents and saltwater drenching, not to mention bruises and scrapes, the party toured Nelson's warships in Portsmouth and saw the place of his death. Maungwudaus was impressed by their treatment: "the officers living in this sea-house were very kind to us. The great sea-war chief took us into the navy yard where they are making many war ships. Another war chief invited us and showed us all his warriors under him in the barracks."[48]

As such descriptions suggest, Maungwudaus employed a variety of nouns, verbs, and metaphors to frame his English hosts and their context in his own terms. London's numerous inhabitants were like "musketoes [sic] in America in the summer season … biting one another to get a living."[49] Queen Victoria was accompanied by "many warriors" when she went out and, although Maungwudaus was impressed by their height, bright and gleaming arms, and horses decorated with much silver and gold, their beards made them look "fierce and savage like our American dogs when carrying black squirrels in their mouths."[50] In Ipswich, their Quaker hosts introduced them to a doctor, F.W. Johnson; after dinner this "medicine man" placed a piece of the cheese which they had just eaten under a microscope and invited them to see the great number of "worms" that were in it. Although very much disconcerted by the experience and anticipating that they would feel the worms biting, Maungwudaus and his party concluded that "our friends must be something like bears, who loves [sic] to eat living worms or maggots."[51] Like his contemporaries Jones and Copway, Maungwudaus performed an Anishinaabe identity on a range of stages in the metropole, those that included both its public spaces – exhibition and lecture halls, streets, and drawing rooms – and, too, the written text.

As did other travellers, Maungwudaus professed to be impressed with certain aspects of England. London was a "wonderful city," with its "many rich" and "many poor"; it also had "many stone inns and lodgings," and St Paul's and the "Council House" (presumably the Houses of Parliament) "are very large buildings indeed."[52] The group were invited to tea almost daily by both the Society of Friends and by the nobility, where the dinnerware and cutlery were made of silver and gold, the servants' hair was powdered white, and the group was given "many handsome presents" and were shown "many things that others have never seen." They were taken to hear Lord John Russell and Sir Robert Peel "talk in the council" and to see the "lower house." Irish politician Daniel O'Connell had them to dinner and "was very kind to us," Maungwudaus wrote. Like the other Ojibwe, they went for a tour of the tunnel under the Thames, with "the ships sailing over us while walking below."[53] They also travelled on the Great Western Railway and witnessed three men from the Zoological Gardens "going up to the country of stars ... with something very large in the shape of a bladder over their heads; they called it a balloon." Moreover, Lord Bloomfield invited them to tour the "big guns at Woolwich; three of us got inside of one of them."[54]

Just as Copway told his readers about his encounters with celebrated figures, so too did Maungwudaus point to the number of times that well-known members of English society welcomed the group and showed them hospitality. As well as O'Connell, "the great war-chief with the big nose, the Duke of Wellington, invited us, and was very kind to us in his house," presenting the group with presents. Sir Augustus d'Este ("cousin to the Queen, son of the Duke of Sussex"), who had also smoothed Peter Jones's way in metropolitan society, frequently had them to his home for tea. "He is a great friend to the Indians; he introduced us to many of his friends." The group visited J.J. Gurney, "the great man of the Quakers," at his home in Norwich, where Gurney and his wife and son gave them "rich presents."[55] Gurney also wrote a testimonial for Maungwudaus to include in his book, in which he spoke of the pleasure the Ojibwe's visit had brought his family. He also reprinted his religious address to the group, which spoke of God's love and his ability to guide them towards peace, his hope that the Bible would be translated into Ojibwe, and his "earnest advice" that they abjure "fire water" in order to embrace industriousness and a sedentary way of life.[56] As well, the Archbishop of Canterbury very kindly gave them a tour of Canterbury Cathedral, telling them it was thirteen hundred years old. "This is the most curious, the largest, and the most beautiful one we have seen. The top of the steeple our arrows could not reach."[57] One of the highlights of such meetings was their audience with the Queen and Prince Albert: the latter they found a "handsome and well built man." The Queen's "house," Maungwudaus thought, was extremely large, "we got tired before we went through all the rooms in it. Great many warriors with their swords and guns stands [sic] outside watching for the enemy." What was more, Victoria had three or four other houses that were as large as this one, and plans were underway to build onto it.[58]

Yet the reverent attitude demonstrated towards the "Great Mother" by his fellow Anishinaabeg does not seem to have affected Maungwudaus. While he found her a "small but handsome" woman, "there are many handsomer women than she is," he confided to his readers. Other aspects of English society also failed to impress him. Steamboats on the Thames were not "as handsome" as their American counterparts, he thought, while London's homes "are rather dark in colour on account of too much smoke."[59] The English officers the group met, while "fine, noble, and dignified looking fellows," whose voices sounded like those of the bullfrog, had only one fault, but it was one that irritated Maungwudaus: "their too many unnecessary ceremonies while eating, such as allow me Sir, or Mrs. to put this on your plate. If you please, sir, thank you, you are very kind, Sir, or Mrs. can I have the pleasure of helping you?" While the mockery might be gentle, Maungwudaus clearly chafed at such niceties. Moreover, like his half-brother, Maungwudaus was not impressed by the English diet. "Many of the Englishmen have very big stomachs, caused by drinking too much ale and porter. Those who drink wine and brandy, their noses look like ripe strawberries."[60]

It was not just England that fell under his critical gaze. From Liverpool, the group sailed to Dublin, where they performed in the city's Rotunda and in the Zoological Gardens in front of audiences of three thousand; they also went to see "Father Mathew," the Irish temperance advocate. The tour also took in Belfast and Londonderry, leaving Maungwudaus thinking that the Irish were "very kind-hearted people," who in the countryside made fires from turf and were often very poor, adding "the British government is over them." In Scotland, they visited Burns's small, straw-roofed cottage, Wallace's Oak Tree near Paisley, and the cities of Glasgow and Edinburgh. Scots were, Maungwudaus decided, very religious, industrious, kind to strangers, strict Sabbath-keepers, and many were teetotal. They did, however, have some curious – if not downright disgusting – habits. Elderly Scotsmen and women were "very fond of snuff," and when they put it in each nostril, their words sound "nasal, something like pig grunting." Even worse, while Edinburgh's new town was "very handsome … the old town is rather filthy. All the dirt is thrown in the streets before people get up, and carts take it away, but still the smell of it is most offensive all day." Even the Scots acknowledged that Edinburgh stank![61] To these Indigenous people, Europeans' ways of dealing with human waste and garbage were puzzling and rather repulsive.

If one incident that brought out both the intolerance and humanitarianism found in Britain stood out for Maungwudaus, it was that of the monkey.[62] While riding through "a town" in Indigenous clothing, the group came upon a monkey, dressed like a man and performing on a music box for an audience of about fifty young men. Upon seeing the Ojibwe, the young men immediately started to mock them, "and made use of very insulting language." The monkey, however, took off his cap and bowed to the group. A nearby gentlemen witnessed the scene and proceeded to lecture the youth:

> Look at the monkey take off his cap and make a bow in saluting these strangers, which of the two the strangers will think are most civilised, you or the monkey? You ought to be ashamed of yourselves. You may consider yourselves better and wiser than those strangers, but you are very much mistaken. Your treatment to them tells them that you are not, and you are so foolish and ignorant, you know nothing about it. I have been travelling five years amongst these people in their own country, and I never, not once, was insulted, but I was always kindly treated and respected by every one of them. Their little children have far better manners than you. Young man, the monkey pays you well for all the pennies you have given him; he is worthy to become your teacher.

The Ojibwe then threw money to the monkey, which he took and put into his master's mouth. As they left, the monkey bowed to them, which prompted a young man to remark "see the teacher making another bow to the Indians," to which another replied "Yes ... this is to teach you, for you are the very one that was making fun and blackguarding the Indians."[63] Even if Maungwudaus and Jones disagreed about the ways in which Anishinaabe people should present themselves for white audiences, nevertheless they shared similar feelings of disgust at being treated like a freak show when in Indigenous clothing. Furthermore, far from being superior in manners and comportment, whites had much to learn about manners and the hospitable treatment of North American Indigenous strangers, something that at least one white "gentleman" recognized.

More than anything else that struck Maungwudaus about Britain, though, was the status and behaviour of English "ladies." The group's dinner with the "fine, noble" English officers also included the "ladies, who were brought to the barracks like sick women." Talkative while eating, "like ravens when feasting on venison," Maungwudaus was reminded of an English prov-erb: "'Thieves and robbers eat and drink a little, and make no noise when they eat." To be sure, he found the women "very handsome," with their small waists, hands, and feet, and long necks. Yet they were also a kind of freak show, with their heads carried "on one side of the shoulder," holding their cutlery with forefingers and thumb, "the two last ones [fingers] are of no use to them, only sticking out like our fish-spears while eating."[64] Even worse, the constant flirting and provocative behaviour that Maungwudaus believed he witnessed did not impress Indigenous men. On leaving the dinner, the officers informed the Ojibwe men that the "ladies" wished to shake their hands. However, the English women then decided the handshake was an insufficient sign of respect, and they wished to be kissed. Maungwudaus and his companions "kissed them according to our custom on both cheeks." That still was not enough: "another officer said to us, 'Gentlemen, our pretty squaws are not yet satisfied, they want to be kissed on their mouths.'" When they did so, "there was a great shout amongst the English war-chiefs. Say-say-gon, our war-chief, then said in our language to the ladies; 'That is all you are good for; as for wives, you are good for nothing.'" As they begged for a translation, Maungwudaus told them that Say-say-gon had expressed a keen desire to be invited back, so that he might kiss the "handsome ladies" again, to which the latter replied, "Did he? Then we will tell our men to invite you again, for we like to be kissed very often; tell him so." Then they put gold rings on fingers and gold pins on our breasts, and when we had thanked them for their kindness, we got in our carriage and went to our apartments."[65]

This, then, was a more pointed critique of the "English ladies" than that offered by Jones, who had seen middle-class Englishwomen as being strangely dressed but, at heart, charitable and sympathetic to Indigenous people. It also went further than Copway's acknowledgment of his attractiveness to European women; not only was he flattered by their attentions, he accepted them as the natural consequences of the superior physiques and personal magnetism of Indigenous men. In contrast, Maungwudaus did not see these women as benevolent or as succumbing to an inevitable attraction; instead, they appear more like sexual predators who pay Indigenous men for sexual favours. His description thus reverses the well-known trope of Indigenous women as sexually profligate beings who would lure European men into liaisons, women no better than prostitutes who offered themselves freely to European men in the colonies for fashionable trinkets (interestingly, Maungwudaus had nothing to say about European men's sexualizing of Indigenous women). Such a passage served as a critique of English women's morality and, equally importantly – given the significance that Anishinaabe society placed on women's productive capacities as wives – highlighted, in the eyes of the Ojibway, their strictly ornamental value.

It is difficult to know how much of this was filtered through Maungwudaus's expectations of proper womanhood, which might well have been shaped both by his Anishinaabe culture and, too, by Methodism's emphasis on female modesty. His characterization of the women's behaviour, though, may have captured some aspects of attitudes toward Indigenous men. Catlin's account of the reaction of English women to the Ojibwe and Iowan people whom he accompanied points to the former's thinly veiled sexual fascination with Indigenous men, a fascination that at times was expressed quite explicitly.[66] As we have seen, the Cadotte-Haynes marriage elicited varying shades of sexually tinged voyeuristic curiosity, albeit much of it emanating from the pens of British male reporters. It is possible that any display of sexual curiosity by middle-class white women unsettled their male counterparts.

Whatever the case, though, Maungwudaus's passage also pointed to a long-standing practice that marked encounters between Indigenous people and Europeans: the use of translation to hide or at least partly cloak Indigenous truths from the latter, particularly when those truths might prove embarrassing to them or could not be expressed in the other party's language.[67] Here, too, he shared much with other travellers. Norton's career had been marked by his role as both interpreter and translator, while Maungwudaus's fellow Anishinaabeg were continuously engaged in attempts to explain their communities' concepts and practices to Europeans and, conversely, to make sense of the latter. In turning his compatriot's dismissal of the women into a compliment, at that particular moment, through speech, Maungwudaus preserved his people's reputation for good manners. Simultaneously, in his text he was able to demonstrate his superior ability to understand and comment on the situation, an ability that surpassed that of his hosts.

The troupe's five-month visit to France also afforded Maungwudaus the chance to muse about another group of Europeans. He found the time there enjoyable, but was not overawed, recounting their meeting with the French court in a matter-of-face tone:

> shook hands with Louis Philippe and all his family in the Park, called St. Cloud; gave them little war dance, shooting with bows and arrows at a target, ball play; also rowed our birch bark canoe in the artificial lake, amongst swans and geese. There were about four thousand French ladies and gentlemen with them. We dined with him in the afternoon in his Palace. He said many things concerning his having been in America

when he was a young man. He gave us twelve gold and silver medals; he showed us all the rooms in his house.

Maungwudaus found the French ladies "handsome, very gay in their dresses, both men and women."[68] Other French women, the "common wives," of Paris, were, he stated, called "industrious fleas," presumably a play on the very popular flea circuses of the period.[69]

To be sure, other events in Paris proved memorable. An invitation by Monsieur Lafontaine, "the great mesmerist," gave the group the chance to pull needles through the flesh of his mesmerized subjects and, as well, to receive a hug and a kiss from one of them, a "young lady." Not only did she call them "my dear," she was also left with their facepaint on her cheeks. While Maungwudaus seemed very pleased with their participation in Lafontaine's work, another visit, this time to a "French gentleman" who made plaster-of-Paris moulds of their heads, left some of the young men in the group "frightened." However, the painting of their likenesses by Monsieur J. Godin, done at Louis-Philippe's request, was less upsetting.[70]

Other aspects of their trip, though, were more than upsetting. As Maureen Konkle points out, Maungwudaus's account was filled with deaths, those of his family and his fellow performers.[71] In Belgium "poor Aunimuckwuh-um and Mishimaung" died from smallpox; the same "dreadful disease" took the war chief Say-say-gon after their return to England. A reader could almost imagine Maungwudaus shaking his head in sorrow, as "these three men would not allow the white doctors to vaccinate them. They said we were very foolish to place ourselves in the care of the whites; – ourselves were saved by this simple remedy, through the kindness of our friends the Quakers."[72] This was not the end of the group's tragedies, though. While in Glasgow and Edinburgh, three of Maungwudaus's children died and were laid to rest "in the burying grounds of our friends the Quakers."[73] Matters did not improve: shortly after burying her children, Maungwudaus's wife died in Newark. "The vicar of that church was very kind to us, in allowing us to bury her remains near the church."[74]

Death touched a number of others in his account. Mrs Catlin and one of the Catlins' younger children died in Paris; Thomas Clarkson, whom the group visited in Ipswich and whose daughter presented them with "a good dinner and handsome presents," expired soon after they met; John Joseph Gurney lost his life in a riding accident while the troupe was in Scotland; and, on the voyage home, sixteen German children and an "English lady" died.[75] And death enters Maungwudaus's story in other ways. While in Edinburgh, they saw "about seventy young men, who are to be medicine men. They had thirty dead bodies, and they were skinning and cutting them same as we do with venison."[76] Equally notable was a hanging that Maungwudaus's group witnessed.

> When we were in Norwich, we saw one man killed; he was killed for killing a woman in Yarmouth for a little money. Many thousand people got together where the man was to be killed, before a large stone house, on a high hill, a long time before the appointed hour arrived. Then they brought the man out they wanted to kill; they made him to stand on a platform with a strong cord around his neck; and when the teacher of wisdom and Christian religion had prayed for him, they pulled down his white cap over his face, and also fastened one end of the cord that was round his neck on a beam over his head. Then another man slipped down the platform he was standing on; he dropped down a little, and was hanging in the air with the cord that was round his neck, his hands tied together behind his back. Then he began to kick and twist about for life, and one of the murderers ran down and caught hold of his legs and pulled him down, and very soon killed him. They said that he was not fit to live on earth, but they believed that he is gone to the happy country in the other world, where he will be out of mischief forever.[77]

An offence committed for very little gain but with grave consequences; "killing" and "murderers" instead of an execution, guards, and a hangman; a huge crowd that gathered to watch the botched hanging (not unlike those who gathered to stare at the Ojibwe); and a "happy country" instead of hell: Maungwudaus's dispassionate tone cloaks his implicit criticism of the procedure. He presented the hanging as something new and novel to his eyes, although it is highly likely that he would have known of capital punishment in Upper Canada, even if he had not witnessed it. His account, though, took an event that would have been all too familiar to his readers, but when framed in a different idiom suggested its barbarity and, by extension, the barbarity of those who condoned it.

Their time in Britain and Europe over, the troupe sailed back to New York. As well as the aforementioned deaths on board, they also saw "seven whales and many porpoises," and witnessed an outbreak of fighting between the German and English passengers over cooking space. This seemed to be a minor scuffle, as "only a few faces got little cut and scratched" and the combatants were punished by the "powerful chief mate" taking a rope to their backs. Maungwudaus much admired the first mate's care of the passengers: he allowed the minister on board to preach every Sunday and was scrupulous about cleanliness, ensuring that the cabins were cleaned regularly inside and out, "that there might be no sickness among us." Such attentiveness to hygiene probably resonated with Maungwudaus, given his recent losses. The man's leadership also drew Maungwudaus's respect: "he was like a father to us," he writes, "all the sailors loved him and were very obedient to him."[78]

Once back in North America, Maungwudaus visited spots that he believed had historical significance for his people, such as Plymouth Rock, "where our forefathers first saw the white man," and Pilgrim Hall. In the United States, he continued his practice of observing and assessing white society, finding the Americans very kind to his group: "they are not so fleshy as the English, but very persevering in all their ways." "Their females," he felt, received more respect than their English counterparts, while the rich in America were called "Top Notches" (in England they were known as "Big Bugs"). Although Americans lacked English manners – putting their feet on tables, chairs, and chimneypieces while smoking or reading the paper, for example – Maungwudaus found that more compatible. "They are not slaves to their civilisations as the English," he believed, "they like to be comfortable, something like ourselves, placing one leg upon the other knee, while basking ourselves in the sun. A real comfort is better than an artificial one to the human nature."[79] Authenticity, it seems, was an admirable trait.

Testimonials and Emotional Ties

While Maungwudaus at times played the "colonial innocent" in his text, his use of testimonials suggested he was a canny and strategic promoter of his troupe and, too, of himself. As well as Gurney's advocacy, Maungwudaus also included a brief endorsement from Catlin, who had promoted and – at least to some degree – managed the troupe during their European sojourn. Others also spoke well of the Ojibwe. In Leicester, Maungwudaus left a lasting impression of his "conduct and spirit." The anonymous writer had formed "'a friendly union, which neither time nor distance can ever destroy' with the son of the wilderness." Furthermore, Maungwudaus had "delighted" the public with his "presence and assistance." Before he left the town, "a remarkable demonstration of gratitude and esteem was manifested." Maungwudaus appeared at a "soiree" and then at an evening's "entertainment" at which thousands witnessed the chief's and his family's performance. Perhaps to suppress any skepticism about this number, the writer assured readers that the fees for this event were very low. Not only did the troupe's display delight, their recent bereavements also elicited sympathy from the people of Leicester. If they excited and thrilled audiences with their displays of war dances (for example), they also could be humanized, their celebrity as "sons of the wilderness" shaped both by an interest in their personal lives and by the mid-nineteenth century's culture of sentiment and domesticity.[80] Such an impression was strengthened by a letter from another who had witnessed their appearances in Leicester. Not only had many of the "excellent of the earth" cherished "the highest sentiments of esteem for this interesting party," their letters to the troupe "breathing a spirit of kindness and piety which cannot fail to produce a salutary impression on the minds of the Indians and their associates in the wilderness," the writer also had been part of a tea held in the city on 27 December 1847. It was attended by more than a thousand of Leicester's poor, including "the lame, the halt, and the blind," and Maungwudaus, sitting alongside a number of ministers, spoke of his people's history, their allegiance to the British Crown, and his troupe's travels in Britain and France.[81]

Other writings suggested how humanitarian and religious circles helped promote and support Maungwudaus and his group. Worcester's Quaker community threw him a party, at which addresses from noted Quakers in London – Edwin Barwin, Letitia Impey, Eliza Humphrey, and R.D. Catchpool, for example – were read. A letter to Maungwudaus from the Reverend Robert Gray Mason, of Leeds, expressed his pleasure in hearing that the former had attracted such a large gathering composed of so many "respectable" people, male and female. Having been told about the group by a "pious and particular" friend in York (and also being an acquaintance of Catlin's), he went to see the group and then told his congregations about them. Mason knew what it was like to be a "stranger in a strange land" and had experienced kindness when on a "foreign shore." While he sympathized greatly with Maungwudaus's recent losses, Mason exhorted him not to be "cast down" and to trust in God. Moreover, he was very happy to hear Maungwudaus speak of his people's need for temperance and the great good that the Christian mission societies had done for them. He closed his letter by mentioning a mutual acquaintance, Rev. Wigg, and was also delighted that Maungwudaus was scheduled to speak at the Wesleyan Missionary Meeting in Nottingham.[82] Perhaps Maungwudaus had managed to put aside his antipathy towards the Methodists, or at least felt the publicity would help his troupe.

It is hard to know, though, what he made of the address of Thomas and Mary Catchpool to the "North American Indians now in this town." Made on behalf of the Colchester Friends, the Catchpools urged Maungwudaus and his group to keep from evil and upon their return home "to leave their wandering life," cultivate crops and raise cattle, teach their children to read, have their wives and daughters make their clothes, abstain from war, and read their Scriptures diligently. By leading a "more civilised" life "you might be helpful to each other," thought the Quakers, and thus able to bear their crosses (the Catchpools did not specify exactly what those might be). They also hoped that the "bright chain of friendship" forged between the "Indians'" forefathers and William Penn would remain so.[83] The couple did not address the irony that, despite their hopes for a "settled" life for Maungwudaus and his people, it was the troupe's mobility that had brought them to the Catchpools. Moreover, they did not realize their characterization of the Ojibwe as wanderers and itinerants did not take into account the latter's attachments to particular territories. Others wrote to Maungwudaus sending their condolences on his wife's death, offering religious precepts that they hoped would provide him some comfort and guidance.[84]

Maungwudaus also included letters from the civic officials, such as Walter Moloney, the resident magistrate of the Belfast District, who wrote to testify to the troupe's "interesting exhibition and respectable behaviour" and, what was more, to ask the city's police to protect them, "as far as possible, from imposition" and to offer them as much help as possible.[85] William Thompson, the mayor of Newark, was very "gratified" by their representation of their "tribe's manner and customs," their acknowledgment of the benefits of the gospel "being preached to heathen," and the fact that Maungwudaus left his wife's remains in his city.[86] Finally, a number of surgeons also wrote: Edmund Smith, formerly of Hudson Bay, wrote on 24 September 1847, while J. Higginbotham of Nottingham was pleased to have received a letter from Maungwudaus, happy to attend him for free, and glad to have been able to have assisted him when his son was ill in that city.[87]

Thus, even if Peter Jones deeply disapproved of his sibling's performances, the testimonials bore witness to the troupe's respectability and good conduct while abroad and the kinds of sympathetic responses they evoked. Moreover, Maungwudaus's account, when placed alongside those of Rankin and Catlin, demonstrates yet again the ways in which mid-nineteenth-century colonial celebrity incorporated – and in many ways depended on – the blurring of private and public boundaries and identities. Body display, sexual intimacy, and even death became part of the colonial celebrity's image.

These writings also demonstrate how, in the words of British historian Catherine Hall, the British Empire was not a "consolidated vision," but rather a "cacophony," a place where stereotypes could and did appear but were never uncontested or the sole means of understanding colonial subjects.[88] For metropolitan audiences, Maungwudaus and his fellow male performers could be fearsome "Red Indians," objects of sexual desire, and loving and bereaved husbands and fathers.

Conclusion

It is tempting and, perhaps, not inaccurate to read in Maungwudaus's account not only knowingness but also insouciance, a bit of cheekiness, directed not just at his British audience but also at his half-brother. Jones's rectitude in public, his black suits and English wife: these choices represented a way of life that Maungwudaus had rejected. Furthermore, by writing his travelogue, Maungwudaus could be seen as allying himself with other performance troupes, providing a type of "voice" for those spoken for by Rankin and Catlin. As historian Sadiah Qureshi argues, Maungwudaus blurred the line between European or Anglo-American managers who displayed – and exploited – colonized performers in Britain; in so doing, he reminds us of "the complexities" of such performances.[89] At the same time, though, he distinguished himself from those who were unable to impress upon the public their histories and subjective thoughts and, too, their impressions of European society. In many ways Maungwudaus resembled Copway, as he moved between depicting himself as a member of a community (albeit with more success than Copway might have been able to achieve) and claiming an individuality that European notions of the "Red Indian" could rarely, if ever, admit. Such possibilities and constraints would endure as other Indigenous performers appeared within the heightened context of late-Victorian and Edwardian imperial modernity.

. 6 .

Performances and Politics at
Empire's Height

Introduction

Five years after Maungwudaus and his troupe returned home, Charles
Dickens published "The Noble Savage" as the lead essay in his journal,
Household Worlds. As literary scholar Grace Moore has pointed out, this
piece is Dickens's "most controversial depiction of the colonial other," one
that other scholars have described as "uncontrolled hysteria" or a "torrent
of vitriol," laced with references to "odious," "disgusting," and "diabolical"
customs and behaviour.[1] The portrait Dickens creates, of people as diverse
as Catlin's 1843–44 troupe of "Ojibbeways Indians" and African "Bushmen,"
is that of degraded savagery, with no nobility to be found. So far as the
Anishnaabe people to which Dickens refers are concerned, their behaviour
consisted of "squatting and spitting," "dancing their miserable jigs after their
own dreary manner." Dickens claimed to have seen through Catlin's efforts to
portray the Anishinaabeg as examples of "symmetry and grace": instead, in
his eyes they were "wretched creatures, very low in the scale and very poorly
formed," as bad as (and possibly worse) than the "Italian Opera in England."[2]

Moore cautions, though, that while clearly racist, Dickens's polemic
should be read with an eye to his changing world view and to his understanding of British society. For one, he may have been using the Anishinaabeg in

order to criticize his fellow Britains, most notably London's East Enders (the Irish also appear in the article in very unflattering ways). Moore also points out that Dickens was known to admire North American Indigenous people; in his other writings he had pointed to settler injustices towards them.[3] Furthermore, he also targets those philanthropists who are overly sentimental about Indigenous people; although he does not name them directly, he would likely have had in mind the humanitarians who supported Peter Jones and Maungwudaus. As his references to Catlin suggest, Dickens castigated those impresarios who orchestrated displays of Indigenous people in the metropole and were responsible for exhibitions that, from his perspective, put on display brutality, primitivism, and degradation.

How many of Dickens's readers approved of "The Noble Savage," nodding their heads in agreement with his descriptions? If they did so, had they also seen Catlin's "Ojibbeways" and Maungwudaus's troupe, or just read about them in the press? It is difficult to know the answer to either question. However, so far as appearances of Indigenous people in London are concerned, the article is notable in a number of ways. For one, as scholars have pointed out, Dickens's depictions of "the savage" reflected a larger shift in attitudes: concepts of "the savage" "as a natural man had given way to the idea that savagery resulted from a process of degeneration from a state of primal grace."[4] Thus, those who followed Maungwudaus would have to contend with changing attitudes and, by the late-nineteenth century, an intensification of imperialist discourses that proclaimed British political, cultural, economic, and racial superiority. Moreover, despite Dickens's dislike of exhibitions of supposedly colonized subjects, "The Noble Savage" admits that, in the years after Maungwudaus and his fellow Anishinaabeg appeared in Britain, such performances could be readily found in London and, indeed, were becoming more common both throughout Britain and around the world.

As historian Roslyn Poignant has pointed out, the growing dispossession of Indigenous peoples in colonial sites, coupled with their entanglement in Western education and mass entertainment, was part of the development of "the modern world as spectacle," displayed in fairgrounds, circuses, exhibitions halls, theatres, and museum spaces. Poignant goes on to argue that the "area in which this engagement took place" can most usefully be called "the show-space," a term that is "more than a collective name for the actual show places." Instead, she sees the "show-space" as a "cultural space that is both a zone of displacement for the performers and a place of spectacle for the onlookers." Furthermore, "it is a chronotopic space ... a conjunction of time and space, where certain stories can 'take place': where historically specific relations of power between coloniser and colonised were made quite visible." Universal exhibitions in particular, in which from the 1860s the technological power and ascendancy of the modern nation-state was made highly visible, attempted to provide concrete and embodied proof of European superiority with displays of reconstructed colonial villages and demonstrations of 'savage' performance."[5]

In many ways, the Ojibwe performances of the 1840s prefigured Poignant's "show-space," as Anishinaabe troupes entered "zones of displacement" in both Upper Canada and the metropole that were undoubtedly places of spectacle for British and European audiences. As we have seen, these places included the performance platform, streets, parks, assembly rooms, and private homes. Moreover, in the British press the Anishinaabe people were juxtaposed as specimens of primitivism with the "marvels" of British technology and scientific knowledge, such as the Thames tunnel. The staging of such displays was meant to remind metropolitan audiences of their own superiority and to impress on the Anishinaabeg themselves their inevitable, and necessary, acquiescence to assimilationist programs of settler society and the colonial state. If the audiences in question were entertained as well as educated, so much the better.

Yet although a useful and insightful concept, "show-space" can be modified, depending on the different colonial contexts and different groups of Indigenous people involved. Maungwudaus, for example, along with other Anishinaabe travellers, particularly Peter Jones and George Copway, insisted that they were fully conscious of being a spectacle and, on some occasions, being viewed as such might be enjoyable. Moreover, as we have seen, displaying oneself as an unsophisticated innocent could also be a stance used to tweak Europeans' sensibility, to use the vantage point of a "Red Indian" to say and write things about the metropole and colonial relationships that might otherwise be difficult to express.

The period of "high imperialism" at the turn of the century saw yet again more arrivals of Indigenous people from the Dominion of Canada. Like their mid-century predecessors, Pauline Johnson and her contemporary John Ojijatekha Brant-Sero stepped onto the Liverpool docks in the 1890s and 1900s with a variety of goals in mind, such as making valuable professional contacts and earning a living performing and lecturing. A number of themes emerge from a close examination of their time in the metropole. For one, contrasting Johnson, a rare example of a North American Indigenous woman traveller and performer, with Brant-Sero helps us see more clearly the gendered dimensions of these appearances, the role gender played in shaping performances of indigeneity. As well, these individuals' travels remind us of the degrees of heterogeneity within those show-spaces that proliferated in late-Victorian and Edwardian British, European, and American cities. To be sure, certain aspects of Johnson's and Brant-Sero's appearances were at times stereotypical, most likely reinforcing their audiences' notions of Indigenous peoples, playing into imperial fantasies and desires, and, indeed, inflected by the discourses and practices of show-spaces. Nevertheless, these performances were not homogenous or completely formulaic.

For one, Johnson and Brant-Sero were not performers whose appearances were directly or solely controlled by a promoter. Although Brant-Sero appeared as part of a theatrical troupe, the majority of his performances and lectures were solo undertakings and bore the hallmark of his individual personality and choices. While Johnson appeared with her manager, Walter McRaye, she also performed by herself and made a number of her own decisions about her career: there is little to suggest that she was manipulated or exploited by an impresario. Moreover, both Johnson and Brant-Sero combined elements of the "Indian poetess" or "heathen redman" with those that challenged the dominant, gendered images and tropes that constituted imperial knowledge of Indigenous peoples. In so doing, they deployed a number of representational strategies and devices. These included historical narratives and knowledge of the central forms of both Indigenous and British culture, including spiritual and political values and practices. Overall, then, Johnson and Brant-Sero's performances were complex and self-conscious displays: they used the metropolis as a stage on which they struggled to craft and perform gendered and racialized identities for the benefit of audiences in England and Canada – and, of course, for themselves.

Grand River Origins

The best known of these imperial travellers, Pauline Johnson, was born in 1861 on the Six Nations Reserve near Brantford, Ontario, her father a Mohawk chief, George Johnson, and her mother an English immigrant, Emily Howells.[6] Johnson was educated, at home and in school, in both English literature and Mohawk history, an education that she drew upon in her career as a writer and performer.[7] Her family enjoyed an elite status on the reserve, and Johnson had access to particular forms of imperial cultural and social capital denied to other Mohawk women.

Fig. 6.1
Chiefswood, E. Pauline Johnson's birthplace,
Onondaga Township, Brant County

However, after her father died in 1884, Johnson and her mother and sister left their home at the Six Nations.[8] She began publishing her poems in the 1880s and started doing performances in 1892, in which she recited her own poetry. At first, she wore only European-style evening dresses for these appearances. By the fall of 1892, however, Johnson also began wearing a fringed buckskin dress of her own design for the first half of her performance, changing into evening dress for the second.[9] In 1894, Johnson travelled to England to look for a publisher for her first book, *The White Wampum*, which was published by Bodley Head in 1895.

While in England, she appeared, as both guest and performer, at various London social evenings hosted by aristocratic women; her biographers generally agree she was the "hit of the season" and achieved the status of "both the cultivated lady and the poetess from the primeval forests" that, to date, had not been forthcoming in Canadian society.[10] In April 1906, Johnson returned to England with her performance partner and manager,

Walter McRaye, and the two signed up with the Keith Prowse entertainment agency in order to hold public performances. Johnson was introduced to and offered the patronage of Lord and Lady Strathcona (Strathcona was the Canadian High Commissioner in London, and Lady Strathcona, as readers of Chapter 4 will remember, was the mixed-race Bella Hardisty), performed at the Imperial Institute's Dominion Day (1 July) party, and, at tea on the House of Commons terrace, met Sir Arthur Pearson, the newspaper magnate who commissioned Johnson to write a number of pieces for his *Daily Express*. Among their various London appearances, Johnson and McRaye performed at London's Steinway Hall in July.[11] During this trip, Johnson met a delegation of British Columbia chiefs, Su-á-pu-luck (Joseph Capilano, Squamish), Chillihitza (Charlie Filpaynem, Okanagan), and Basil David (Shuswap), who had arrived in London in early August, their goal a royal audience to discuss imperial restrictions on their access to fish and game and white settlers' encroachment on their lands; this encounter precipitated a very close friendship with Capilano. Having obtained their audience with the King and Queen on August 13, the chiefs returned to Canada two days later.[12] Johnson and McRaye followed them in mid-November and, although Johnson is said to have returned to England the next year, nothing is known about that transatlantic trip.[13] She continued to tour Canada and the United States and published in North American periodicals. Johnson died in 1913 of breast cancer, her last years lived in poverty.[14]

To some degree John Brant-Sero's life resembled that of Johnson, although it has received far less attention from Canadian scholars and there are considerably more gaps in biographical accounts. Unlike Johnson, though, both his parents were Mohawk, his mother a descendant of Joseph Brant and his father, Dennis Sero, a member of the Bay of Quinte (near Kingston, Ontario) Tyendinaga Mohawks. As well, Brant-Sero's childhood and young adulthood were less privileged than Johnson's. Born on the Six Nations reserve in 1867, Brant-Sero was educated at the reserve school and the New England Company's Mohawk Institute, where he learnt carpentry. As a young man, Brant-Sero worked in Toronto as a machine hand, where he also developed a love of theatre and appeared as an actor on the city's stage. In 1891 he left for England, where he claimed to have been cast in a number of productions, including the American *On the Frontier* in Liverpool. In that city, as we saw in Chapter 4, he fathered a child with Mary Ann McGrath, then married Frances Baynes Kirby, a forty-eight-year-old widow of a British clergyman, added "Brant" to his name, returned to Canada with his new wife, and established their home in Hamilton.[15]

In Canada, Brant-Sero presented himself as an authority on Mohawk history and culture, sat on the Ontario Historical Society's executive board, and worked as an informant and translator for the provincial archaeologist. In 1900, Brant-Sero travelled to Chicago and began a United States lecture tour on the history and customs of the Mohawk. He then went to South Africa, where he tried to enlist for the British in the South African War, but was refused on the grounds of his race. Upon returning to England in 1900, Brant-Sero read a paper before the British Association for the Advancement of Science, was elected a fellow of the Anthropological Institute of Great Britain and Ireland (although he resigned in 1902), and attracted "enthusiastic crowds" with his lectures, augmented with lantern illuminations and music. On 13 February 1902, 1,311 Liverpudlians turned out to hear him speak about "Canada and the Indians."[16]

Brant-Sero spent the rest of his life in England, writing papers and giving interviews and talks on his homeland and peoples. Some of his public appearances, to be sure, were more notable or flamboyant: such as his Liverpool arraignment in the city's police court on charges of failure to provide child support for his son with Mary McGrath.[17] In August 1908, he was a contestant in a Folkestone male beauty contest, in which he wore "full Indigenous dress, with feathery headgear." The reporter took special note of his "jet-black hair, which fell over the nape of his neck."[18] He also travelled to Germany. As historian Karl Markus Kreis tells us, in 1909 Brant-Sero appeared in Dresden with a group of Indigenous performers, lectured and presented work the following year at Berlin's Geographical Society, and published an article attacking German fiction writer Karl May's descriptions of "Indians."[19] In 1914, Brant-Sero died at West London Hospital, of "acute pneumoccocal meningitis."[20]

Educating the Metropole

Like Maungwudaus, George Copway, Peter Jones, and John Norton, both Johnson and Brant-Sero travelled to the United States in various capacities. Yet, like their predecessors, Johnson's and Brant-Sero's tours of England have a meaning and specificity that differentiate them from their American travels. They appeared in a metropole in which it would have been extremely difficult, if not impossible, to escape the presence of the British Empire: popular and elite culture were saturated with imperial imagery and representations; discussions of the Empire were the subject of numerous newspaper articles and editorials, not to mention political conferences that attracted Dominion and imperial politicians; and imperial exhibitions and, notably, Victoria's Diamond Jubilee of 1897 brought together representatives from a range of colonies and Dominions.[21] Empire, it would have seemed to these travellers, was everywhere.

In this context, Johnson and Brant-Sero claimed a particular relationship to the imperial power. Their ties to Britain, they argued, had been forged within the upheavals of the American Revolution and the War of 1812, a relationship that, from their perspective, could not be subsumed under the categories of "colonizer" and "colonized." As did their predecessors, neither Johnson nor Brant-Sero rejected their formal and informal education in British culture and history. Nevertheless, neither were they content that Europeans should continue seeing their relationship with Indigenous people as that of paternal guidance, in which unlearned children were led to enlightened adulthood.[22] Johnson and Brant-Sero's presence in Britain as self-identified Indigenous people who assumed an authoritative and knowledgeable position vis-à-vis the British public also sought to disrupt another imperial, masculinist position: that of the "seeing-man" or "lord-of-all-I-survey." By the late-nineteenth century, this persona, which appeared at exhibitions, in learned anthropological and scientific gatherings, and through imperial policy-making, assumed a position of knowledge about Indigenous peoples, a knowledge that might have little to do with their own subjectivities, their own knowledge of their histories and social practices.[23] Such a stance harkened back to earlier colonial ethnography and cartography: it was not, after all, a new or novel phenomenon for Europeans to assert imperial superiority through the display of knowledge about colonial subjects. Furthermore, it certainly was not new for the Indigenous people of the Great Lakes area to fall under the scrutiny of ethnographers; from the 1840s on, Americans Henry Schoolcraft, Horatio Hale, and Lewis Henry Morgan had produced studies of Anishinaabe and Haudenosaunee communities (in Schoolcraft's case, such work was done with the assistance of his mixed-race wife, Jane Johnston, the daughter of a Scots-Irish fur-trader father and an Ojibwe mother).[24] By the time Johnson and Brant-Sero appeared on British and European stages, though, they were faced with a large and ever-growing body of anthropological knowledge that was presented as based in scientific bodies of "facts" about Indigenous people from both North America and beyond. Moreover, such knowledge was being institutionalized in museums and universities.[25] As historian Sadiah Qureshi has pointed out, this information was no longer being gathered exclusively from displayed peoples, as anthropologists increasingly travelled to the latter's homelands to study the cultural and social aspects of their communities. Displays of Indigenous people increasingly became seen as "spectacle, visual extravagance, and frivolity."[26]

It's not clear if Johnson and Brant-Sero appreciated the full impact of such changes; however, there is no doubt they saw that their position afforded them the chance to critique both settler government's actions and metropolitan ignorance of their peoples. Writing from the vantage point of the late-nineteenth century, in the aftermath of the Riel uprising and the increasing encroachment of the Dominion government's control over the Indigenous population, Johnson saw a history of colonial domination as being a problem for Indigenous peoples. As well as her writings on this subject, she repeatedly used the "Indian" clothing she wore in her performances – itself a hybrid of various First Nations dress – to make a political point.[27] Indigenous history, though, was not simply a narrative of exploitation and domination by Europeans. Upon returning to England in 1906, Johnson continued to insist that the British public should be "enlightened" about the Six Nations government, one inherited from the original Five Nations Confederacy. In her article, "The Lodge of the Law-Makers: Contrasts Between the Parliaments of the White Man and the Red," commissioned by the *Daily Express*, Johnson confronted and gazed upon the central symbol of the British empire and "civilization": the Houses of Parliament. In this essay, she compared the men in charge of British government and their effects on it to the government of Indigenous peoples. Johnson characterized English democracy as fickle, inconstant, and subject to whims and caprices, feminine characteristics that, at various moments, Europeans had attributed to Indigenous people. As did Maungwudaus and Copway, she also reversed the imperial pattern of the European venturing into unknown territory and took her readers into a familiar space, the Houses of Parliament, or the "abode of the wise men of this nation." Here she discovered "the tongues of these mighty men beneath the tower proclaim[ing] their dominion over all the wildernesses of mankind in these island kingdoms of the East."[28]

Yet for all their might and their aggressive speech, these "old men and young" who were "debating with great spirit" were no matches for Indigenous statesmen. Here Johnson sought to overturn another colonial stereotype of Indigenous masculinity: that of the monosyllabic and ignorant "Indian." Her assessment of British political debate found it lacking in diplomacy, marked by a poverty of symbolism, and possessed of far less respect or knowledge of the rhetoric prized by Indigenous politicians. As would Brant-Sero, in her public performances Johnson took great pains to construct Iroquois masculinity not as martial "savagery" but rather as comprised of the skilled and wise use of rhetoric, diplomacy, and statesmanship, deployed in ways that were superior to the efforts of British men.

Johnson made two other important points about gendered forms of government in this article. She critiqued the rigidity of British customs concerning the eldest son's succession to his father's peerage and compared this practice to that of the Iroquois, who chose the most capable son to be chief. Furthermore, "will the white man who considers us a savage, unenlightened race wonder if I told him that the fate of our 'Senate' lies in the hands of the women of our tribes?" Like Brant-Sero, who also reminded his international audiences of the importance of the role of women in Iroquois politics, Johnson believed that this feature of Iroquois society rendered it far more "progressive" and advanced than that of the imperial power. "I have heard that the daughters of this vast city cry out for a voice in the Parliament of this land. There is no need for an Iroquois woman to clamour for recognition in our councils; she has had it for upwards of four centuries." Johnson then explained the role of the clan matron, "the eldest woman of each of the noble families," in choosing men of their families as Iroquois chiefs. "From her cradle-board she is taught to judge men and their intellectual qualities, their aptness for public life, and their integrity." Her decision was unquestioned and final and, when the chief's title was conferred, the chief matron "may if she so desires, enter the council-house and publicly make an address to the chiefs, braves, and warriors assembled, and she is listened to not only with attention, but respect." Johnson concluded by pointing out that "there are fifty matrons possessing this right in the Iroquois Confederacy. I have not yet heard of fifty white women even among those of noble birth who may speak and be listened to in the lodge of the law-makers here."[29] Thus, gender roles and relations within Haudenosaunee society were far more egalitarian than those of Britain, a country where women did not play a part in the "lodge" of Westminster and where, in rallies, public concerts, and at Speaker's Corner in Hyde Park, the gendered nature of this "lodge" was being hotly contested.

Johnson thus challenged and reversed the dominant colonial narrative of Indigenous women's lives, one that, as we have seen, had been a tale told many times in both settler and metropolitan society. Such a narrative was predicated on Indigenous women's suffering in conditions of servitude and subjection to Indigenous men, a state alleviated only by the enlightened intervention of Christian missionaries and British civilization.[30] Moreover, by suggesting a different role for women in Haudenosaunee society, Johnson also attempted to create a concept of its masculinity that she felt was far superior to British middle-class "manliness." In her eyes, not only were Iroquois men more gifted in rhetoric and diplomacy and not reducible to the physicality of a "warrior," they also were more egalitarian men who welcomed women's strength and wisdom instead of fearing and denigrating them.

Brant-Sero, too, presumed to lecture Britain – instead of being lectured – about Indigenous peoples. As a self-styled expert on Mohawk customs and traditions, Brant-Sero assumed the status of an educator, one who was able to impart knowledge to an imperial audience that he felt was likely to be ignorant or hold distorted stereotypes of Indigenous Canadians. In his delivery of papers to learned organizations or lectures to public audiences on Mohawk history, political organization, and religion, Brant-Sero thus challenged an important trope of imperial policy towards Indigenous peoples, one initially set in place by the British government and then elaborated on by Dominion officials: that of the pitiful "Indian," ignorant and unlearned, mired in superstition, and lacking education, social norms, and economic and political organization.

Indigenous men were well-versed in government, education, and religion and therefore should not be considered as subjugated by a paternalistic imperial government. They also claimed a history of recurring military alliance with Britain. This history could be deployed strategically to challenge contemporary imperial policy. In his 1901 letter to *The Times* about his experiences in South Africa, Brant-Sero identified himself as "a humble Canadian Mohawk Indian, hailing from the Six Nations Reserve, Brant County, Ontario." He had gone to the Cape colony to enlist in a mounted rifle regiment, but "not being a man of European descent, I was refused to do active service in Her Majesty's cause as did my forefathers in Canada." Brant-Sero's problem had been, it seemed, the fact that "I was too genuine a Canadian"; he was pronounced "unfit" by an officer who "simply remarked, very good-naturedly, 'There is nothing serious; don't you worry.'" Brant-Sero did find a position at the Queenstown remount depot, where his duties "consisted in taking animals up to the front and bossing the Kaffirs."[31]

After realizing his quest for a military position was futile, Brant-Sero resigned and went to Cape Town, where he happened to meet William Merritt, a Canadian major in the Colonial Division and "an old friend" from Brant-Sero's days with the Ontario Historical Society. Merritt attempted to help Brant-Sero, but, after numerous inquiries, found that "the authorities refuse absolutely to enlist others than of European descent to do the fighting in the war." However, Merritt felt "you deserve every credit for your patriotism, which, however, is nothing more than I should expect from one of our faithful allies and friends, the Six Nations Indians." Brant-Sero went on to point out that a "history of Canada cannot be written impartially without recounting the warlike deeds of the Six Nations. We believe we have an interest in the empire, bought by the blood of our ancestors." The readers of *The Times* were then given a short history of Joseph Brant's alliance with the British in 1776 and the Six Nations' subsequent migration north to the Grand River and Bay of Quinte (where they were now peaceful and prosperous).[32]

Brant-Sero's use of Merritt's testimony attested to his own respectability and fitness to serve the empire, past and present, but, more importantly, the letter was also a testimony to the ironies, contradictions, and hypocrisies of empire: those men deemed suitable imperial allies in one context were not even credible imperial subjects in another. They might appear onstage as members of Wild West shows, a show-space performance that could be encouraged and possibly even celebrated. However, in the theatre of imperial warfare they were to be kept firmly in the wings, their place backstage at the depot, not centre stage on the field of battle. Furthermore, his account also suggests how particular notions of gender and race – including his own – might have shaped imperial practices. Brant-Sero's letter testifies to the desire of the imperial authorities to keep non-white men, particularly South Asians, out of the field of battle, as they feared that, if such men defeated white opponents, they might then decide to overthrow British colonizers "at home."[33] Brant-Sero's experience also suggests that, by the late-nineteenth century, Mohawk men were not included in the pantheon of "martial races," those Scots, Sikhs, and Gurkhas who were seen as paragons of military masculinity, their strengths as fierce fighters indispensable to the Empire's security.[34] Thus, in the gendered and racial hierarchy of early-twentieth-century imperialism, Mohawk men were able only to exercise power over – in the case of "the Kaffirs" that Brant-Sero "bossed around" – other, even more subordinate, men. Although he did not elaborate on this point, Brant-Sero, like Johnson, appears to have subscribed to imperial discourses of racial hierarchies in which certain Indigenous people occupied a higher status than others, discourses that some Indigenous people mobilized and put to their own use.[35]

Johnson and Brant-Sero, then, created for their audiences the personas of a "Indigenous woman" and a "Indigenous man" as vehicles who, again and again, gazed upon, assessed, and found British society wanting, not least through its "unenlightened" notions of gender relations. Yet it would be misleading to focus only on this dimension of Brant-Sero's and Johnson's writings and speeches, to see them as simply the defenders of Indigenous societies, who refused both the imperial gaze and imperial society. Unlike Maungwudaus, who portrayed himself as a "Red Indian" untutored in the ways of Europeans, both Johnson and Brant-Sero presented themselves very clearly and consciously to the British public as "educated Indians," who, because of their backgrounds, were fluent in English, aware of English society's cultural and social mores and manners, and did not feel out of place on London's concert platforms or in its drawing rooms and lecture halls. The theme of Indigenous progress – again, particularly that of Indigenous men – through the acceptance of at least some British customs and education also ran through their writings, particularly those of Brant-Sero.[36] To no small extent, this position was, as we have seen, a refutation of "ignorant savagery," the kind of stereotype that "The Noble Savage" dealt in. Brant-Sero asserted the ability of Indigenous peoples to learn from other cultures (while not denying their own) when and if necessary (just as Europeans had been dependent on Indigenous knowledge for their very survival in North America). It was also part of claiming a kinship between themselves and their imperial audiences, part of the process of establishing the fundamental humanity of those who had been seen as only barely possessing such an attribute. While others, such as Jones and Nahneebahweequa, had appealed to their metropolitan audiences' emotional sensibilities, Brant-Sero instead reminded the latter that they shared with Indigenous people the capacity and ability to acquire and deploy knowledge. Although he was by no means above playing on his audiences' senses, particularly when it came to personal display, nevertheless Brant-Sero insisted, with Johnson, that they be seen as intelligent, rational human beings.

Both also made a point about the specificity of Indigenous identities when they discussed Indigenous "progress" through their use of British institutions. As the previous passages suggest, they often lectured their audiences on the adaptability of, and advancements made by, the Six Nations, especially the Mohawk.[37] However, both Johnson and Brant-Sero felt that the Six Nations presented a special case: from the Six Nations had come men who were teachers, lawyers, government officials, and other professionals; the Six Nations were a model of agricultural productivity (albeit part of their economic heritage and not just because of British beneficence in teaching them farming); the conduct of Indigenous men and women on the reserve was marked by morality and dignity.[38] As Johnson put it to an interviewer from *The Gazette*, "I am an Iroquois, and, of course, I think the Iroquois are the best Indians in civilization and birth, just as you English think you are better than the Turks."[39]

Not only did they use colonial history to demonstrate their particular position within the empire, Johnson and Brant-Sero's privileging of the "Iroquois" also constituted a refusal of imperialist attempts to homogenize Indigenous peoples. As First Nations and other scholars argue, the "Indian" was a European creation, one that collapsed a huge variety of languages, political structures, social and cultural systems, and spiritual beliefs (and in fact denied that such things even existed) into the colonial stereotype of the half-clothed, impassive, and warlike (albeit to be admired for "his" martial qualities) male "savage."[40] Brant-Sero and Johnson asserted the specific patterns of Iroquois history and political and social organization, including their different gender relations and roles, in the face of British popular culture that saw "Indians" in the terms of boys' adventure tales and Wild West shows: Plains peoples who wore loin cloths and sometimes eagle-feathered bonnets, "natural" horsemen armed with rifles and tomahawks.[41] Such images and symbols, of course, not only helped contribute to a stereotype of Indigenous peoples as masculine and often omitted Indigenous women entirely; they also suggested that Indigenous masculinity was one-dimensional, having no meaning other than that of violent corporeality.

It was this one-dimensional masculinity that Brant-Sero and Johnson, in both their speeches and their personas, attempted to subvert. However, as the passages quoted above suggest, both had far less to say to their British audiences about Mohawk women's role in modernity. To be sure, Johnson and Brant-Sero emphasized the role of women in political decision-making as an important feature of Iroquois society. When asked by a *Daily News* reporter if the Six Nations' traditions were "handed down from father to son," Brant-Sero replied, "no, no, from mother to daughter. In our Indian tribes the woman is of more importance than the man. They preserve the customs and were the depositories of the traditions of the race. If a warrior died in battle, it was the women who recorded his deeds and preserved his memory. They were better educated than the men."[42] Yet, when Brant-Sero argued that, while his people's role outside reserves was growing, it was Indigenous men, not women, who were in "every profession and calling," although they did not care for the ministry or for shopkeeping.[43] He jokingly suggested during his time in Chicago that "Indian girls" could be usefully employed as domestic servants, being brought from "Reservation Schools" and led to "the graceful arts of smashing crockery and reasoning with the Ice Man." Such a comment implied Brant-Sero was aware of the domestic training schemes set up by the United States government for Indigenous girls and young women, and that he saw them (as did others, albeit for different reasons) as a failure and waste of time.[44] In his account, Indigenous women were best confined, literally and metaphorically, to the reserve and to one – albeit critically important – culture. In contrast, their male counterparts were eager participants in multiple aspects of modern Canadian society. Brant-Sero's vision of Indigenous women therefore denied them the cultural complexity he himself embraced, for redeeming the "Iroquois man" from a limited notion of "his" capacities was as much an act of self-redemption as an assertion of collective racial pride. While Brant-Sero felt free to play with and transgress racial boundaries of identity and culture, his contravention stopped short when it came to the delineations of gender.

For Johnson's part, in her poetry and prose Indigenous women receive greater attention, and their historical and contemporary "plight" under colonialism is highlighted and decried.[45] Yet, as Veronica Strong-Boag and Carole Gerson point out in their biographical study of Johnson, Johnson herself held notions of gender relations in Haudenosaunee society that often tended towards essentialist, organic conceptions of women's and men's positions in it.[46] Like Brant-Sero, Johnson applauded such women as cultural guardians, but in designating them the "keepers of tradition," she tended to place them outside the very milieus in which she herself participated, milieus much closer to those of her own English mother than to her female Haudenosaunee relatives. Why she felt compelled to rescue and redeem the reputation of Haudenosaunee men is not an easy question to answer. It may well have been that in focusing on them, constructing their masculinity in a more multi-dimensional manner, and allowing them to "travel" across the boundaries of English and Haudenosaunee culture, Johnson was shaping representations of these men that were similar, yet not identical, to her own. It may have been too personally and politically difficult for her to create an "Iroquois woman" whose life and subjectivity mirrored her own, given that her notions of Iroquois cultural survival were invested in women's embodiment of "tradition": as the daughter of a white mother, Johnson's relationship to the Haudenosaunee was a complicated one, since membership was reckoned through matrilineal ties. Yet an "Iroquois man" who successfully embodied hybridity might reassure Johnson, concerned about her people's entanglements with modernity, that such an encounter would not end in tragedy for the Haudenosaunee. Although, as we shall see, Johnson's performances were those of Indigenous and European womanhood, her use of the pen name "Tekahionwake" hints at the adoption of a masculine persona, as it had been her grandfather's name (it is doubtful, though, whether her English audience would have associated it with either a male or female Mohawk identity). Finally, in her writings about gender in Haudenosaunee society, Johnson may also have been thinking about her father. George Johnson crossed a number of ethnocultural boundaries, both in his marriage to Emily Howells and in his work as an interpreter and mediator between the colonial government and Haudenosaunee society.

Furthermore, as we have seen in the case of Jones and Copway, Johnson and Brant-Sero dealt not only with the mingling of races and cultures but also with "movement through space and time," a mobility they shared with other imperial travellers.[47] Not only had Johnson and Brant-Sero "moved" literally across the Atlantic, in their writings and interviews they sought to reverse the process, to transport their audiences across the Atlantic to not just Canada but, more specifically, to Haudenosaunee territory. For Brant-Sero, such a movement might be through space to the Six Nations community at the Grand River, or it might be through time to the bodies of Mohawk men fighting alongside their colonial allies in the War of 1812. Johnson also used this rhetorical strategy of temporal and geographic movement on a number of occasions, in such articles as "The Lodge of the Law-Makers." She made even more extensive use of it in her comparison of Iroquois and English religion, "A Pagan in St Paul's," an article also commissioned for the London paper, the *Daily Express*, during her 1906 visit. (Her readers may well have been familiar with its Queen Anne statue in the cathedral's courtyard, on the plinth of which is the figure of a feathered "Indian," whose foots rests on a severed European head.) Taking her audience inside the cathedral, Johnson transported them from a service taking place to the Onondaga longhouse on the Six Nations reserve.[48] In this piece, as in others, Johnson adopted the stance of a "Red Indian," an innocent being enlightened by her forays into the empire's centre, a position of potential naïveté that Johnson herself, with her family background and childhood experiences, most certainly did not occupy. And while terms such as "Red Indian" and "paleface" may have reinforced imperial stereotypes, placed alongside Johnson's challenge to Christianity they suggested a heightened degree of performativity to her writing, a degree of self-awareness that mocked the imperial power's ignorance of the complexity of Haudenusaunee spirituality.[49]

Fig. 6.2
Pauline Johnson in her "English" evening gown, 1894

Playing Indian, Playing European

If Johnson had less to say to her British audiences about the place of Indigenous women in modernity, she herself continuously and repeatedly represented herself as one in which English and Haudenosaunee cultures were entangled, an identity that involved various forms of racial crossings. Such a performance distinguished both Johnson and Brant-Sero from Maungwudaus, whose appearances, while no less strategic, were consistently those of an "Indian" of the Upper Canadians woods. In many ways they harkened back to the use by Jones and his contemporaries of both the black suit of the European missionary and Anishinaabe clothing.

To be sure, Johnson crafted a persona of an "authentic Indian," but then complicated matters by also being photographed performing as an upper-class "British" woman, resplendent in the gowns and hairstyles of late-Victorian high fashion.[50] In 1894 she proudly modelled her "first English dinner dress," purchased at John Barker's in Kensington, part of the West End's elegant and modern shopping centres."[51] High fashion – the draped, embroidered, and velvet- or lace-trimmed gowns, the moulded waists produced by corsets, and the upswept hairstyles – was as much a part of Johnson's public appearances as her loosely cut, fringed buckskin dresses with their feathers and beads, her wampum belts, and her loose, shoulder-length hair. In choosing the dress of London's West End, Johnson also linked herself with that late-Victorian and Edwardian milieu identified as "the locus of middle- and upper-class women's amusement, social life, and politics."[52]

As Strong-Boag and Gerson point out, in many ways Johnson resembled a "New Woman," a category that was the subject of considerable discussion in turn-of-the-century England.[53] After all, she was an independent female traveller, a woman who supported herself and who appeared in public, as well as publishing her prose and poetry, in order to make her living. But far from being the "unmanageable wife, frustrated spinster, and street-corner demagogue," typologies which theatre historians Joel Kaplan and Sheila Stowell have suggested represented "new womanhood" on the West End stage, Johnson personified Kaplan and Stowell's first category, that of the "liberated bachelor girl."[54] As part of that persona, Johnson was also fond of outdoors recreation. Her love of canoeing, in particular, was presented as part of her Indigenous heritage, although it could also be read as symptomatic of the late-nineteenth-century urban middle-class need for rest and

Fig. 6.3
Pauline Johnson in her Indigenous performance dress

rejuvenation through "nature" (a need that frequently conflated Indigenous peoples with the landscape that was providing this respite).[55]

Not only was Johnson part of the New Woman's world of increased freedom of movement, economic self-sufficiency, and consumption, she also was a public performer, part of late-Victorian and Edwardian London's myriad forms of theatrical representation.[56] To be sure, Johnson and her manager used carefully delineated boundaries of genre and space to guard her appearances. On her first trip to London, Johnson appeared in private recitals in aristocratic homes, often at the invitation of women patrons, thereby cultivating a class-based aura of refinement that helped domesticate her status as an "exotic colonial."[57] Her 1906 performances, while for "public" consumption, were held on concert-hall platforms, not in the mass commercialism of the music-hall or Gaiety stages, venues noted for representations of racialized "others" or "New Women."[58] Nor did she participate in displays of Canadian Indigenous peoples in colonial exhibitions; in fact, it might be said that she deliberately kept aloof from them. Just like Nahneebahweequa in her refusal to appear before Victoria in "Indian" dress, Johnson was aware of the need to deploy her public image carefully, conscious of the possibility of being misjudged by audiences.

Yet if Johnson did not wish to be part of the music hall or exhibition, in many ways she adapted a particular theatrical style of the late-nineteenth century (albeit not the new theatre of George Bernard Shaw, Oscar Wilde, or Harley Granville Barker). While her recitals were not accompanied by lavish sets, lighting, or props, they made use of grand theatrical gestures, poses, and vocal styling that, in all likelihood, Johnson had perfected from her trips to West End theatres, as well as from elocutionists in Canada. At venues such as Daly's and the Lyceum, she had seen well-known actors such as Eleanora Duse, Sarah Bernhardt, Ellen Terry, and Henry Irving, known for their interpretations of classical and Shakespearean plays.[59] Her recitals also featured the spectacle of her body, first clothed in the bricolage of her "Indian" clothing and then costumed in European evening dress. Such choices were not simply whims on Johnson's part; rather, they were made within the moral economy of imperialism, one in which clothing served many purposes and carried a number of political messages. As historian Antoinette Burton has argued for South Asian travellers in London during the 1880s, "Indigenous" dress might be both a source of unwelcome attention and one of pride.[60] Wearing both moccasins and evening slippers, fringed buckskin and décolletage, could be a means of playing with boundaries, a way of appropriating identities – such as that of "the lady" – denied to colonized

Fig. 6.4
Pauline Johnson, canoeing on the Grand River, 1890s.

women by colonial authorities. Such shifting forms of representations of femininity were Johnson's assertion of her capacity to cope with both sets of racialized femininities, removing Johnson herself, Mohawk women specifically, and Indigenous women in general from the realm of Wild West shows and a particular racist stereotype (one increasing in popularity in Canada) of the drunken, dirty, illiterate, and potentially dangerous "squaw," the kind of image that Bella Hardisty would have encountered as Lady Strathcona in elite metropolitan circles in personal and painful ways.[61] Moreover, the ease with which Johnson switched identities on stage underscored that these racially charged categories of womanhood were as artificial as the forms of dress that represented them. Johnson's mixed-race background, her (relatively) more privileged upbringing, and her ease with English cultural forms gave her the confidence to move between "Indian" dress and English clothing with a degree of ease. In this regard, then, her presentation of self differed considerably from that of Nahneebahweequa's; in some ways, not least her flair and confidence, Johnson more closely resembled John Norton, Copway, and Brant-Sero.

But in addition to its significance within colonial ways of seeing and assigning meanings, switching identity through dress was also common to British popular culture in this period. Music-hall stars, such as Vesta Tilley, for example, were noted for cross-dressing; moreover, actresses attired in the height of fashion appeared with growing frequency on West End stages throughout the decades of Johnson's London trips.[62] As well, Johnson's performance partner, Walter McRaye, dramatized "habitant" (Quebec peasant) songs and dances, routines that were not unlike the "Scotch," "Irish," and "Yorkshiremen" sketches of the music hall – not least because McRaye, like the "stage Irishmen," was decidedly not a habitant.[63]

Brant-Sero's appearances upon the stage are not as well-recorded as Johnson's. The only extant description of his Wild West frontier show, produced in Britain, appears in a 1900 interview he gave in Chicago. His participation in this type of production was not, of course, unusual for Indigenous peoples during this period.[64] But in *On the Frontier*, Brant-Sero claimed to have played not one of the Mohawks, but instead a white man, Bill Morley. That, Brant-Sero stated, "was my strong part, for I spoke to those real Indians – whom I had brought with me from Canada – in genuine Mohawk, and it never failed to bring the house down." In the same interview, Brant-Sero also claimed to have appeared in one of Joe Murphy's Toronto productions as a "stocky Hibernian lad, playing a fiddle at an Irish wake."[65] His desire to emphasize "Indian authenticity" by his leadership of "real Indians" to whom he spoke Mohawk also played to the late-Victorian desire for colonial subjects' authenticity. Brant-Sero's "lectures," for example, were advertised in ways that highlighted his performance of "Mohawk" music. One wonders how the majority of his audiences would have known how to "authenticate" his claim.[66]

To no small degree, of course, Brant-Sero's theatre appearances were probably dictated simply by financial exigency. How many ways of making a living "abroad" were open to him, after all? As did Maungwudaus, both Johnson and Brant-Sero profited from – indeed, built their careers in the metropolis on – the opportunities afforded them by the fascination of imperial audiences with "exotic others" (although curiously enough neither of them showed any public awareness or interest in the other).[67] Yet Brant-Sero's economic situation is not the only issue to consider. Like Johnson's use of European women's clothing, his choice of dress must also be analyzed as part of the multiple contexts – with their opportunities for "repetition and reiteration" of his persona – in which he and Johnson moved and which they embodied.[68] For one, his appearances can be seen as part of late-Victorian

Fig. 6.5
John Ojijatekha Brant-Sero, n.d.

Fig. 6.6
John Ojijatekha Brant-Sero, London, c. 1912

and Edwardian British masculine theatrical performance. In publicity photographs, Brant-Sero appears somewhat of a dandy, whose taste for sartorial display placed him on a cultural spectrum between the music hall's Champagne Charlie and a Wildean cultivation of detail. In Brant-Sero's case, his hair, not the buttonhole or tie, probably served as a means for self-expression.[69] His use of Indigenous dress was, to be sure, an assertion of Haudenosaunee "identity," but it also could be viewed as a rebuke to the sobriety and dullness of turn-of-the-century respectable British male attire, yet another assertion that he was constructing Mohawk masculinity as *not* being confined to a "fraught and narrow cultural space."[70] In other photographs, though, Brant-Sero donned a black suit, the type of clothing favoured by Jones; like Jones, though, it is likely that his hair and skin colour prevented him from blending into the (European) crowd.

And in his most flamboyant and obviously performative appearance, the Folkestone male beauty pageant, Brant-Sero appears to have been playing with a number of gendered and racial signs and tropes. He had often praised the physiques and clothing of his Mohawk ancestors, so it is possible that he was constructing and celebrating the physical manifestations of a performed Indigenous masculinity. He also may have been "reiterating and repeating" his refutation, a point he made in a number of press interviews, of the commonly held imperialist belief that his people were a "dying race."[71] Instead, Brant-Sero himself might literally embody his counter-argument: that they were very much alive and were thriving. In both his celebration of Indigenous masculinity and his determination to disrupt Europeans' notions of his people, Brant-Sero resembled both Norton and Copway's insouciance and outward equanimity in front of metropolitan audiences.

His bodily display also may have been part of the late-Victorian and Edwardian "strong man" craze, linked to the transatlantic cult of the muscular male body. By 1908, Brant-Sero had spent enough time in and around England's theatres to be aware of this genre that, as historian Dave Russell has pointed out, reflected the concerns of the metropolis over imperialism and national efficiency and sought to assuage them.[72] Yet in his case, Brant-Sero's physical display could tweak, not placate, imperial anxieties over white men's lack of physical "development" and "progress," even though he did come in second to the captain of the Folkestone life-boat team.[73] While I have no evidence to suggest that he consciously modelled himself on the well-known African-American boxer Jack Johnson, who, as Gail Bederman has shown, openly taunted white men about their physical and sexual capabilities, Brant-Sero's use of a specifically racially inflected form of masculine physical display, his insistence on Mohawk men's superiority, and even his relationships with white women suggest a similar dynamic may have been at work. In these aspects of his life, Brant-Sero also bore a marked resemblance to Copway.[74]

Nor should we overlook Brant-Sero's pleasure in taking part in such a spectacle. Brant-Sero was noted for having a sense of humour, and may have relished the transgressive and ironic aspects of appearing in a Wild West show as a white man, as a male beauty-pageant contestant who represented "Indians," and on other occasions donning a suit and reciting Shakespeare: reversals, although with "different trajectories of power relations," of black-face performances in late-Victorian minstrel shows.[75] Brant-Sero was unlikely to have used the phrase "hybridity" to describe his behaviour or persona; nevertheless, his interviews suggest he was no great respecter of the borders of imperialism, the segregation of imperial ruler and imperial "knowledge" from *supposed* imperial subjects. Just as Johnson may have used two sets of clothing to make political points about the artificiality of imperialism's constructions of "respectable womanhood," Brant-Sero displayed little patience with the binary categories of the imperial power's definitions of masculinity, its cleavage of "men" into the hierarchies of "civilized" and "savage." He enjoyed, for example, telling his audiences about Mohawk men's history of martial prowess and then startling them by showing how the "classics" of English literature, such as *Othello*, could be transposed into Mohawk.[76]

Of course, Johnson and Brant-Sero did not suddenly invent themselves as a Mohawk woman or man within the British context. Unlike Burton's colonial travellers, who by and large learned the meanings of being an "Indian" through their travels to Britain, they had been performing being "Indigenous" in white society in Canada and the United States, a production that was well rehearsed before either set foot on a British stage.[77] Yet it was one thing to appear before audiences in the context of settler society, either reciting poetry about the 1885 Riel uprising or performing in a Wild West production, a context in which the relations of power between colonized and colonizer were being clearly drawn over issues such as treaties, residential schooling, and the suppression of Indigenous cultural practices.[78] Movement through time and space does appear to have been somewhat easier to achieve for Brant-Sero and Johnson in the context of imperial London or Liverpool.[79] Just as earlier British audiences with humanitarian leanings may have found it easier to support John Sunday, Jones, and Nahneebahweequa than did Upper Canadians, there may well have been less at stake for British audiences who came to hear Johnson's recitations or listen to Brant-Sero's lectures. Metropolitan audiences need not feel directly responsible for the plight of Indigenous peoples under colonialism or as threatened and challenged by Brant-Sero and Johnson's harsher denunciations of imperial policy and practices. It was the British monarch, after all, not the "Canadian" parliament, to whom Indigenous people appealed as a more just and impartial authority, one whose relationship with Indigenous nations predated provincial and national governments.[80]

The Perils and Possibilities of Performance

Nevertheless, Johnson's and Brant-Sero's freedom to play with boundaries in front of an audience less invested in their specific imperial histories should not be confused with an audience somehow "liberated" from particular forms of imperial knowledge. As cultural historian Peter Bailey has argued, both artists and audiences in the period's music halls shared a form of knowledge of working-class life that united those on both sides of the proscenium.[81] In a similar vein, both these performers shared with their audiences a familiarity with the stereotypes of the "Indian." But knowingness might have its limits, and, by its very nature, performance was a dangerous affair. No matter the degree of careful planning and rehearsal, any number of things might go awry. An audience might hear the performer's words imperfectly or not at all; cues might be jumped or missed completely. Despite Johnson and Brant-Sero's constant reminders that they, too, shared their audiences' membership in the British Empire and therefore possessed their own form of imperial "knowingness," nevertheless their audiences may have watched them from a very different vantage point. And despite the multiple possibilities of hybridity and the potentially liberating aspects of performance, I suspect that neither Brant-Sero nor Johnson could entirely escape the images of either savagery or of passive acceptance of the inevitable (death or assimilation) that constituted many Britons' knowledge of Indigenous culture. Witness, for example, the attitudes evident in the press coverage of the 1844 Cadotte-Haynes marriage. Brant-Sero and Johnson were still forced to contend with a general public that in other venues understood the meanings of "Indian" through very narrowly defined and stereotypical meanings of the masculine corporeal, an audience that played its part in other types of imperial spectacles, other "show-spaces," by appreciating either the "noble savage" or the "vicious warrior."[82] Was it likely that English audiences would attach a confederated form of government, or the significance of clan mothers, to the body of meanings that already comprised the image of the "Indian"? It is difficult to know how certain aspects of Johnson and Brant-Sero's messages about the relationship of the Haudenosaunee and Indigenous peoples to Britain were received: whether, for example, their stance of simultaneous refusal of and commitment to "empire" was read reductively, as one of an "either/or." The specificities of their position and histories may simply not have occurred to those who gathered to hear Johnson recite her poetry or watched Brant-Sero parade on the Folkestone pier.

The distinctions and differences between these two performers also remind us not to overlook the varying configurations of social relations in which performances have been embedded, those "conditions of [performances'] emergence and operation."[83] Johnson's family background, her informal education in English culture at the hands of her English mother, and her performances of English "gentility" allowed her to enter the world of the English aristocracy, to gain their patronage and "take tea" at Westminster. While he did not lack a circle of patrons, not least his English wife, Frances Kirby, Brant-Sero did not have Johnson's social connections; such wealth and influence might have allowed him to concentrate on his less-spectacular exploits, such as anthropological lectures (although, as I have noted, he seems to have enjoyed his theatrical career). Yet while class distinctions shaped the kinds of opportunities open to Johnson and Brant-Sero, they were not the only social relations to do so. Johnson's need to appear "respectable" as either a "Mohawk" or "English" woman dictated, as I have suggested, her choices of performance venue, while Brant-Sero, for his part, appeared on both the lecture platform *and* the popular stage. Financial needs certainly played a role in his decision to do so, but I would speculate that Brant-Sero did not risk masculine "respectability" in choosing a wider range of venues. Despite the new opportunities that the metropole offered middle-class women, for Johnson it may have been far too great a gamble to appear in venues that featured risqué songs, gestures, and poses (not to mention costumes).[84] In popular culture, the line separating chaste "Indian poetesses" from promiscuous "squaws" was one all too easily crossed in the eyes of white audiences, a situation to which Johnson was sensitive.[85] While Brant-Sero's appearance in a Wild West production might have been viewed askance by some, nevertheless it did not preclude him from giving papers to learned societies. Moreover, while Johnson and Brant-Sero were interviewed by the press and were also able to write about their impressions of England, as we have seen, other Indigenous women and men were unable to do so, either because they did not speak English or were "spoken for" by a promoter.

Conclusion

It is difficult – perhaps impossible – to know what their travels meant to Johnson and Brant-Sero on a personal level. Unlike many of their non-Indigenous Canadian counterparts who travelled to Britain and Europe during this period, they did not leave travel diaries, nor did they bequeath historians much in the way of travel correspondence.[86] But to see Johnson and Brant-Sero or their Anishinaabe predecessors as public performers, or to raise questions about their reception, does not mean that they must be relegated to the realm of "inauthenticity" and thus dismissed as simply "white men's – or imaginary – Indians."[87] Rather, it is more fruitful to see such performances by colonial subjects as part of the complex strategies of representation and negotiation that they forged from the very limited menu offered by imperialism's contingencies, strategies described by anthropologist James Clifford as a "pragmatic response, making the best of given (often bad) situations."[88] As Clifford argues, in this process "an ability to sustain and rearticulate a sense of who one is by appropriating, cutting, and mixing cultural forms appears as a significant alternative to homogenizing, normalizing disciplines exercised at national and transnational levels."[89]

Furthermore, we cannot examine these responses and rearticulations without considering the many ways in which gender relations were both integral to and shaped by them. While Johnson and Brant-Sero brought their own cultural and political understandings to their imperial performances of Haudenosaunee femininity and masculinity, simultaneously the conditions and contexts of imperial modernity, which they helped shape, also moulded the choices they made and the messages they tried to convey. To no small degree, the "agency" they exercised resided within the power relations of turn-of-the-century imperialism and not solely as an oppositional power relation.[90] To make that observation is not to deny that rearticulations of gender and race might produce unpredictable results, such as a Mohawk man writing to The Times to protest his exclusion from imperial warfare. As cultural historian Della Pollock argues, performances can generate transformation, a surplus that can "generate something more: more agency, more pleasure and possibility, more conflict and contention."[91] But Johnson and Brant-Sero's travels within the matrix of imperial modernity remind us that such surpluses, such transformations, and such pleasures, possibilities, and conflicts are produced within – not detached from – historically specific places and times.

To be sure, as we have seen, the challenges Brant-Sero and Johnson faced were not dissimilar to that experienced by those who had gone before them in the 1830s and 1840s: no matter how cogently Maungwudaus couched his critique of British society, he too was at risk of being seen as both savage and freak show. Yet Johnson and Brant-Sero also brought to the metropolitan stage their specific histories and modes of performance, which both gestured to and cut across cultural boundaries, testifying to the many changes the nineteenth century had brought to the Six Nations of the Grand River. They also encountered a changed context for performances of indigeneity in metropolitan show-spaces, a context in which their messages about complexity and cultural adaptation were in danger of being drowned out by carnivalesque spectacles of "savage others." Nevertheless, Brant-Sero and Johnson also contrived to create their own "show-stages," platforms they deployed for their own complicated engagements with and travels through empire.

. 7 .

An Ending – and an Epilogue

Indigenous peoples' mobility has always been seen as a
problem ... First we were too mobile to make any claims
to the land, then we were seen as not mobile enough, and
therefore backwards. Reserves were imposed on us to restrict
our movement and our claim to the land. But there was always
movement – for potlatching or trading or intermarriage, or
along waterways for fishing.[1]
>   *Sarah Hunt*

As the above quote from Sarah Hunt, a Kwagiulth scholar of critical indigenous geographies at the University of British Columbia suggests, mobility has
had a vital, if often fraught, relationship to the lives of Indigenous peoples
under settler colonialism. But as she points out, despite the wishes of the
government, "there was always movement." To be sure, *Travellers through
Empire* looks at movement often undertaken precisely because of the colonial
state's actions: the Indigenous people's mobility explored in this book took
place at a time when many men, women, and children in the British world
were "on the move," their voyages having direct and often deleterious effects
on Indigenous peoples' lives. It also, though, suggests that such Indigenous
movement had multiple dimensions, multiple valences, and involved multiple actors, as Indigenous travellers petitioned the Crown, appealed to
humanitarian sentiment, reminded British audiences of military alliances,
performed Indigenous culture, and became part of imperial networks, public
and intimate.

Travel, it is sometimes claimed, broadens the mind. By venturing into new places and encountering previously unmet societies and their residents, their novel sights, smells, and sounds, human beings educate themselves and become transformed in this process. For one, that was how many nineteenth-century North Americans who ventured across the Atlantic to Britain and Europe conceived of their voyages: as entertainment, to be sure, but also as education.[2]

For the men, women, and children who people the pages of this book, travel might well be an education, yet it might not constitute the kind of liberal pedagogy that nineteenth-century travel writers and enthusiasts contemplated. "Education" for many of these travellers could mean an introduction to the technological wonders of the Liverpool docks, to the throngs of people and goods that populated London, or to the pleasures of steamer trips around Scotland's lakes and coasts. It might also, though, constitute an unpleasant, if not completely surprising, reminder that being an Indigenous person exposed to metropolitan audiences meant levels of public visibility and scrutiny that were not always welcome. For children, such scrutiny could be more intimate, never-ending, and even more complicated. Not only there was no refuge or sanctuary to which they could retreat, but the eyes that assessed and judged them were those of family and friends, not strangers: aunts, uncles, cousins, and grandparents, who were charged with these children's material and emotional well-being. Movement across the Atlantic could also mean a less-than-voluntary habituation to new emotional regimes, one in which children had to learn new codes of expressing affection and gratitude and, conversely, ways of suppressing feelings of homesickness and dislocation.

Yet travel overseas could also introduce them to circles of friends and supporters, those who could assist John Norton, Peter Jones, and Nahneebahweequa (for example) in their struggles over land rights and efforts to ensure their communities' future. Such circles were not entirely new, as they were often linked to settler colonial connections and networks. Moreover, Indigenous communities had, after all, their own histories of valuing alliances and friendships, so perhaps it is not surprising that these men and women were so open to forging connections with those predisposed to help, to offer sympathy and succour. The physical and affective comfort they might provide these travellers in Britain, thus, should not be overlooked or dismissed as inconsequential. But crossing borders and oceans also meant entering networks that were shot through with emotional connections and codes, and, too, encountering reactions from audiences that were heavily freighted with emotions, whether those of pleasure, puzzlement, or a squeamish curiosity that might lead to outright revulsion. And as Chapter 3 has shown, movement and mobility might result in even more intimate connections, which could lead to the formation of new families, new networks, and new emotional communities.

Moreover, in the case of adults, because of their high levels of visibility, overseas travel also offered them the opportunity to educate, as well as be educated. As a number of these chapters have shown, many of these men and women crafted embodied histories, cultural landscapes, and ethnographies of their own communities for, they hoped, the edification of their British audiences. The particular places in which they did so differed: it might occur in the dining hall of Cambridge University, as John Norton lectured and performed his "war dance"; be delivered from the temperance and missionary-hall platforms where Peter Jones and George Copway preached about the benefits of Christianity for the Mississauga; or be presented on the stages where Pauline Johnson and John Brant-Sero gave their public performances in late-Victorian and Edwardian London. In many cases, they also provided their audiences with written texts, whether in the form of travelogues, histories, or periodical and press interviews. Their desire to explain themselves and their people to imperial authority and imperial audiences was coupled with an equally strong desire to speak back to them, as these travellers assessed, analyzed, and critiqued metropolitan men and women and the societies they had created. Wherever and however it occurred, the work of the Indigenous travellers as public pedagogues is a persistent, recurring theme throughout this book.

To be sure, the context in which they delivered such messages changed. Over the period this book covers, British imperial power expanded significantly beyond the North American settler frontier into many other parts of the globe (including the settler colonies of Australia, Aotearoa New Zealand, and the Cape Colony). Representatives of humanitarian networks in London called metropolitan attention to settler violence, the result of such expansion; and metropolitan society saw a growing number of Indigenous people arrive in its midst, often as participants (willing or not) in imperial exhibitions and displays (such as Wild West Shows). It also saw a shift in discourses around race: in the eyes of some influential British thinkers, "noble savages" became decidedly less noble, decidedly more savage. Not surprisingly, the reworking of imperial power and changes in British society had consequences for the ways in which these travellers' messages were heard and understood. While John Norton certainly found support from the humanitarians and abolitionists who welcomed him into their circles of affection and sympathy, he was also confronted by an imperial government who, so far as land claims were concerned, wished to turn responsibility for Upper Canada's Indigenous population over to settler colonial authorities, the very group that had thwarted Norton and his allies at the Grand River. At certain moments, though, metropolitan audiences, including that of the Crown, were more receptive to hearing about settler injustices and the need for humanitarian intervention. Such was the case in the 1830s and 1840s.

By the late-nineteenth century, the growth of mass popular culture in Britain, itself often imbued with representations of white British imperial supremacy, may have offered new opportunities for Indigenous performers, particularly around sport and feats of physical prowess.[3] It did so, though, in a context in which fears of white racial degeneration were rife, so that a Haudenosaunee man's desire to contribute to British imperial military dominance could not be allowed. While Pauline Johnson no doubt benefited from the presence of well-connected Canadian imperial patrons in London (such as the Strathconas, whose authority and visibility were themselves linked to imperial networks of commerce and emigration) and from changing attitudes towards the presence of middle-class women in public life, she also had to tread carefully in her public performances of Mohawk womanhood, lest she be relegated to the realm of show-spaces and treated merely as an exotic curiosity. The circumstances surrounding the presence of the fur-trade children in Britain meant that, no matter what the decade, their Cree background was meant to be subsumed by their British ancestry. It took courage, determination, and a certain amount of cultural capital (an advanced education at Scotland's universities, for example), for an individual such as Alexander Isbister to consistently identity himself as both Cree and Scottish – and to do so as a political activist.

Furthermore, the growing numbers of colonized people who appeared in metropolitan spaces may have placed an additional onus on these travellers. They might have needed, for example, to ensure that the specificities of their histories and geographies were not subsumed, not just by British imperial discourses but also by the claims of others with similar grievances with colonial governments, similar problems with settler violence, similar encroachments on their traditional territories. Furthermore, they may have had to differentiate themselves from those who had been brought by promoters to be displayed: one thinks of the careful ways in which Johnson managed her image and referred to the Mohawk as a special people, different even from other Canadian Indigenous communities. However, it is difficult to answer such questions definitively. Certainly Norton, Jones, and Copway were well aware of the troubles that settler colonialism had brought to other Indigenous nations in North America. Witness, for example, Norton's discussion of the Cherokee, Jones's relationship with the Haudenosaunee, and Copway's experiences in the American Midwest. In addition, Jones would have read about the situation of recently emancipated slaves in the Caribbean and missionary work in the Pacific and India, working as he did within the context of the global missionary movement. In the case of other travellers, apart from a few scattered, but perhaps telling, comments – Nahneebahweequa's remark about the "poor slave" who, unlike her people, could claim citizenship and land in Upper Canada, or Brant-Sero's allusion to the "kaffirs" over whom he exercised authority at the Cape – they left few explicit comparisons of themselves to other colonized people around the Empire. Following that, it doesn't seem that they actively sought to create alliances with people from other colonies, the kinds of coalitions that by the end of the nineteenth century would result in anti-imperialist conferences and activism.[4] To be sure, such a topic deserves more attention from Canadian historians. However, so far as these travels through empire were concerned, the frameworks these travellers drew upon were those of their own nations and communities, their points of connection within imperial networks, primarily with sympathetic and supportive elements of settler society, and – more commonly – within the metropole.[5]

Finally, while my focus throughout *Travellers through Empire* has been on the travellers themselves, it is worth considering if and how their voyages can help us rethink the history of the British Empire. To some extent, answering this question relies on being able to gauge audience perception and reception, something that can only be uneven and partial. For every written reaction we have, whether that of Headley, who wrote of Norton's Cambridge appearance (whether with approval or ambivalence), that of Richard Cobden, who doubted George Copway's authenticity, and those of the British relatives and schoolteachers who wrote about a fur-trade child's progress (or supposed lack of it), there would have been many others whose thoughts about these visitors were not recorded or have been lost. Of course, these travellers were not unique; as we know, others had come before them and continued to do so. But perhaps the point is not so much looking for a singularity or uniqueness that might add new dimensions to our understanding of British imperialism. Rather, by placing these travellers' experiences alongside those studied by other scholars, we can see the extent to which the metropole was a space widely claimed by multiple colonial subjects across the nineteenth century. As Coll Thrush, historian of Indigenous travel to London, whom we saw earlier, has argued, we need to acknowledge "the deep entanglement of London's places, people and histories with Indigenous places, peoples and histories, and vice versa."[6] Although I agree with Thrush, I would also say that the "deep entanglement" of which he speaks extended beyond the city's boundaries. It encompassed other urban centres, such as Bristol, Birmingham, Manchester, Liverpool, Glasgow, Edinburgh, Ayr, Inverness, Dublin, and Belfast, and it ranged across a number of public and semi-public places, such as those cities' streets, military mess halls, lecture halls, theatres, schools, and the drawing and dining rooms of these travellers' elite hosts. It also extended into domestic spaces, such as parlours, kitchens, gardens, and bedrooms. While British North America's settler government was doing its best to sequester Indigenous people, their presence in Britain suggests the obverse: a history of mingling, meeting, and entanglement that came close to spanning the country's breadth and length, reaching into its "heart" in multiple ways.

Epilogue: Memory and Indigenous Voyages into the Twenty-First Century

In 1823, John Norton vanished into the American interior, his movements lost to the historian's curious eye. In a similar manner, after 1851 it is no longer possible to trace the lives of Duncan and Donald McTavish: they too disappear from the historical record. Others suffered a similar fate.

Yet although it might be tempting, given the long-standing desire of the Canadian nation-state to assimilate Indigenous people into Canadian society (albeit never as equal members) and thus to make them vanish as "Indians," nonetheless it would be unwise to think that the memory of these travellers did not live on. To be sure, they were not the subject of the large-scale commemorative undertakings that marked the late-nineteenth and early twentieth century, a period in which English and French-Canadians crafted historical narratives of their pasts in pageants, statues, and written accounts. While such enterprises incorporated Indigenous people, they did so as foils for their central narratives, either that of the triumph of British progress and liberalism or the survival of French-Canada in a hostile New World, not as historical actors with their own motivations, desires, and trajectories.[7]

But the men and women in this book did leave a trace in Canada's historical memory. It is true that a historian seeking to discover how John

Fig. 7.1
John Norton Statue, Landscape of Nations Monument,
Queenston Heights, Ontario

Norton, Catherine Sutton, Peter Jones, George Copway, or John Brant-Sero have been publicly remembered would find a commemorative record more fragmented, frequently more local in its nature, and often more recent than that of figures such as Jacques Cartier. On 2 October 2016, for example, under an early fall downpour, a large crowd gathered to witness the unveiling of the Landscape of Nations, a memorial created at Queenston Heights in the Niagara peninsula to honour the many Indigenous allies who fought alongside Europeans in the War of 1812. Costing $1.4 million, the memorial is the product of collaborative work between Six Nations artist Raymond Skye and landscape architect Tom Ridout. It includes a Two Row Wampum trail, a memory circle, a white pine Tree of Peace, and prominent statues of John Norton and John Brant.[8] The Landscape has many purposes, one of them being to re-establish peace between those Indigenous nations who fought on different sides during the war. Moreover, it is meant to remind the non-Indigenous public that Norton, Brant, and their contemporaries played a significant role in both the Battle of Queenston Heights and overall, in the defence of "Canada." Tellingly, while non-Indigenous coverage ranged from celebrating such a defence to pointing to Canada's colonial treatment of Indigenous people (and the shoddy commemoration of Indigenous people's role in the war), it was Ava Hill, chief of the Six Nations, who pointed out that "people will be reminded of how much our people did to defend our lands, their lives and the lives of their allies."[9] The memorial does not, though, tell viewers of Norton's complicated history of travel and mobility.

Peter Jones, for his part, has been remembered with at least three plaques. One marks his and Eliza's home, Echo Villa, while the other two (one in English and one in Ojibwe) have been placed at the New Credit Council House, the work of the Historic Sites and Monuments Board and the Mississauga of the New Credit First Nation. While both remember Jones as a Mississauga chief and as an important Methodist minister, responsible for many Mississauga conversions, they diverge in other, perhaps more telling, ways that testify to the importance of place in shaping public memory. The plaque at Echo Villa in Brantford tells visitors of Jones's Welsh-Mississauga ancestry, his translation of the Gospels and hymns into Ojibwe, and of his trips to England.[10] At the New Credit, Jones's life is framed within the context of settler colonialism: residents and visitors are told that he "helped his people survive the impact of European settlements which had brought them close to extinction" and that his work to convert them and induce them "to adapt to European ways" was done "as his Band's fishing and hunting territories disappeared." While Jones himself, then, is depicted as not being

Fig. 7.2

E. Pauline Johnson stamp, 1960

entirely free of colonizing imperatives and motives, the plaque also credits him with advocating education, being "the first" to make Ojibwe a written language, and advocating in 1826 that the Band settle at the Credit River and take up farming. The text ends by telling readers that the band moved to the New Credit in 1847 as a result of "settler encroachment," forcing it to leave "the thriving village it had built."[11] Interestingly enough, though, at neither Echo Villa nor at the New Credit would a reader learn anything of Eliza Field Jones, "the white lady who married an Indian."

The public memory of others in this book is dispersed, whether at the level of their Indigenous communities or in local, non-Indigenous historical societies and memories and by the work of historians, all of which are often disseminated through websites and social media.[12] Yet, if there is one individual from *Travellers through Empire* whose memory has been perpetuated in a range of fora, it is E. Pauline Johnson. There is no doubt that Johnson's memory has been a contested, sometimes contentious, one, not least because of her sale of wampum and other fraught aspects of her relationship with her Haudenosaunee community.[13] Moreover, as historian Dianne Dodd has pointed out, the Canadian government has demonstrated considerable ambivalence at times about including Johnson in official memory, at least so far as recognition from the Historic Sites and Monuments Board has been concerned.[14] Nevertheless, she too has been remembered by the Canadian government with a stamp and with a plaque that sits on the site of her restored childhood home, Chiefswood, now a National Historic Site. The plaque's text combines Johnson's achievements as a poet and dramatic reciter who travelled to Great Britain and throughout North America with a commemoration of Chiefswood itself, "a wedding gift" built by her father, the "greatly respected" Six Nations leader Chief G.H.M. Johnson, for Johnson's English mother, "a cousin of the well-known American novelist William Dean Howells." But like Eliza Field Jones, Emily Howells is not named.[15]

In addition to these more conventional ways of remembering Johnson and her travels across the boundaries of nation, race, and belonging, Johnson's legacy as a performer lived on. Twentieth-century Indigenous performers Frances Nickawa, Ethel Brant Monture, and Bernice Loft Winslow self-consciously and openly adopted both aspects of Johnson's performance style and her material into their recitals of poetry and prose. Not only that, all three women crossed national borders in pursuit of work, opportunities to perform, and, in Winslow's case, as a result of her marriage to Massachusetts businessman Arthur H. Winslow.[16] In all three cases, Johnson's memory was maintained through an embodied, performative medium.

What, though, of memories of these travellers in Britain? While the topic of Indigenous people's commemoration and public memory in Britain is worthy of its own study, it seems that the record is an uneven, even more fragmented, one than that in the Canadian context.[17] As historian Wendy Webster has argued, the memory of Britain's imperial past in the mid-twentieth century has been diverse and complex: the former settler colonies, including Canada, figure in this memory, but primarily vis-à-vis their white residents.[18] However, the repatriation of Indigenous artifacts also has, at least at the institutional level, brought the relationship between Indigenous nations in Canada and British imperialism into public consciousness in Britain.[19] But like Canada, local memory is, I think, an important part of this story. On 24 February 1945, the *Dunfermline Press* told its readers of the town's connection to North American Indigenous people though the travels of a local man who, in the newspaper's words, "Became an Indian Chief;

Fig. 7.3
Ethel Brant Monture, by Irma Council, c. 1950s

Fig 7.4
Frances Nickawa, 1924

Story of Dunfermline Burgess. Squaw's Residence in Town." J. McMurray of Toronto had come into possession of John Norton's letters and had written to the town clerk for information about his Scottish background.[20] In the summer of 2009, Fife Council remembered the presentation to Norton of the Freedom of Dunfermline with a short biography.[21]

As well, the contemporary fascination with tracing ancestry through tracking DNA has led some British people to "discover" they have North American Indigenous ancestry, a phenomenon, the media suggested, that might be the result of early modern visits to Britain by North American Indigenous people, whether on diplomatic missions or as exhibition displays. The figures of Pocahontas and, in the words of American historian Alden Vaughan, "Native American slaves," also were invoked as possible ancestors.[22] More to the point, perhaps, the memory of fur-trade families is present in the Orkney Islands, where it is located in a clearer, more detailed, understanding of the shared histories of fur-trade encounters, the embodied and material legacies of those intimate meetings between Cree women and Orcadian men.[23]

Memories of the late-eighteenth and nineteenth centuries are not the only things to consider, though. Although the twentieth-century history of Canadian Indigenous movement and mobility across national borders still awaits its historian(s), nevertheless a number of examples, suggest continuities in the histories of Indigenous mobility. Furthermore, these are not obscure or hidden histories. Indigenous men from across Canada volunteered to fight in both world wars, while, in the aftermath of World War One, the travels of Deskeheh (Levi General), the Cayuga political leader from the Grand River who took the hereditary council's claim to sovereignty to first London's Privy Council and then the League of Nations, has been the subject of a number of book chapters.[24] The stories of the Kahnawake, Akwesasne, and Grand River Mohawk ironworkers who helped create emblems of urban modernity (such as Manhattan's skyscrapers) have been the subject of a number of scholarly articles and public recollections.[25] In 1949, Elliott Moses (Delaware) led a delegation of men from the Grand River to participate in an international ploughing match in England, a trip that in some ways echoed John Norton's voyages.[26] As Coll Thrush has pointed out, in the 1970s and 1980s, First Nations leaders and activists were highly visible in London, their trips overseas aimed at drawing the British government's attention to its treaty obligations (particularly in the context of the repatriation of Canada's constitution).[27] Most recently, Alexis Nakota, Sioux Nation Chief, and Tony Alexis, Treaty 6 Grand Chief, along with other members of the Alexis Lakota Sioux Nation and the Paul First Nation travelled to the Vatican and met with Pope Francis.[28]

While these twentieth-century voyages have taken place in different contexts, they also display a striking continuity with their nineteenth-century predecessors. As this book has demonstrated, such mobility should not be viewed as a new phenomenon, the product of a twentieth-century modernity that can be juxtaposed alongside long-standing habits of immobility, whether imposed by the Canadian state or the product of Indigenous traditions. Following in their predecessors' footsteps, twentieth-century travellers have used mobility to protest government's actions, to seek out opportunities for work, to create new networks of family and kin, and to claim citizenship in both the Canadian nation-state and their Indigenous communities.

As the travels – and travails – of these late-eighteenth- and nineteenth-century men, women, and children demonstrate, movement across geographic, cultural, and intimate borders needs to be considered as part of Indigenous people's history, not an interesting sideshow or the province of a few exceptional individuals. Their narratives tell us much about their entangled experiences with nineteenth-century settler colonialism, experiences that also were forged within the orbit of an expanding British Empire. Equally importantly, they tell us much about these travellers' courage, creativity, and determination to tell their own stories and those of their people to those willing to listen to them. It is their persistence across the nineteenth century, their repetition and reiteration, that stands out, reminding twenty-first-century historians (not to mention their audiences) of Indigenous peoples' insistence that they tell their own stories, narrate their own lives and those of their communities, to both settler and metropolitan audiences. And in all of this they remind us that these are, indeed, shared histories.

Notes

Introduction

1 The historiography on imperial expansion during this period, including that of the British Empire, is extensive. See, for example, Ballantyne and Burton, *Empires and the Reach of the* Global; Bayly, *The Birth of the Modern World*; Belich, *Replenishing the Earth*; Hall, ed., *Cultures of Empire*.

2 Examples of work on earlier Indigenous travellers from North America include Anderson, *The Betrayal of Faith*; Eric Hindraker, "The 'Four Indian Kings,'"; Jewitt, "Extraordinary Arrivals"; Pratt, *American Indians in British Art*; Vaughan, "Sir Walter Raleigh's Indian Interpreters"; Vaughan, *Transatlantic Encounters*.

3 Thomas, *Islanders*, 3; Carey and Lydon, eds., *Indigenous Networks*; Chang, *The World and All the Things Upon It*; Somerville, *Once Were Pacific*.

4 The literature on such changes is voluminous. For discussions that pertain to Upper Canada, see Benn, *The Iroquois in the War of 1812*; Miller, *Compact, Contract, Covenant*; Smith, *Sacred Feathers*; Rogers and Smith, eds., *Aboriginal Ontario*; Schmalz, *The Ojibwa of Southern Ontario*; Taylor, *The Divided Ground*.

5 Miller, "Victoria's 'Red Children'"; Carlson, "Rethinking Dialogue and History"; Benn, *Mohawks on the Nile*.

6 Holly, "Transatlantic Indians," 527; Zacek, "Roundtable on *The Red Atlantic*, 1121.

7 Such challenges, along with the question of Indigenous modernity and mobility, have been addressed most recently in a thematic issue of *Cultural and Social History* 9, no. 4 (2012). In particular, see Antoinette Burton's introduction to this issue, "Travelling Criticism," 491–6.

8 The pioneering work on fur-trade relationships is Brown, *Strangers in Blood*; Peterson and Brown, eds., *The New People*; and Van Kirk, *"Many Tender Ties."* Other work on imperial and settler intimacies includes Basson, *White Enough to Be American?*; Burton and Ballantyne, "Introduction: The Politics of Intimacy in an Age of Empire," in Burton and Ballantyne, eds., *Moving Subjects*; Ellinghaus, *Taking Assimilation to Heart*; Ghosh, *Sex and the Family in Colonial India*; Grimshaw, "Interracial Marriages and Colonial Regimes"; McGrath, "Consent, Marriage, and Colonialism"; Pascoe, "Miscegenation Law, Court Cases, and Ideologies of 'Race'"; Salesa, *Racial Crossings"*; Stoler, *Carnal Knowledge*; Stoler, ed., *Haunted by Empire*.

9 Feest, ed., *Indians and Europe*; Moses, *Wild West Shows*; Poignant, *Professional Savages*; Qureshi, *Peoples on Parade*; Crais and Scully, *Sara Baartman and the Hottentot Venus*.

10 Indigenous performers' relationship to anthropology is discussed in Poignant, *Professional Savages*, and Quereshi, *Peoples on Parade*, especially Part Three, "The Natural History of Race," 185–270.

11 Smith, *Sacred Feathers*; Smith, *Mississauga Portraits*; Haig-Brown, "Seeking Honest Justice in a Land of Strangers."

12 Qureshi, *Peoples on Parade*, 33, 105–6, 146; Flint, *The Transatlantic Indian*, 82–5.

13 The most comprehensive coverage of John Brant-Sero's career can be found in Petrone, "Brant-Sero, John Ojijatekha." For Johnson, see Strong-Boag and Gerson, *Paddling Her Own Canoe*; Monture, "The Challenge to Haudenosaunee Nationhood: Performing Politics, Translating Culture," Chapter 2 in his *We Share Our Matters – Teionkwakhashion Tsi Niionkwariho:ten*, 63–106; Flint, *The Transatlantic Indian*, 269–86.

14 Brown, *Strangers in Blood*; Peterson and Brown, *The New Peoples*; Van Kirk, *"Many Tender Ties."* See Stoler, "Tense and Tender Ties."

15 Fullagar, *The Savage Visit*, 3.

16 Ibid., 12.

17 Ibid.

18 Ibid., 183.

19 Flint, *The Transatlantic Indian*, 10.

20 Ibid., 287.

21 Morgan, "Rethinking Nineteenth-Century Transatlantic Worlds."

22 Weaver, *The Red Atlantic*.

23 Thrush, *Indigenous London*. Both Weaver's and Thrush's books were

published well after this project had been conceptualized, researched, and (particularly for Thrush's work) written.

24 See, for example, McNairn on Smith's work ("As the Tsunami of Histories, Part Two," 423). While the literature on "cultural brokers" is useful in some regards, not least because it suggests the agency and critical role of Indigenous people in North American encounters with Europeans, its focus is primarily on such encounters within the North American context. See, for example, Szaz, ed., *Between Indian and White Worlds*; Schenck, *William W. Warren*.

25 Flint, Chap. 2, "The Romantic Indian" and Chap. 8, "Sentiment and Anger: British Women Writers and Native Americans," in *The Transatlantic Indian*; Weaver, Chap. 5, "Fireside Travelers, Armchair Adventurers, and Apocryphal Voyages," in *The Red Atlantic*. While she does not ignore Indigenous voices, Fullagar's *The Savage Visit* focuses on the meaning of eighteenth-century travellers' visits to metropolitan imperial culture.

26 In her contribution to the *Journal of American Studies'* roundtable on *The Red Atlantic*, Pennock points to the problems of trying to incorporate all Weaver's subjects into the *Red Atlantic* framework (Jace Weaver, "Roundtable on the *The Red Atlantic*," 1115). See also Holly, "Transatlantic Indians in the Early Modern Era." Moreover, as McNairn has noted, seeing the settler colony of Upper Canada through the lens of Atlantic studies can result in a distortion of its history ("As the Tsunami of Histories, Part One").

27 This is a point that Holly makes, particularly in the context of Alden Vaughan's book, on the problems of a wider sweep of time in studies of Indigenous mobility ("Transatlantic Indians," 525–6). To be sure, Thrush is careful to contextualize the people in his book, using the insights of ethnohistory to explain their reactions and perspectives on London.

28 While still a relatively small field within imperial history, work on the history of childhood and imperialism includes Buettner, *Empire Families*; Boucher, *Empire's Children*; Robinson and Sleight, eds., *Children, Childhood and Youth in the British World*; Smith, *Imperial Girls, 1880–1915*.

29 Ballantyne, *Webs of Empire*; Laidlaw, *Colonial Connections*; Lester, *Imperial Networks*; Magee and Thompson, *Empire and Globalisation*. For a discussion of the question of webs and Indigenous peoples, see Elbourne, "Imperial Networks and Indigenous People"; McDonnell, "Facing Empire: Indigenous Histories in Comparative Perspective."

30 For example, Poignant, *Professional Savages* and Quereshi, *Peoples on Parade*.

31 Laidlaw, *Colonial Connections*, 35.

32 Thrush, *Indigenous London*, 107.

33 Ballantyne, "Writing," Part Four in *Webs of Empire*, 179–246.

34 Scholars in Native American and literary studies have explored these publications, particularly those of George Copway. Ruoff and Smith, eds., *George Copway (Kahgegagahbowh)*, "George Copway: Canadian Ojibwa Methodist and Romantic Cosmopolite" in Peyer, *The Tutor'd Mind*; Fulford, *Romantic Indians*, 280–91; Walker, *Indian Nation*, 84–110; Konkle, *Writing Indian Nations*, 189–97, 205–23. See also Benn, "Missed Opportunities," and Benn, "Introduction," in Klinck and Talman, eds. *The Journal of Major John Norton, 1816*.

35 Morgan, "'Write Me. Write Me.'"

36 This question is explored in a number of the essays in Carey and Lydon, eds., *Indigenous Networks*.

37 For Indigenous biography in Canadian history, see Greer, *Mohawk Saint*; Smith, *Mississauga Portraits* and *Sacred Feathers*; Carter and McCormack, "Lifelines: Searching for Aboriginal Women."

38 For example, Burton, *At the Heart of the Empire*; Perry, *Colonial Relations*.

39 Lambert and Lester, "Imperial Spaces, Imperial Subjects," in Lambert and Lester, eds., *Colonial Lives*.

40 Little has been written in the Upper Canadian context about this question. For early colonial America, see Brown, "The Anglo-Algonquian Gender Frontier."

41 Weaver's work has been criticized for its inattention to gender in shaping the *Red Atlantic* (Zacek, "Roundtable," 1121); see also his acknowledgment of this problem (Weaver, "Roundtable," 1124). In contrast, Thrush's work encompasses more Indigenous women, not least because he does not confine himself to North America, and in certain chapters (most notably Chap. 6, "Civilization Itself Consents: Disciplining Bodies in Imperial Suburbia, 1861–1914") gender figures as a category of analysis in his work.

42 For the concept of emotional frontiers, see Vallegårda, Alexander, and Olsen, "Emotions and the Global Politics of Childhood," 15–20. My thanks to Kristine Alexander for sharing this chapter prior to its publication and for directing me to the rich historiography on emotions.

43 Flint, *The Transatlantic Indian*, 87.

44 For a range of scholarship on the history of the emotions, see Eustace, Lean, Livingston, Plamper, Reddy, and Rosenwein, "*AHR* Conversation:

The Historical Study of Emotions"; Scheer, "Are Emotions a Kind of Practice?"; Rosenwein, "Worrying About Emotions in History"; Plamper, "The History of Emotions." Although eschewing the term "history of emotions," in separate articles Phillips and Wickberg have explored related areas: see Phillips, "On the Advantages and Disadvantages"; Wickberg, "What Is the History of Sensibilities?" Studies that integrate emotions as part of political culture include Eustace, *Passion Is the Gale*; Eustace, *1812*; Reddy, *The Navigation of Feeling*.

45 See, though, Lorenzkowski, *Sounds of Ethnicity*; also Morgan, "'Better Than Diamonds.'"

46 Rosenwein, "Worrying About Emotions in History," 842; Scheer, "Are Emotions a Kind of Practice," 209; Eustace, "*AHR* Conversation," 1525.

47 Vallegårda, Alexander, and Olsen, "Emotions and the Global Politics of Childhood," 14.

48 Plamper, "*AHR* Conversation," 1527.

49 These questions are raised in Deloria, "Places Like Houses"; Ellinghaus, "Strategies of Elimination." But see also Maynard, "Transcultural/Transnational Interaction and Influences on Aboriginal Australia."

Chapter One

1 Klinck, "John Norton." Kuwoki (or Keowee) was in present-day South Carolina. See also, Benn, "Introduction" to the Reissue of *The Journal of Major John Norton, 1816*. For Norton' birth certificate, see "Norton, John," Office of Public Records.

2 Gadsden, *Some Observations on the Two Campaigns*, 79.

3 Shannon, "King of the Indians"; also Calloway, *White People, Indians, and Highlanders*.

4 Ball, *The Statistical Account of Scotland*, vol. 10, *Fife, 1791–1799*, 157.

5 Ibid., 158–60.

6 Ibid., 172.

7 Ibid., 169.

8 Ibid., 172.

9 Ibid., 160.

10 Ibid., 173.

11 The Scottish Statistical Accounts are discussed in Withers, "How Scotland Came to Know Itself."

12 Klinck, "John Norton."

13 Maclean and Fernie, *The Statistical Account of Scotland*, vol. 10, *Fife, 1791–1799*, 271.

14 Ibid., 277–80.

15 Ibid., 276.

16 Ibid., 320.

17 Ibid., 321.

18 Klinck, "John Norton."

19 Ibid.

20 Willig, *Restoring the Chain of Friendship*, 161–95.

21 Ibid., 163–4.

22 Johnston, "The Six Nations in the Grand River Valley," 170.

23 Other nations settled on the Grand River's banks, with the Upper Cayuga and Oneida closest to the Mohawk and the Lower Cayuga and Delaware further south, nearer Lake Erie (ibid., 170).

24 Ferris, *The Archaeology of Native-Lived Colonialism*, 127.

25 Ibid.

26 Ibid, 129–30.

27 The effects of the Revolutionary War on the Haudenosaunee and Brant's role in these developments are explored in Taylor, *The Divided Ground*, esp. Part Four, "Limits."

28 Willig, *Restoring the Chain of Friendship*, 126–7; Monture, *We Share Our Matters – Teionkwakhasion Tsi Niionkwariho:ten*, 41–4.

29 According to Willig, the Haldimand Grant was – unfortunately for the Six Nations – vaguely worded in its discussion of alienation of Indigenous lands to parties other than the Crown. While it didn't expressly forbid such transactions, neither did it directly sanction them (*Restoring the Chain of Friendship*, 126–7). See also Monture, *We Share Our Matters – Teionkwakhasion Tsi Niionkwariho:ten*, 46–7.

30 Willig, *Restoring the Chain of Friendship*, 130.

31 Ibid., 131–50.

32 Monture has suggested it is likely that Brant sent Norton with the confidence of the Grand River Council, who would have seen Norton as a trusted outsider, a "useful ally who had the potential to effect positive change" (*We Share Our Matters – Teionkwakhasion Tsi Niionkwariho:ten*, 56). Although Monture recognizes that Brant's perspectives were not shared by all members of the Confederacy, he also argues that Brant "often drew upon a traditional understanding of Six Nations sovereignty to promote a peaceful nation-to-nation relationship" with the British, while

simultaneously challenging the latter's assumption of dominance over the Haudenosaunee (30). See also Johnston, "The Six Nations in the Grand River Valley," and Paxton, *Joseph Brant and his World*.

33 Klinck, "Biographical Introduction," *Journal of John Norton*, xli.

34 Ibid., xlviii.

35 Ibid. For Lombard Street, see White, *London in the Nineteenth Century*, 163.

36 Klinck, "Biographical Introduction," xliii. During Norton's sojourn in England, William Claus, deputy superintendent general of Indian Affairs in Canada, brought together a number of men from the Grand River who were not happy with either Brant or Norton; he also invited Seneca delegates from Buffalo Creek (on the American side of the border) and other Iroquois who were opposed to Brant. According to Willig, those who supported Brant and Norton refused to attend, thus allowing Claus to secure the council's disavowal of Norton, a motion that was then passed on to English officials. As Willig points out, Claus (the grandson of Sir William Johnson) lacked the extent of his father's and grandfather's experience with the Confederacy, was determined to assert the Indian Department's authority over Indigenous people, and was firmly opposed to any claims of Indigenous sovereignty (Willing, *Restoring the Chain of Friendship*, 174–6).

37 Klinck, "Biographical Introduction," xliii.

38 Stephen, "William Allen."

39 Klinck, "John Norton."

40 Headley manuscript, 7–44. Norton's Cambridge appearance is also discussed in Fulford, *Romantic Indians*, 212–13.

41 Headley manuscript, 36–7.

42 Ibid., 44.

43 Ibid.

44 Ibid., 46.

45 Ibid., 50.

46 Ibid., 52–3.

47 Ibid., 53.

48 Ibid., 58.

49 Ibid., 56–7.

50 Phillips, "Making Sense out/of the Visual," 603.

51 Thrush, *Indigenous London*, 141.

52 For such interest, see Wilson, *The Island Race*; Harriet Guest, "Ornament and Use."

53 Headley manuscript, 37.

54 Jasanoff, *Edge of Empire*.

55 Headley manuscript, 57.

56 Norton to William Wilberforce, 29 Aug. 1895, Ayer MS 654.

57 Norton to John Owen, 28 Jan. 1807, Ayer MS 654.

58 Norton to Bath and West of England Agricultural Society, 24 Dec. 1804, Ayer MS 654.

59 Bhabha, "Of Mimicry and Man." Deloria makes related points about attempts to assimilate Indigenous Americans in his *Indians in Unexpected Places*, 230.

60 Huneault, "Miniature Objects of Cultural Covenant."

61 In another portrait, said to have been painted by Solomon Williams, c.1804, Norton is depicted holding a tomahawk, but the background is highly suggestive of romantic views of Scotland. http://vitacollections.ca/sixnationsarchive/2686551/data?n=1

62 Klinck, "Biographical Introduction," lvii. Klinck attributes the portrait to "Williams."

63 Ibid., 90.

64 John Owen to Miss Ansted, 20 Jan. 1806, John Norton Papers, Newberry Library.

65 Allen, *The Life of William Allen*, 78.

66 Wilberforce and Wilberforce, *The Life of William Wilberforce*, vol. 3, 188.

67 Norton to Owen, 19 Aug. 1805, John Norton Papers, Newberry Library.

68 Ibid., 29 Aug. 1805. Women's role in male sociability is discussed in Harvey, "The History of Masculinity"; also Cohen, "'Manners' Make the Man."

69 Norton to Robert Barclay, 15 Jan. 1806, and to Samuel Thornton, 25 March 1806, Ayer MS 654. "Goreghwens" appears to have been the Mohawk name that Norton gave Miss Agatha (presumably one of Barclay's relatives or close friends).

70 Norton to Owen, 12 Aug. 1806, Ayer MS 654. Masculinity and politeness are discussed in Harvey, "The History of Masculinity," esp. 301–5; Cohen, "'Manners' Make the Man," 325–9. Davidoff and Hall have explored the evangelicals' conceptions of manliness in *Family Fortunes*.

71 Norton to Barclay, 15 Jan. 1806, Ayer MS 654.

72 Norton to Owen, 19 Aug. 1807, Ayers MS 654.

73 Hoock, *Empire of the Imagination*, 179–83.

74 Russell, *The Theatres of War*.

75 Norton to Owen, 29 Aug. 1805, Ayer MS 654.

76 Norton to Wilberforce, 29 Aug. 1805, Ayer MS 654.

77 Norton to Owen, 29 Aug. 1805, Ayer MS 654.

78 Morgan, *Public Men and Virtuous Women*, 32–3; also Cohen, "'Manners' Make the Man."

79 Klinck, "Biographical Introduction," xxxviii.

80 Norton to Thornton, 25 Mar. 1806, Ayer MS 654. It is not clear who the "older brother" is in Norton's letter.

81 Norton to Barclay, 15 Jan. 1806, Ayer MS 654. I have not been able to substantiate the identities of the family members to whom Norton refers.

82 Norton to Owen, 12 Aug. 1806, Ayer MS 654. The little buck was probably his son John, who accompanied Norton and his new wife, Catherine, to Britain in 1815.

83 Ibid. Family relations were also of great interest to Norton as he travelled through Cherokee country, not least because of his own background (Klinck, "Biographical Introduction," lxix).

84 Norton to: Barclay, 20 Oct. 1806; Owen, 18 Aug. 1806, 28 Jan. 1807, Ayer MS 654.

85 Lord Percy to Norton, 31 Oct. 1808, Norton Fonds, Archives of Ontario.

86 Kelsey, "Tekarihogen, John Brant."

87 Klinck, "John Norton."

88 Norton to Owen 18 Aug. 1806; see also a copy of a speech delivered by Joseph Brant at Fort George, 28 July 1806. Ayer MS 654.

89 Norton, *The Journal of Major John Norton, 1816*, 160.

90 Ibid., 14–15. Whites in Nashville also recounted narratives of their community's brutality to the Cherokee during the war (29).

91 For example, ibid., 38, 41–3, 131–4.

92 Ibid., 32, 38–40, 45; his discussions of Cherokee history also included accounts of intertribal warfare (31–4, 79–108).

93 See, for example, ibid., 79–108.

94 Ibid., 70. Norton told a similar story to other Cherokee (ibid, 56, 109).

95 Ibid., 128.

96 For example, ibid., 15, 22.

97 Ibid., 57.

98 Ibid., 69.

99 Ibid., 112–14.

100 Ibid., 69; also 67, 115, 140, 142.

101 Ibid., 32, 57. Gender relations within Cherokee society in this period are discussed in Purdue, "Women, Men, and American Indian Policy."

102 Norton, *The Journal of Major John Norton*, 128.

103 Ibid., 182–3.

104 Ibid., 62, 67–8, 74, 111.

105 Ibid., 64.

106 Ibid., 50.

107 Ibid., 73–4. For other such examples, see ibid,, 114, 117, 128, 140–1. Norton also commented on other family configurations, such as a household comprised of Onondaga, Cherokee, and British ethnicities (37). He also met a Mohawk woman who married a Cherokee; she had met him while following her sister, who had done the same (67).

108 Salesa has pointed out that mixed-race relationships were not always treated as problematic (*Racial Crossings*).

109 Norton, *The Journal of John Norton, 1816*, 71.

110 Ibid., 114.

111 Ibid., 114, 157.

112 Ibid., 26.

113 Ibid., 44.

114 Ibid., 27.

115 Ibid., 142.

116 Chalmers, *Historical and Statistical Account of Dunfermline*, 327, 385–5, 402.

117 Henderson, *Annals of Dunfermline*.

118 Klinck, "Biographical Information," lxxxi; also Hunter, "Johnstone, Christian Isobel."

119 Klinck, "Biographical Information," lxxxi.

120 Brown, "Patterns and Problems of 'Placing': Company Offspring in Britain and Canada after 1821," Chapter 8 in her *Strangers in Blood*; Van Kirk, "*Many Tender Ties*." A similar phenomenon took place in the East India Company (Ghosh, *Sex and the Family in Colonial India*, 97).

121 J.O. Johnstone to Norton, Dec. 1815, Norton Papers, Archives of Ontario.

122 Andrew Shearer, town clerk, Dunfermline, to J.M. Murray, 11 May 1944, ibid.

123 Duke of Northumberland to Norton, 23 June 1816, ibid.

124 Ibid.

125 Norton to Duke of Northumberland, 6 Feb. 1817, as quoted in Klinck, "Biographical Introduction," lxxxiii.

126 Benn, "'Give Us Hopes of Finding Some Relief': 1815 and Beyond," Chapter 8 in his *The Iroquois in the War of 1812*.

127 Klinck, "Biographical Introduction," lxxxviii.

128 Ibid., lxxxix. See also Elbourne, "Broken Alliance."

129 Klinck, "Biographical Introduction," lxxxix.

130 Barclay to Norton, 7 Apr. 1817 and 30 Sept. 1823, Norton Papers, Archives of Ontario.

131 J.O. Johnstone to Norton, 4 Aug. 1819, ibid.

132 Klinck, "Biographical Introduction," lxxxvii.

133 Ibid.

134 Ibid., xc.

135 Catherine Norton to Christian Johnstone, n.d., Norton Papers, Archives of Ontario.

136 Norton to Colonel John Harvey, n.d., ibid. Harvey was a fellow veteran of 1812.

137 John Norton, Jr, to Norton, n.d., ibid.

138 Robert Thomson to Norton, 28 July 1823, ibid.

139 Ibid., 8 Aug. 1823.

140 Hagerman was a prominent militia captain and conservative politician, while Beardsley had served as defence counsel for prisoners charged with treason at the Ancaster "Bloody Assizes" in 1814 (and would go on to support William Lyon Mackenzie). Fraser, "Hagerman, Christopher Alexander," and Nelles, "Beardsley, Bartholomew Crannell."

141 Klinck, "Biographical Introduction," xciii.

142 Ibid., xciv.

143 Ibid.

144 Ibid, xcv.

145 Ibid, xcvi.

146 Cronk, "Editor's Introduction," xx.

147 Pybus, *Epic Journeys of Freedom*; Colley, *The Ordeal of Elizabeth Marsh*.

148 Hoock, *Empires of the Imagination*, 1–2; also Fisher, "Asians in Britain: Negotiations of Identity through Self-Representation," in Wilson, ed., *A New Imperial History*, 91–112.

149 Hoock, 397, n1. Taleb's account was the first published travel narrative of Europe by a south Asian.

150 For a discussion of the trajectory of scholarly interest in Native Americans, see Conn, *History's Shadow*.

Chapter Two

1 The implications of mid-nineteenth-century British North American liberalism for Indigenous people are discussed in Brownlie, "A Persistent Antagonism."

2 Elbourne, "The Sin of the Settler"; Lester, "British Settler Discourse"; Zoë Laidlaw, "'Aunt Anna's Report.'"

3 Radforth, "Performance, Politics, and Representation"; Chute, *The Legacy of Shingwaukonse*; Schmalz, *The Ojibwa of Southern Ontario*; Ferris, "Changing Continuities: Ojibwa Territorial Communities in Southwestern Ontario," Chapter 3 in his *The Archaeology of Native-Lived Colonialism*; Bohaker, "Anishinaabe Toodaims."

4 This condensed account owes much to Smith, *Sacred Feathers*.

5 Henry Steinhauer, another convert from the Rama area, travelled to England with John Ryerson in 1854. However, little appears to have survived about his experiences overseas. Krystyna Z. Sieciechowicz, "Teinhauer, Henry Bird."

6 Smith, *Mississauga Portraits*.

7 Smith, "The Outsider: Peter Jacobs, or Pahtahsega (c. 1810–1890)," Chapter 4 in *Mississauga Portraits*.

8 Work on Copway is extensive and includes Smith, "Kahgegagahbowh"; Smith, "The Life of George Copway"; Ruoff and Smith, eds., *George Copway*; Peyer, "George Copway: Canadian Ojibwa Methodist and Romantic Cosmopolite," Chapter 6 in his *The Tutor'd Mind*; Fulford, "Kag-ge-ga-gah-bowh/George Copway," Chapter 18 in his *Romantic Indians*; Walker, "The Terms of George Copway's Surrender," Chapter 5 in her *Indian Nation*; Konkle, *Writing Indian Nations*, 189–97, 205–23; Rex, "Survival and Fluidity," 13; Morgan, "Kahgegagahbowh's (George Copway) Transatlantic Performance."

9 Smith, "Kahgegagahbowh: Canada's First Literary Celebrity in the United States; in Ruoff and Smith, eds., *George Copway*, 32–8.

10 Norton's conception of an Indigenous territory is discussed in Willig, *Restoring the Chain of Friendship*, 170. It does seem, though, that Norton's vision did not include the involvement of white governors.

11 Ibid., 44–6.

12 "George Copway, the Chippewa Chief, has gone to Nicaragua, to join Walker's army," *The Weekly Raleigh Register*, 1 Apr. 1857.

13 Smith, *Mississauga Portraits*, 208.

14 The Credit Mississauga had considered a wholesale move to the area, but on the whole decided to remain. Shortly after, on being invited by the Six Nations Council, they moved to the Grand River to form the New Credit reserve.

15 Smith, "Nahnebahwequay"; Haig-Brown, "Seeking Honest Justice"; also her "The 'Friends' of Nahnebahwequa."

16 Smith, *Sacred Feathers*; Graham, *Medicine Man to Missionary*; Grant, *Moon of Wintertime*; Petit, "'To Civilize and Christianize'"; Stoehr,

"Salvation from Empire"; Schmalz, *The Ojibwa of Southern Ontario*, esp. Chap. 7, "Early Reserves: 'We Must Go Begging.'"

17 Stoehr, "Salvation from Empire."

18 On this topic, see Bohaker, "Anishinaabe Toodaims"; and Ferris, *Archaeology of Native-Lived Colonialism*, ch. 3.

19 Ferris, *Archaeology of Native-Lived Colonialism*, 35–8.

20 Vaughan, *Transatlantic Encounters*.

21 Copway, *Running Sketches*, 46–8.

22 Elbourne, "The Sin of the Settler"; Lester, "British Settler Discourse and the Circuits of Empire"; Laidlaw, "'Aunt Anna's Report.'"

23 Hall, *Civilizing Subjects*, 315–22.

24 Davidoff and Hall, *Family Fortunes*; Thorne, *Congregational Missions*; Twells, *The Civilising Mission*.

25 Altick, *The Shows of London*; Crais and Scully, *Sara Baartman and the Hottentot Venus*.

26 Peter Jones, *Christian Guardian*, 29 Feb. 1832, File 2, Box 3, Peter Jones Papers.

27 In particular, see Lester, "British Settler Discourse and the Circuits of Empire."

28 Hall, *Civilizing Subjects*, 120–39.

29 Peter Jones, *Christian Guardian*, 11 Jan. 1832, Peter Jones Papers.

30 Peter Jones, *Missionary Notices*, June 1838, 402, Peter Jones Papers.

31 Ibid. When Peter Jacobs appeared in front of British missionary audiences, he noted that two-thirds of his listeners were women (*Missionary Notices*, June 1843, 510, Peter Jones Papers).

32 Morgan, *Public Men and Virtuous Women*, 132–9.

33 Peter Jones, *The Witness*, 30 July 1845, Peter Jones Papers.

34 Morgan, "Turning Strangers into Sisters?"

35 See, for example, Peter Jones, "The Substance of a Sermon, Preached at Ebenezer Chapel, Chatham, Nov. 20, 1831, in Aid of the Home Missionary Society," Peter Jones Papers. For Copway, see his *Recollections of a Forest Life*.

36 Jones, "The Substance of a Sermon"; also "*Kahkewaquonaby*, the North American Indian Chief and Missionary," *Caledonian Mercury* 28 July 1845; *The Witness*, 30 July 1845; *The Ladies' Own Journal and Miscellany*, 2 Aug. 1845; *Edinburgh Advertiser*, 5 Aug. 1845 ("Clippings, 1827–1856," File 4, Box 8, Peter Jones Papers).

37 Bhabha, "Of Mimicry and Man."

38 For a discussion of nostalgia, see Rosaldo, "Imperialist Nostalgia."

39 While in Ayr in 1845, Jones wrote to Eliza to tell her of reading a Glasgow

newspaper article that attacked him and his brother, John, as not true Indians and claimed Jones was not a chief. Jones believed it was the work of his enemy, Upper Canadian Indian Department official Samuel Peters Jarvis (Peter Jones to Eliza Jones, 19 Nov. 1845, Box 3, File 6, Peter Jones Letterbook [letters to Eliza Field Jones, 1833–1848], Peter Jones Papers). Richard Cobden voiced his suspicions about Copway to fellow Congress organizer and reformer Joseph Sturge, hoping that Sturge would "not find it necessary to resort to the Ogibbeway [sic] Chief – who I think is a humbug" (Cobden to Sturge, 18 Nov. 1850, cited in Howe, ed., *The Letters of Richard Cobden*, 256).

40 Copway, *Running Sketches*, 52.

41 Fulford and Hutchings provide brief useful discussion of these movements in "Introduction: The Indian Atlantic," in their *Native Americans and Anglo-American Culture*, 9–13.

42 Konkle, *Writing Indian Nations*, 191–2; Stoehr, "Salvation from Empire."

43 Konkle discusses Copway's relationship to his father and the latter's decision to stop drinking (*Writing Indian Nations*, 191–2, 215–16).

44 Copway, *Running Sketches*, 255.

45 Miller provides a comprehensive discussion of Ojibwa treaty-making and Ojibwa leaders in Chapter 6, "'From Our Lands We Receive Scarcely Anything': The Upper Canadian Treaties, 1818–1862," in his *Compact, Contract, Covenant*.

46 Hutchings, "'The Nobleness of the Hunter's Deeds,'" 225.

47 For the use of theatre and theatrical techniques of display in eighteenth- and mid-nineteenth-century metropole and colony, see Hall, *Civilizing Subjects*, 280–2; also Wilson, *The Island Race*. Peter Jacobs also appeared in Indigenous dress for missionary audiences.

48 Jones, *Christian Guardian*, 29 Feb. 1832.

49 Ibid.

50 Copway, *Running Sketches*, 85.

51 Ibid., 46–8.

52 Ibid., 112.

53 Ibid., 49–50.

54 Ibid., 85.

55 Ibid., 275.

56 Ibid., 276–7.

57 Burton, *At the Heart of the Empire*, 6. Coll Thrush also makes the point that Indigenous travellers from other British settler colonies crafted similar critiques (*Indigenous London*).

58 Catherine Sutton to ?, n.d., 59, William Sutton Journals, Sutton Papers.

59 See, for example, Nahnebahwequay: "To the Friends of New York," *Friends' Intelligencer* 5, no. 4 (1861); "Is There Hope for the Indian?" *Christian Guardian*, 28 May 1862; "To My Beloved Friends in England," n.d., Sutton ledger, Sutton Papers. For a discussion of the languages of starving and pity, see Black-Rogers, "Varieties of 'Starving.'" My thanks to Heidi Bohaker for alerting me to Black-Rogers's article.

60 Nahneebahweequa, "Friends of New York," *Friends' Intelligencer*, 1861, Sutton Papers.

61 Nahnebahwequay, "Memorial," *Colonial Intelligencer, or Aborigines' Friend*, 1860, 149–53, Sutton Papers.

62 N.a., *Colonial Intelligencer, or Aborigines' Friend*, 1860, 155, Sutton Papers.

63 For Copway, see *Running Sketches*, 58–65, 304–32.

64 Johnston, "British Missionary Publishing." As cultural theorist Chris Rojek has argued, religious and celebrity cultures both diverge and resemble each other in various ways (*Celebrity*, 48, 98). Joseph Roach's work on public intimacy demonstrates its links to traditional religious beliefs and popular religion ("Public Intimacy," 16).

65 These themes are discussed in the following chapters in *Theatre and Celebrity in Britain*: Luckhurst and Moody, "Introduction: The Singularity of Theatre Celebrity"; Shearer West, "Siddons, Celebrity, and Regality: Portraiture and the Body of the Aging Actress"; Felicity Nussbaum, "Actresses and the Economies of Celebrity, 1700–1800."

66 For example, "Kahkewaquonaby, The North American Indian Chief and Missionary," *Caledonian Mercury*, 28 July 1845, Peter Jones Papers.

67 Copway, *Running Sketches*, 297.

68 Ibid., 299, 339.

69 The crowd who turned out for his address at the London Tavern was judged by the press to be so large (500 to 600) that additional rooms needed to be used ("Temperance Festival," *The Leeds Mercury*, 19 Oct. 1850). However, the "attendance was scanty" for a temperance demonstration in London at which he spoke; the result of "some mismanagement or error in the public announcement of the meeting" ("Temperance Demonstration," *Daily News*, 3 Dec. 1850).

70 See, for example, "A Red Indian Chief," *Caledonian Mercury*, 3 Oct. 1850.

71 See, for example, "The North American Indians," *The Leeds Mercury*, 21 Sept. 1850.

72 "The Ojibbeway Missionary," *The Bury and Norwich Post*, and *Suffolk Herald*, 11 Sept. 1850; "Temperance Festival," *The Morning Chronicle*,

15 Oct. 1850; "North American Indians," *Dundee Courier*, 27 Nov. 1850.

73 "Printed Testimonials," File 8, Box 3, Peter Jones Papers.

74 Eliza Jones, 18 July 1838, Diary, Peter Jones Papers.

75 Ibid., 14 Sept. 1838.

76 Peter Jones, "Letter to John Jones," *Christian Guardian*, 29 Feb. 1832, 59, Peter Jones Papers. Jones was probably referring to King Philip, or Metacom, the Wampanaog leader who led attacks against the English in Plymouth colony.

77 Copway, *Running Sketches*, 42, 52. William and Richard Rathbone belonged to a prominent Liverpool Quaker family of merchants; they were involved in a number of reform causes that included abolition, parliamentary and municipal reform, and Catholic emancipation. In 1837–38, William served as the city's mayor (Gordon, "Rathbone, William"). Edward Rushton also was prominent in Liverpool politics and causes such as Catholic emancipation, prison reform, and the abolition of capital punishment. Rushton's career is briefly discussed in the entry devoted to his father, the poet and radical Edward Rushton (Royden, "Rushton, Edward").

78 Copway, *Running Sketches*, 97, 116, 121. For Joseph Brotherton, the Salford MP, and supporter of education reform, abolition of both slavery and capital punishment, and the peace movement, see Shapely, "Brotherton, Joseph." When Cobden met Copway, the free-trade advocate and parliamentary reformer was the MP for Yorkshire's West Riding; as well as becoming a leading supporter of international peace, he had become involved in colonial reform (Taylor, "Cobden, Richard"). Lord Brougham most likely refers to Henry Peter Brougham, Lord Chancellor, free-trade champion, and advocate of legal and social reform (Lobban, "Brougham, Henry Peter"). Gambardilli is likely a misspelling of the last name of Spiridione Gambardella, the Italian portrait painter who exhibited at the Royal Academy from 1842 to 1854 (N.a., *Notes and Queries*).

79 Copway, *Running Sketches*, 125. Sir Edwin Saunders was a leader in the professionalization of dentistry and Queen Victoria's dentist; he also provided free dental services to London's poor from 1840 to 1852 (Power, "Saunders, Sir Edwin"). Jane Franklin's interest in travel and reform, as well as her time in Tasmania, may have prompted her interest in Copway (Middleton, "Franklin, Jane"). Mr Simpkinson may have been the barrister and QC Sir John Augustus Francis, who was married to Jane Franklin's sister Mary Griffin. John and Mary Simpkinson's son Francis served with his uncle, Sir John Franklin (Hodgman, "Simpkinson de Wesselow").

For Wiseman, see Richard J. Schiefen, "Wiseman, Nicholas Patrick Stephen (1802–1865)," *Oxford Dictionary of National Biography*, Oxford University Press, 2004; online edn, May 2011 [accessed 27 March 2017].

80 Ibid, 278.

81 Copway, *Running Sketches*, 148–52.

82 Ibid., 268.

83 Pratt, *American Indians in British Art*, 145.

84 Morgan, *Public Men and Virtuous Women*, 112–13.

85 Peter Jacobs, *Missionary Notices*, June 1843, 512–15, Peter Jones Papers.

86 Smith, *Sacred Feathers*, 141–2.

87 Peter Jones to Eliza Jones, 7 June 1837, Peter Jones Letterbook, Peter Jones Papers.

88 Vaughan, *Transatlantic Encounters*, 78, 217.

89 Mrs Ward, "Observations Regarding Kahkewahquonaby's Health," n.d. 1831. File 2, Box 3, Peter Jones Papers.

90 N.a., *Missionary Notices*, Sept. 1837, 705, Peter Jones Papers.

91 Samson Occom, the Mohegan Presbyterian minister who toured Britain from 1766 to 1768 to fundraise for Indigenous American education, also wore a plain black suit and was painted in it (Vaughan, *Transatlantic Encounters*, 191–206).

92 *Aberdeen Journal*, 13 Aug. 1845, Peter Jones Papers.

93 *Aberdeen Journal*, 13 Aug. 1845; *Edinburgh Advertiser*, 5 Aug. 1845, Peter Jones Papers.

94 Peter Jones to Eliza Jones, 29 Oct. 1845, Peter Jones letterbook, Peter Jones Papers.

95 Ibid., 29 June 1845. Radforth points out that John Sunday refused to wear "Indian" clothing when he appeared before the Prince of Wales during the latter's 1860 tour of British North America ("Performance, Politics, and Representation," 17–18). My thanks to Patricia Kennedy for pointing out the other reasons why Jones might wish to eschew his Ojibwe clothing.

96 Nahneebahweequa, *The Colonial Intelligencer or Aborigines' Friend*, 1860, 156, Sutton Papers.

97 Mattingly, *Appropriat[ing] Dress*, 124. See also Radforth, "Performance, Politics, and Representation," for discussions of Aboriginal dress during the Prince of Wales's tour.

98 Copway, *Running Sketches*, 42–3.

99 Ibid., 54. The *Liverpool Mercury* and other English newspapers covered Copway's appearances and movements. See *Liverpool Mercury*: "An Address to the People of the United States. The Indians of the Western

Continent of America," 30 July 1850; "The Rev. George Copway and the Western American Indian," 2 Aug. 1850; "Peace Congress at Frankfort-on-the-Main," 11 Aug. 1850; "The Rev. George Copway, the Indian Chief," 16 Aug. 1850; "Teetotalism Among the American Indians," 20 Aug. 1850; "The Peace Congress at Frankfort-on-the-Main"; also *Daily News*, 23 Aug. 1850; "Teetotalism Among the American Indians," *Manchester Times*, 24 Aug. 1850; "Meeting of the Peace Congress at Frankfort," *Daily News*, 27 Aug. 1850; "Peace Congress at Frankfort," *Manchester Times*, 31 Aug. 1850; "Temperance Festival," *John Bull* 19 Oct. 1850.

100 Copway, *Running Sketches*, 330–1.

101 Ibid., 223.

102 Ibid.

103 Burton, *Heart of the Empire*, 185.

104 Thanks to Elizabeth Elbourne for reminding me of that complication. See Altick, *The Shows of London*.

105 Crais and Scully, *Sara Baartman*; also Qureshi, *Peoples on Parade*.

106 See Burton, "Introduction: Traveling Criticism?" 492.

107 There is now an extensive literature on humanitarian and paternalism within the mid-nineteenth-century British Empire. See, for example, Lester and Dussart, *Colonization and the Origins of Humanitarian Governance*.

Chapter Three

1 Burton and Ballantyne, *Moving Subjects*, 4.

2 Salesa, *Racial Crossings*, 2.

3 The literature here is quite large, but see: Salesa, *Racial Crossings*; Stoler, *Carnal Knowledge*; Stoler, ed., *Haunted by Empire*; Grimshaw, "Interracial Marriages"; Wanhalla, *In/visible Sight*; McGrath, "Consent, Marriage, and Colonialism"; Pascoe, "Miscegenation Law, Court Cases"; Perry, *On the Edge of Empire*; Carter, *The Importance of Being Monogamous*; Basson, *White Enough to Be American*.

4 Beckles, "Taking Liberties"; Hodes, *White Women, Black Men*; Blunt, *Domicile and Diaspora*. For discussions of comparisons of intimate relations across transnational networks and empires, see Stoler, "Tense and Tender Ties."

5 Hodes, *The Sea Captain's Wife*; Ellinghaus, *Taking Assimilation to Heart*;

Haskins and Maynard, "Sex, Race, and Power"; Altena, "The Lady and the Indian."

6 For Canada, the "classic" works are Van Kirk, *"Many Tender Ties"*; Brown, *Strangers in Blood*. See also Van Kirk, "From 'Marrying-in' to 'Marrying-out'"; Stewart, *The Ermantingers*; and Ellinghaus, Chapters 2 and 3, in her *Taking Assimilation to Heart*.

7 Salesa, *Racial Crossings*, 2.

8 While the marriage of English-born Emily Howells to George Johnson, the Mohawk chief and interpreter, is not discussed in this chapter, it too falls under the rubric of a significant "racial crossing," not least because it produced the writer and performer E. Pauline Johnson, whose voyages to London are discussed in Chapter 6.

9 Smith, *Sacred Feathers*, 134.

10 Eliza Field Diary, 19 Mar. 1832, Box 4, File 4, Peter Jones Papers 17-Series 2 File list.

11 Ibid.

12 Ibid., 17 Feb. 1832.

13 Ibid., 15 Mar. 1832. "Mama" was Eliza's stepmother, as her biological mother had died in childbirth in 1820. For a discussion of Eliza Field's background as the daughter of a devout Christian and well-off factory owner, Charles Field, see Smith, *Sacred Feathers*, 130–5.

14 Field Diary, 28 June 1832, Peter Jones Papers.

15 Ibid., 31 Oct. 1832.

16 See, for example, her entries for 1832: 1, 17, 23 Feb.; 12, 20 Mar.; 25 Apr.; 24 June; 10 Aug; 4 Sept.; 31 Oct., Field Diary, Peter Jones Papers.

17 Peter Jones to Eliza Field, 9 Apr. 1833, Peter Jones Letterbook, Box 3, File 4, Peter Jones Papers.

18 Ibid., 1 May 1833.

19 Ibid.

20 See my discussion of this article in Chapter 2.

21 Peter Jones to Eliza Jones, 7 June 1837, Peter Jones Letterbook. This incident is also discussed in Chapter 2.

22 See, for example, ibid., 10 July 1834; 5 July 1837; 17 Apr. 1838; 19 Nov. 1845; 25 Nov. 1845.

23 Smith, *Sacred Feathers*.

24 Ellinghaus, *Taking Assimilation to Heart*, 78.

25 Peter Jones to Eliza Jones, 1845: 6, 12, July; 4, 9 Nov., Peter Jones Letterbook.

26 Ibid. 6 July 1845.

27 Sutton's support for her cause is discussed in Haig-Brown, "The 'Friends' of Nahnebahwequa," 146–7.

28 William Sutton, "Memo," n.d. (c. 1865), William Sutton journals, Sutton Papers.

29 "William Sutton Obituary," *Christian Guardian*, 13 June 1894, Sutton Papers.

30 Smith, *Sacred Feathers*, 213.

31 Haig-Brown, "The 'Friends' of Nahnebahwequa," 135.

32 Smith, *Sacred Feathers*, 215.

33 Ibid.

34 I explore these complications more fully in "'The Joy My Heart Has Experienced.'"

35 For a discussion of the Enfranchisement and Indian acts, particularly as they pertain to Indigenous women, see Fiske, "Political Status of Indigenous Indian Women."

36 Petition, "Catherine Sutton to Superintendent, Indian Affairs," 6 June 1899, Sutton Family History Binder, Sutton Papers.

37 I do not wish to suggest that Jones did not draw on his Anishinaabe background in his intimate life, or that evangelicals had a monopoly on companionate ideals. However, in Jones's correspondence to Eliza, the influence of Methodism is quite apparent. His great love for their sons may, though, have also stemmed from Anishinaabe society's attitudes towards children.

38 Smith, "Kahgegagahbowh: Canada's First Literary Celebrity in the United States," in Ruoff and Smith, *Life, Letters, and Speeches*, 29.

39 For a discussion of Copway's literary abilities, see Rex, "Survivance and Fluidity," 26–7, n2.

40 Copway, *Reflections on a Forest Life*, 116–17.

41 See Rex, "Survivance and Fluidity," 13.

42 Copway, *Running Sketches*, 282–3.

43 Smith, "Kahgegagahbowh," 38.

44 Ibid., 45. There are conflicting years for Frances Minnehaha's birth: the 1891 Canadian Census gives it as about 1860, whereas the 1901 Census and her death certificate state 1863. Her headstone at Brantford's Greenwood Cemetery, though, states 1863 (see Fig. 3.9). Census of Canada, Year: 1891; Census Place: Port Dover, Norfolk South, Ontario; Roll: T-6356; Family No.: 152. Census of Canada, Year: 1901; Census Place: Port Dover (Village), Norfolk (south/sud), Ontario; Page: 8; Family No: 85; Archives of Ontario;

Toronto, Ontario, Canada; Series: MS 935; Reel: 275. The Census data and death certificate can be found at ancestry.ca

45 There are a number of references to Howell in the scholarship on Copway, including the fact that she was a published writer and poet. However, I have not been able to locate her work. See, for example, Rex, "Survivance and Fluidity," 26, n2, 26; also Smith, "Kahgegagahbowh."

46 Smith, "Kahgegagabowh," 43–4.

47 Elizabeth Copway to George Copway, as cited in Smith, "Kahgegagahbowh," 57, n75. It isn't clear why Elizabeth needed to beg his forgiveness.

48 Ibid., 45.

49 Ibid., 47.

50 Year: 1891; Census Place: Port Dover, Norfolk South, Ontario; Roll: T-6356; Family No: 152; Year: 1901; Census Place: Port Dover (Village), Norfolk (south/sud), Ontario; Page: 8; Family No: 85. Elizabeth died 19 Jan. 1904 (Archives of Ontario; Series: MS935; Reel: 116).

51 Katherine T. Corbett, "Called Home," 168. My thanks to one of the anonymous reviewers for drawing my attention to Corbett's work.

52 For their marriage, see http://homepages.rootsweb.ancestry.com/~maryc/toro5p2.htm; also http://www.brantmasons.com/images/website_DDGM_2007_Trestle_Board.pdf

53 Brant-Sero's life is discussed in more detail in the following chapter. He was born and raised at the Six Nations, and both Brant-Sero's parents were Mohawk. His mother, Ellen Funn, was a descendant of Joseph Brant, and his father, Dennis Sero, was part of the Bay of Quinte Mohawks. Petrone, "Brant-Sero, John Ojijatekha."

54 N.a., "A Mohawk Chief's Romance," *The Derby Mercury*, 29 July 1896.

55 Birth Certificate #333, Issued 9 Apr. 1894, John Edward Brant, b. 20 Feb. 1894, General Register Office England, Application Number 136065–1.

56 N.a., "A Mohawk Chief's Romance."

57 "The Six Nations Celebrate the Jubilee," *The Globe*, 16 Oct. 1897.

58 *British Columbia Archival Union List*, John Edward Brant entry; *Online Census of England*, 1901, Parish of Blackburn, 14 Larkhill Road, p. 22, RG13/391; United States Department of Justice, Immigration, and Naturalization, *Record of Border Crossings*, List E, 20 Dec. 1925. John Edward Brant-Sero is listed as a "commercial salesman," born in England. My thanks to Marian Press, formerly of OISE/U of T's Education Commons, for her help in locating Brant-Sero and other individuals through the online British census.

59 "A Mohawk Chief's Romance."

60 See *British Columbia Archival Union list*, John Edward Brant entry.

61 For a discussion of Kirby's collection, see Arni Brownstone, "Treasures of the Bloods"; also Hamilton, *Collections and Objections*, 116, 119, 127. Thanks to Sarah Carter for telling me about Kirby's trip and pointing me to Brownstone's article.

62 N.t., n.a., *The Era*, Issue 2996, 22 Feb. 1895.

63 See Brownstone, "Treasures," 27.

64 Hamilton, *Collections and Objections*, 229, n35.

65 While I initially believed that he had left Frances Kirby in Canada, they are listed as living together in the 1901 Census in Liscard, Cheshire (English Census online, RG13/3401). See J. Obed Smith, Assistant Superintendent of Emigration, Department of the Interior, London, to The Secretary, Department of Indian Affairs, 20 Nov. 1914, *Estate of John Brant-Sero*, M-2635, RG-10, Library and Archives Canada. Petrone also believed that the couple separated before his departure for England (Petrone, "Brant-Sero, John Ojijatekha").

66 For McGrath, see "A Mohawk Chief's Romance"; also *English Census Online*, 1891, Blackburn, p. 24, RG12/3395.

67 My sources are not forthcoming on the question of sexuality in any of these relationships. The "longing" that the Joneses speak of in their diaries and letters may well have included both emotional and sexual desire; however, it is difficult – and probably ahistorical – to separate these elements out neatly, particularly as they were bound up with religious beliefs and values. Ellinghaus also points to the difficulty of discussing sexual desire and attraction in these relationships, but suggests that, late in the nineteenth century, some white women expressed a frank desire for a relationship with an Indigenous man based on sexualized fantasies (*Taking Assimilation to Heart*, 103–4).

68 As well as acting as an advisor to the Ontario Provincial Archaeologist, David Boyle, Brant-Sero gave a number of papers to learned societies in Chicago and Britain (Morgan, "'A Wigwam to Westminster,'" 322–3).

69 Petrone, "Brant-Sero, John Ojijatekha."

70 Ibid., 332–3.

71 Lambert and Lester, "Imperial Spaces, Imperial Subjects," 2.

72 Ibid., 12.

73 I have explored these questions further in "'Write me. Write me.'"

74 Rex, "Survivance and Fluidity," 13–14.

75 Haskins and Maynard, "Sex, Race, and Power," 216.

76 Hall and Rose, "Introduction," 24.

77 Eliza Field Jones Diary, 1833, Peter Jones Papers: 21, 24 Sept.; 28, 29 Oct.; 20 May 1838; 29 July 1838.

78 Ibid., 16, 17 Oct. 1833.

79 Ibid., 24 Sept. 1833.

80 For a discussion of these developments in Canada, see Carter, *The Importance of Being Monogamous*.

81 I do not wish to suggest that this was somehow a "better" situation for these couples and children or that Canada practised a more benevolent form of colonial rule, particularly when we consider the large-scale establishment of residential schools later in the nineteenth century and, in 1960s, the "scoop" of Indigenous children from their communities for adoption by white couples. I simply wish to call attention to the different conditions for the mixed-race couples in this book, ones shaped by their particular circumstances and relationships to colonial institutions and international networks.

82 For a discussion of this shift, see Hall, *Civilizing Subjects*.

83 There is a very large literature on this subject, but see Carter, "Categories and Terrains of Exclusion"; Titley, *A Narrow Vision*; Harris, *Making Indigenous Space*.

Chapter Four

1 These children's experiences have been explored by Van Kirk, *"Many Tender Ties"*; Brown, *Strangers in Blood*; Fuchs, "Native Sons of Rupert's Land." For other work on the movement of fur-trade families, see McCormack, "Lost Women"; Jackson, *Children of the Fur Trade*; Barman, *French Canadians, Furs, and Indigenous Women*, esp. Chap. 10, "Enabling Sons and Daughters."

2 Hudson's Bay Company Biographical File, "Davis, John."

3 Will of John Davis, 1825, Box 1, File 7, Miscellaneous Papers Items 130–67, n.d., Davis Family Fonds.

4 To be sure, Vincent was not entirely trustworthy. In 1817 he had taken a second wife, prompting his first country wife, Cree-English Jane Renton, to return to her people at Moose Factory; he did, though, provide for his and Jane Renton's children and for both women (Van Kirk, *"Many Tender*

Ties," 116; Brown, "Vincent, Thomas (d. 1832)."

5 Morley, "Davis, Mathilda."

6 W.L. Hardisty to Matilda Davis, 1 Aug. 1870, File 22 Hardisty Correspondence 1869–70, Davis Family Fonds. Hardisty regretted that Davis would no longer take boys at the school, but thanked her for all she had done for his sons.

7 Morley, "Davis, Mathilda"; Abraham Cowley to John Davis, 6 July 1875, File 18, Cowley Correspondence, 1866–75, Davis Family Fonds. Upon Davis's death in 1873, though, the school eventually left the family's hands. The property became a private residence and was known as "Twin Oaks," which now features in historic tours of Winnipeg. Most recently the Davis School House/Twin Oaks has been featured on a walking tour of Red River. See "People of the Red River Settlement: A Self-Directed Drive and Stroll Tour," www.routesonthered.ca, accessed 24 Aug. 2009.

8 The role of siblings and other relatives – aunts, uncles, cousins – in the nineteenth-century English middle class is discussed by Davidoff, "Forgotten Figures."

9 Matilda Davis to George Davis, 30 May 1843, File 2, Davis Family Fonds.

10 Matilda Davis to George and ? Davis, n.d., Davis Family Fonds.

11 Van Kirk discusses the racially charged tensions that arose as Indigenous women increasingly became less acceptable marriage partners or companions, as fur traders chose to marry either mixed-race women or white women ("Daughters of the Country," Chap. 5 in her *Many Tender Ties"*). Van Kirk also points to attempts by the relatives of fur traders to disinherit children on the grounds of their illegitimacy (*"Many Tender Ties,"* 117).

12 While there is genealogical information to be found about John and Nancy/Ann Davis, my attempts to track her uncle through the thicket of present-day genealogical information have been, unfortunately, unsuccessful.

13 Janet (or Jane) Braby to Matilda Davis, 16 May 1862, File 23 Albert Hodgson Correspondence and Financial Papers, 1862–69, Davis Family Fonds. Braby is listed in the 1861 English census as fifty years old, born in Walworth, and living at 2 Norfolk Place with nine-year-old Albert Hodgson and fifty-two-year-old Harriet Howarth (1861 England Census, RG 9; Piece: 402; Folio: 3; Page: 3; GSU roll: 542631, ancestry.ca). Albert was the son of Catherine Davis, Matilda's younger sister, and John Hodgson. Hodgson was the son of Charlotte Yorkston, a Cree-Scottish woman, and John Hodgson Sr. He was also Catherine's cousin through Nancy

Hodgson Davis, his father's sister (http://www.redriverancestry.ca/DAVIS-JOHN-1785.php; http://www.redriverancestry.ca/HODGSON-JOHN-1763.php; http://www.redriverancestry.ca/HODGSON-JOHN-1826.php.

14 Braby to Matilda Davis, 16 May 1862, File 23 Albert Hodgson Correspondence, Davis Family Fonds.

15 Van Kirk, "Isbister, Alexander Kennedy."

16 Braby to Matilda Davis, 16 May 1862, File 23 Albert Hodgson Correspondence, Davis Family Fonds.

17 The Forest School is still in operation today; see http://www.forest.org.uk/

18 D. Grey to Matilda Davis, 5 Apr. 1863, File 23 Albert Hodgson Correspondence, Davis Family Fonds.

19 "Bill for Forest School, Walthamstow," Easter 1865, File 3, Rosser Correspondence, 1863–68, Davis Family Fonds; also Henry Rosser to Matilda Davis, 13 Oct. 1863, ibid. In this letter, Rosser mentions that "Abbie" must cost her at least one hundred pounds a year. Rosser is listed in the school's 1863–1865 register as being in the care of Henry Rosser, 166 Fenchurch Street, London (Brian Hardcastle, Alumni Relations, Forest School, email communication, 22 June 2010).

20 D. Grey to Matilda Davis, 5 Apr. 1863, File 23 Albert Hodgson Correspondence, Davis Family Fonds.

21 Albert Hodgson to Matilda Davis, 20 Nov. 1864 and n.d. Dec 1863 or 1864, Davis Family Fonds.

22 Albert Hodgson to Matilda Davis, n.d. Dec. 1863 or 1864, Davis Family Fonds.

23 Albert Hodgson to Matilda Davis, 20 Nov. 1864, Davis Family Fonds.

24 D. Grey to Matilda Davis, 9 June 1865, Davis Family Fonds.

25 Ibid.

26 Prospectus for "The Nest," c. 1850s, File 23, No. 1163–4, Davis Family Fonds. See also O'Brien, *The Nest Academy*, 6–9; also Berry, "Recovered Identities," 51.

27 The prospectus for "The Nest" lists "Miss Millar" as being the Superintendent "for the Board and Education of Young Gentlemen." In the 1871 Scottish census Millar had become Marion Fyfe, 47, married to George Fyfe, and living in Jedburgh (1871 Scotland Census, Jedburgh Parish, Line 11, www.ancestry.co.uk-1871 Scotland Census; accessed 12 Feb. 2007). My thanks to Marion Press, Education Commons, OISE/UofT, for this search.

28 Marion Millar to Matilda Davis, 30 Jan. 1866, Davis Family Fonds.

29 Ibid., 6 Nov. 1866.

30 Ibid., 24 Nov. 1866.

31 Marion Millar to Matilda Davis, 5 Feb. 1867, File 11, John Davis Correspondence 1862–70, Davis Family Fonds.

32 John Davis to: George Davis, 4 Oct. 1867; Catherine Davis, 21 Nov. 1867; Matilda Davis 4 July 1868; File 11, Davis Family Fonds. Albert Hodgson to George Davis, 6 Apr. 1867, File 23, Albert Hodgson Correspondence, Davis Family Fonds.

33 John Davis to Matilda Davis 4 July 1868, File 11, John Davis Correspondence 1862–1870, Davis Family Fonds.

34 Alice Davis to John Davis, 6 Nov. 1870, Davis Family Fonds.

35 John Davis to Matilda Davis 4 July 1868, Davis Family Fonds.

36 For Alexander Christie, see Bowsfield, "Christie, Alexander." Charles Christie told Matilda Davis that Dr Cowan's son was attending The Nest, as the family was making preparations to send son Willie to join his brother Johnny there (14 Dec. 1865, Davis School Correspondence, Davis School Fonds). Dr Cowan refers to William Cowan, the Scottish-born fur trader and physician; he married Harriette Sinclair, the Cree-Scottish daughter of the prominent fur trader and merchant James Sinclair (Ronaghan, "Cowan, William").

37 John Davis to his sisters, 9 Oct. 1869, John Davis Correspondence, 1862–1870.

38 1871 Scotland Census, Jedburgh Parish. It is not clear if the boys who were from other parts of the British Empire or abroad were mixed-race or of English descent.

39 See Buettner, "Sent Home to Britain: British Education, Status, and Returns Overseas," for a discussion of the English schools that catered to the Indian-born children of British colonial officials (Chapter 4 in her *Empire Families*). Much of the work on the education of mixed-race children focuses on the colonial context. However, Durba Ghosh also points to the small, yet significant, number of those children born in the early 1800s to South Asian mothers and British fathers employed in the East India Company who were sent to relatives and school in Britain and Europe (Ghosh, *Sex and the Family*, 126–8). While more work remains to be done on this topic, I would argue that it provides a useful point of convergence and comparison for the Hudson's Bay Company and the East India Company, commercial enterprises deeply intertwined with imperial expansion.

40 Warren Sinclair, "Davis," 885–90, Metis Genealogies, Warren Sinclair Fonds.

41 Matilda Hunt to Matilda Davis, 25 Aug. 1868, File 26, Matilda J. Hunt

Correspondence, 1868–69, Davis Family Fonds. Henry appears to have been Matilda Hunt's brother.

42 Hunt to Davis, 20 Mar. 1869, Davis Family Fonds.

43 According to Sinclair, in 1874 Albert married a Métis woman, Frances Edith Davis (she may have been his cousin). Sinclair, *Metis Genealogies*, Warren Sinclair Fonds.

44 Matilda Smith to Matilda Davis, 6 Feb. 1865 and 25 Sept. 1865, File 3, Correspondence 1861–65, Matilda Davis School Fonds.

45 Hunt to Davis, 20 Mar. 1869, File 26, Matilda J. Hunt Correspondence, 1868–69, Davis Family Fonds.

46 Anne Thomas's background is discussed briefly in Peel, "Thomas, Thomas," in *Dictionary of Canadian Biography*, vol. 6, University of Toronto/Université Laval, 2003–, accessed December 13, 2016, http://www.biographi.ca/en/bio/thomas_thomas_6E.html.

47 Alexander Christie to Matilda Davis, n.d., p. 39, File 1, Matilda Davis School Fonds.

48 C. Christie to Matilda Davis, 4 Dec. 1864, File 3, 1861–65, Matilda Davis School Fonds; Alex Christie to Emma Christie, 29 Jun. 1868, File 16, Christie Correspondence, 1862–68, Davis Family Fonds.

49 Letitia Hargrave to Mrs Dugald MacTavish, 17 Sept. 1847, Macleod, ed., *The Letters of Letitia Hargrave*, 177. The academy's problems are also discussed in Van Kirk, although she points out that the school was successful in inculcating the values of Victorian "ladyhood" in many of its female pupils (*"Many Tender Ties,"* 149 and 151).

50 N (or M?) Christie to Matilda Davis, 4 Apr. 1868, File 16, Christie Correspondence, 1862–68, Davis Family Fonds.

51 Lydia Christie to Matilda Davis, 30 June n.y., File 16, Christie Correspondence, 1862–68, Davis Family Fonds.

52 Other families wrote to Davis, asking whether she would be able to take their own offspring, who would be sent from a number of outlying areas and fur-trade posts. Alex Christie to Matilda Davis, 28 July 1867, File 4, Correspondence, 1866–70, Matilda Davis School Fonds; Arabella Cowley to Matilda Davis, 17 Sept. 1866, File 18, Cowley Correspondence, 1866–75, Davis Family Fonds; Eleanora Campbell to Matilda Davis, 17 Jan. 1868, File 6, School Correspondence and Accounts, Davis Family Fonds.

53 Abraham Cowley to George Davis, 6 July 1875, File 18, Cowley Correspondence, 1866–75, Davis Family Fonds.

54 Myers, *Antipodal England*, 127. My thanks to Kristine Moruzi for alerting me to Myers's work.

55 Myers, "'Verily the Antipodes of Home': Narrating Domesticity in the Bush," Chap. 4 in *Antipodal England*; also Chilton, *British Female Migration*.

56 Davidoff, "Forgotten Figures."

57 Vallegårda, Alexander, and Olsen, "Emotions and the Global Politics of Childhood," 13–14.

58 "Mr Ballenden" was John Ballenden, the fur trader and justice of the peace who had married Sarah McLeod, the Cree-Scottish daughter of Chief Trader Alexander Roderick McLeod. The Ballenden marriage became the subject of considerable controversy in Red River and the subject of a slander trial; its aftermath is discussed later in this chapter. Sylvia Van Kirk, "Ballenden, John."

59 Christie to Ross, 25 Mar. 1851, File 22, Ross Family Fonds.

60 Van Kirk, "Isbister, Alexander Kennedy."

61 Christie to Ross, 3 Mar. 1852, File 22, Ross Family Fonds.

62 Letitia Hargrave to Mrs Mactavish, 30 Sept. 1851, Hargrave Papers.

63 See Van Kirk, *"Many Tender Ties"* and Brown, *Strangers in Blood*. A few wives went with their husbands to the Canadas (Stewart, *The Ermatingers*).

64 Brown, "Keith, George." According to Brown, Nanette Keith was the "country daughter" of James Sutherland, a North West Company clerk.

65 Letitia Hargrave to James Hargrave, 18 Mar. 1852, Hargrave Papers. Hargrave's writings are discussed in Devereux and Venema, eds., *Women Writing Home*, xxix–xxxiii, 185–232.

66 Letitia Hargrave to James Hargrave, 28 Mar. 1852, Hargrave Papers.

67 Ghosh, *Sex and the Family in Colonial India*, 143–7.

68 1841 and 1851 Scotland Census, Ancestry.com, accessed 15 Jan. 2008. My thanks to Marian Press for locating this information.

69 "Prospectus, Miss Evershed's Boarding School," n.d., Ross Family Fonds.

70 "Miss Carnaby's Boarding School, Inverness," n.d., Ross Family Fonds. It's not clear if any members of the Ross family attended the Evershed or Carnaby school: the 1851 Scottish census of her household lists six pupil boarders but none, it seems, were from fur-trading families (1851 Scotland Census).

71 Letitia Hargrave to Letitia MacTavish, 9 Sept. 1844, *The Letters of Letitia Hargrave*, 185.

72 G. Barnston to James Hargrave, 14 Nov 1824, Hargrave Papers.

73 Although Letitia Hargrave spelt it "MacTavish," John George's correct surname was "McTavish." For his career, including his casting aside of his country wife, Nancy McKenzie, see Van Kirk, "Mctavish, John George."

74 Letitia Hargrave to Letitia MacTavish, 1 Dec. 1840, *The Letters of Letitia Hargrave*, 83–4.

75 Letitia Hargrave referred to her as "Jane" Ross, while the Red River Ancestry site calls her "Jean." For consistency's sake, I have kept the name "Jane." http://www.redriverancestry.ca/ROSS-DONALD-1798.php.

76 Letitia Hargrave to Letitia MacTavish, 6 June 1840, *The Letters of Letitia Hargrave*, 45.

77 Ibid., 7–14 June 1840, 47–8.

78 Ibid., 2 Sept. 1840, 74.

79 Letitia Hargrave to Dugald MacTavish, 2 Sept. 1840, *The Letters of Letitia Hargrave*, 81.

80 See Hargrave's other descriptions of indigenous women in fur-trade country (Letitia Hargrave to Mary MacTavish, 1 Sept. 1840, *The Letters of Letitia Hargrave*, 73). Such attitudes are also discussed in Hall, *Civilizing Subjects*, 221; Morton, "Separate Spheres in a Separate World"; Myers, *Antipodal England*, 73–7.

81 Fears of racial degeneration in India are discussed in Buettner, *Empire Families*, esp. Chaps. 1 and 2. For Indonesia, see Stoler, *Carnal Knowledge*.

82 See Dyer, "Shopping and the Senses."

83 Letitia Hargrave to James Hargrave, 18 Feb. 1852, Hargrave Papers. It is not clear which "old Mowat" was Maggie's father. Two Edward Mowats are listed in the Red River Ancestry website, one born in in 1778 and one in 1786. Both men had children with Cree women (Mary and Margaret Stewart, respectively) and both had daughters named Margaret. http://www.redriverancestry.ca/MOWAT-EDWARD-1778.php and http://www.redriverancestry.ca/MOWAT-EDWARD-1786.php

84 This description of the Reverend James, a Church of England minister at Red River, comes from Letitia Hargrave to Mrs Dugald MacTavish, 28 Aug. 1846, *The Letters of Letitia Hargrave*, 222. It's clear she did not care for the James family, as she told her mother in the same letter, "they plague me very much as I have plenty to do and they have no mercy."

85 Letitia Hargrave to James Hargrave, 5–10 Oct. 1851, *The Letters of Letitia Hargrave*, 264. It is not clear who "Mr Smith" was: he may have been William Smith (1828–1884), a Cree-English employee of the company who was married to Charlotte Mowat, the daughter of Margaret and Edward Mowat. If so, he would have been Maggie Mowat's brother-in-law, which might explain his concern for her well-being. http://www.redriverancestry.ca/SMITH-WILLIAM-1828.php

86 Isabella Hardisty to Richard Hardisty, 16 Jan. 1845, Hardisty Family Papers.

87 Dennison and Coleman, *Historic Nairn*, 3, 40, 57.

88 Stephens, rev. Milne, "Cumming, Roualeyn George Gordon"; Beignet, "Cumming, Constance Frederica Gordon." See also, Rampini, *A History of Moray and Nairn*, 394, 400–2.

89 "The Late Mrs. Lamb," *Nairnshire Telegraph*, 29 Nov. 1923. My thanks to Marion Press and Allen Barron, Museum Company secretary and director, Nairn. The Bank House has been described as representing a "confident and forward-looking time in Nairn's history" (Dennison and Coleman, *Historic Nairn*, 70).

90 Forbes and Macgowan, *A History of Nairnshire Farming Society, 1798–1998*, 53, 84–5; Rae and Lawson, *Doctor Gregor of Nairn*, 105, 126–7, 234.

91 For this overview of the Lamb family, see Marion Press, "Lamb Family Tree," compiled Aug. 2008, author's personal files. For Alexander James Lamb, see *Thacker's Indian Directory* (1917), 135; Roderick Lamb, "List or Manifest of Alien Passengers for the United States," 18 April 1916.

92 Lamb, John William, 1901 Scotland Census, Parish: Perth; ED: James Murrays Royal Asylum; Page: 5; Line: 19; Roll: CSSCT1901_126, Ancestry. ca, accessed 17 Feb. 2016; Lamb, John William (Regimental # 32152), Attestation Papers, 4 Jan. 1915, RG–150, Accession 1992–93/166, Box 5333–43.

93 Van Kirk, "Ballenden, John," in *Dictionary of Canadian Biography*, vol. 8, University of Toronto/Université Laval, 2003–, accessed February 18, 2016, http://www.biographi.ca/en/bio/ballenden_john_8E.html; also her "'The Reputation of a Lady.'"

94 "Deaths, Annie Ballenden McMurray," *Dundee Courier and Argus*, 5 May 1862.

95 See PRO, PROB 11/2257/667. HBRS, 3 (Fleming) "Wills," 1864, 44.

96 "Marriage Announcement," *Pall Mall Gazette*, 4 May 1871.

97 William Norris, *England and Wales Death Index: 1916-2007*, Ancestry.ca, accessed 16 Feb. 2016. William and Frances had one child, Edith Frances Fearne Denys Norris, born Apr. 1872 in Kensington, England and Wales Birth Index, 1837–1915, 302, Ancestry.ca, accessed 16 Feb. 2016.

98 "Death Announcement, Alexander Roderick McLeod Ballenden," *Dundee Courier and Daily Argus*, 16 Aug. 1861.

99 Van Kirk, *"Many Tender Ties"*; Brown, *Strangers in Blood*.

100 Alexander Christie to Donald Ross, n.m. 1844, File 22, Ross Family Fonds.

101 Christie to Ross, 25 Mar. 1851, Ross Family Fonds.

102 Christie to Ross, 3 Mar. 1852, Ross Family Fonds.

103 Van Kirk, *"Many Tender Ties,"* 168.

104 It seems that the baby was left with a nurse at Fort Chipewyan and died while still an infant (ibid. 276, n76). Catherine and her husband settled in St Thomas, Upper Canada, upon his retirement (Stewart, *The Ermatingers*, 4). See also "Ermatinger, Francis," *Hudson's Bay Company Biographical Sheets.*

105 http://www.redriverancestry.ca/CHRISTIE-ALEXANDER-1792.php; "Christie, Alexander Jr," *Hudson's Bay Company Biographical Sheets.*

106 Donald McTavish to Josette McKenzie, 1 May 1849, Peter and Josette McKenzie Family Fonds.

107 "McTavish, Alexander," *Hudson's Bay Company Biographical Sheets.*

108 "McKenzie, Peter," *Hudson's Bay Company Biographical Sheets.*

109 Cameron, *A History and Description of the Town of Inverness*, 52, 95; Rose and Anderson, *New Statistical Account of Scotland*, 17.

110 Cameron, *A History and Description*, 48, 50; Barron, *The Northern Highlands in the Nineteenth Century*, 179.

111 Newton, *Inverness*, 47.

112 Duncan McTavish to Josette McKenzie, n.d. 1840, Peter and Josette McKenzie Family Fonds.

113 "Board and Education," *Inverness Courier*, 13 May 1830.

114 "Old Inverness. Noted Boys' Boarding School," *Inverness Courier*, 31 Aug. n.y.; Anderson, *Inverness Before Railways*, 56–7.

115 Duncan McTavish to Josette Monier McKenzie, n.d., 1840, Peter and Josette McKenzie Family Fonds.

116 Donald McTavish to Josette McKenzie, n.d. May 1838, ibid.

117 Donald McTavish to Josette McKenzie, 22 July 1841, ibid.

118 For example, 11 Oct. 1837, 19 Dec. 1838, 12 Aug. 1840, in Barron, *The Northern Highlands in the Nineteenth Century*, 211, 239, 281.

119 Ibid, 230.

120 Ibid, 287.

121 Donald McTavish to Josette McKenzie, 22 July 1841, Peter and Josette McKenzie Family Fonds.

122 Donald McTavish to Josette McKenzie, 1 May 1849, Ibid.

123 G. Wills (?), Deputy Sheriff, to Superintendent LaTrobe, 17 Jan. 1842, Unit 37, File 2089, Inward Correspondence Files, PROV Victoria Archives.

124 Alistair McKenzie, Deputy Sheriff, to Superintendent LaTrobe, 9 Nov. 1842, ibid.

125 "Garryowen," *The Chronicles of Early Melbourne*, 107.

126 Ibid., 203–16, 346–62.

127 Ibid., 194–5.

128 "Hospital Subscribers," 3 July 1845, and "Temperance Pic Nic," 11 Nov. 1845, *Port Phillip Herald*.

129 "The Census for the Town," *Port Phillip Gazette*, 27 May 1846.

130 "English Extracts. The Indian Marriage at St. Martin's Church," *Port Phillip Herald*, 13 Sept. 1844.

131 "Return of Clerks in the Public Departments at Port Phillip with the Dates of Their Appointments and Salaries," Feb. 1848, Unit 30, File 953, Inward Correspondence Files, PROV Victoria Archives; n.a., *The Civil Establishment of the Colony of Victoria*, 191.

132 Alistair McKenzie to Superintendent LaTrobe, 17 Oct 1850, Unit 140, File 1777, Inward Correspondence Files, PROV Victoria Archives.

133 Donald McTavish to Superintendent Latrobe, 22 July 1844, ibid., File 1253.

134 Donald McTavish to Superintendent Latrobe, 12 Sept. 1848, ibid., File 1966.

135 Ibid.

136 Lambert and Lester, eds., *Colonial Lives*, 2.

137 Jacobs, *White Mother to a Dark Race*, xxxi.

138 For historiography on residential schooling in Canada, see Miller, *Shingwauk's Vision* and Milloy, *A National Crime*.

139 Reford, "Smith, Donald Alexander, 1st Baron Strathcona and Mount Royal." See also McDonald, *Lord Strathcona*, 405.

140 "The Late Mrs. Lamb," *Nairnshire Telegraph*, 20 Nov. 1923.

141 Buettner, "Sent Home to School: British Education, Status, and Returns Overseas," in *Empire Families*.

142 Van Kirk, "'What If Mama Was an Indian?'" 207–17; Henrietta Ross Black to James Ross, n.d. c. 1854, p. 495, Alexander Ross Fonds. This Ross family was not related to that of Donald Ross.

143 Smith, "'Gentlemen, This Is No Ordinary Trial,'" 364–80; FitzGerald and Muszynski, "Negotiating Female Morality." Smith mentions Matilda Davis as "the most powerful moulding force in the elevation of young girls in Red River" (377). For an exploration of shifting concepts of race in mid-nineteenth-century England, see Hall, *Civilizing Subjects*.

144 "Weekly Lessons," n.d., Box 1, File 7, Miscellaneous Papers and Items 130–67, n.d., Matilda Davis School Fonds.

145 Penny Russell's and Robert Ross's studies of manners in, respectively, colonial Australia and the Cape Colony provide a useful springboard for such considerations. (Russell. *Savage or Civilised?*; Ross, *Status and Respectability*).

146 Alexander Christie to Donald Ross, 25 Mar. 1851 and 3 Mar. 1852, Ross Family Fonds. In both letters, Christie, who was living at his home, Newlands (near Aberdeen), thanked Ross for sending him buffalo tongues.

147 Van Kirk, "Isbister, Alexander Kennedy."

148 Ibid.

Chapter Five

1 "Arrival Extraordinary," *Bell's New Weekly Messenger*, 12 Nov. 1843, 3.

2 "Presentation of the Ojjibaway Indians to the Queen," ibid., 24 Dec. 1843.

3 Smith, *Sacred Feathers*, 169.

4 Brode, "Rankin, Arthur."

5 *Bell's New Weekly Messenger*, 24 Dec. 1843; also *The Times*, 24 Nov., 22, 29 Dec. 1843.

6 "Grotesque," *Oxford English Dictionary Online* (accessed 30 May 2013).

7 Baignent, "Bullock, William."

8 Dippie, Mulvey, Troccoli, and Heyman, *George Catlin and His Indian Gallery*.

9 *Bell's Life in London and Sporting Chronicle*, 31 Dec. 1843.

10 *Bell's Weekly Messenger*, 14 Jan. 1844. See also, "Royal Gifts to the Ojibbeways," *Bell's Weekly Messenger*, 21 Jan. 1844. Catlin also ran advertisements in *The Observer*: 14 Jan., 17, 24 Mar. 1844.

11 *Bell's Weekly Messenger*, 14 Apr. 1844.

12 *The Observer*, 14 Apr. 1844.

13 Taylor also was a Colonial Office clerk. Reger, "Taylor, Sir Henry (1800–1886)."

14 "The 'Strong Wind' in St. Martin's Church," *Punch*, 20 Apr. 1844.

15 "Important – To the Ladies," *Punch*, 27 Apr. 1844.

16 Myers, *Antipodal England*, 73–7.

17 This would not be the last time *Punch* played with categories of race and gender in its articles. See, Chaney, "Heartfelt Thanks to *Punch*"; Codell, "Imperial Differences and Culture Clashes"; Yan, "(Ad)Dressing Women."

18 Rankin, *A Short History and Description*, 2.

19 Ibid., 5–6.

20 Schmalz, *The Ojibwa of Southern Ontario*, 111–19.

21 Ibid., 9.

22 Ibid., 13–14. A toxopholite is a lover of, or one devoted to, archery.

23 Over the course of the nineteenth century, hunting became synonymous

with Indigenous masculinity in a number of colonial sites; it also, though, became a source of tension between Indigenous and European men. See, for example, Vibert, "Real Men Hunt Buffalo"; Gillespie, "'I Was Well Pleased with Our Sport Among the Buffalo.'"

24 Rankin, *A Short History*, 14–15.

25 Ibid., 16.

26 Ibid., 16–17.

27 Ibid., 17.

28 Ibid., 18.

29 Ibid., 17.

30 Ibid., 18–19.

31 Ibid., 19.

32 Historians have long pointed to the ways in which constructs of white middle-class motherhood became suffused with sentiment during the nineteenth century. See, for example, Davidoff and Hall, *Family Fortunes*; also my discussion of missionary attitudes towards Ojibwe mothers: "Turning Strangers into Sisters."

33 Ibid, [Repeat title]19–20.

34 Charles Stuart, "An Adventure in Canada," in Rankin, *A Short History*, 21–30.

35 Genealogical details about Haynes and Cadotte can be found at http://person.ancestry.ca/tree/20988346/person/1064585154/facts and http://person.ancestry.ca/tree/20988346/person/1040763057/facts accessed 15 Dec. 2016. Cadotte's second wife appears under various names in these sources as either Celenise or Sarah.

36 Hancock, *An Emigrant's Five Years*, 240–1.

37 Kingston, *Western Wanderings*, 188–9.

38 Baraga, *The Diary of Bishop Frederic Baraga*, 209.

39 Cadotte was also annoyed that Baraga had given Sarah's dresses to Polly Johnson, "whom he hates." Diary entry, 17 Dec. 1860, *The Diary of Bishop Frederic Baraga*, 211.

40 Ibid.

41 Work on Maungwudaus's tour includes Smith, *Mississauga Portraits*, 126–63; Konkle, *Writing Indian Nations*, 205, 209–12; Flint, *The Transatlantic Indian*, 53–85; Qureshi, *Peoples on Parade*, 105–6; Thrush, *Indigenous London*, 6–13.

42 Smith, *Sacred Feathers*, 187.

43 Ibid., 188.

44 Ibid., 186–8.

45 Maungwudaus, *An Account of the Chippewa Indians*.
46 See, for example, Konkle, *Writing Indian Nations*; also Flint, *The Transatlantic Indian*.
47 Maungwudaus, *An Account*, 3.
48 Ibid.
49 Ibid.
50 Ibid., 4.
51 Ibid., 11.
52 Ibid., 3–4.
53 Ibid., 4.
54 Ibid., 5.
55 Ibid., 7.
56 "Joseph John Gurney Address," in Maungwudaus, *An Account*, 13–14.
57 Maungwudaus, *An Account*, 6.
58 Ibid., 4.
59 Ibid.
60 Ibid., 5.
61 Ibid., 8.
62 See also, Konkle, for a discussion of the incident with the monkey, *Writing Indian Nations*, 211–12. This was not the first Indigenous visit in which a monkey featured: Inuit visitors to London in 1767 were shown a Piccadilly menagerie in which one was displayed. They were said to have thought it a small Inuk (Thrush, *Indigenous London*, 117).
63 Maungwudaus, *An Account*, 9.
64 Ibid., 5.
65 Ibid., 5–6. Flint also discusses this aspect of Maungwudaus's account (*The Transatlantic Indian*, 63).
66 Catlin, *Adventures of the Ojibbeway and Ioway Indians*, 22, 25–6, 27, 30–1, 50–1.
67 For a range of discussions of the roles of interpreters and translators in settler-Indigenous encounters, see Eves, "Finding Place to Speak"; Taylor, *The Divided Ground*, 309–12; Van Toorn, *Writing Never Arrives Naked*, 152–74.
68 Maungwudaus, *An Account*, 6.
69 Ibid., 7.
70 Ibid., 6–7.
71 Konkle, *Writing Indian Nations*, 211.
72 Maungwudaus, *An Account*, 7.

73 Ibid., 8.

74 Ibid., 9.

75 Ibid., 7, 9.

76 Ibid., 8.

77 Ibid., 7–8.

78 Ibid., 9–10.

79 Ibid., 11.

80 Maungwudaus, *An Account of the Chippewa Indians*, Microfiche Version, Library and Archives Canada, 1978, 14. This version includes pages that are missing from the British Library edition.

81 Ibid., 15.

82 Ibid., 20.

83 Ibid., 21–2.

84 See, for example, Sarah Wegham, who wrote from Edinburgh, 5 May 1847; Harriet Gross, who wrote to Maungwudaus from Leicester, 26 Nov. 1847; and A. Wilson, who wrote 10 Dec. 1847, anxious about Maungwudaus's health, as well as other letters of condolence. Henry George Maungwudaus, *An Account of the Chippewa Indians*, 22, 24.

85 Walter Moloney, 26 Nov. 1846, ibid., 20.

86 William Thompson, 7 Dec. 1847, ibid., 23.

87 Edmund Smith, 24 Sept. 1847, ibid., 20; J. Higginbotham, 9 Dec. 1847, ibid., 23.

88 Hall, *Civilizing Subjects*, 274–6.

89 Qureshi, *Peoples on Parade*, 106; also Flint, *The Transatlantic Indian*, 82–5.

Chapter Six

1 Moore, *Dickens and Empire*, 64. The description of "The Noble Savage" as "uncontrolled hysteria" comes from critic Sheila M. Smith.

2 Dickens, "The Noble Savage," 337.

3 Moore, *Dickens and Empire*, 67.

4 Ibid. Moore's quote is from Shearer West, ed., *The Victorians and Race* (Aldershot, Hants.: Ashgate Publishing, 1996), 37.

5 Poignant, *Professional Savages*, 7. See also Ryan, *Picturing Empire*, 140–82.

6 The Six Nations reserve on the Grand became the most populous and wealthiest of its kind in Canada and the largest Iroquois settlement in North America. See Weaver, "The Iroquois," 182–5; Morgan, "Site of Dispossession."

7 Biographies of Johnson include Strong-Boag and Gerson, *Paddling Her*

Own Canoe; Rose, "Johnson, Emily Pauline"; Keller, *Pauline*; Johnston, *Buckskin and Broadcloth*. See also Monture, *We Share Our Matters – Teionkwakhashion Tsi Niionkwariho:ten.*, 63–106.

8 Strong-Boag and Gerson, *Paddling Her Own Canoe*, 50.

9 For a discussion of that costume, see ibid., 110–14.

10 See, for example, Johnston, *Buckskin and Broadcloth*, 102–3; Keller, *Pauline*, 106.

11 The most thorough discussion of this trip is in Johnston, *Buckskin and Broadcloth*, 106–7.

12 Ibid., 106–7.

13 Ibid., 108. There are gaps in our knowledge of Johnson's life, as her sister is said to have burned her personal correspondence after her death (ibid., 209).

14 Ibid., 202–8.

15 See "The Six Nations Celebrate the Jubilee," *The Globe*, 16 October 1897. The most complete account of Brant-Sero's life is Petrone, "Brant-Sero, John Ojijatekha."

16 Petrone, "Brant-Sero, John Ojijatekha."

17 Ibid.; see also Chapter 3.

18 "Male Beauty Show at the Victorian Fair," *Folkestone Daily News*, 27 August 1908.

19 Kreis, "John O. Brant-Sero's Adventures in Europe." Many thanks to Dr Kreis for sharing with me this article, and other work on German appearances of "show-Indians."

20 *Folkestone Daily News*, 27 August 1908.

21 There is a very large body of literature that attests to Empire's saturation of London's public spaces in this period. See, for example, Mackenzie, ed., *Imperialism and Popular Culture*; Mackenzie, ed., *Propaganda and Empire*; Bell, *The Idea of Greater Britain*; Coombes, *Reinventing Africa*, 187–216; Smith, "'Almost Pathetic ... but Also Very Glorious.'"

22 See, for example, an interview with Johnson in *The Gazette*, n.d., June 1894, which was reprinted in the *Ottawa Daily Free Press*.

23 See Pratt, *Imperial Eyes*, 201–8.

24 Deloria, *Playing Indian*; Conn, *History's Shadow*.

25 Coombes, *Reinventing Africa*.

26 Qureshi, *Peoples on Parade*, 269–70.

27 *The Gazette*, June 1894.

28 Tekahionwake, "The Lodge of the Law-Makers," *Daily Express*, 14 August 1906.

29 Ibid.

30 Such narratives were often told by missionaries in the Canadian context; see Morgan, *Public Men and Virtuous Women*, 133. For British feminists' use of such narratives and images, see Burton, *Burdens of History*.

31 Brant-Sero, "A Canadian Indian and the War," *The Times*, 2 January 1901. Johnson, for her part, did not see African-Canadians or Chinese-Canadians as full members of the Canadian nation. As Strong-Boag and Gerson point out, "her imagination was inevitably caught within the confines of the racial thinking of her age" (*Paddling Her Own Canoe*, 184).

32 Brant-Sero, "A Canadian Indian and the War." Brant-Sero's letter was also reprinted 17 January in the *Ottawa Citizen*, including *The Times*'s editorial reply, which justified his exclusion because the war "between two white races ... waged in the presence of an enormously preponderant population of a totally different character. In such a war, it was thought better not to call in the aid of races who habitually furnish a whole army of defenders of the empire."

33 Brendon, *The Decline and Fall of the British Empire*, 227–8.

34 While Mohawk men were among the contingent that travelled up the Nile to relieve General Gordon at Khartoum, they do not figure in discourses of the martial races. See Benn, *Mohawk on the Nile*; also Streets, *Martial Races*.

35 This question is addressed in Jane Carey, "A 'Happy Blending'? Māori Networks, Anthropology, and 'Native' Policy in New Zealand, the Pacific, and Beyond," in Carey and Lydon, eds., *Indigenous Networks*, 184–215.

36 Brant-Sero, "A Canadian Indian."

37 Although on other occasions Johnson wrote about western Indigenous communities and, in some of her works published in Britain, she suggested a pan-Indigenous identity and nationalism that might transcend specificities of language group, tribe, and clan (Van Steen, *Pauline Johnson*, 60–2).

38 Johnson, *The Gazette*; Brant-Sero, "Views of a Mohawk Indian," *Journal of American Folklore* 18 (1905): 160–2, 161 (Brant-Sero clipping file, Woodland Cultural Centre).

39 Johnson, *The Gazette*.

40 Berkhofer, *The White Man's Indian*; also Francis, *The Imaginary Indian*.

41 For such stereotypes, see Moyles and Owram, *Imperial Dreams*.

42 See also his interview with the *Daily News*, reprinted in the Toronto *Evening Telegram*, 18 January 1901, and in "Views of a Mohawk Indian," Brant-Sero clipping file, Woodland Cultural Centre.

43 *Evening Telegram*, 18 January 1901, ibid.

44 These programs are discussed in Jacobs, *White Mother to a Dark Race*; also Haskins, *Matrons and Maids*.

45 Johnson, "A Cry from an Indian Wife" and "A Red Girl's Reasoning" in Van Steen, *Pauline Johnson*, 60–2 and 103–42.

46 Strong-Boag and Gerson, *Paddling Her Own Canoe*, 92–5.

47 See Burton, *At the Heart of the Empire*, 20.

48 Johnson, "A Pagan in St. Paul's Cathedral (Iroquois Poetess's Impressions in London's Cathedral)," in Ruoff, ed., *The Moccasin Maker*, 139. The statue, a memorial to the early British empire in North America, is discussed in Thrush, *Indigenous London*, 82.

49 For an analysis of Johnson's rhetoric and imagery that leans towards her reinforcing stereotypes, see Monture, "The Challenge to Haudenosaunee Nationhood," Chapter 2 in *We Share Our Matters – Teionkwakhashion Tsi Niionkwariho:ten*.

50 Although Leighton has argued that Canadian audiences often "interpreted her change of clothing as a barometer of her assimilation" and were reluctant to see her evening gown as *also* being a costume ("Performing Pauline Johnson," 148–9).

51 Rappaport, *Shopping for Pleasure*, 151.

52 Ibid.

53 Strong-Boag and Gerson, "Finding Her Way as a New Woman," Chapter 2 in *Paddling Her Own Canoe*.

54 Kaplan and Stowell, *Theatre and Fashion*, 61.

55 For Johnson's love of canoeing, see Strong-Boag and Gerson, *Paddling Her Own* Canoe, 101, 115, 141. For wilderness tourism in Ontario during this period, see Jasen, *Wild Things*.

56 See, for example, Gardner and Rutherford, eds., *The New Woman*; Kaplan and Stowell, *Theatre and Fashion*; Bratton, ed., *Acts of Supremacy*; Booth and Kaplan, eds., *The Edwardian Theatre*.

57 For a discussion of Johnson's performing career, see Strong-Boag and Gerson, *Paddling Her Own Canoe*, 104–21. As they point out, prior to her appearances in "Indian" costume, she could be classified as an elocutionist, a category which would be considered more respectable than "actress." However, after she donned her buckskin costume, "no single term serves as a ready substitute" (105). I believe the term "performer" captures her appearances and presentation of self.

58 See Peter Bailey, "'Naughty but Nice': Musical Comedy and the Rhetoric of the Girl, 1892–1914," in Booth and Kaplan, eds., *The Edwardian Theatre*,

36–60; Pickering, "Mock Blacks and Racial Mockery: The 'Nigger' Minstrel and British Imperialism," in Bratton, ed., *Acts of Supremacy*, 179–236; Bratton, "Irrational Dress," in Gardner and Rutherford, eds., *The New Woman*.

59 Johnston, *Buckskin and Broadcloth*, 102.

60 Burton, *At the Heart of the Empire*, 19, 132, 136, 152. Dress was a crucial means of regulation for various parties within imperial contexts, from European missionaries to indigenous nationalists. Morgan, *Public Men and Virtuous Women*, 132–4; De Alwis, "'Respectability,' 'Modernity,' and the Policing of 'Culture'"; Gouda, "Gender and Hyper-masculinity."

61 Carter, "Categories and Terrains of Exclusion."

62 Bratton, "Irrational Dress," in Gardner and Rutherford, eds., *The New Woman*, 85–100; also her "Beating the Bounds: Gender Play and Role Reversal in the Edwardian Music Hall," in Booth and Kaplan, eds., *The Edwardian Theatre*, 86–110; Kaplan and Stovell, *Theatre and Fashion*.

63 Dave Russell, "The Making of the Edwardian Music Hall," in Booth and Kaplan, eds.. *Edwardian Theatre*, 61–85.

64 For these productions in Europe, see Mulvey, "Among the Sag-a-Noshes"; Haberland, "Nine Bella Coolas in Germany"; Nalla Clerici, "Indigenous Americans in Columbus's Home Land: A Show Within a Show"; and Daniele Florentine, "'Those Red-Brick Faces': European Press Reactions to the Indians of Buffalo Bill's Wild West Show," in Feest, ed., *Indians and Europe*. For a slightly later "Indian" performer in Europe, see McBride, *Molly Spotted Elk*.

65 N.a., "Visit of Brant-Sero. Direct Descendant of Famous Mohawk Chief in Chicago. Comes to See Tall Wigwams. Will Study People and Habits Here with Indian Scholar's Eye and Traveler's Breadth of View," *Chicago Evening Post*, 19 April 1900 (Brant-Sero clipping file, Woodland Cultural Centre). Brant-Sero may have been referring to Murphy's Minstrels, a blackface troupe that toured southern Ontario (Lenton-Young, "Variety Theatre," 183).

66 For a discussion of Johnson that locates her within current theoretical analyses of performance, see Veronica Strong-Boag, "A Red Girl Speaks."

67 Johnson apparently knew of Brant-Sero's performances but does not seem to have thought much of him (Strong-Boag and Gerson, *Paddling Her Own Canoe*, 257, n43).

68 The phrase "repetition and reiteration" comes from Butler, *Gender Trouble*, 140–1.

69 Kaplan and Stowell, *Theatre and Fashion*, 3.

70 Christopher Breward, "Sartorial Spectacles," 241.

71 Brant-Sero, "Views of a Mohawk Indian." He also made this point in his letter in *The Times*.

72 Russell, "The Making of the Edwardian Music Hall," Booth and Kaplan, eds.. *Edwardian Theatre*, 73–4.

73 "Male Beauty Show at the Victorian Fair," *Folkestone Daily News*, 27 August 1908.

74 Bederman, "Remaking Manhood Through Race and 'Civilization,'" Chapter 1 in her *Manliness and Civilization*.

75 My thanks to Mansour Bonakdarian for suggesting this mimicry.

76 "During his lecture, to illustrate the flexibility of the Mohawk tongue, he recited a short scene from *Othello* in English and immediately followed with the same lines in Mohawk. It was an off-hand translation, but nothing could better have persuaded his audience that he was no novice in either English or Mohawk" (n.a., "Visit of Brant-Sero").

77 Burton, *At the Heart of the Empire*, 19.

78 See Titley, *A Narrow Vision*.

79 Leighton points out that Canadian audiences "thrilled to her evocations of Indigenous experiences and injustices, which they were able to read as relegated to the past" ("Performing Pauline Johnson," 159). Correspondence between non-Indigenous executive members of the Ontario Historical Society hints that Brant-Sero's interpretations of the British-Mohawk alliance were not always welcomed wholeheartedly (James H. Coyne to David Boyle, 28 July, 6 October 1898, Ontario Historical Society Correspondence, 1898–1903).

80 Such relationships have been discussed in Miller, "Victoria's 'Red Children'"; also Carlson, "Rethinking Dialogue and History."

81 Peter Bailey, "Music Hall and the Knowingness of Popular Culture," in Bailey, *Popular Culture and Performance*.

82 Those images are discussed in Moyles and Owram, *Imperial Dreams and Colonial Realities*.

83 Pollock, "Making History Go," 8.

84 See Strong-Boag and Gerson, *Paddling Her Own Canoe*, 104–5. See, for example, Kaplan and Stowell, "The Suffrage Response," in *Theatre and Fashion*, which examines suffragists' use of fashion as a means of responding to attacks on their femininity.

85 As Strong-Boag and Gerson point out, her earlier poetry dealt with

sensuality and eroticism; however, her performances were carefully constructed to avoid overt sexual displays or connotations (*Paddling Her Own Canoe*, 112–13, 143–5).

86 Such travel diaries and correspondence are discussed in Morgan, "A Happy Holiday." Johnson's major qualms about her London appearances appear to have been not about her dealings with the aristocracy, but with the metropolis's literary circles (Keller, *Pauline*, 81).

87 This is largely the interpretation of Johnson offered by Francis, *The Imaginary Indian*.

88 James Clifford, "Mixed Feelings," 366. See also Butler, *Bodies That Matter*, 7.

89 Clifford, "Mixed Feelings," 366.

90 Butler, *Bodies That Matter*, 15.

91 Pollock, "Making History Go," 8.

Chapter Seven

1 Sarah Hunt, quoted in Slobodian, "First Nations Show They Won't Be Fenced In."

2 See, for example, Morgan, *"A Happy Holiday."*

3 Thrush, *Indigenous London*, 175–203.

4 Schneer, *London 1900*.

5 See, for example, Rutherford, "Indigenous Peoples, Colonialism, and Canada." For Australia, see John Maynard, "Marching to a Different Beat: The Influence of the International Black Diaspora on Aboriginal Australia," in Carey and Lydon, eds., *Indigenous Networks*, 262–72.

6 Thrush, *Indigenous London*, 13.

7 For an overview of these commemorations, see my "The Heyday of Public Commemorations in Canada, 1870s–1920s," Chap. 3 in *Commemorating Canada*.

8 Cheevers, "National Campaign Launched"; Law, "Native Memorial Unveiled."

9 Chief Ava Hill, quoted in Law, "Native Memorial Unveiled." See also Gould, "Overlooked First Nations War Heroes Recognized"; LaFleche, "First Nations Allies."

10 http://www.ontarioplaques.com/Plaques/Plaque_Brantford01.html

11 http://www.ontarioplaques.com/Plaques/Plaque_Brant24.html. To the best of my knowledge, the Ojibwe text in the plaque attributed to the

Mississauga of the New Credit tells the same story; I have not been able to find an English translation. It does differ, though, in that it has a raised engraving of one of Jones's portraits in the upper-left-hand corner.

12 For example, http://nativeamericanwriters.com/copway.html; http://www.firstpeople.us/FP-html-Wisdom/GeorgeCopway.html; http://www.heritagemississauga.com/page/Peter-Jones; http://www.stoneskingston.ca/indigenous-history/the-mississaugas-and-peter-jones/ https://prezi.com/2irxodfnrgg7/nahnebahwequay-catherine-sutton/; https://feministjuice.wordpress.com/2012/10/17/standing-upright-woman/

13 Hamilton and Monture have discussed Johnson's sale of wampum. Hamilton, *Collections and Objections*, 114–15; Monture, "The Challenge to Haudenosaunee Nationhood," Chap. 2 in his *We Share Our Matters – Teionkwakhashion Tsi Niionkwariho:ten*.

14 Dodd, "Canadian Historic Sites and Plaques."

15 http://ontarioplaques.com/Plaques/Plaque_Brant11.html

16 Brown, "Frances Nickawa"; Morgan, "Performing for 'Imperial Eyes.'"

17 There has been more research on the memory of Indigenous people in settler societies. For example, Coombes, ed., *Rethinking Settler Colonialism*; Veracini, *The Settler Colonial Present*; Furniss, *The Burden of History*. For Britain, see Thrush, "The City of Long Memory: Remembering and Reclaiming Indigenous London, 1982–2013," Chap. 6 in his *Indigenous London*.

18 Webster, *Englishness and Empire*. My thanks to Angela Woollacott for pointing me to Webster's work.

19 For example, Peers and Brown, *Pictures Bring Us Messages*.

20 N.a., "Became an Indian Chief. Story of Dunfermline Burgess. Squaw's Residence in Town," *Dunfermline Press*, 24 Feb. 1945, Norton Papers. It is possible that Dunfermline's Norton Place was named after him (Pitcairn, *The Old "Fitpaths,"* 283–4).

21 Fife Council, "Mohawk Chief Teyoninhokarawen Gets Freedom of Dunfermline," 26 June 2009.

22 Rincon, "Native American DNA Found in UK."

23 Kath Gourlay, "Scotland's Lost Braves"; N.a., "Orcadians Head to Canada." My thanks to Mark Abley for pointing me to these articles. See also McCormack, "Lost Women." McCormack's article includes a number of interviews and oral histories with Orcadian families about their Cree or Chipewyan ancestors.

24 Moses, "Six Nations Veterans and Political Change." Deskaheh's travels are discussed in Joëlle Rostkowski, "The Redman's Appeal for Justice:

Deskaheh and the League of Nations," in Feest, ed., *Indians and Europe*; Monture, *We Share Our Matters – Teionkwakhashion Tsi Niionkwariho:ten*, 116–30.

25 For example, see Reid, "Illegal Alien?"; Blanchard, "High Steel!"; Einhorn, "Warriors of the Sky." For popular memory, both Indigenous and non-Indigenous, see http://www.aboriginalironworkers.ca/tradition; http://www.sites.si.edu/exhibitions/exhibits/archived_exhibitions/booming/main.htm; http://dailycommercialnews.com/Labour/News/2015/5/Skywalkers-Mohawk-ironworkers-honoured-with-new-US-coin-1007985W/.

26 Morgan, "Mr. Moses Goes to England: Twentieth-Century Mobility and Networks at the Six Nations Reserve, Ontario," in Lydon and Carey, eds., *Indigenous Networks*, 167–83.

27 Thrush, *Indigenous London*, 212–17.

28 http://globalnews.ca/news/2671516/we-asked-for-prayers-for-our-people-alberta-first-nation-chief-meets-with-pope/

Bibliography

Primary Sources

ARCHIVAL SOURCES

Archives of British Columbia
British Columbia Archival Union List, John Edward Brant entry, www.aabc.
bc.ca/access/aabc/archbc/display/UVICARch-325

Archives of Ontario
F440, John Norton Fonds
MU5422, Ontario Historical Society Correspondence, Series C, 1898–1903

Glenbow Museum and Archives
M-5908-1442, Series 23-1, Hardisty Family Papers

Grey Roots Archival Collection, Owen Sound, Ontario
Sutton Papers

Hudson's Bay Company Archives
Hudson's Bay Company Biographical Files:
"Davis, John." http://www.gov.mb.ca/chc/archives/hbca/biographical/d/davis_
john.pdf., accessed 2 Feb. 2012.
"McKenzie, Peter." http://www.gov.mb.ca/chc/archives/hbca/biographical/
index.html, accessed 2 Feb. 2012.
"McTavish, Alexander." http://www.gov.mb.ca/chc/archives/hbca/
biographical/index.html, accessed 2 Feb. 2012.

Library and Archives Canada

C–84, Hargrave Papers

RG–10, M–2635, *Estate of John Brant-Sero*

RG–150, Accession 1992–93/166, Box 5333–43, Lamb, John William (Regimental # 32152), Attestation Papers

Newberry Library

John Norton Papers, 1804–1816, Ayer MS 654, Edward E. Ayer Collection

New York State Public Library

Headley Manuscript, BD 13350

Public Archives of Manitoba

Davis Family Fonds

E.235, Warren Sinclair Fonds, E.235

M65, Roll 1, MG2 C24 Matilda Davis School Fonds

M309–311 Ross Family Fonds

M11427, Peter and Josette McKenzie Family Fonds

MG 2 C14, Ross, Alexander Fonds

Victoria State Archives, Melbourne

PROV Victoria Archives 473, Inward Correspondence Files: Series 19, Units 30, 37, and 140, File 2089.

Victoria University Library, Toronto

Peter Jones Papers, Special Collections.

Woodland Cultural Centre, Brantford, Ontario

John Brant-Sero Clipping File

NEWSPAPERS

Bell's Life in London and Sporting Chronicle (1843)

Bell's New Weekly Messenger (1843)

Bell's Weekly Messenger (1844)

Daily Express (1906)

Daily News (1850)

Derby Mercury (1896)

Dundee Courier and Daily Argus (1861 and 1862)
Era (1895)
Folkestone Daily News (1908)
Gazette (1894)
Globe (1897)
John Bull (1850)
Leeds Mercury (1850)
Liverpool Mercury (1850)
Manchester Times (1850)
Nairnshire Telegraph (1923)
Observer (1844)
Pall Mall Gazette (1871)
Port Phillip Gazette (1846)
Port Phillip Herald (1844–45)
Punch (1844)
The Times (1901)
Weekly Raleigh Register (1857)

ONLINE CENSUS (ACCESSED THROUGH ANCESTRY.CA)

Ontario (Port Dover) 1891, 1901
England (London, Blackburn) 1861, 1891
Scotland (Jedburgh, Perth) 1841, 1851, 1871, 1901

PUBLISHED PRIMARY SOURCES

Allen, William. *The Life of William Allen with Selections from His Correspondence in Three Volumes*. vol. 1. London: Charles Gilpin, 1846.
Ball, Rev. Andrew. *The Statistical Account of Scotland*. Vol. 10: *Fife, 1791–1799*. Edited by John Sinclair. New introduction by R.G. Grant. Wakefield, UK: E.P. Publishing, 1978.
Baraga, Bishop. *The Diary of Bishop Frederic Baraga: First Bishop of Marquette, Michigan*. Edited by Regis M. Walling and Rev. N. Daniel Rupp. Translated by Joseph Gregorich and Rev. Paul Prud'homme. Detroit: Wayne State University Press, 1990.
Barron, James. *The Northern Highlands in the Nineteenth Century, Newspaper Index and Annals*. Vol. 2, *1825–1841*. Inverness: Robert Carruthers and Son, 1907.

Cameron, George A. *A History and Description of the Town of Inverness.* Inverness: Kenneth Douglas, James Smith, and Donald Fraser, 1847.

Catlin, George. *Adventures of the Ojibbeway and Ioway Indians in England, France, and Belgium.* Vol. 2. London: Published by the Author, 1852.

Chalmers, Peter. *Historical and Statistical Account of* Dunfermline. Edinburgh: Wm. Blackwood and Sons, 1844.

Cheevers, Melinda. "National Campaign Launched to Fund Native Memorial. Landscape of Nations to Be Built at Queenston Heights," *Niagara This Week*, 10 Jun 2015. [http://www.niagarathisweek.com/news-story/5669242-national-campaign-launched-to-fund-native-memorial/].

Copway, George. *Recollections of a Forest Life.* New York: C. Gilpin, 1850.

– *Running Sketches of Men and Places in England, France, Germany, Belgium, and* Scotland. (New York: J.C. Riker, 1851).

Devereux, Cecily, and Kathleen Venema, eds. *Women Writing Home, 1700–1920. Female Correspondence across the British Empire.* Vol. 3, *Canada.* London: Pickering and Chatto, 2006.

Dickens, Charles. "The Noble Savage," *Household Words*, 11 June 1853, 337–9.

Gadsden, Christopher. *Some Observations on the Two Campaigns against the Cherokee Indians, in 1760 and 1761.* Charles Town, SC: Peter Timothy, 1762.

Gould, Havard. "Overlooked First Nations War Heroes Recognized Two Centuries Later," *CBC News*, 2 Oct. 2016 [http://www.cbc.ca/news/canada/war-1812-first-nations-memorial-1.3786289].

Gourlay, Kath. "Scotland's Lost Braves," *The Scotsman*, 28 Aug. 2001 [http://www.electricscotland.com/history/canada/lost_braves.htm].

Hancock, William. *An Emigrant's Five Years in the Free States of America.* London: T. Cautley Newby, 1860.

Henderson, Ebenezer. *Annals of Dunfermline.* Glasgow: John Tweed, 1879.

Howe, Anthony, ed. *The Letters of Richard Cobden.* Vol. 2, *1848–1853.* Oxford: Oxford University Press, 2010.

Kingston, William H.G. *Western Wanderings; or, a Pleasure Tour in the Canadas.* London: Chapman and Hall, 1856.

Klinck, Carl F., and James J. Talman, eds. *The Journal of Major John Norton, 1816.* Introduction to the Reissue and Additional Notes by Carl Benn. Toronto: The Champlain Society, 1966 and 2011.

LaFleche, Grant. "First Nations Allies Finally Get Their Due," *St Catharines Standard*, 3 Oct. 2016 [http://www.stcatharinesstandard.ca/2016/10/03/lafleche-first-nations-allies-finally-get-their-due].

Law, John. "Native Memorial Unveiled at Queenston Heights," *Niagara Falls Review*, 2 Oct. 2016 [http://www.niagarafallsreview.ca/2016/10/02/

native-memorial-unveiled-at-queenston-heights].

Macleod, Margaret Arnett, ed. *The Letters of Letitia Hargrave*. Toronto: Champlain Society, 1947.

Maungwudaus (George Henry). *An account of the Chippewa Indians, who have been traveling among the Whites, in the United States, England, France and Belgium. Written by, the self-taught Indian, etc.* Boston: Published by the author, 1848. British Library Historical Print Edition, 1977.

– *An account of the Chippewa Indians, who have been traveling among the Whites, in the United States, England, France and Belgium. Written by, the self-taught Indian, etc.* Boston: Published by the author, 1848. Microfiche Version, Library and Archives Canada, 1978.

N.a. "Orcadians Head to Canada for Family Powwow. Islanders and Canada's Native Cree Indians Celebrate Ancient Bonds and Friendship," *Sunday Herald*, 29 Jan. 2005 [http://www.heraldscotland.com/news/12402082. Orcadians_head_to_Canada_for_family_powwow_I_slanders_and_ Canada_apos_s_native_Cree_Indians_celebrate_ancient_bonds_and_ friendship/].

Norris, William. *England and Wales Death Index: 1916–2007,* Ancestry.ca accessed 16 Feb. 2016.

Rankin, Arthur. *A Short History and Description of the Ojibbeway Indians Now on a Visit to England*. London: n.p., 1844.

Rincon, Paul. "Native American DNA found in UK," *BBC News*, 4 May 2007 [http://news.bbc.co.uk/2/hi/science/nature/6621319.stm].

Rose, Rev. Dr, and George Anderson. "Parish of Inverness," *New Statistical Account of Scotland*. Vol. 14, *Inverness, Ross and Cromarty*. Edinburgh: William Blackwood and Sons, 1845.

Slobodian, Mayana C. "First Nations Show They Won't Be Fenced In," *Guardian Weekly*, 29 July 2016, 289.

Thacker's Indian Directory (1917).

Wilberforce, Robert Isaac and Samuel Wilberforce. *The Life of William Wilberforce*. vol. 3 London: John Murray, 1838.

SECONDARY SOURCES

Altena, Marga. "'The Lady and the Indian': Representing an Inter-ethnic Marriage in Dutch and Canadian News Media (1906–1928)." *International Journal of Canadian Studies/Revue international d'études canadiennes* 38 (2008): 119–47.

Altick, Richard D. *The Shows of London*. Cambridge, MA.: The Belknap Press of Harvard University Press, 1978.

Anderson, Emma. *The Betrayal of Faith: The Tragic Journey of a Colonial Native Convert*. Cambridge, MA: Harvard University Press, 2007.

Anderson, Isabel Harriet. *Inverness Before Railways*. Inverness: A. and W. Mackenzie, 1885.

Baignent, Elizabeth. "Bullock, William (bap. 1773, d. 1849)," *Oxford Dictionary of National Biography*, see ed. H.C.G. Matthew and Brian Harrison (Oxford: Oxford University Press, 2004); online ed., ed. Lawrence Goldman, September 2013 [http://www.oxforddnb.com.myaccess.library. utoronto.ca/view/article/3923 accessed 25 February 2016].

Bailey, Peter. *Popular Culture and Performance in the Victorian City*. Cambridge: Cambridge University Press, 1998.

Ballantyne, Tony, and Antoinette Burton. *Empires and the Reach of the Global*. Harvard: Belknap Press, 2012.

– *Webs of Empire: Locating New Zealand's Colonial Past*. Vancouver: University of British Columbia Press, 2013.

Basson, Lauren L. *White Enough to Be American? Race Mixing, Indigenous People, and the Boundaries of State and Nation*. Chapel Hill, NC: University of North Carolina Press, 2008.

Barman, Jean. *French Canadians, Furs, and Indigenous Women in the Making of the Pacific Northwest*. Vancouver: University of British Columbia Press, 2014.

Bayly, C.A. *The Birth of the Modern World, 1780–1914*. Malden, MA: Blackwell Publishing, 2004.

Beckles, Hilary M. "Taking Liberties: Enslaved Women and Anti-slavery in the Caribbean," in *Gender and Imperialism*, edited by Clare Midgley. Manchester: Manchester University Press, 1998, 137–57

Bederman, Gail. *Manliness and Civilization: A Cultural History of Gender and Race in the United States, 1880–1917*. Chicago: University of Chicago Press, 1995.

Beignet, Elizabeth. "Cumming, Constance Frederica Gordon," *Oxford Dictionary of National Biography* 2010 [accessed 23 May 2013].

Belich, James. *Replenishing the Earth: The Settler Revolution and the Rise of the Anglo World, 1783–1939*. Oxford: Oxford University Press, 2009.

Bell, Duncan. *The Idea of Greater Britain: Empire and the Future of World Order, 1860–1900*. Princeton: Princeton University Press, 2007.

Benn, Carl. *The Iroquois in the War of 1812*. Toronto: University of Toronto Press, 1998.

– "Missed Opportunities and the Problem of Mohawk Chief John Norton's Cherokee Ancestry," *Ethnohistory* 59, no. 2 (Spring 2012): 261–91.

– *Mohawks on the Nile: Natives Among the Canadian Voyageurs in Egypt, 1884–1885.* Toronto: Natural Heritage Books, 2009.

Berkhofer, Robert F. *The White Man's Indian: Images of the American Indian from Columbus to the Present.* New York: Alfred Knopf, 1978.

Berry, Susan. "Recovered Identities: Four Métis Artists in Nineteenth-Century Rupert's Land," in *Recollecting: Lives of Aboriginal Women of the Northwest and Borderlands*, edited by Sarah Carter and Patricia A. McCormack. Edmonton: Athabasca University Press, 2011, 29–60.

Bhabha, Homi. "Of Mimicry and Man: The Ambivalence of Colonial Discourse," in his *The Location of Culture*. London: Routledge, 1994, 85–92.

Black-Rogers, Mary. "Varieties of 'Starving': Semantics and Survival in the Subarctic Fur Trade, 1750–1850," *Ethnohistory* 33, no. 4 (Fall 1986): 353–83.

Blanchard, David. "High Steel! The Kahnawake Mohawk and the High Construction Trade," *Journal of Ethnic Studies* 11, no. 2 (1983): 41–60.

Blunt, Alison. *Domicile and Diaspora: Anglo-Indian Women and the Spatial Politics of Home.* Malden, MA: Blackwell Publishing, 2005.

Bohaker, Heidi. "Anishinaabeg Toodaims: Contexts for Politics, Kinship, and Identity in the Eastern Great Lakes," in *Gathering Places: Aboriginal and Fur Trade Histories*, edited by Carolyn Podruchny and Laura Peers. Vancouver: University of British Columbia Press, 2010, 93–119.

Booth, Michael R., and Joel H. Kaplan, eds. *The Edwardian Theatre: Essays on Performance and the Stage.* Cambridge: Cambridge University Press, 1996.

Boucher, Ellen. *Empire's Children: Child Emigration, Welfare, and the Decline of the British World.* Cambridge: Cambridge University Press, 2014.

Boulware, Tyler. *Deconstructing the Cherokee Nation: Town, Region, and Nation among Eighteenth-Century Cherokee.* Gainsville, FL: University Press of Florida, 2011.

Bowsfield, Hartwell. "Christie, Alexander," in *Dictionary of Canadian Biography*, vol. 10. University of Toronto/Université Laval, 2003– . Accessed 13 December 2016 [http://www.biographi.ca/en/bio/christie_alexander_10E.html].

Bratton, J.S., ed. *Acts of Supremacy: The British Empire and the Stage, 1790–1930.* Manchester: Manchester University Press, 1991.

Breward, Christopher. "Sartorial Spectacles: Clothing and Masculine Identities in the Imperial City, 1860–1914," in *Imperial Cities: Landscape, Display and Identity*, edited by Felix Driver and David Gilbert. Manchester:

Manchester University Press, 1999, 238–53.

Brendon, Piers. *The Decline and Fall of the British Empire, 1781–1997.* London: Vintage Books, 2008.

Brode, Patrick. "Rankin, Arthur," in *Dictionary of Canadian Biography*, vol. 12. University of Toronto/Université Laval, 2003– [http://www.biographi.ca/en/bio/rankin_arthur_12E.html, accessed 25 February 2016].

Brown, Jennifer S.H. "Frances Nickawa: 'A Gifted Interpreter of the Poetry of Her Race,'" in *Recollecting: Lives of Aboriginal Women of the Northwest and Borderlands*, edited by Sarah Carter and Patricia A. McCormack. Edmonton: Athabasca University Press, 2011, 263–402.

– "Keith, George," in *Dictionary of Canadian Biography*, vol. 8. University of Toronto/Université Laval, 2003– [http://www.biographi.ca/en/bio/keith_george_8E.html, accessed 14 December 2016].

– *Strangers in Blood: Fur Trade Company Families in Indian Country.* Vancouver: University of British Columbia Press, 1980.

– "Vincent, Thomas (d. 1832)," in EN:UNDEF:public_citation_publication, vol. 6, University of Toronto/Université Laval, 2003– [http://www.biographi.ca/en/bio/vincent_thomas_1832_6E.html, accessed 31 December 2016].

Brown, Kathleen M. "The Anglo-Algonquian Gender Frontier," in *Negotiators of Change: Historical Perspectives on Native American Women*, edited by Nancy Shoemaker. New York: Routledge, 1995, 26–48.

Brownlie, Robin Jarvis. "A Persistent Antagonism: First Nations and the Liberal Order," in *Liberalism and Hegemony: Debating the Canadian Liberal Revolution*, edited by Jean-François Constant and Michel Ducharme. Toronto: University of Toronto Press, 2009, 298–321.

Brownstone, Arni. "Treasures of the Bloods," *Rotunda* 38, no. 2 (Winter 2005–06): 22–30.

Buettner, Elizabeth. *Empire Families: Britons and Late Imperial India.* London: Oxford University Press, 2004.

Burton, Antoinette. *At the Heart of the Empire: Indians and the Colonial Encounter in Late-Victorian Britain.* Berkeley: University of California Press, 1998.

– *Burdens of History: British Feminists, Indian Women, and Imperial Culture, 1865–1918.* Chapel Hill: University of North Carolina Press, 1994.

– "Travelling Criticism? On the Dynamic Histories of Indigenous Modernity," *Cultural and Social History* 9, no. 4 (2012): 491–6.

– and Tony Ballantyne, eds. *Moving Subjects: Gender, Mobility, and Intimacy in an Age of Global Empire.* Urbana and Chicago: University of Illinois Press, 2009.

Butler, Judith. *Bodies That Matter: On the Discursive Limits of "Sex."* New York: Routledge, 1993.

– *Gender Trouble: Feminism and the Subversion of Identity.* London: Routledge, 1990.

Calloway, Colin. G. *White People, Indians, and Highlanders: Tribal Peoples and Colonial Encounters in Scotland and America.* Oxford: Oxford University Press, 2008.

Carey, Jane, and Jane Lydon, eds. *Indigenous Networks: Mobility, Connections and Exchange.* London: Routledge, 2015.

Carlson, Keith Thor. "Rethinking Dialogue and History: The King's Promise and the 1906 Aboriginal Delegation to London," *Native Studies Review* 16, no. 2 (2005): 1–38.

Carter, Sarah. "Categories and Terrains of Exclusion: Constructing the 'Indian Woman' in the Early Settlement Era in Western Canada," in *In the Days of Our Grandmothers,* edited by Mary-Ellen Kelm and Lorna Townsend. Toronto: University of Toronto Press, 2006, 146–69.

– *The Importance of Being Monogamous: Marriage and Nation Building in Western Canada to 1915.* Edmonton and Athabasca: University of Alberta and Athabasca University Press, 2008.

– and Patricia A. McCormack, "Lifelines: Searching for Aboriginal Women of the Northwest and Borderlands," in *Recollecting: Lives of Aboriginal Women of the Northwest and Borderlands,* edited by Carter and McCormack. Edmonton: Athabasca University Press, 2011, 29–60.

Chaney, Michael A. "Heartfelt Thanks to *Punch* for the Picture: Frederick Douglass and the Transnational Jokework of Slave Caricature," *American Literature* 82, no. 1 (March 2010): 57–90.

Chang, David A. *The World and All the Things Upon It: Native Hawaiian Geographies of Exploration.* Minneapolis: University of Minnesota Press, 2016.

Chilton, Lisa. *British Female Migration to Canada and Australia, 1860s–1930.* Toronto: University of Toronto Press, 2007.

Chute, Janet. *The Legacy of Shingwaukonse: A Century of Native Leadership.* Toronto: University of Toronto Press, 1998.

Clifford, James. "Mixed Feelings," in *Cosmopolitics: Thinking and Feeling Beyond the Nation,* edited by Pheng Cheah and Bruce Robbins. Minneapolis: University of Minnesota Press, 1998.

Codell, Julie F. "Imperial Differences and Culture Clashes in Victorian Periodicals' Visuals: The Case of *Punch,*" *Victorian Periodicals Review* 39, no. 4 (Winter 2006): 410–28.

Cohen, Michèle. "'Manners' Make the Man: Politeness, Chivalry, and the Construction of Masculinity, 1750–1830," *Journal of British Studies* 44, no. 2 (April 2005): 312–29.

Colley, Linda. *The Ordeal of Elizabeth Marsh: A Woman in World History*. New York: Anchor Books, 2007.

Coombes, Annie E., ed. *Reinventing Africa: Museums, Material Culture and Popular Imagination*. New Haven and London: Yale University Press, 1994.

– ed. *Rethinking Settler Colonialism: History and Memory in Australia, Canada, Aoteroa New Zealand, and South Africa*. Manchester: Manchester University Press, 2006.

Conn, Steven. *History's Shadow: Native Americans and Historical Consciousness in the Nineteenth Century*. Chicago: University of Chicago Press, 2008.

Corbett, Katherine T. "Called Home: Finding Women's History in Nineteenth-Century Cemeteries," in *Her Past Around Us: Interpreting Sites for Women's History*, edited by Polly Wells Kaufman and Katharine T. Corbett. Malabar, Florida: Krieger Publishing, 2003, 163–88.

Crais, Clifton, and Pamela Scully. *Sara Baartman and the Hottentot Venus: A Ghost Story and a Biography*. Princeton, NJ: Princeton University Press, 2009.

Cronk, Douglas. "Editor's Introduction," in *Wacousta or, The Prophecy: A Tale of the Canadas*, by John Richardson. Ottawa: Carleton University Press, 1990.

Davidoff, Leonore. "Forgotten Figures: Aunts, Uncles, Nieces, Nephews, and Cousins," Chapter 4 in her *Thicker Than Water: Siblings and Their Relations, 1780–1920*. Oxford: Oxford University Press, 2012.

– and Catherine Hall, *Family Fortunes: Men and Women of the English Middle Class, 1780–1850*. Chicago: University of Chicago Press, 1987.

De Alwis, Malathi. "'Respectability,' 'Modernity,' and the Policing of 'Culture.' in Colonial Ceylon." In *Gender, Sexuality, and Colonial Modernities*, edited by Antoinette Burton. London: Routledge, 1999, 177–92.

Deloria, Philip J. "Places Like Houses, Banks, and Continents: An Appreciative Reply to the Presidential Address," *American Quarterly* 58, no. 1 (March 2006): 23–9.

– *Indians in Unexpected Places*. Lawrence, Kansas: University Press of Kansas, 2004.

– *Playing Indian*. New Haven: Yale University Press, 1998.

Dennison, E. Patricia, and Russel Coleman. *Historic Nairn: The Archaeological Implications of Development*. Edinburgh: Historic Scotland in Association with Scottish Cultural Press, 1999.

Dippie, Brian, Christopher Mulvey, Joan Carpenter Troccoli, and Therese

Thau Heyman. *George Catlin and His Indian Gallery*. Washington, DC: Smithsonian American Art Museum and W.W. Norton & Company, 2002.

Dodd, Diane. "Canadian Historic Sites and Plaques: Heroines, Trailblazers, The Famous Five," CRM: *The Journal of Heritage Stewardship* 6, no. 2 (Summer 2009): 29–66.

Dyer, Serena. "Shopping and the Senses: Retail, Browsing, and Consumption in 18th-Century England," *History Compass* 12, no. 9 (Sept. 2014): 694–703.

Einhorn, Arthur C. "Warriors of the Sky: The Iroquois Iron Workers," *European Review of Native American Studies* 13, no. 1 (1999): 25–34.

Elbourne, Elizabeth. "Broken Alliance: Debating Six Nations' Land Claims in 1822," *Cultural and Social History* 9, no. 4 (Dec. 2012): 497–595.

– "Imperial Networks and Indigenous People in the Early Nineteenth Century," in *Rediscovering the British World*, edited by Phillip Buckner and R. Douglas Francis. Calgary: University of Calgary Press, 2005, 59–85.

– "The Sin of the Settler: The 1835–36 Select Committee on Aborigines and Debates Over Virtue and Conquest in the Early Nineteenth-Century British White Settler Empire," *Journal of Colonialism and Colonial History* 4, no. 3 (Winter 2003).

Ellinghaus, Katherine. "Strategies of Elimination: 'Exempted' Aborigines, 'Competent' Indians and Twentieth Century Assimilation Policies in Australia and the United States," *Online Journal of the Canadian Historical Association* 18, no. 2 (2007): 202–25 [accessed 12 Aug. 2008].

– *Taking Assimilation to Heart: Marriages of White Women and Indigenous Men in the United States and Australia, 1887–1937*. Lincoln and London: University of Nebraska Press, 2006.

Eustace, Nicole. *1812: Passion Is the Gale: Emotion, Power, and the Coming of the American Revolution*. Chapel Hill: University of North Carolina Press, 2008.

– *War and the Passions of Patriotism*. Philadelphia: University of Pennsylvania Press, 2012.

– Eugenia Lean, Julie Livingston, Jan Plamper, William M. Reddy, and Barbara H. Rosenwein. "AHR Conversation: The Historical Study of Emotions," *American Historical Review* 117, no. 5 (Dec. 2012): 1486–531.

Eves, Rosalyn Collings. "Finding Place to Speak: Sarah Winnemucca's Rhetorical Practices in Disciplinary Spaces," *Legacy: A Journal of American Women Writers* 31, no. 1 (2014): 1–22.

Feest, Christian, ed. *Indians and Europe: An Interdisciplinary Collection of Essays*. Aachen, The Netherlands: Rader Verlag, 1987.

Ferris, Neal. *The Archaeology of Native-Lived Colonialism: Challenging History in the Great Lakes*. Tucson, AZ: University of Arizona Press, 2009.

Fisher, Michael. "Asians in Britain: Negotiations of Identity Through Self-Representation," in *A New Imperial History: Culture, Identity and Modernity in Britain and the Empire, 1660–1840*, edited by Kathleen Wilson. Cambridge: Cambridge University Press, 2004, 91–112.

Fiske, Jo-Anne. "Political Status of Indigenous Indian Women: Contradictory Implications of Canadian State Policy," in *In the Days of Our Grandmothers: A Reader in Aboriginal Women's History in Canada*, edited by Mary-Ellen Kelm and Lorna Townsend. Toronto: University of Toronto Press, 2006, 336–66.

FitzGerald, Sharron A., and Alicja Muszynski. "Negotiating Female Morality: Place, Ideology and Agency in the Red River Colony," *Women's History Review* 16, no. 5 (2007): 661–80.

Flint. Kate. *The Transatlantic Indian, 1776–1930*. Princeton: Princeton University Press, 2009.

Forbes, Patricia R., and Alan J. Macgowan. *A History of Nairnshire Farming Society, 1798–1998*. Nairn: Nairnshire Farming Society, 1998.

Francis, Daniel. *The Imaginary Indian: The Image of the Indian in Canadian Culture*. Vancouver: Arsenal Pulp Press, 1992.

Fraser, Robert L. "Hagerman, Christopher Alexander," in *Dictionary of Canadian Biography*, vol. 7, University of Toronto/Université Laval, 2003– [http://www.biographi.ca/en/bio/hagerman_christopher_alexander_7E. html, accessed 10 September 2013].

Fuchs, Denise. "Native Sons of Rupert's Land, 1760 to the 1860s," PhD thesis, University of Manitoba, 2000.

Fulford, Tim. *Romantic Indians: Native Americans, British literature, and Transatlantic Culture, 1756–1830*. New York: Oxford University Press, 2006.

– and Kevin Hutchings, eds. *Native Americans and Anglo-American Culture: The Indian Atlantic*. New York: Cambridge University Press, 2009.

Fullagar, Kate. *The Savage Visit: New World People and Popular Imperial Culture in Britain, 1710–1795*. Berkeley, CA: University of California Press, 2012.

Furniss, Elizabeth. *The Burden of History: Colonialism and the Frontier Myth in a Rural Canadian Community*. Vancouver: University of British Columbia Press, 1999.

Gardner, Viv, and Susan Rutherford, eds. *The New Woman and Her Sisters: Feminism and Theatre, 1850–1914*. Manchester: Harvester Wheatsheaf, 1992.

Garryowen [Edmund Finn]. *The Chronicles of Early Melbourne*. Melbourne: Ferguson and Mitchell, 1888.

Ghosh, Durba. *Sex and the Family in Colonial India: The Making of Empire.* Cambridge: Cambridge University Press, 2006.

Gillespie, Greg. "'I Was Well Pleased with Our Sport Among the Buffalo': Big-Game Hunters, Travel Writing, and Cultural Imperialism in the British North American West, 1847–72," *Canadian Historical Review* 83, no. 4 (Dec. 2002): 555–85.

Gordon, Alexander. "Rathbone, William (1757–1809)," rev. M.W. Kirby, *Oxford Dictionary of National Biography* (Oxford, 2004) [accessed 16 July 2011].

Gouda, Frances. "Gender and Hyper-masculinity as Post-Colonial Modernity During Indonesia's Struggle for Independence, 1945 to 1949," in *Gender, Sexuality, and Colonial Modernities,* edited by Antoinette Burton. London: Routledge, 1999, 161–74.

Graham, Elizabeth. *Medicine Man to Missionary: Missionaries as Agents of Change Among the Indians of Southern Ontario, 1784–1867.* Toronto: P. Martin Associates, 1975.

Grant, John Webster. *Moon of Wintertime: Missionaries and the Indians of Canada in Encounter Since 1534.* Toronto: University of Toronto Press, 1984.

Greer, Alan. *Mohawk Saint: Catherine Tekakwitha and the Jesuits.* New York: Oxford University Press, 2005.

Grimshaw, Patricia. "Interracial Marriages and Colonial Regimes in Victoria and Aotearoa/New Zealand," *Frontiers: A Journal of Women's Studies* 23, no. 3 (2002): 12–28.

Guest, Harriet. "Ornament and Use: Mai and Cook in London," in *A New Imperial History: Culture, Identity and Modernity in Britain and the Empire, 1660–1840,* edited by Kathleen Wilson. Cambridge: Cambridge University Press, 2004, 317–45.

Haig-Brown, Celia. "The 'Friends' of Nahnebahwequa," in *With Good Intentions: Euro-Canadian and Aboriginal Relations in Colonial Canada,* edited by Celia Haig-Brown and David Nock. Vancouver: University of British Columbia Press, 2006, 132–57.

– "Seeking Honest Justice in a Land of Strangers: Nahnebahwequa's Struggle for Land," *Journal of Canadian Studies/Revue e'études canadiennes* 26, no. 4 (Hiver 2001/2002 Winter): 143–72.

Hall, Catherine. *Civilizing Subjects: Metropole and Colony in the English Imagination, 1830–1867.* Chicago: University of Chicago Press, 2002.

– ed. *Cultures of Empire: Colonizers in Britain and the Empire in the Nineteenth and Twentieth Centuries, a Reader.* Manchester: Manchester University Press, 2000.

– and Sonya O. Rose. "Introduction: Being at Home with the Empire," in *At Home With the Empire: Metropolitan Culture and the Imperial World*, edited by Hall and Rose. New York: Cambridge University Press, 2006, 1–31.

Hamilton, Michelle. *Collections and Objections: Aboriginal Material Culture in Southern Ontario*. Montreal and Kingston: McGill-Queen's Press, 2010.

Harris, Cole. *Making Indigenous Space: Colonialism, Resistance, and Reserves in British Columbia*. Vancouver: University of British Columbia Press, 2002.

Harvey, Karen. "The History of Masculinity, Circa 1650–1800," *Journal of British Studies* 44, no. 2 (April 2005): 296–311.

Haskins, Victoria K. *Matrons and Maids: Regulating Indian Domestic Service in Tucson, 1914–1934*. Tucson: University of Arizona Press, 2014.

– and John Maynard. "Sex, Race, and Power: Aboriginal Men and White Women in Australian History," *Australian Historical Studies* 126 (2003): 191–216.

Hatley, Tom. *The Dividing Paths: Cherokees and South Carolinians Through the Era of Revolution*. New York: Oxford University Press, 1995.

Hindraker, Eric. "The 'Four Indian Kings' and the Imaginative Construction of the First British Empire," *William and Mary Quarterly* 53, no. 3 (July 1996): 487–526.

Hodes, Martha. *The Sea Captain's Wife: A True Story of Love, Race, and War in the Nineteenth Century*. New York: W.W. Norton and Co., 2006.

– *White Women, Black Men: Illicit Sex in the Nineteenth-Century South*. New Haven: Yale University Press, 1997.

Hodgman, V.W. "Simpkinson de Wesselow, Francis Guillemard (1819–1906)," *Australian Dictionary of Biography* [http://adb.anu.edu.au/biography/simpkinson-de-wesselow-francis-guillemard-2664/text3711, accessed 17 July 2011].

Holly, Nathaniel F. "Transatlantic Indians in the Early Modern Era," *History Compass* 14, no. 10 (October 2016): 522–32.

Hoock, Holger. *Empire of the Imagination: Politics, War, and the Arts in the British World, 1750–1850*. London: Profile Books, 2010.

Huneault, Kristina. "Miniature Objects of Cultural Covenant: Portraits and First Nations Sitters in British North American," *Canadian Art Review* (*RACAR*) 30, no. 1/2 (2005): 87–100.

Hunter, Fred. "Johnstone, Christian Isobel (1781–1857)." *Oxford Dictionary of National Biography*, online ed., edited by David Cannadine. Oxford: Oxford University Press, 2004 [accessed April 2, 2017].

Hutchings, Kevin. "'The Nobleness of the Hunter's Deeds': British Romanticism, Christianity, and Ojibwa Culture in George Copway's

Recollections of a Forest Life," in *Native Americans and Anglo-American Culture: The Indian Atlantic*, edited by Tim Fulford and Kevin Hutchings. New York: Cambridge University Press, 2009, 217–40.

Jacobs, Margaret. *White Mother to a Dark Race: Settler Colonialism, Maternalism, and the Removal of Indigenous Children in the American West and Australia, 1880–1940.* Lincoln and London: University of Nebraska Press, 2009.

Jackson, John C. *Children of the Fur Trade: Forgotten Métis of the Pacific Northwest.* Missoula, MT: Mountain Press, 1996.

Jasanoff, Maya. *Edge of Empire: Lives, Culture, and Conquest in the East, 1750–1850.* New York: Knopf, 2005.

Jasen, Patricia. *Wild Things: Nature, Culture, and Tourism in Ontario, 1791–1914.* Toronto: University of Toronto Press, 1995.

Jewitt, John. "Extraordinary Arrivals: Native American Visitors to London, 1710–1844," MA thesis, University of Kent at Canterbury, 1998.

Johnson, E. Pauline. *The Moccasin Maker.* Edited by A. Lavonne Brown Ruoff. Tucson: University of Arizona Press, 1987.

Johnston, Anna. "British Missionary Publishing, Missionary Celebrity, and Empire," *Nineteenth-Century Prose* 32, no. 1 (Fall 2005): 20–47.

Johnston, Charles M. "The Six Nations in the Grand River Valley, 1784–1847," in *Aboriginal Ontario: Historical Perspectives on the First Nations*, edited by Edward S. Rogers and Donald B. Smith. Toronto: Dundurn Press, 1994, 167–81.

Johnston, Sheila M.F. *Buckskin and Broadcloth: A Celebration of E. Pauline Johnson – Tekahionwake, 1861–1913.* Ottawa: Natural History/Natural Heritage, 1997.

Kaplan, Joel H., and Sheila Stowell. *Theatre and Fashion: Oscar Wilde to the Suffragettes.* Cambridge: Cambridge University Press, 1994.

Keller, Betty. *Pauline: A Biography of Pauline Johnson.* Toronto: Douglas and McIntyre, 1981.

Kelsey, Isabel T. "Tekarihogen, John Brant," *Dictionary of Canadian Biography*, vol. 6. University of Toronto/Université Laval, 2003– [http://www.biographi.ca/en/bio/tekarihogen_1794_1832_6E.html, accessed 4 July 2013].

Klinck, Carl F. "John Norton," *Dictionary of Canadian Biography.* Vol. 6, *1821–1835* [http://www.biographi.ca/en/bio/norton_john_6E.html, accessed 4 July 2013].

Konkle, Maureen. *Writing Indian Nations: Native Intellectuals and the Politics of Historiography, 1827–1863.* Chapel Hill: University of North Carolina Press, 2004.

Kreis, Karl Markus. "John O. Brant-Sero's Adventures in Europe," *European Review of Native American Studies* 15, no. 2 (2010): 27–30.

Laidlaw, Zoë. "'Aunt Anna's Report': The Buxton Women and the Aborigines Select Committee, 1834–37," *Journal of Imperial and Commonwealth History* 32, no. 2 (May 2004): 1–28.

– *Colonial Connections: Patronage, the Information Revolution and Colonial Government*. London: Routledge, 2005.

Lambert, David, and Alan Lester, eds. *Colonial Lives Across the British Empire: Imperial Careering in the Long Nineteenth Century*. Cambridge: Cambridge University Press, 2006.

Leighton, Mary Elizabeth. "Performing Pauline Johnson: Representations of the 'Indian Poetess' in the Periodical Press, 1892–95," *Essays on Canadian Writing*, 65 (1998), 141–62.

Lenton-Young, Gerald. "Variety Theatre," in *Early Stages: Theatre in Ontario, 1800–1914*, edited by Ann Saddlemyer. Toronto: University of Toronto Press, 1990, 166–213.

Lester, Alan. "British Settler Discourse and the Circuits of Empire," *History Workshop Journal* 54, no. 1 (Autumn 2002): 24–48.

– *Imperial Networks: Creating Identities in Nineteenth-Century South Africa and Britain*. London: Routledge, 2001.

– and Fae Dussart. *Colonization and the Origins of Humanitarian Governance: Protecting Aborigines Across the British Empire*. Cambridge: Cambridge University Press, 2014.

Linkon, Sherry Lee. "Reading Lind Mania: Print Culture and the Construction of Nineteenth-Century Audiences," *Book History* 1 (1998): 94–106.

Lobban, Michael. "Brougham, Henry Peter, first Baron Brougham and Vaux (1778–1868)," *Oxford Dictionary of National Biography* (Oxford, 2004) [accessed 17 July 2011].

Lorenzkowski, Barbara. *Sounds of Ethnicity: Listening to German North America, 1850–1914*. Winnipeg: University of Manitoba Press, 2010.

Luckhurst, Mary, and Jane Moody. "Introduction: The Singularity of Theatre Celebrity," in *Theatre and Celebrity in Britain, 1660–2000*, edited by Mary Luckhurst and Jane Moody. Basingstoke, UK: Palgrave Macmillan, 2005, 1–14.

Mackenzie, John M., ed. *Imperialism and Popular Culture*. Manchester: Manchester University Press, 1992.

– ed. *Propaganda and Empire: The Manipulation of British Public Opinion, 1880–1960*. Manchester: Manchester University Press, 1984.

Magee, Gary B., and Andrew S. Thompson. *Empire and Globalisation:*

Networks of People, Goods and Capital in the British World, c. 1850–1914. Cambridge: Cambridge University Press, 2010.

Mattingly, Carol. *Appropriat[ing] Dress: Women's Rhetorical Style in Nineteenth-Century America*. Carbondale and Edwardsville: Southern Illinois University Press, 2002.

Maynard, John. "Transcultural/transnational Interaction and Influences on Aboriginal Australia," in *Connected Worlds: History in Transnational Perspective*, edited by Ann Curthoys and Marilyn Lake. Canberra: ANU E-Press, 2005, 195–208.

McBride, Bunny. *Molly Spotted Elk: A Penobscot in Paris*. Norman, OK: University of Oklahoma Press, 1995.

McCormack, Patricia A. "Lost Women: Native Wives in Orkney and Lewis," in *Recollecting: Lives of Aboriginal Women of the Canadian Northwest and Borderlands*, edited by Sarah Carter and Patricia A. McCormack. Edmonton, AB: Athabasca University Press, 2011, 61–88.

McDonald, Donna. *Lord Strathcona: A Biography of Donald Alexander Smith*. Toronto: Dundurn Press, 2002.

McDonnell, Michael A. "Facing Empire: Indigenous Histories in Comparative Perspective," in *The Atlantic World in the Antipodes: Effects and Transformations Since the Eighteenth Century*, edited by Kate Fullagar. Newcastle upon Tyne, UK: Cambridge Scholars Publishing, 2012, 220–36.

McGrath, Ann. "Consent, Marriage, and Colonialism: Indigenous Australian Women and Colonizer Marriages," *Journal of Colonialism and Colonial History* 6, no. 3 (2005): 1–24.

McNairn, Jeffrey L. "As the Tsunami of Histories of Atlantic and Liberal Revolutions Wash Up in Upper Canada: Worries from a Colonial Shore," Parts I and II, *History Compass* 14, no. 9 (September 2016): 407–17 and 418–29.

Middleton, Dorothy. "Franklin, Jane, Lady Franklin (1792–1875)," *Oxford Dictionary of National Biography* (Oxford, 2004) [accessed 17 July 2011].

Miller, J.R. *Compact, Contract, Covenant: Aboriginal Treaty-making in Canada*. Toronto: University of Toronto Press, 2009.

– *Shingwauk's Vision: A History of Native Residential Schools*. Toronto: University of Toronto Press, 1996.

– "Victoria's 'Red Children': The 'Great White Mother' and Native-Newcomer Relations in Canada," *Native Studies Review* 17, no. 1 (2008): 1–23.

Milloy, John. *A National Crime: The Canadian Government and the Residential School System, 1879–1986*. Winnipeg: University of Manitoba Press, 1999.

Monture, Rick. *We Share Our Matters – Teionkwakhashion Tsi Niionkwariho:ten: Two Centuries of Writing and Resistance at Six Nations of the Grand River.* Winnipeg: University of Manitoba Press, 2014.

Moore, Grace. *Dickens and Empire: Discourses of Class, Race and Colonialism in the Work of Charles Dickens.* Aldershot, UK: Ashgate Publishing, 2004.

Morgan, Cecilia. "'Better Than Diamonds': Sentimental Strategies and Middle-Class Culture, Canada West," *Journal of Canadian Studies* 32, no. 3 (Winter 1997–98): 125–48.

– *Commemorating Canada: History, Heritage, and Memory 1850s-1990s.* Toronto: University of Toronto Press, 2016.

– *"A Happy Holiday": English-Canadians and Transatlantic Tourism, 1870–1930.* Toronto: University of Toronto Press, 2008.

– "'The Joy My Heart Has Experienced': Eliza Field Jones and the Transatlantic Missionary World, 1830s–1840s," in Tolly Bradford and Chelsea Horton, eds., *Mixed Blessings: Indigenous Encounters with Christianity in Canada.* Vancouver: University of British Columbia Press, 2016, 83–101.

– "Kahgegagahbowh's (George Copway's) Transatlantic Performance: *Running Sketches,* 1850," *Cultural and Social History Journal* 9, no. 4 (Fall 2012): 527–48.

– "Performing for 'Imperial Eyes': Bernice Loft and Ethel Brant Monture, Ontario, 1930s–1960s," in *Contact Zones: Aboriginal and Settler Women in Canada's Colonial Past,* edited by Myra Rutherdale and Katharine Pickles. Vancouver: University of British Columbia Press, 2005, 65–89.

– *Public Men and Virtuous Women: The Gendered Languages of Religion and Politics in Upper Canada, 1781–1850.* Toronto: University of Toronto Press, 1996.

– "Rethinking Nineteenth-Century Transatlantic Worlds: With and Through 'Indian Eyes,'" *Victorian Studies* 52, no. 2 (Winter 2010): 255–62.

– "Site of Dispossession, Site of Persistence: The Haudenosaunee (Six Nations) at the Grand River Territory in the Nineteenth and Twentieth Centuries," in *Indigenous Communities and Settler Colonialism: Land Holding, Loss and Survival in an Interconnected World,* edited by Alan Lester and Zee Laidlaw. New York: Palgrave Macmillan, 2015, 192–213.

– "Turning Strangers into Sisters? Gender and the Work of Missionary Colonization in Upper Canada," in *Sisters or Strangers?: Immigrant Women, Minority Women, and the Racialized "Other,"* edited by Marlene Epp, Franca Iacovetta, and Frances Swyripa. Toronto: University of Toronto Press, 2004, 23–48.

– "'A Wigwam to Westminster': Performing Mohawk Identity in Imperial Britain, 1890s–1900s," *Gender and History* 25, no. 2 (Aug. 2003): 319–41.

– "'Write Me. Write Me': Native and Métis Letter-Writing across the British Empire, 1800–1870," in *Writing the Empire: Interventions from Below*, edited by Kirsty Reid and Fiona Paisley. London: Routledge Press, 2014, 141–56.

Morley, Marjorie G. "Davis, Mathilda," in *Dictionary of Canadian Biography*, vol. 10. University of Toronto/Université Laval, 2003– [http://www.biographi.ca/en/bio/davis_mathilda_10E.html, accessed 9 July 2013].

Morton, Suzanne. "Separate Spheres in a Separate World: African–Nova Scotian Women in Late 19th-Century Halifax County," *Acadiensis* 22, no. 2 (Spring 1993): 61–83.

Moses, John. "Six Nations Veterans and Political Change at the Grand River Reserve, 1917–1924," in *Aboriginal Peoples and the Canadian Military: Historical Perspectives*, edited by P. Whitney Lackenbauer and Craig Leslie Mantle. Kingston: Canadian Defence Academy Press, 2007, 131–5.

Moses, L.M. *Wild West Shows and the Image of American Indians, 1883–1933*. Albuquerque, NM: University of New Mexico Press, 1996.

Moyles, R.G., and Doug Owram. *Imperial Dreams and Colonial Realities: British Views of Canada, 1880–1914*. Toronto: University of Toronto Press, 1988.

Myers, Janet C. *Antipodal England: Emigration and Portable Domesticity in the Victorian Imagination*. Albany: SUNY Press, 2009.

N.a., *The Civil Establishment of the Colony of Victoria for the Year 1851*. Melbourne: Public Record Office, 1976.

N.a., *Notes and Queries*, vol. 12, no. 3 (10 Feb. 1917): 114 [http://nq.oxfordjournals.org/content/s12-III/59/114-e.extract, accessed 17 July 2011].

Nelles, H.V. "Beardsley, Bartholomew Crannell," in *Dictionary of Canadian Biography*, vol. 8. University of Toronto/Université Laval, 2003– [http://www.biographi.ca/en/bio/beardsley_bartholomew_crannell_8E.html, accessed 10 September 2013].

Newton, Norman S. *Inverness: Highland Town to Millennium City*. Derby: Breedon Books, 2003.

Nussbaum, Felicity. "Actresses and the Economies of Celebrity, 1700–1800," in *Theatre and Celebrity in Britain, 1660–2000*, edited by Mary Luckhurst and Jane Moody. Basingstoke, UK: Palgrave Macmillan, 2005, 146–68.

O'Brien, Garrett. *The Nest Academy Jedburgh: "A healthy situation for young gentlemen."* Jedburgh: The Crochet Factory, 1990.

Pascoe, Peggy. "Miscegenation Law, Court Cases, and Ideologies of 'Race' in Twentieth-Century America," *The Journal of American History* 83, no. 1 (June 1996): 44–69.

Paxton, James W. *Joseph Brant and His World: Eighteenth-century Mohawk Warrior and Statesman*. Toronto: James Lorimer and Co., 2008.

Peers, Laura, and Alison K. Brown. *"Pictures Bring Us Messages" / Sinaakssiiksi aohtsimaahpihkookiyaawa: Photographs and Histories from the Kainai Nation*. Toronto: University of Toronto Press, 2007.

Pennock, Caroline Dodds, "Roundtable on *The Red Atlantic*," *Journal of American Studies* 50, no. 4 (Nov. 2016): 1113–16.

Perry, Adele. *Colonial Relations: The Douglas-Connelly Family and the Nineteenth-Century Imperial World*. Cambridge: Cambridge University Press, 2015.

– *On the Edge of Empire*. Toronto: University of Toronto Press, 2000.

Peterson, Jacqueline, and Jennifer S.H. Brown, eds. *The New Peoples: Being and Becoming Métis in North America*. Winnipeg: University of Manitoba Press, 1985.

Petit, Jennifer Loretta Jane. "'To Civilize and Christianize': Native Industrial Schools in Canada." PhD thesis, University of Calgary, 1997.

Petrone, S. Penny. "Brant-Sero, John Ojijatekha," in *Dictionary of Canadian Biography*, vol. 14. University of Toronto/Université Laval, 2003– [http://www.biographi.ca/en/bio/brant_sero_john_ojijatekha_14E.html, accessed 28 October 2015].

Peyer, Bernd C. *The Tutor'd Mind: Indian Missionary-Writers in Antebellum America*. Amherst: University of Massachusetts Press, 1997.

Phillips, Mark Salber. "On the Advantages and Disadvantages of a Sentimental History for Life." *History Workshop Journal* 61, no. 1 (Spring 2008): 49–64.

Phillips, Ruth B. "Making Sense out/of the Visual: Aboriginal Presentations and Representations in Nineteenth-Century Canada," *Art History* 27, no. 4 (Sept. 2004): 591–615.

Plamper, Jan. "The History of Emotions: An Interview with William Reddy, Barbara Rosenwein, and Peter Stearns," *History and Theory* 49, no. 2 (May 2010): 237–65.

Pitcairn, Sheila. *The Old "Fitpaths" and Streets of Dunfermline*. N.p.: Millennium Publishers, n.d.

Poignant, Roslyn. *Professional Savages: Captive Lives and Western Spectacle*. New Haven: Yale University Press, 2004.

Pollock, Della. "Making History Go," in *Exceptional Spaces: Essays in*

Performances and History, edited by Pollock. Chapel Hill: University of North Carolina Press, 1998, 1–45.

Power, D'A. "Saunders, Sir Edwin (1814–1901)," rev. Patrick Wallis, *Oxford Dictionary of National Biography* (Oxford, 2004) [accessed 17 July 2011].

Pratt, Mary Louise. *Imperial Eyes: Travel Writing and Transculturation*. London: Routledge, 1992.

Pratt, Stephanie. *American Indians in British Art, 1700–1840*. Tulsa, OK: University of Oklahoma Press, 2005.

Purdue, Theda. "Women, Men, and American Indian Policy: The Cherokee Response to 'Civilization,'" in *Negotiators of Change: Historical Perspectives on Native American Women*, edited by Nancy Shoemaker. London: Routledge, 1995, 90–114.

Pybus, Cassandra. *Epic Journeys of Freedom: Runaway Slaves of the American Revolution and Their Global Quest for Liberty*. Boston: Beacon Press, 2006.

Qureshi, Sadiah. *Peoples on Parade: Exhibitions, Empire, and Anthropology in Nineteenth-Century Britain*. Chicago: University of Chicago Press, 2011.

Radforth, Ian. "Performance, Politics, and Representation: Aboriginal People and the 1860 Royal Tour of Canada," *Canadian Historical Review* 84, no. 1 (March 2003): 1–32.

Rae, Isabel, and John Lawson. *Doctor Gregor of Nairn*. Nairn: Douglas Publishing, 1994.

Rampini, Charles. *A History of Moray and Nairn*. Edinburgh and London: Charles Blackwood and Sons, 1897.

Rappaport, Erika Diane. "'The Bombay Debt': Letter Writing, Domestic Economies, and Family Conflict in Colonial India," *Gender and History* 16, no. 2 (Aug. 2004): 233–60.

– *Shopping for Pleasure: Women in the Making of London's West End*. Princeton: Princeton University Press, 2000.

Reford, Alexander. "Smith, Donald Alexander, 1st Baron Strathcona and Mount Royal," in *Dictionary of Canadian Biography*, vol. 14, University of Toronto/Université Laval, 2003–[http://www.biographi.ca/en/bio/smith_donald_alexander_14E.html, accessed 22 February 2016].

Reger, Mark. "Taylor, Sir Henry (1800–1886)," *Oxford Dictionary of National Biography*, see online ed., edited by Lawrence Goldman, Oxford: Oxford University Press, 2004 [accessed 26 February 2016].

Reid, Gerald F. "Illegal Alien? The Immigration Case of Mohawk Ironworker Paul K. Diablo," *Proceedings of the American Philosophical Society* 151, no. 1 (Mar. 2007): 61–78.

Rex, Cathy. "Survival and Fluidity: George Copway's *The Life, History and Travels of Kah-ge-ga-gah-bowh.*" *Studies in American Indian Literature* 18, no. 2 (Summer 2006): 1–33.

Roach, Joseph. "Public Intimacy: The Prior History of 'It'," in *Theatre and Celebrity in Britain, 1660–2000*, edited by Mary Luckhurst and Jane Moody. Basingstoke, UK: Palgrave Macmillan, 2005, 15–30.

Rogers, Edward S., and Donald M. Smith, eds. *Aboriginal Ontario: Historical Perspectives on the First Nations*. Toronto: Dundurn Press, 1994.

Rojek, Chris. *Celebrity*. London: Reaktion, 2001.

Ronaghan, N. E. Allen. "Cowan, William," in *Dictionary of Canadian Biography*, vol. 13, University of Toronto/Université Laval, 2003– [http://www.biographi.ca/en/bio/cowan_william_13E.html, accessed 13 December 2016].

Rosaldo, Renato. "Imperialist Nostalgia," *Representations* 26 (Spring 1989): 107–22.

Rose, Marilyn J. "Johnson, Emily Pauline," in *Dictionary of Canadian Biography*, vol. 14, University of Toronto/Université Laval, 2003– [http://www.biographi.ca/en/bio/johnson_emily_pauline_14E.html, accessed 9 January 2017].

Rosenwein, Barbara H. "Worrying About Emotions in History," *American Historical Review* 107, no. 3 (June 2002): 821–45.

Ross, Robert. *Status and Respectability in the Cape Colony: A Tragedy of Manners*. Cambridge: Cambridge University Press, 1999.

Royden, Michael. "Rushton, Edward (1756–1814)," *Oxford Dictionary of National Biography* (Oxford, 2004) [accessed 17 July 2011].

Ruoff, A. Lavonne Brown, and Donald B. Smith, eds. *George Copway (Kahgegagahbowh): Life, Letters and Speeches*. Lincoln, Nebraska: University of Nebraska Press, 1997.

Russell, Gillian. *The Theatres of War: Performance, Politics, and Society, 1793–1815*. Oxford:Clarendon Press, 1995.

Russell, Penny. *Savage or Civilised? Manners in Colonial Australia*. Sydney: University of New South Wales Press, 2010.

Rutherford, Scott. "Indigenous Peoples, Colonialism, and Canada," in *Canada and the Third World: Overlapping Histories*, edited by Karen Dubinsky, Sean Mills, and Scott Rutherford. Toronto: University of Toronto Press, 2016, 15–36.

Ryan, James R. *Picturing Empire: Photography and the Visualization of the British Empire*. Chicago: University of Chicago Press, 1997.

Salesa, Damon Ieremia. *Racial Crossings: Race, Intermarriage, and the Victorian British Empire*. Oxford: Oxford University Press, 2011.

Scheer, Monique. "Are Emotions a Kind of Practice (And Is That What Makes Them Have a History)? A Bourdieuian Approach to Understanding Emotions," *History and Theory* 51, no. 2 (May 2012): 193–220.

Schenck, Theresa M. *William W. Warren: The Life, Times, and Letters of an Ojibwe Leader*. Lincoln, NB: University of Nebraska Press, 2007.

Schiefen, Richard J. "Wiseman, Nicholas Patrick Stephen (1802–1865)," *Oxford Dictionary of National Biography* (Oxford, 2004) [accessed 27 March 2017].

Schmalz, Peter S. *The Ojibwa of Southern Ontario*. Toronto: University of Toronto Press, 1991.

Schneer, Jonathan. *London 1900: The Imperial Metropolis*. New Haven: Yale University Press, 1999.

Shannon, Timothy J. "King of the Indians: The Hard Fate and Curious Career of Peter Williamson," *The William and Mary Quarterly* 66, no. 1 (Jan. 2009): 3–44.

Shapely, Peter. "Brotherton, Joseph (1783–1857)," *Oxford Dictionary of National Biography* (Oxford, 2004) [accessed 17 July 2011].

Sieciechowicz, Krystyna Z. "Steinhauer, Henry Bird," in *Dictionary of Canadian Biography*, vol. 11, University of Toronto/Université Laval, 2003– [http://www.biographi.ca/en/bio/steinhauer_henry_bird_11E.html, accessed 12 September 2013].

Smith, Donald B. "KAHGEGAGAHBOWH (Kahkakakahbowh, Kakikekapo) (George Copway)," in *Dictionary of Canadian Biography*, vol. 9, University of Toronto/Université Laval, 2003–[http://www.biographi.ca/en/bio/kahgegagahbowh_9E.html, accessed April 2, 2017].

– "The Life of George Copway or Kah-ge-ga-gah-bowh (1818–1869) – and a Review of his Writings," *Journal of Canadian Studies/ Revue d'études canadiennes* 23, no. 4 (1988): 5–38.

– *Mississauga Portraits: Ojibwe Lives from Nineteenth-Century Canada*. Toronto: University of Toronto Press, 2013.

– "Nahnebahwequay," in *Dictionary of Canadian Biography*, vol. 9, University of Toronto/Université Laval, 2003– [http://www.biographi.ca/en/bio/nahnebahwequay_9E.html. accessed 12 September 2013].

– *Sacred Feathers: The Reverend Peter Jones (Kahkewaquonaby) and the Mississauga Indians*. Toronto: University of Toronto Press, 1987.

Smith, Erica. "'Gentlemen, This Is No Ordinary Trial': Sexual Narratives in the Tale of the Reverend Corbett, Red River, 1863," in *Reading Beyond*

Words: Contexts for Indigenous History, edited by Jennifer S.H. Brown and Elizabeth Vibert. Peterborough: Broadview Press, 1996, 364–80.

Smith, Tori. "'Almost Pathetic … But Also Very Glorious': The Consumer Spectacle of the Diamond Jubilee," *Histoire sociale/Social History* 58 (Novembre-November 1996): 333–56.

Somerville, Alice Te Punga. *Once Were Pacific: Māori Connections to Oceania*. Minneapolis: University of Minnesota Press, 2012.

Stephen, Leslie. "Allen, William (1770–1843)." Rev. G.F. Bartle. In *Oxford Dictionary of National Biography*, edited by H.C.G. Matthew and Brian Harrison. Oxford: Oxford University Press, 2004. Online ed., edited by David Cannadine, 2004 [accessed April 2, 2017].

Stephens, H.M., rev. Lynn Milne. "Cumming, Roualeyn George Gordon," *Oxford Dictionary of National Biography*, 2010 [accessed 23 May 2013].

Stewart, W. Brian. *The Ermantingers: A Nineteenth-Century Ojibwa-Canadian History*. Vancouver: University of British Columbia Press, 2007.

Stoehr, Katherine Murton. "Salvation from Empire: The Roots of Anishinaabe Christianity in Upper Canada, 1650–1840," PhD thesis, Queen's University, 2008.

Stoler, Ann Laura. *Carnal Knowledge and Imperial Power: Race and the Intimate in Colonial Rule*. Berkeley and Los Angeles: University of California Press, 2002.

"Tense and Tender Ties: The Politics of Comparison in North American History and (Post) Colonial Studies." *Journal of American History* 88, no. 3 (Dec. 2001): 829–65.

– ed. *Haunted by Empire: Geographies of Intimacy in North American History*. Durham, NC: Duke University Press, 2006.

Streets, Heather. *Martial Races: The Military, Race, and Masculinity in British Imperial Culture, 1857–1914*. Manchester: Manchester University Press, 2004.

Strong-Boag, Veronica. "A Red Girl Speaks," in *Painting the Maple: Essays on Race, Gender, and the Construction of Canada*, edited by Strong-Boag, Sherrill Grace, Avigail Eisenberg, and Joan Anderson. Vancouver: University of Vancouver Press, 1998, 130–54

– and Carole Gerson. *Paddling Her Own Canoe: The Times and Texts of E. Pauline Johnson*. Toronto: University of Toronto Press, 2000.

Szaz, Margaret Connell, ed. *Between Indian and White Worlds: The Cultural Broker*. Norman, OK: University of Oklahoma Press, 1994.

Taylor, Alan. *The Divided Ground: Indians, Settlers, and the Northern Borderlands of the American Revolution*. New York: Vintage Books, 2006.

Taylor, Miles. "Cobden, Richard (1804–1865)." *Oxford Dictionary of National Biography* (Oxford, 2004) [http://www.oxforddnb.com.myaccess.library. utoronto.ca/view/article/5741, accessed 17 July 2011].

Thomas, Nicholas. *Islanders: The Pacific in the Age of Empire.* New Haven: Yale University Press, 2010.

Thorne, Susan. *Congregational Missions and the Making of an Imperial Culture in Nineteenth-Century Britain.* Stanford: Stanford University Press, 1999.

Thrush, Coll. *Indigenous London: Native Travellers at the Heart of the Empire.* New Haven: Yale University Press, 2016.

Titley, E. Brian. *A Narrow Vision: Duncan Campbell Scott and the Administration of Indian Affairs.* Vancouver: University of British Columbia Press, 1986.

Toorn, Penny van. *Writing Never Arrives Naked: Early Aboriginal Cultures of Writing in Australia.* Canberra: Aboriginal Studies Press, 2006.

Twells, Alison. *The Civilising Mission and the English Middle Class, 1792–1850: The "Heathen" at Home and Overseas.* Basingstoke, UK: Palgrave Macmillan, 2009.

Vallegårda, Karen, Kristine Alexander, and Stephanie Olsen. "Emotions and the Global Politics of Childhood," in *Childhood, Youth and Emotions in Modern History: National, Colonial, and Global Perspectives*, edited by Stephanie Olsen. Basingstoke, UK: Palgrave Macmillan, 2015, 1–34.

Van Kirk, Sylvia. "Ballenden, John," in *Dictionary of Canadian Biography*, vol. 8, University of Toronto/Université Laval, 2003– [http://www.biographi. ca/en/bio/ballenden_john_8E.html, accessed 18 February 2016].

– "Isbister, Alexander Kennedy," in *Dictionary of Canadian Biography*, vol. 11, University of Toronto/Université Laval, 2003– [http://www.biographi.ca/ en/bio/isbister_alexander_kennedy_11E.html, accessed 16 February 2016].

– "From 'Marrying-in' to 'Marrying-out': Changing Patterns of Aboriginal/ non-aboriginal Marriage in Colonial Canada." *Frontiers: A Journal of Women's Studies* 23, no. 3 (2002): 1–8.

– *"Many Tender Ties": Women in Fur Trade Society, 1670–1870.* Winnipeg: Watson and Dwyer, 1980.

– "McTavish, John George," in *Dictionary of Canadian Biography*, vol. 7, University of Toronto/Université Laval, 2003– [http://www.biographi.ca/ en/bio/mctavish_john_george_7E.html, accessed 14 December 2016].

– "'The Reputation of a Lady': Sarah Ballenden and the Foss-Pelly Scandal," *Manitoba History* 11 (Spring 1986) [http://www.mhs.mb.ca/docs/mb_ history/11/fosspellyscandal.shtml accessed 17 Feb. 2016].

– "'What If Mama Was an Indian?' The Cultural Ambivalence of the

Alexander Ross Family," in *The New Peoples: Being and Becoming Métis in North America*, edited by Jacqueline Peterson and Jennifer S.H. Brown. Winnipeg: University of Manitoba Press, 1985, 207–17.

Van Steen, Marcus. *Pauline Johnson: Her Life and Work*. Toronto: Musson Book Co., 1965.

Vaughan, Alden T. *Transatlantic Encounters: American Indians in Britain, 1500–1776*. Oxford: Oxford University Press, 2006.

Vaughan, Alden. "Sir Walter Raleigh's Indian Interpreters, 1584–1618," *The William and Mary Quarterly* 59, no. 2 (Apr. 2002): 341–76.

Veracini, Lorenzo. *The Settler Colonial Present*. Basingstoke, UK: Palgrave Macmillan, 2015.

Vibert, Elizabeth. "Real Men Hunt Buffalo: Masculinity, Race, and Class in British Fur Traders' Narratives," *Gender and History* 8, no. 1 (Apr. 1996): 4–21.

Walker, Cheryl. *Indian Nation: Native American Literature and Nineteenth-Century Nationalisms*. Durham, NC: Duke University Press, 1997.

Wanhalla, Angela. *In/visible Sight: The Mixed Descent Families of Southern New Zealand*. Wellington, NZ: Bridget Williams Books, 2009.

Webster, Wendy. *Englishness and Empire, 1939–1965*. Oxford: Oxford University Press, 2007.

Weaver, Jace. *The Red Atlantic: American Indigenes and the Making of the Modern World, 1000–1927*. Chapel Hill: University of North Carolina, 2014.

– "Roundtable on *The Red Atlantic*," *Journal of American Studies* 40 (2016): 1122–6.

Weaver, Sally M. "The Iroquois: The Consolidation of the Grand River Reserve in the Mid-Nineteenth Century, 1847–1875," in *Indigenous Ontario: Historical Perspectives on the First Nations*, edited by Edward S. Rogers and Donald B. Smith. Burlington, ON: Dundurn Press, 1994, 182–212.

West, Shearer. "Siddons, Celebrity, and Regality: Portraiture and the Body of the Aging Actress," in *Theatre and Celebrity in Britain, 1660–2000*, edited by Mary Luckhurst and Jane Moody. Basingstoke, UK: Palgrave Macmillan, 2005, 191–213.

White, Jerry. *London in the Nineteenth Century*. London: Vintage Books, 2008.

Wickberg, Daniel. "What Is the History of Sensibilities? On Cultural Histories, Old and New." *American Historical Review* 112, no. 3 (June 2007): 661–84.

Willig, Timothy D. *Restoring the Chain of Friendship: British Policy and the Indians of the Great Lakes, 1783–1815*. Lincoln and London: University of Nebraska Press, 2008.

Wilson, Kathleen. *The Island Race: Englishness, Empire, and Gender in the Eighteenth Century.* London: Routledge, 2003.

– ed. *A New Imperial History: Culture, Identity and Modernity in Britain and the Empire, 1660–1840.* Cambridge: Cambridge University Press, 2004.

Withers, Charles W.J. "How Scotland Came to Know Itself: Geography, National Identity, and the Making of a Nation, 1680–1790." *Journal of Historical Geography* 21, no. 4 (1995): 371–97.

Yan, Shu-Chuan. "(Ad)Dressing Women: Fashion and Body Image in *Punch*, 1850s–1860s." *Women's Studies* 43, no. 6 (2014): 750–73.

Zacek, Natalie. "Roundtable on *The Red Atlantic*," *Journal of American Studies* 50, no. 4 (Nov. 2016): 1118–22.

Index